I've been wanting to write a tournament arc
since I was a little kid. Now that I've done it,
I see it's a ridiculously hard thing to pull off.

KOHEI HORIKOSHI

SHONEN JUMP Manga Edition

STORY & ART KOHEI HORIKOSHI

TRANSLATION & ENGLISH ADAPTATION **Caleb Cook**
TOUCH-UP ART & LETTERING **John Hunt**
DESIGNER **Shawn Carrico**
EDITOR **Mike Montesa**

BOKU NO HERO ACADEMIA © 2014 by Kohei Horikoshi
All rights reserved.
First published in Japan in 2014 by SHUEISHA Inc., Tokyo.
English translation rights arranged by SHUEISHA Inc.

The stories, characters and incidents mentioned in this publication are entirely fictional.

Printed in the U.S.A.

Published by VIZ Media, LLC
P.O. Box 77010
San Francisco, CA 94107

10 9 8
First printing, August 2016
Eighth printing, April 2020

viz.com

PARENTAL ADVISORY
MY HERO ACADEMIA is rated T for Teen
and is recommended for ages 13 and up.
This volume contains fantasy violence.

shonenjump.com

MY HERO ACADEMIA

Shoto Todoroki: Origin

My Hero
Academia
Vol. 5

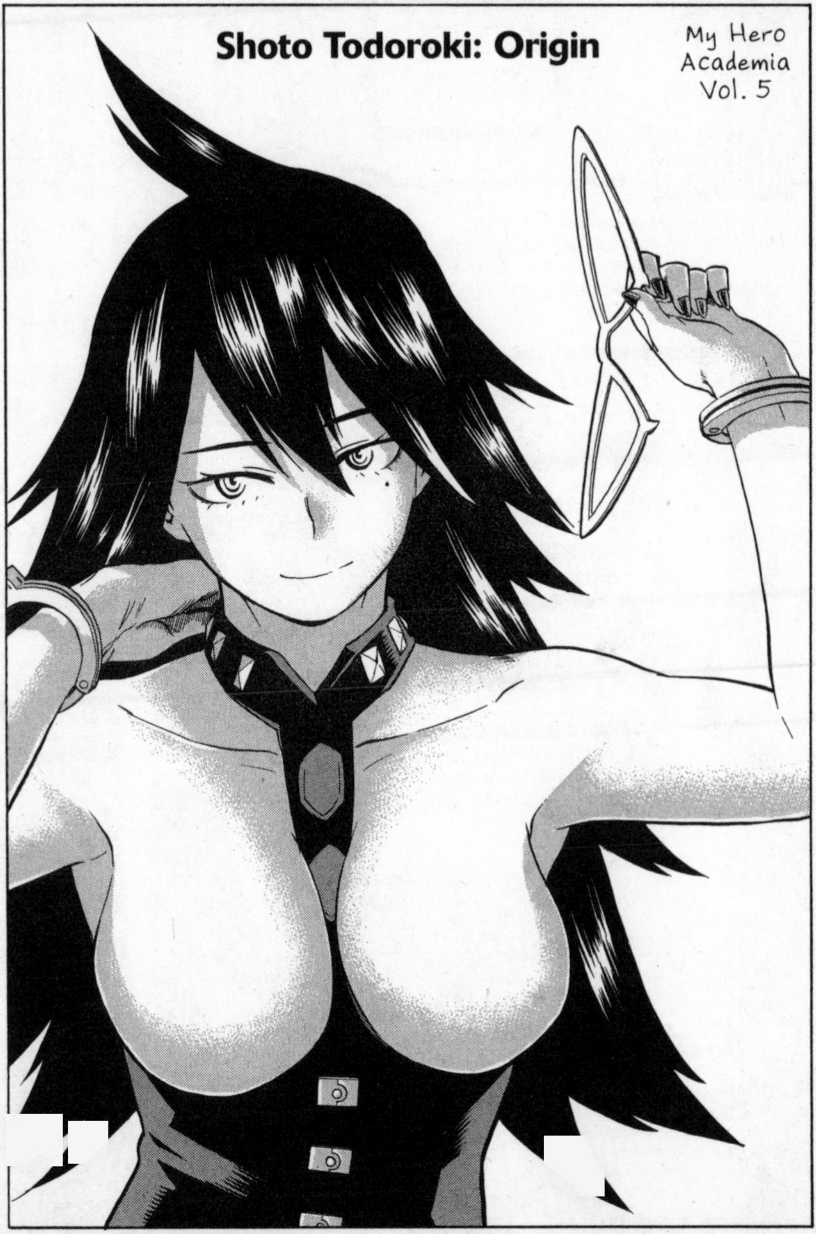

KOHEI HORIKOSHI

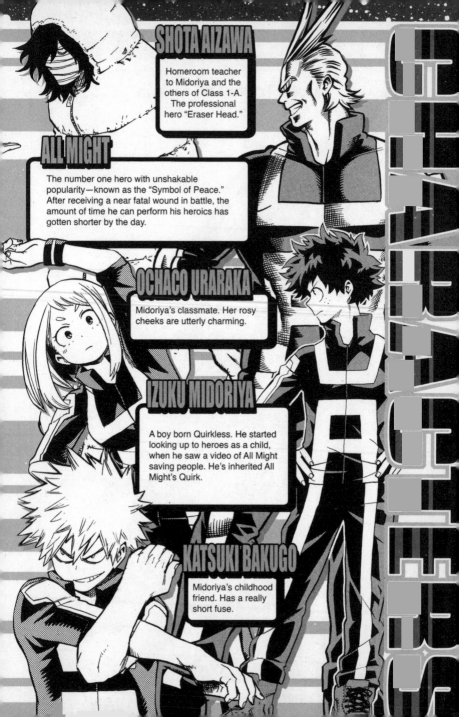

SHOTA AIZAWA

Homeroom teacher to Midoriya and the others of Class 1-A. The professional hero "Eraser Head."

ALL MIGHT

The number one hero with unshakable popularity—known as the "Symbol of Peace." After receiving a near fatal wound in battle, the amount of time he can perform his heroics has gotten shorter by the day.

OCHACO URARAKA

Midoriya's classmate. Her rosy cheeks are utterly charming.

IZUKU MIDORIYA

A boy born Quirkless. He started looking up to heroes as a child, when he saw a video of All Might saving people. He's inherited All Might's Quirk.

KATSUKI BAKUGO

Midoriya's childhood friend. Has a really short fuse.

STORY

One day, people began manifesting special abilities that came to be known as "Quirks," and before long, society became full of these super-powered humans. But with the advent of these exceptional individuals came an increase in crime, and governments were unable to deal with the situation. At the same time, others emerged to oppose the spread of evil! As if straight from the comic books, these heroes keep the peace and are even officially authorized to fight crime. Our story begins when a certain Quirkless boy and lifelong hero fan meets the world's number one hero, starting him on his path to becoming the greatest hero ever!

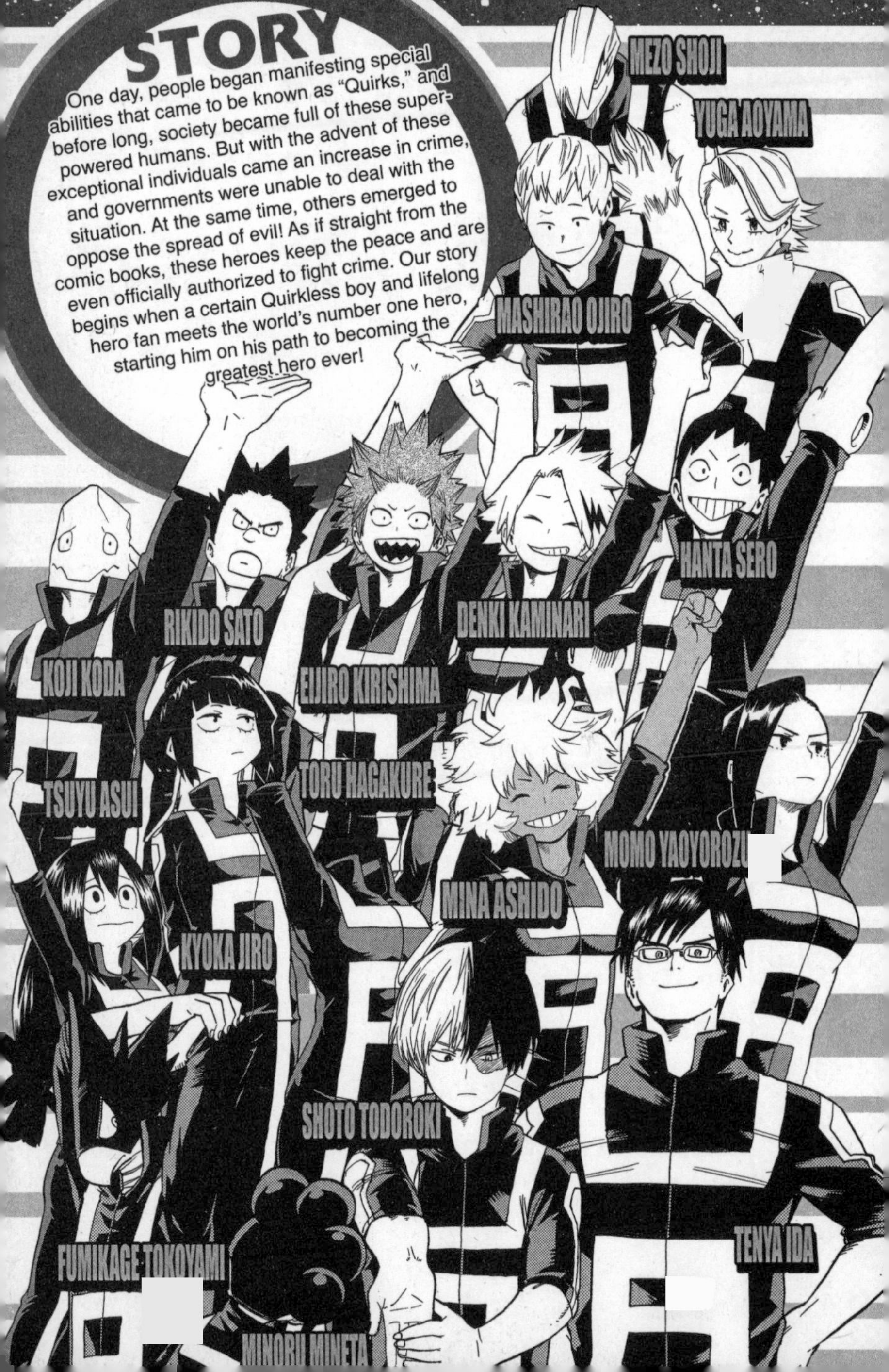

MEZO SHOJI
YUGA AOYAMA
MASHIRAO OJIRO
HANTA SERO
DENKI KAMINARI
RIKIDO SATO
KOJI KODA
EIJIRO KIRISHIMA
MOMO YAOYOROZU
TORU HAGAKURE
TSUYU ASUI
MINA ASHIDO
KYOKA JIRO
SHOTO TODOROKI
TENYA IDA
FUMIKAGE TOKOYAMI
MINORU MINETA

MY HERO ACADEMIA

Shoto Todoroki: Origin

Vol. 5

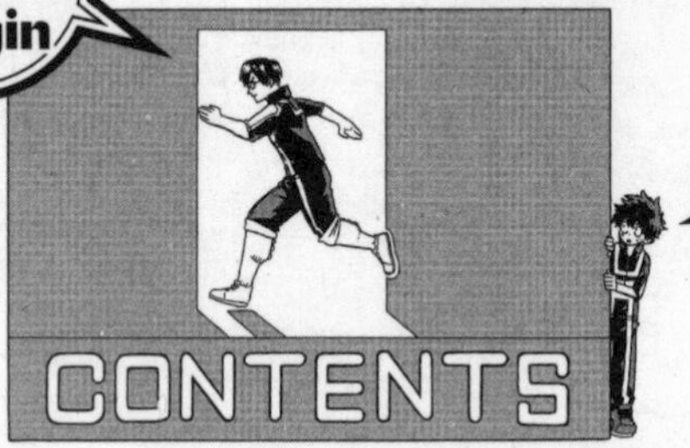

CONTENTS

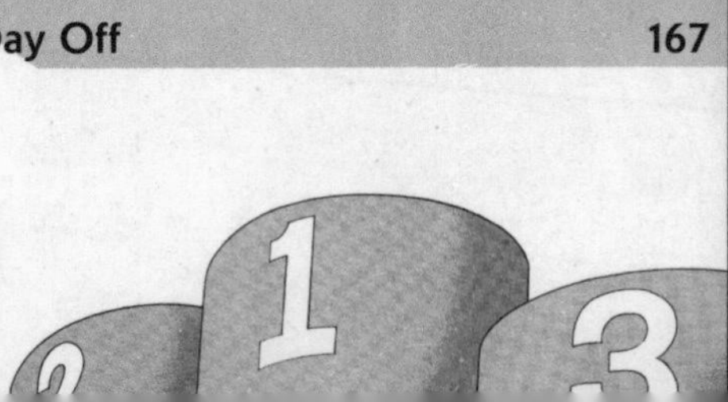

1
3

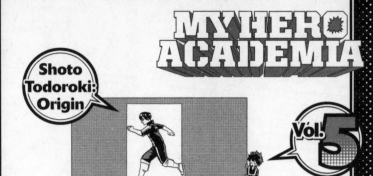

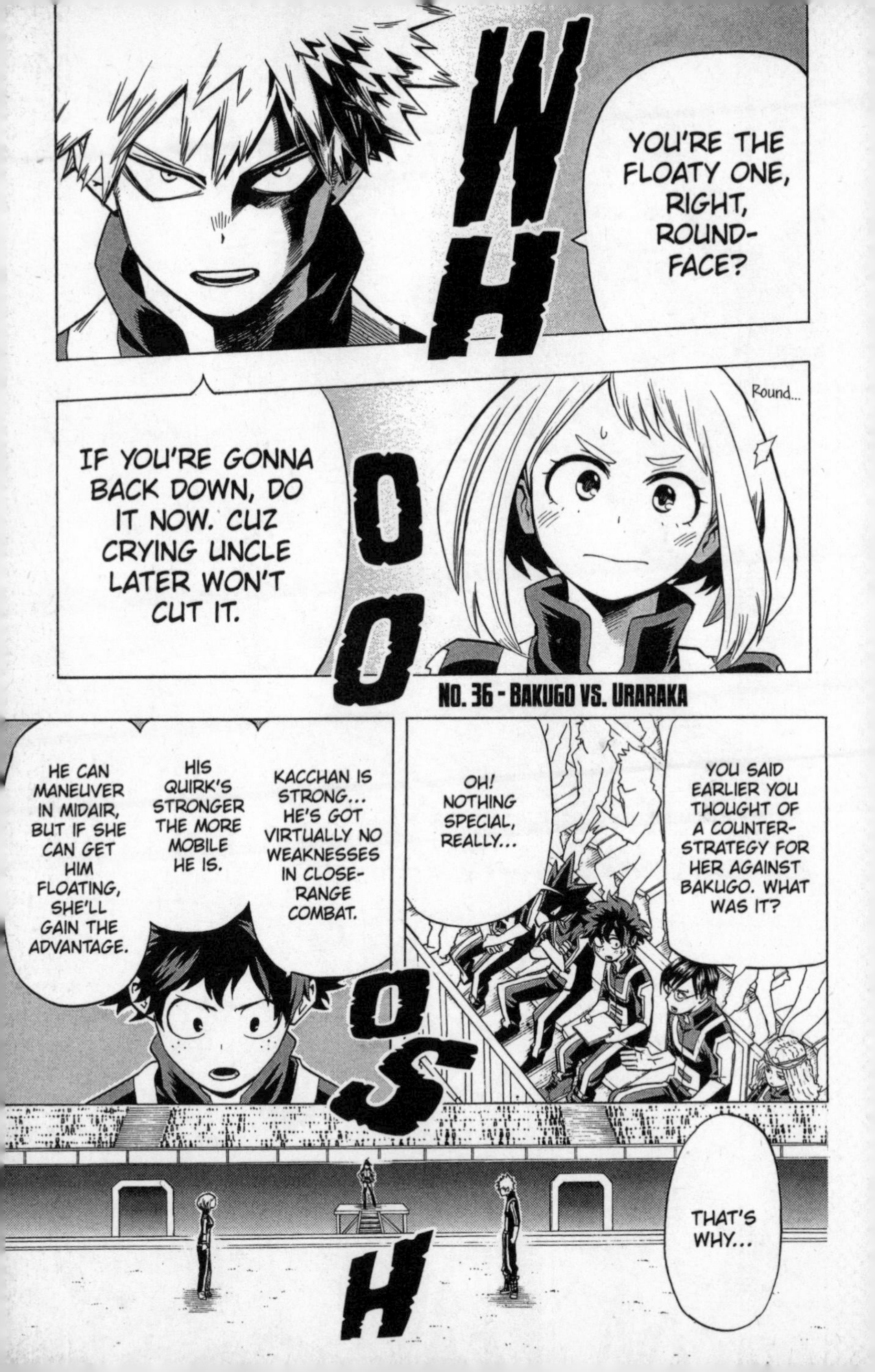
WHOOOSH
YOU'RE THE FLOATY ONE, RIGHT, ROUND-FACE?
Round...
IF YOU'RE GONNA BACK DOWN, DO IT NOW. CUZ CRYING UNCLE LATER WON'T CUT IT.
NO. 36 - BAKUGO VS. URARAKA
YOU SAID EARLIER YOU THOUGHT OF A COUNTER-STRATEGY FOR HER AGAINST BAKUGO. WHAT WAS IT?
OH! NOTHING SPECIAL, REALLY...
KACCHAN IS STRONG... HE'S GOT VIRTUALLY NO WEAKNESSES IN CLOSE-RANGE COMBAT.
HIS QUIRK'S STRONGER THE MORE MOBILE HE IS.
HE CAN MANEUVER IN MIDAIR, BUT IF SHE CAN GET HIM FLOATING, SHE'LL GAIN THE ADVANTAGE.
THAT'S WHY...

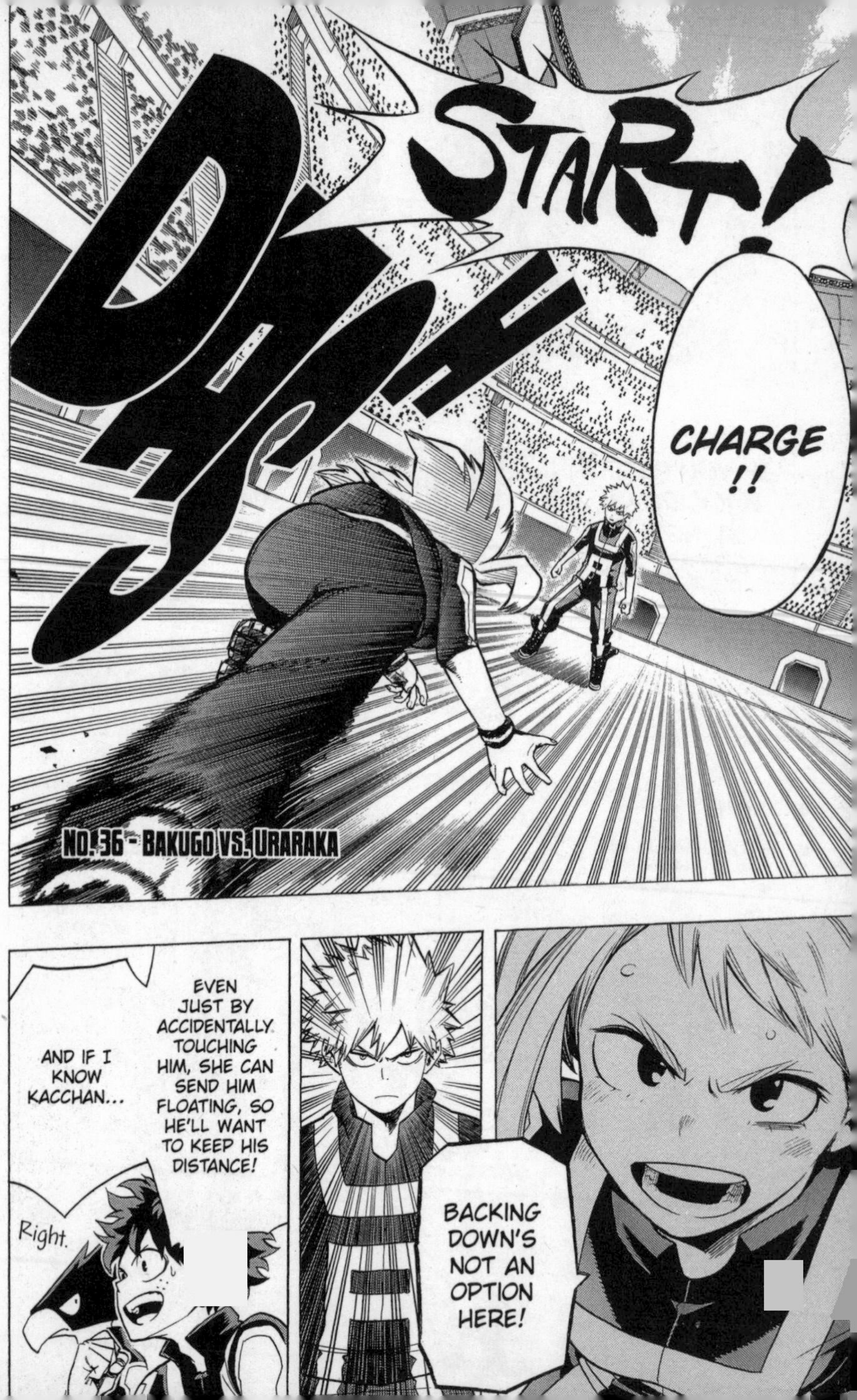
START!
CHARGE !!
DASH
No. 36 - Bakugo vs. Uraraka
BACKING DOWN'S NOT AN OPTION HERE!
EVEN JUST BY ACCIDENTALLY TOUCHING HIM, SHE CAN SEND HIM FLOATING, SO HE'LL WANT TO KEEP HIS DISTANCE!
AND IF I KNOW KACCHAN...
Right.

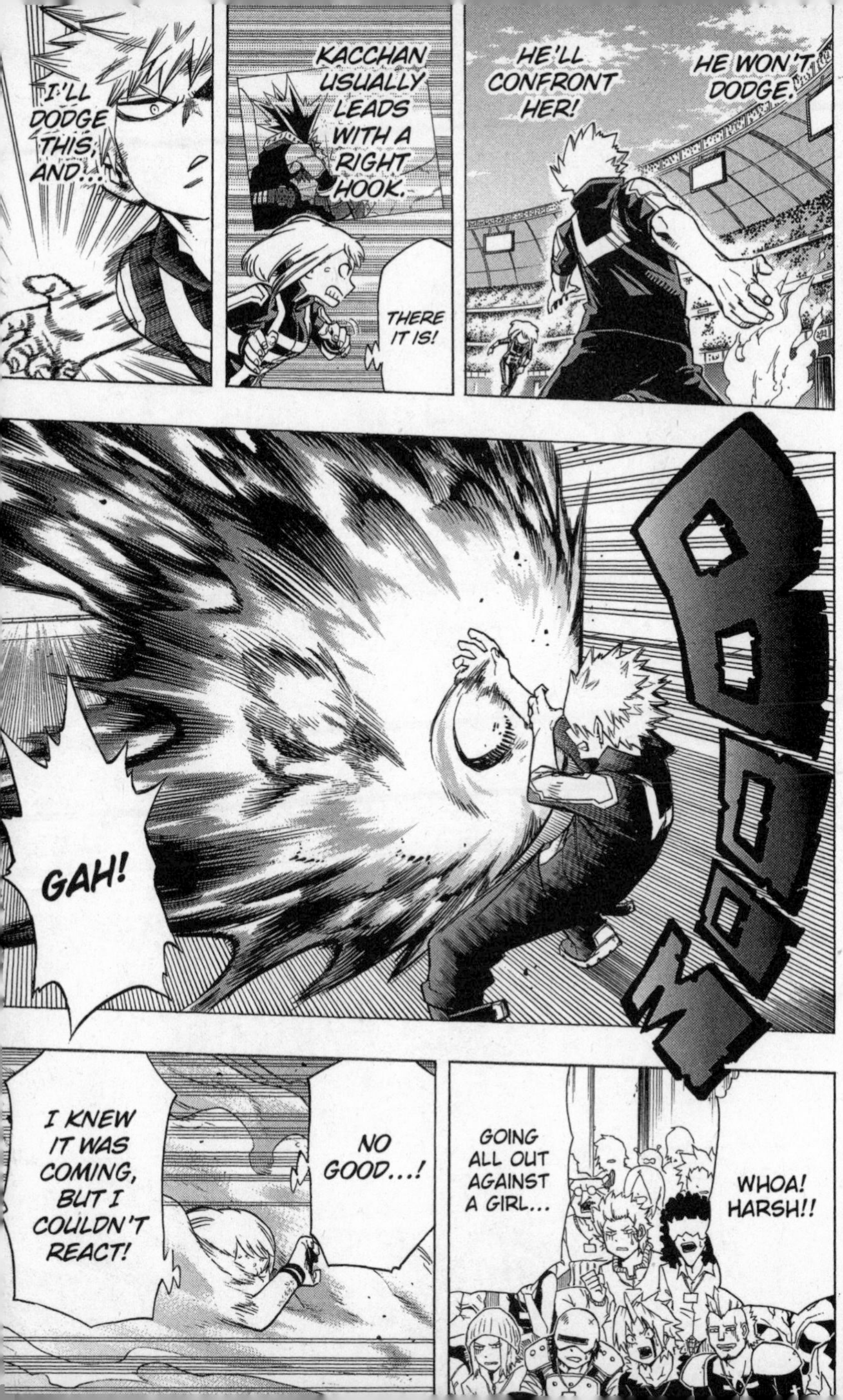
HE WON'T DODGE.
HE'LL CONFRONT HER!
KACCHAN USUALLY LEADS WITH A RIGHT HOOK.
THERE IT IS!
I'LL DODGE THIS, AND...
BOOOM
GAH!
WHOA! HARSH!!
GOING ALL OUT AGAINST A GIRL...
NO GOOD...!
I KNEW IT WAS COMING, BUT I COULDN'T REACT!

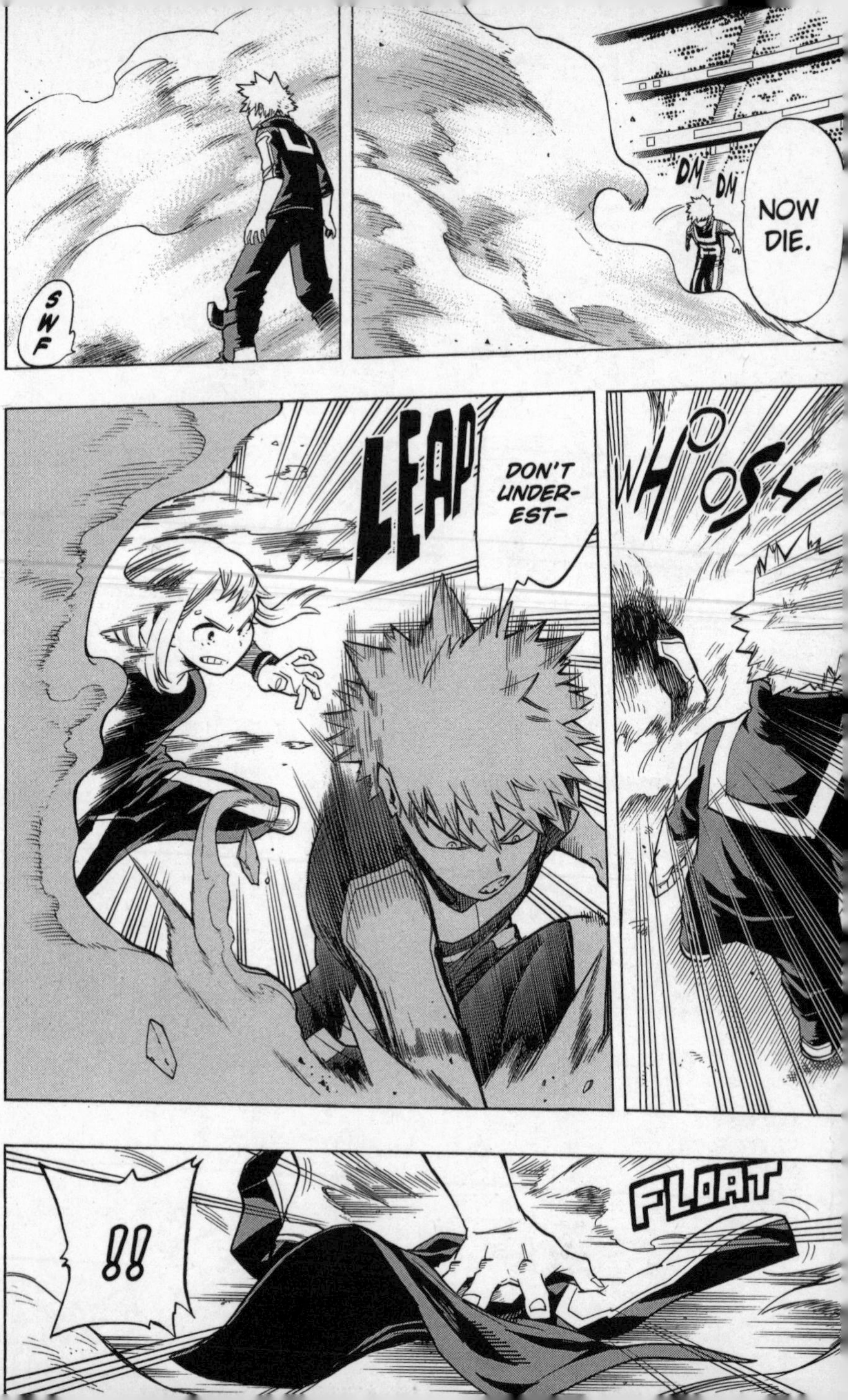
NOW DIE.
DM DM
SWF
WHOOSH
LEAP
DON'T UNDER-EST-
FLOAT
!!

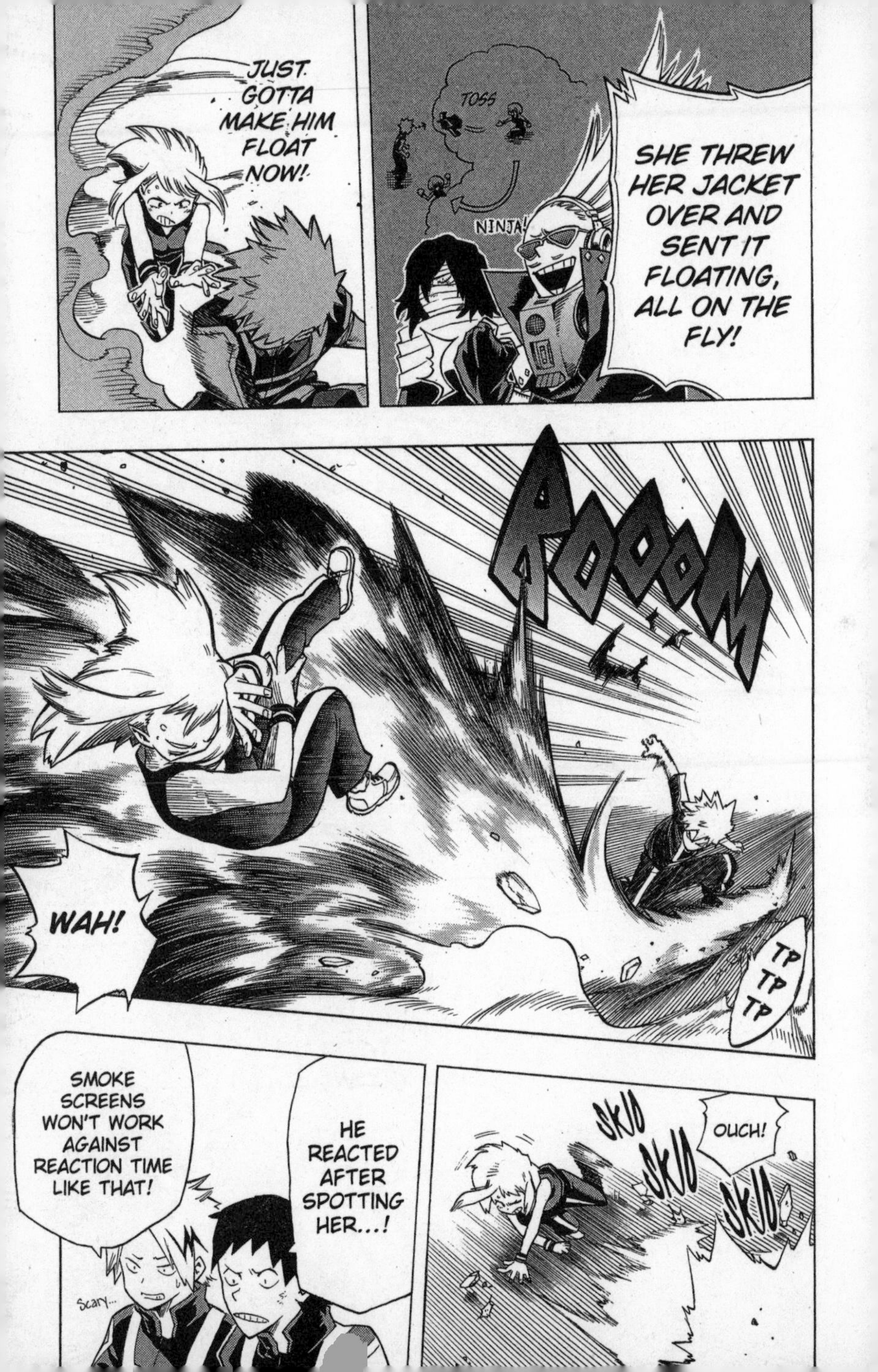
SHE THREW HER JACKET OVER AND SENT IT FLOATING, ALL ON THE FLY!
NINJA!
TOSS
JUST GOTTA MAKE HIM FLOAT NOW!
BOOOM
TP TP TP
WAH!
OUCH!
SKID
SKID
SKID
HE REACTED AFTER SPOTTING HER...!
SMOKE SCREENS WON'T WORK AGAINST REACTION TIME LIKE THAT!
Scary...

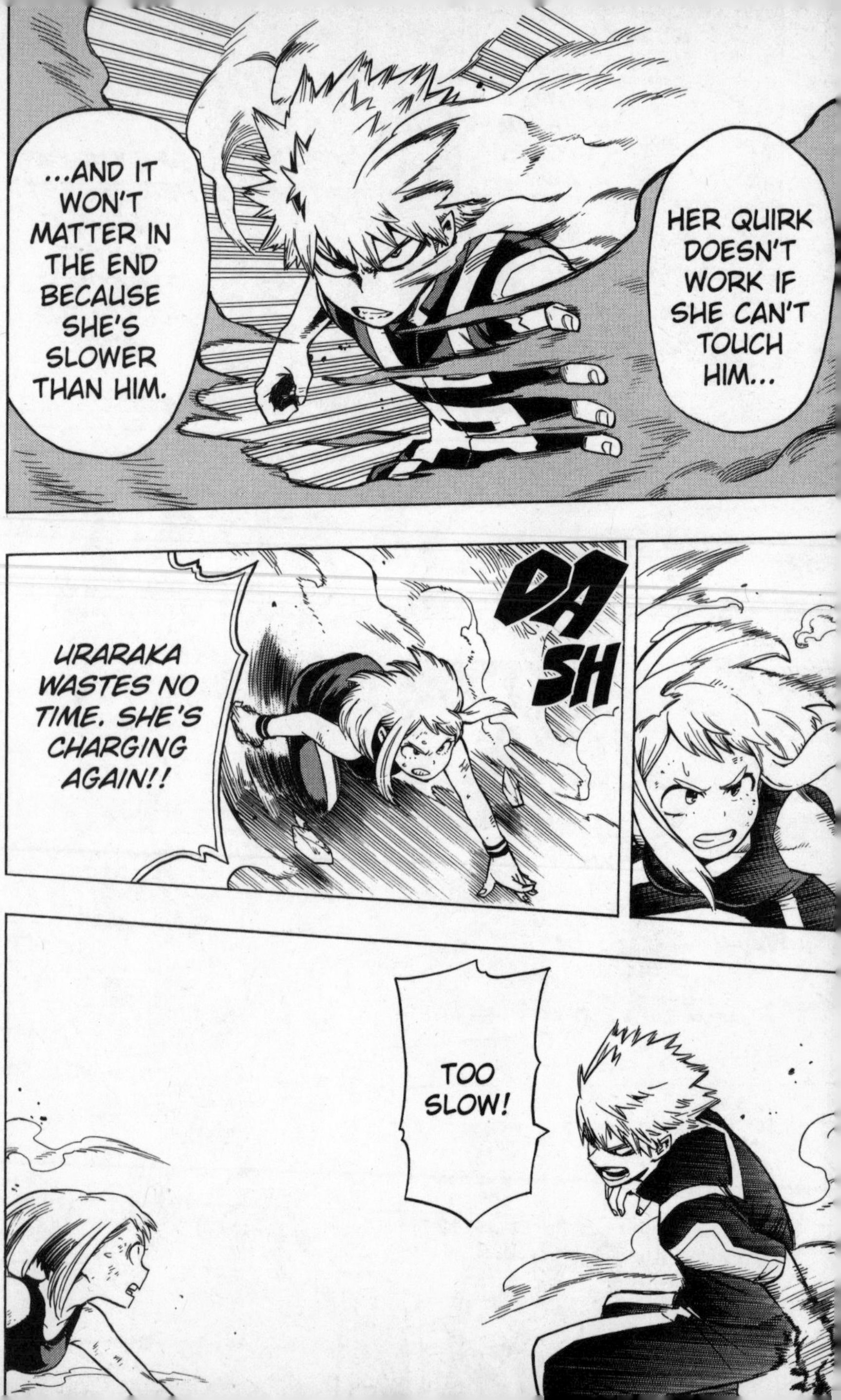
HER QUIRK DOESN'T WORK IF SHE CAN'T TOUCH HIM...
...AND IT WON'T MATTER IN THE END BECAUSE SHE'S SLOWER THAN HIM.
DASH
URARAKA WASTES NO TIME. SHE'S CHARGING AGAIN!!
TOO SLOW!

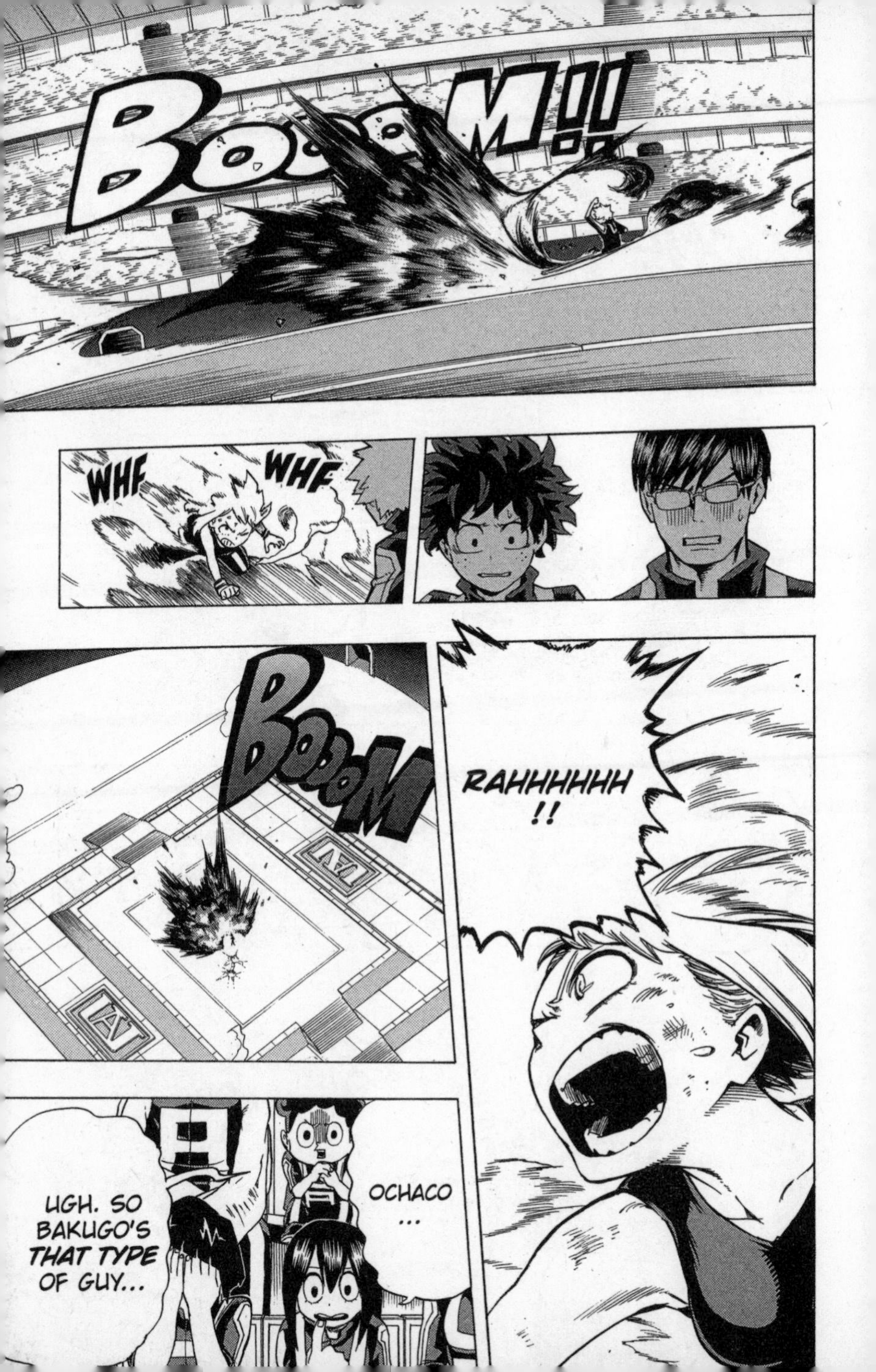

BOOOM!!!
WHF
WHF
RAHHHHHH !!
BOOOM
OCHACO ...
UGH. SO BAKUGO'S THAT TYPE OF GUY...

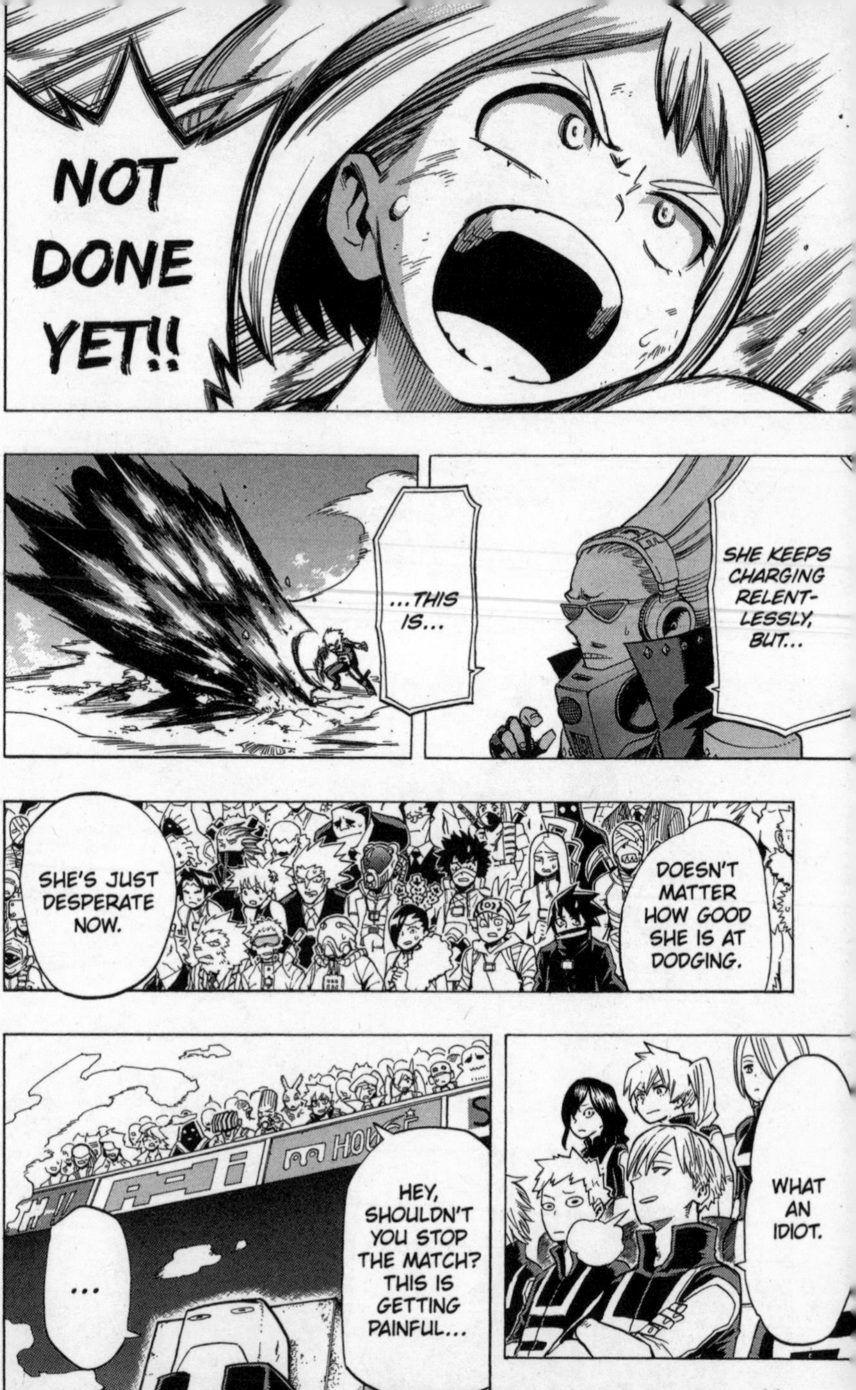
NOT DONE YET!!
SHE KEEPS CHARGING RELENT-LESSLY, BUT...
...THIS IS...
DOESN'T MATTER HOW GOOD SHE IS AT DODGING.
SHE'S JUST DESPERATE NOW.
WHAT AN IDIOT.
HEY, SHOULDN'T YOU STOP THE MATCH? THIS IS GETTING PAINFUL...
...

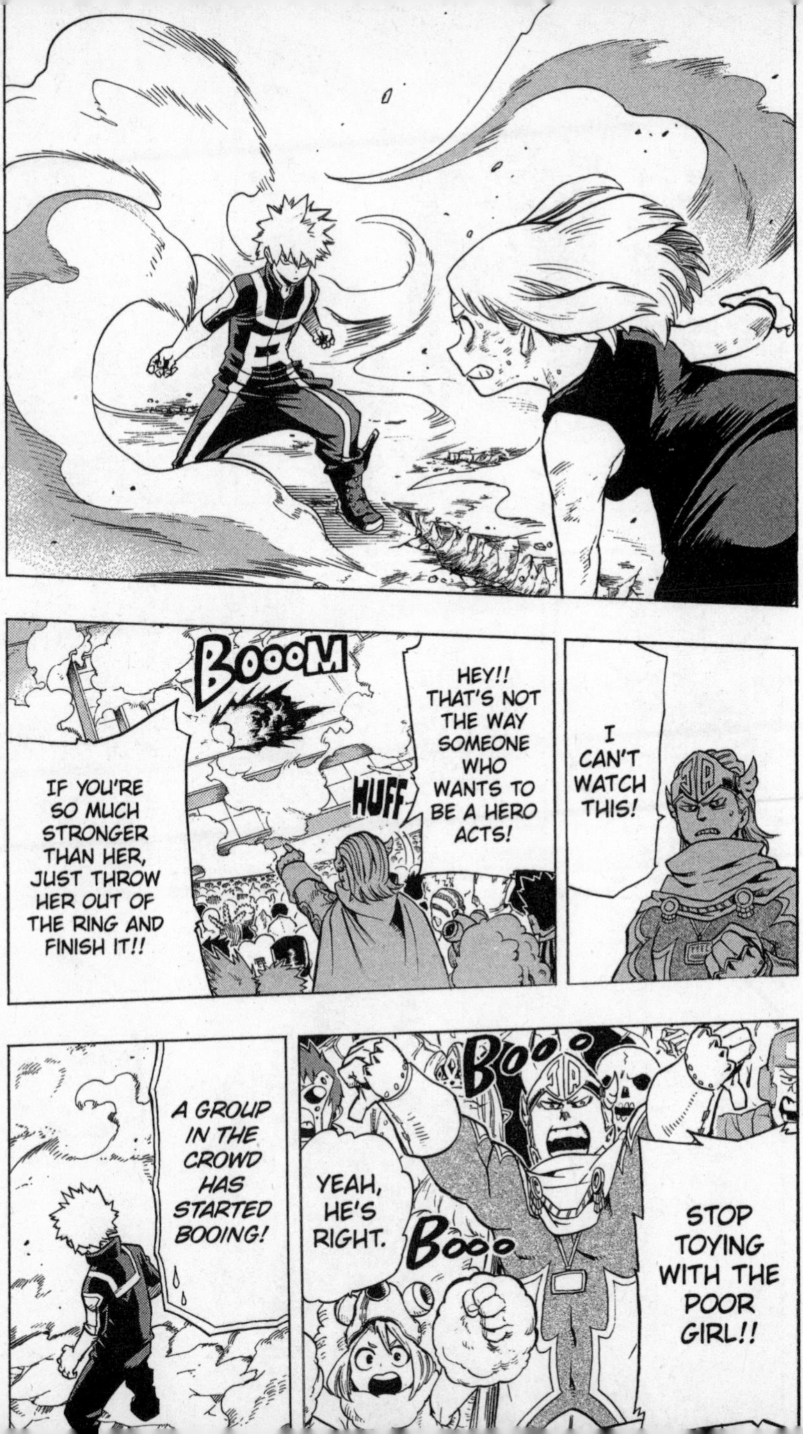
I CAN'T WATCH THIS!
BOOOM
HEY!! THAT'S NOT THE WAY SOMEONE WHO WANTS TO BE A HERO ACTS!
HUFF
IF YOU'RE SO MUCH STRONGER THAN HER, JUST THROW HER OUT OF THE RING AND FINISH IT!!
BOOO
STOP TOYING WITH THE POOR GIRL!!
YEAH, HE'S RIGHT.
BOOO
A GROUP IN THE CROWD HAS STARTED BOOING!

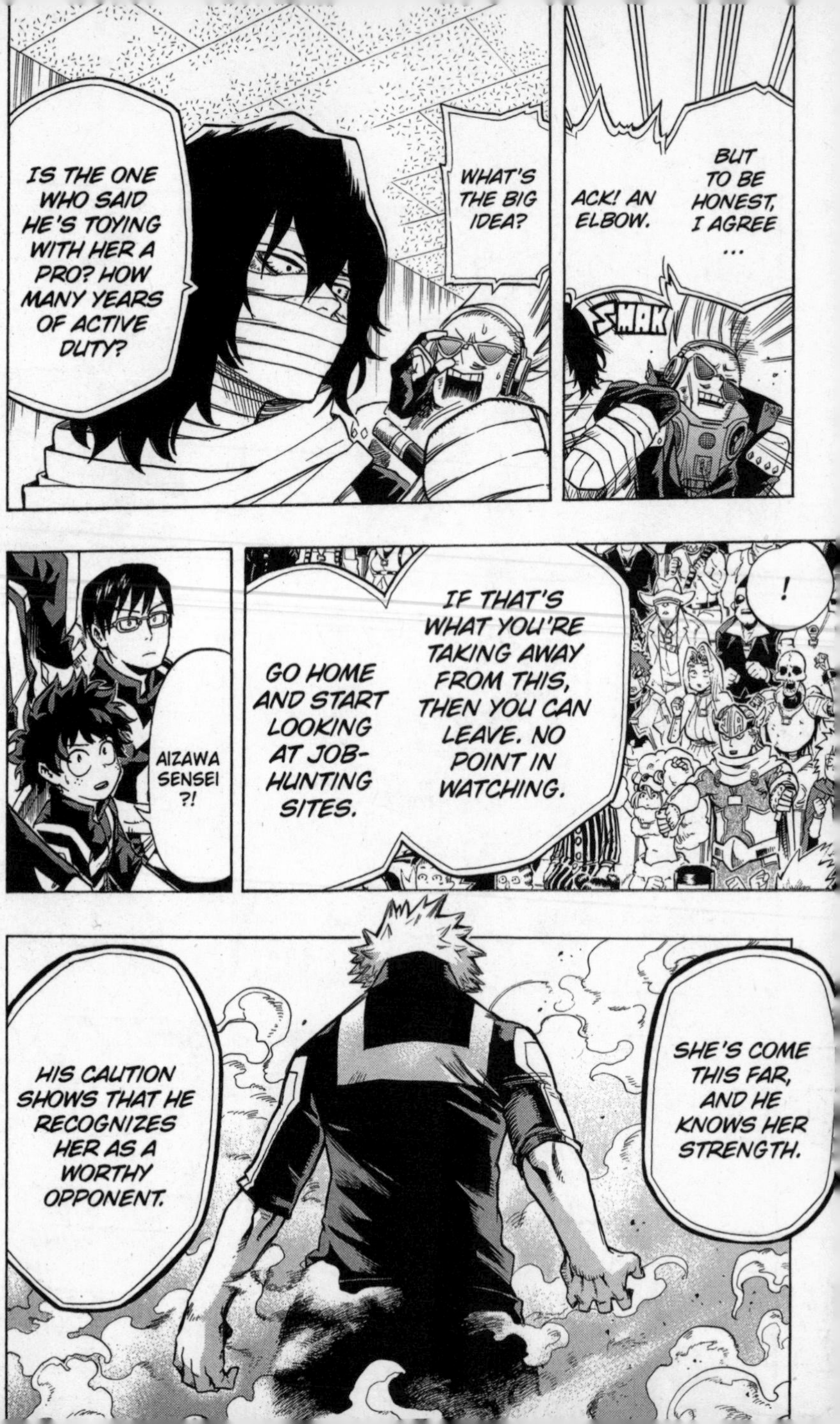
BUT TO BE HONEST, I AGREE ...
ACK! AN ELBOW.
SMAK
WHAT'S THE BIG IDEA?
IS THE ONE WHO SAID HE'S TOYING WITH HER A PRO? HOW MANY YEARS OF ACTIVE DUTY?
!
IF THAT'S WHAT YOU'RE TAKING AWAY FROM THIS, THEN YOU CAN LEAVE. NO POINT IN WATCHING.
GO HOME AND START LOOKING AT JOB-HUNTING SITES.
AIZAWA SENSEI ?!
SHE'S COME THIS FAR, AND HE KNOWS HER STRENGTH.
HIS CAUTION SHOWS THAT HE RECOGNIZES HER AS A WORTHY OPPONENT.

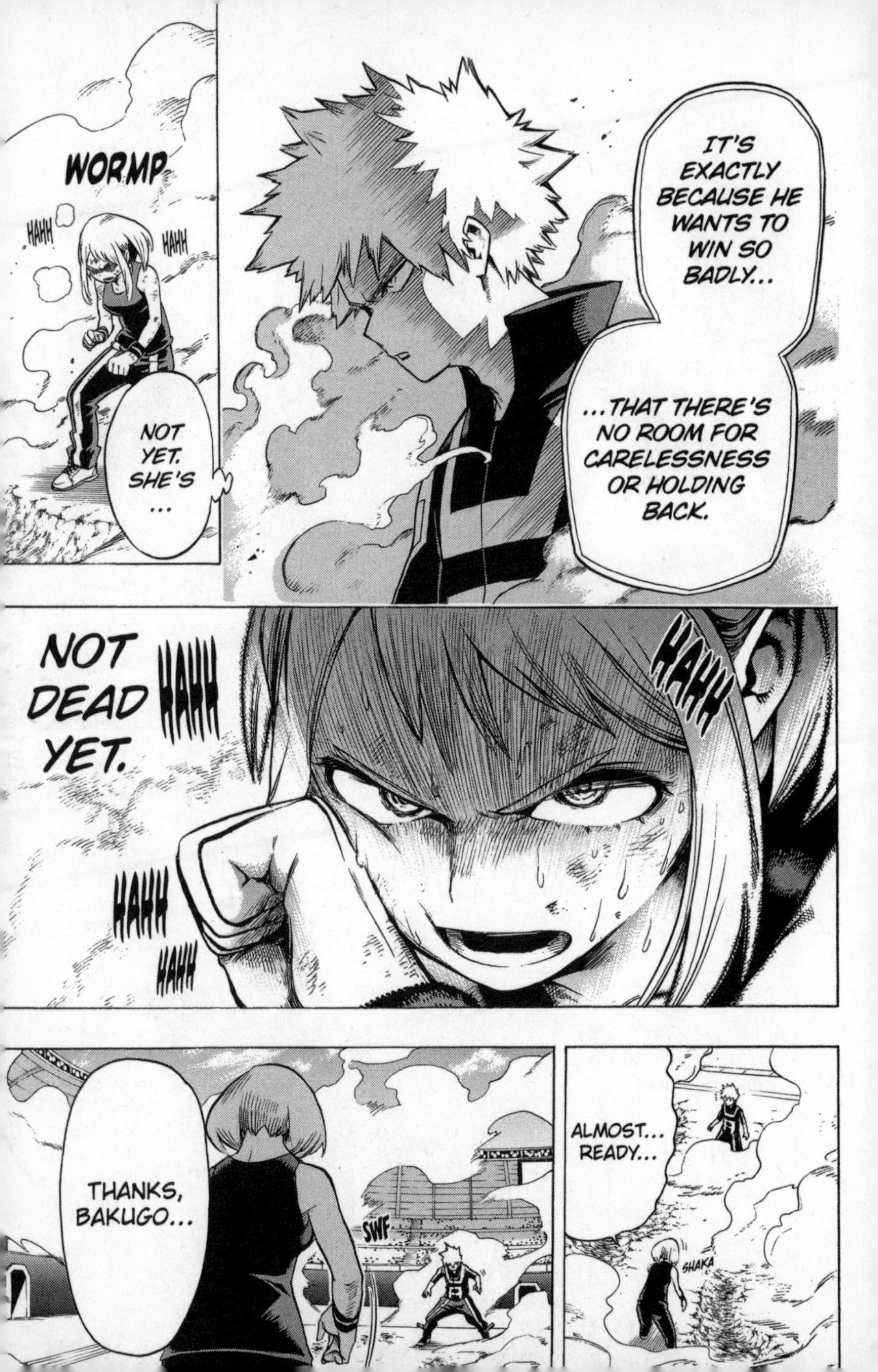
IT'S EXACTLY BECAUSE HE WANTS TO WIN SO BADLY...
...THAT THERE'S NO ROOM FOR CARELESSNESS OR HOLDING BACK.
WORMP
HAHH
HAHH
NOT YET. SHE'S ...
HAHH
NOT DEAD YET.
HAHH
HAHH
HAHH
ALMOST... READY...
SHAKA
THANKS, BAKUGO...
SWF

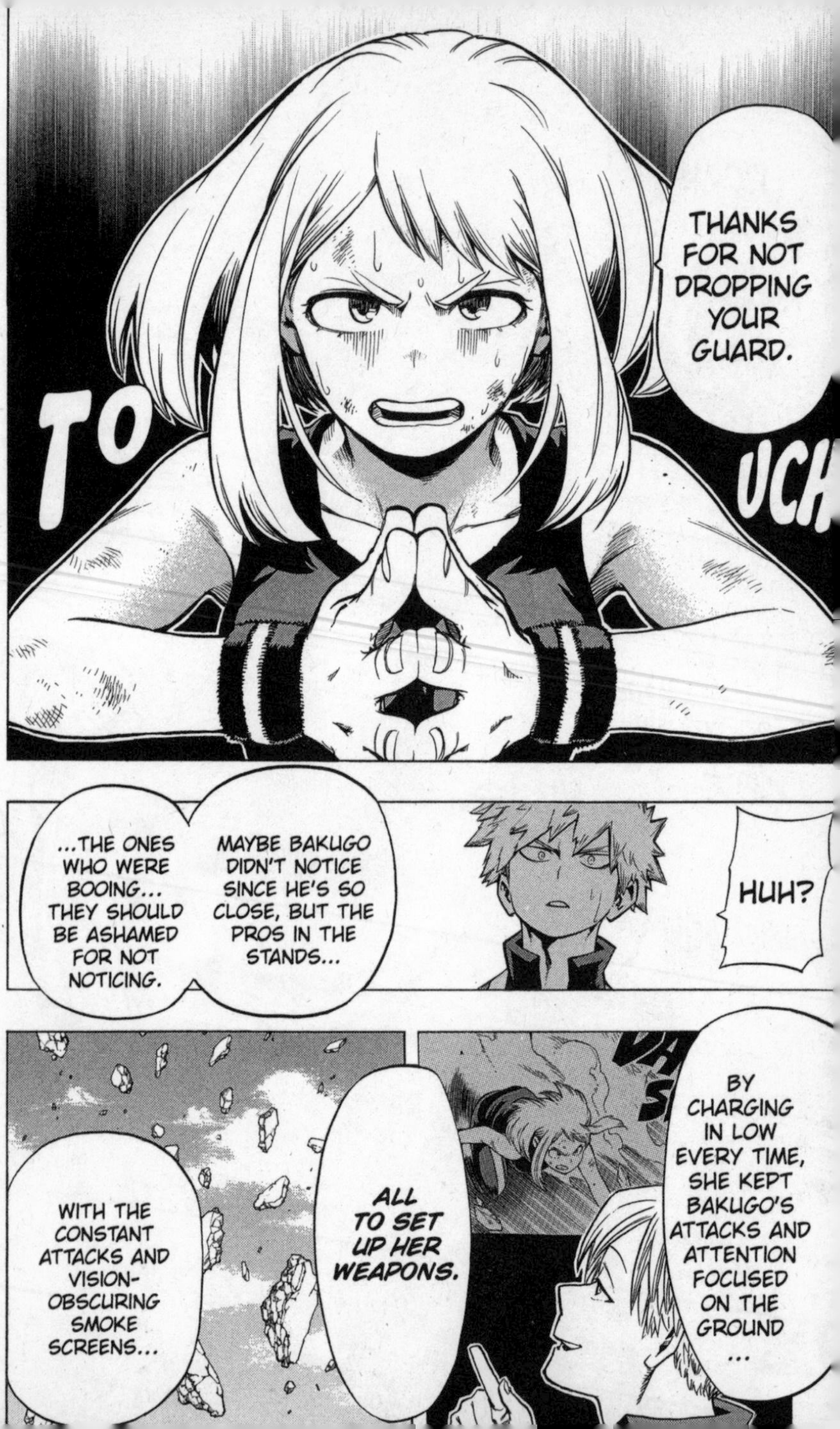
THANKS FOR NOT DROPPING YOUR GUARD.
TO
UCH
HUH?
MAYBE BAKUGO DIDN'T NOTICE SINCE HE'S SO CLOSE, BUT THE PROS IN THE STANDS...
...THE ONES WHO WERE BOOING... THEY SHOULD BE ASHAMED FOR NOT NOTICING.
BY CHARGING IN LOW EVERY TIME, SHE KEPT BAKUGO'S ATTACKS AND ATTENTION FOCUSED ON THE GROUND...
ALL TO SET UP HER WEAPONS.
WITH THE CONSTANT ATTACKS AND VISION-OBSCURING SMOKE SCREENS...

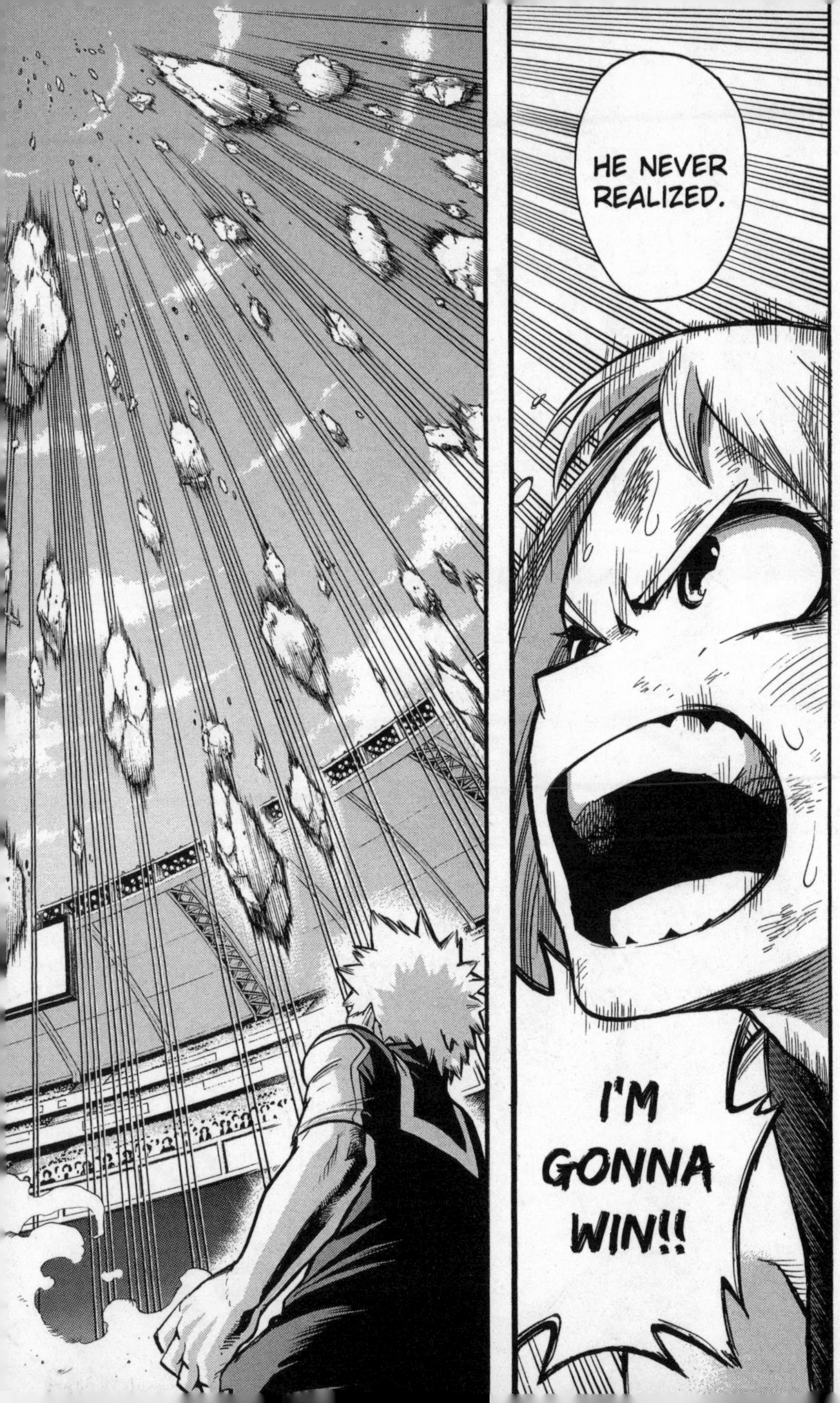
HE NEVER REALIZED.
I'M GONNA WIN!!

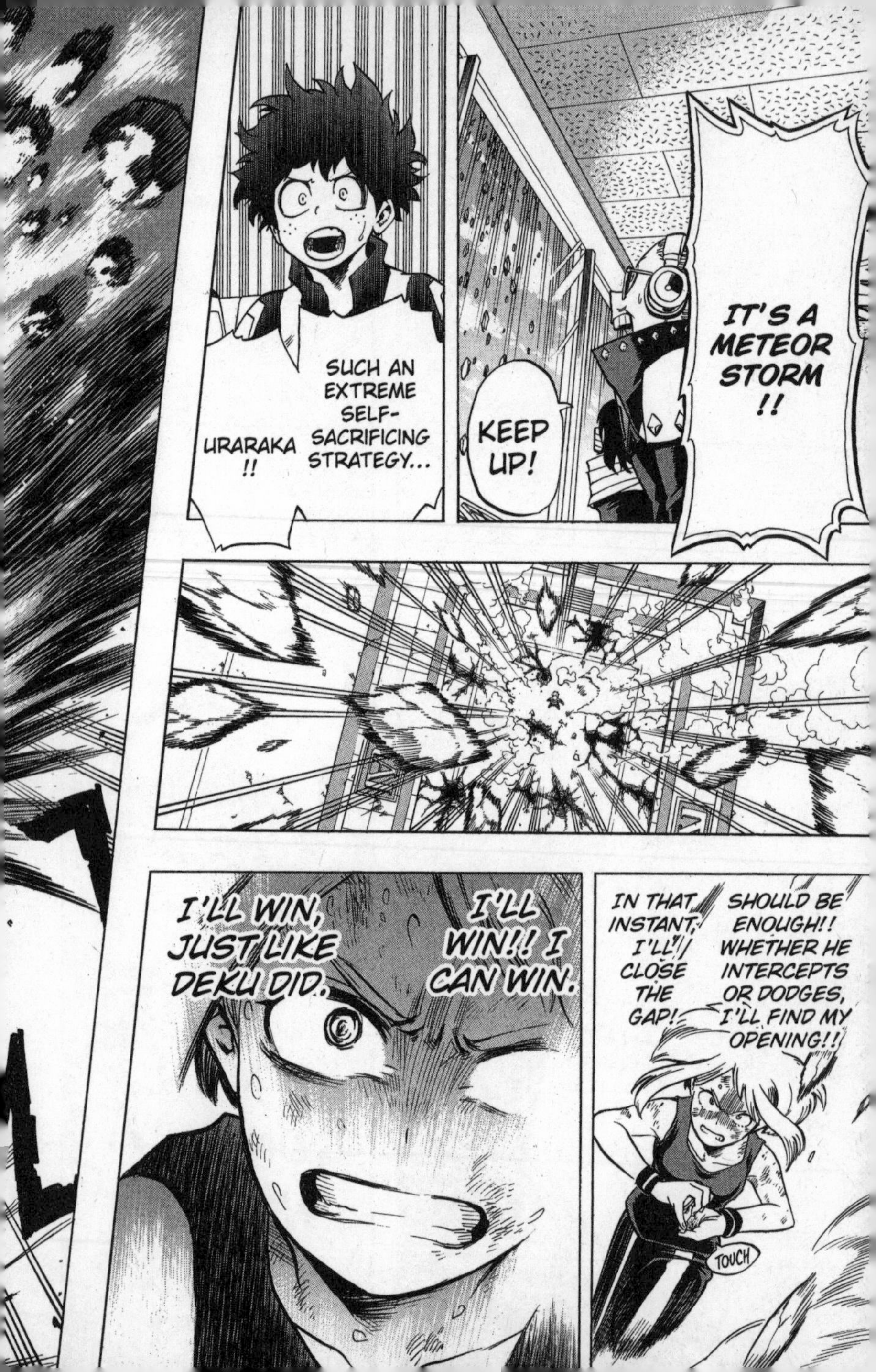
IT'S A METEOR STORM!!
KEEP UP!
SUCH AN EXTREME SELF-SACRIFICING STRATEGY...
URARAKA!!
SHOULD BE ENOUGH!! WHETHER HE INTERCEPTS OR DODGES, I'LL FIND MY OPENING!!
IN THAT INSTANT, I'LL CLOSE THE GAP!
TOUCH
I'LL WIN!! I CAN WIN.
I'LL WIN, JUST LIKE DEKU DID.

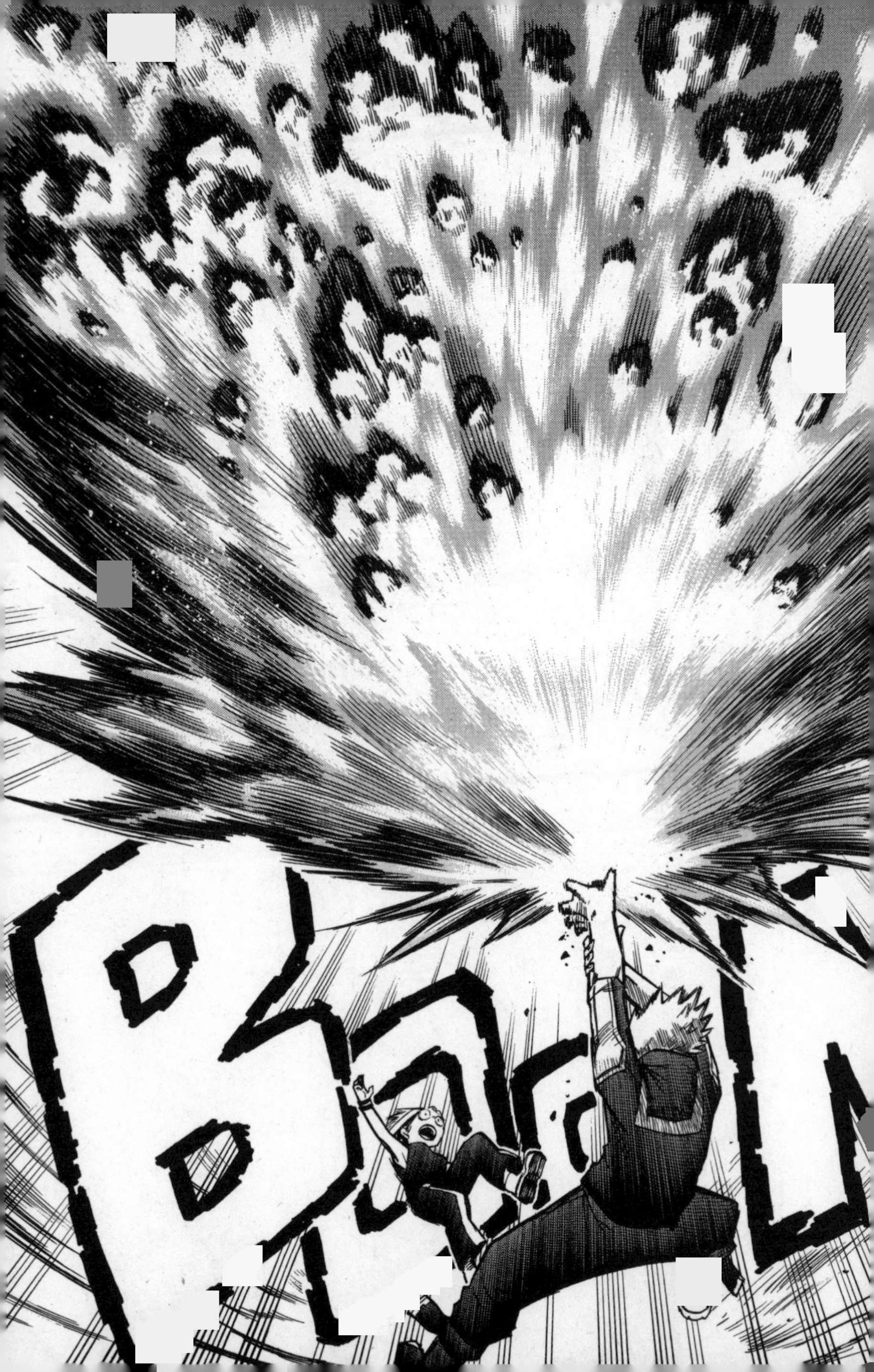

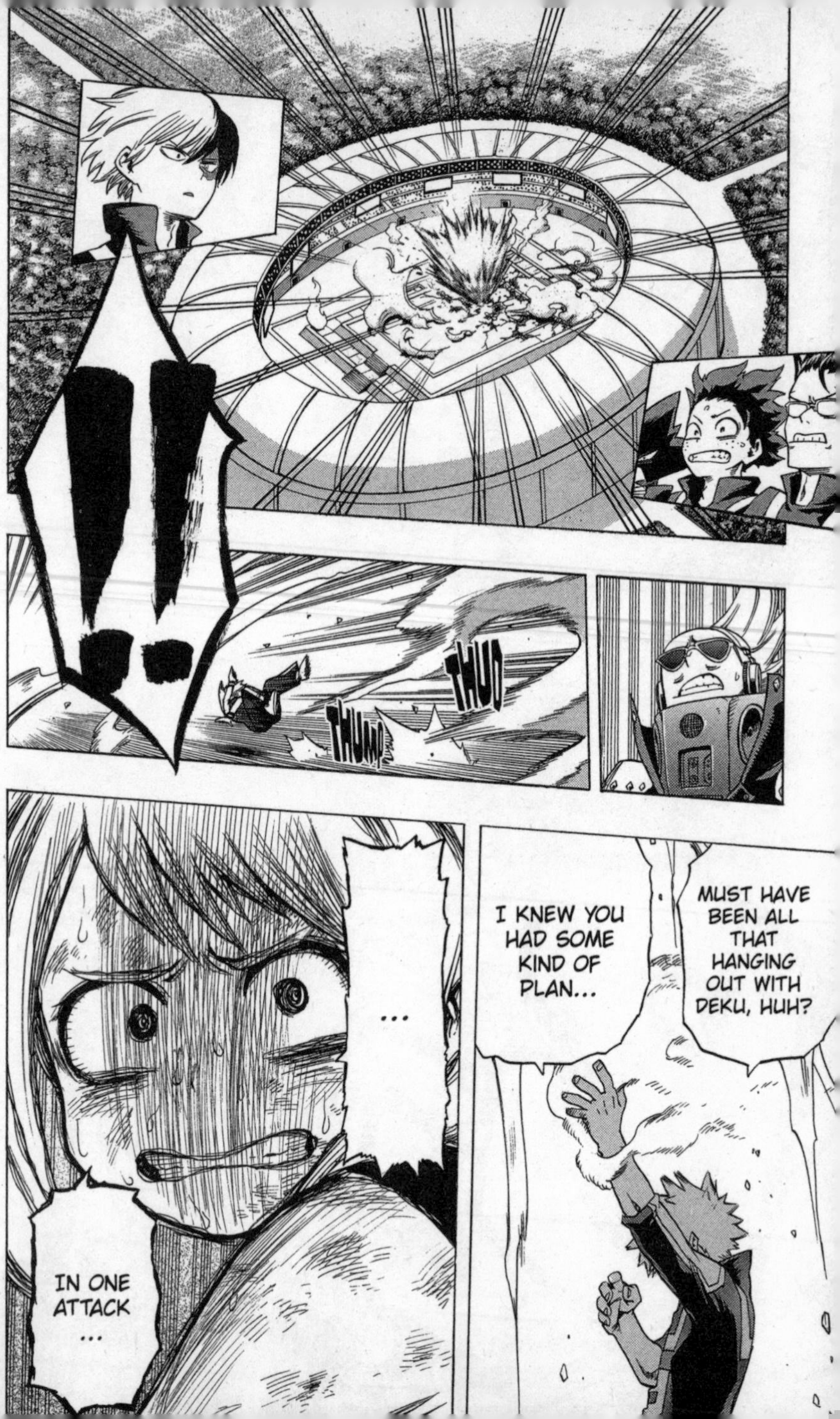
THUD
THUMP
MUST HAVE BEEN ALL THAT HANGING OUT WITH DEKU, HUH?
I KNEW YOU HAD SOME KIND OF PLAN...
...
IN ONE ATTACK ...

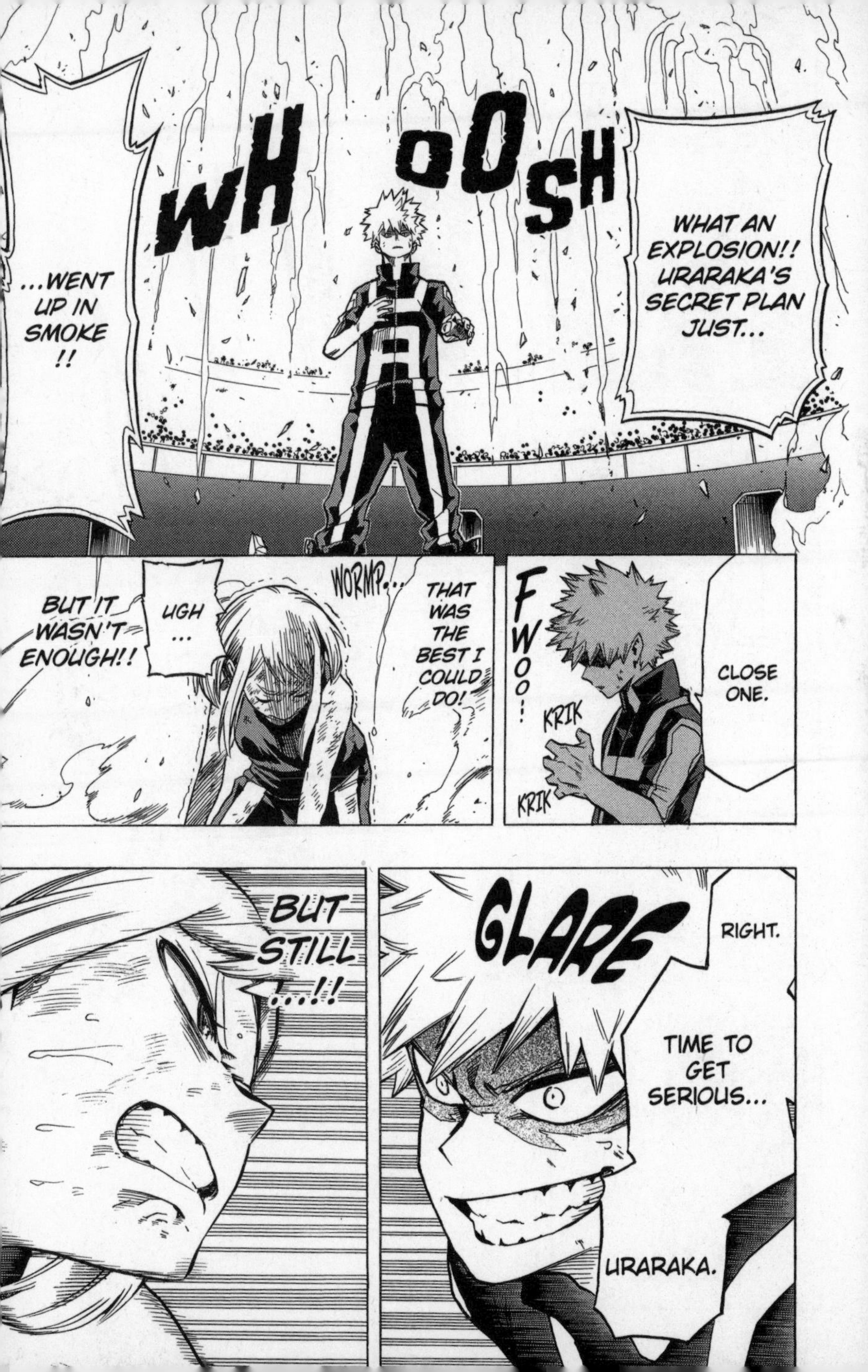
WHAT AN EXPLOSION!! URARAKA'S SECRET PLAN JUST...
WHOOSH
...WENT UP IN SMOKE!!
FWOO!!
KRIK
KRIK
CLOSE ONE.
WORMP...
THAT WAS THE BEST I COULD DO!
UGH...
BUT IT WASN'T ENOUGH!!
GLARE
RIGHT.
TIME TO GET SERIOUS...
URARAKA.
BUT STILL...!!

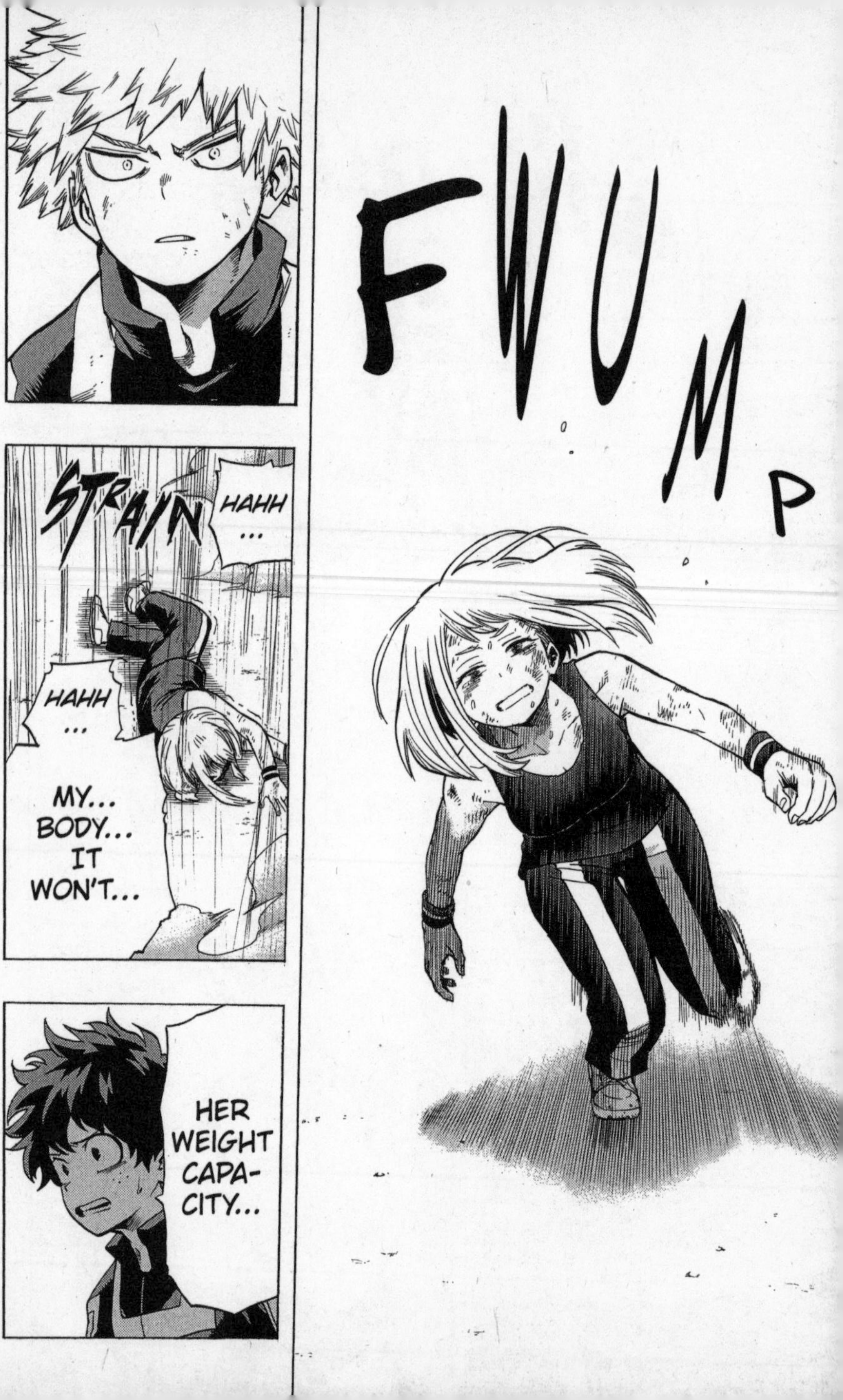
FWUMP
HAHH...
STRAIN
HAHH...
MY... BODY... IT WON'T...
HER WEIGHT CAPA-CITY...

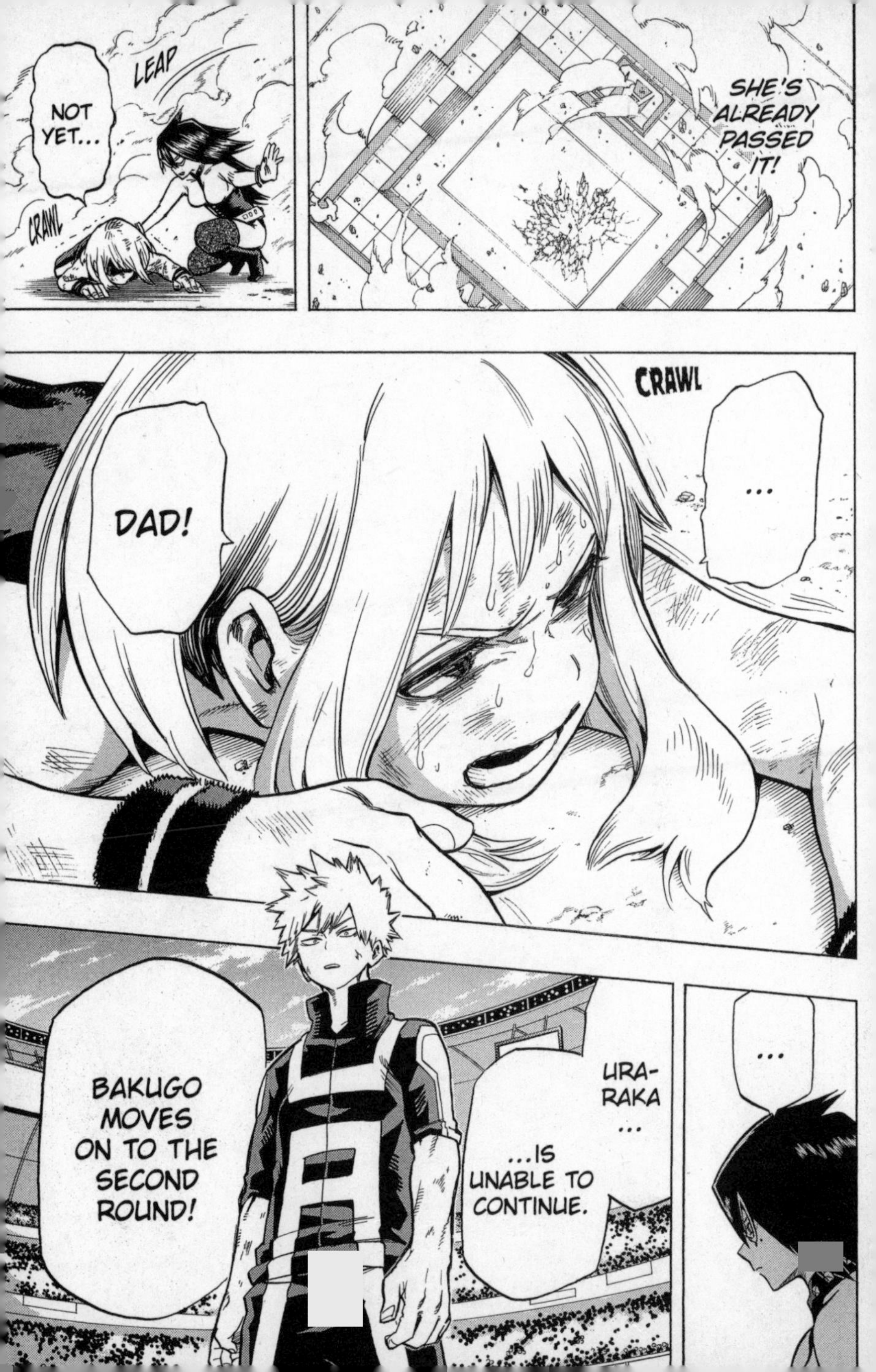
SHE'S ALREADY PASSED IT!
LEAP
NOT YET...
CRAWL
CRAWL
...
DAD!
...
URA-RAKA ...
...IS UNABLE TO CONTINUE.
BAKUGO MOVES ON TO THE SECOND ROUND!

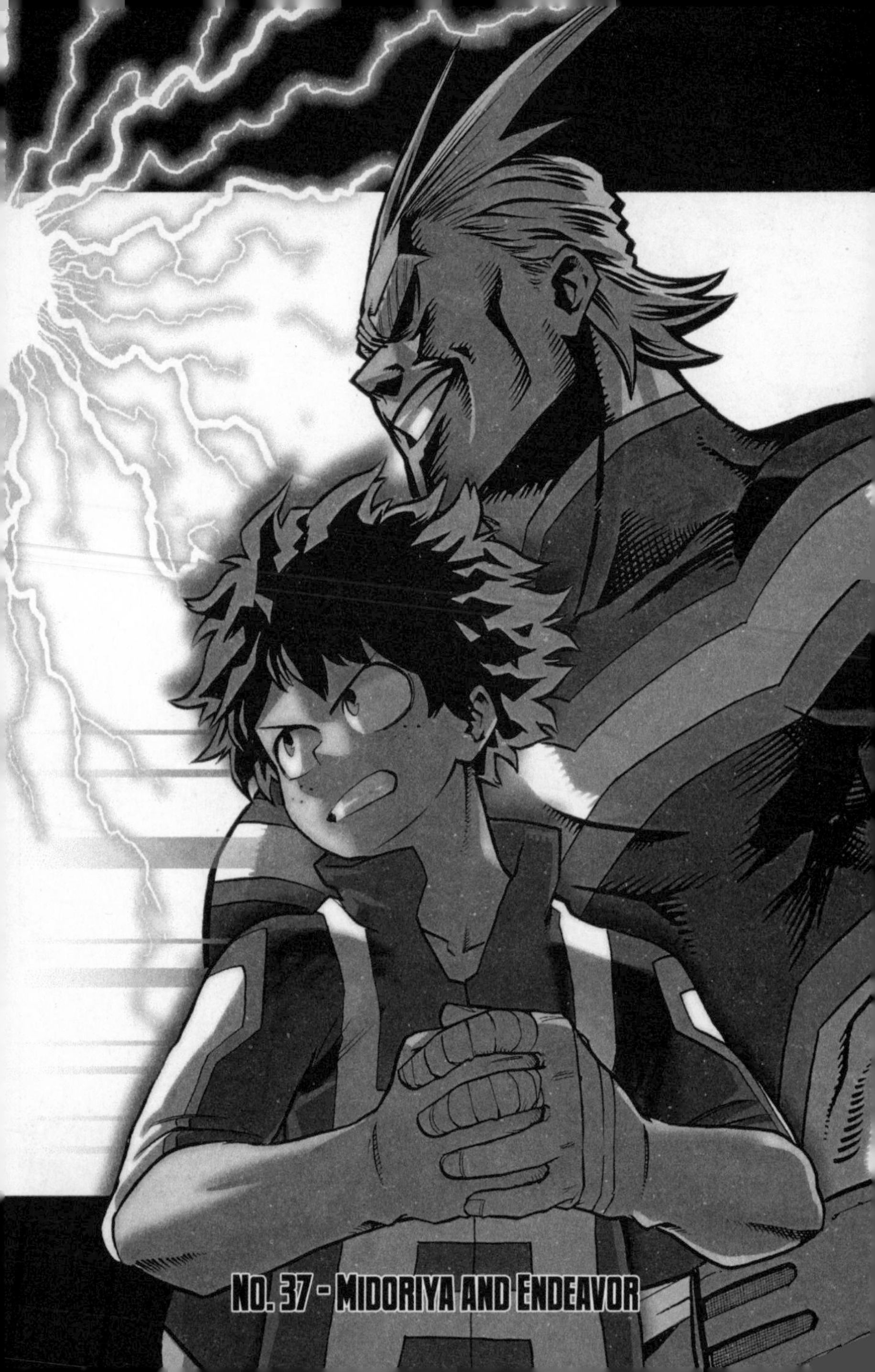
No. 37 - Midoriya and Endeavor

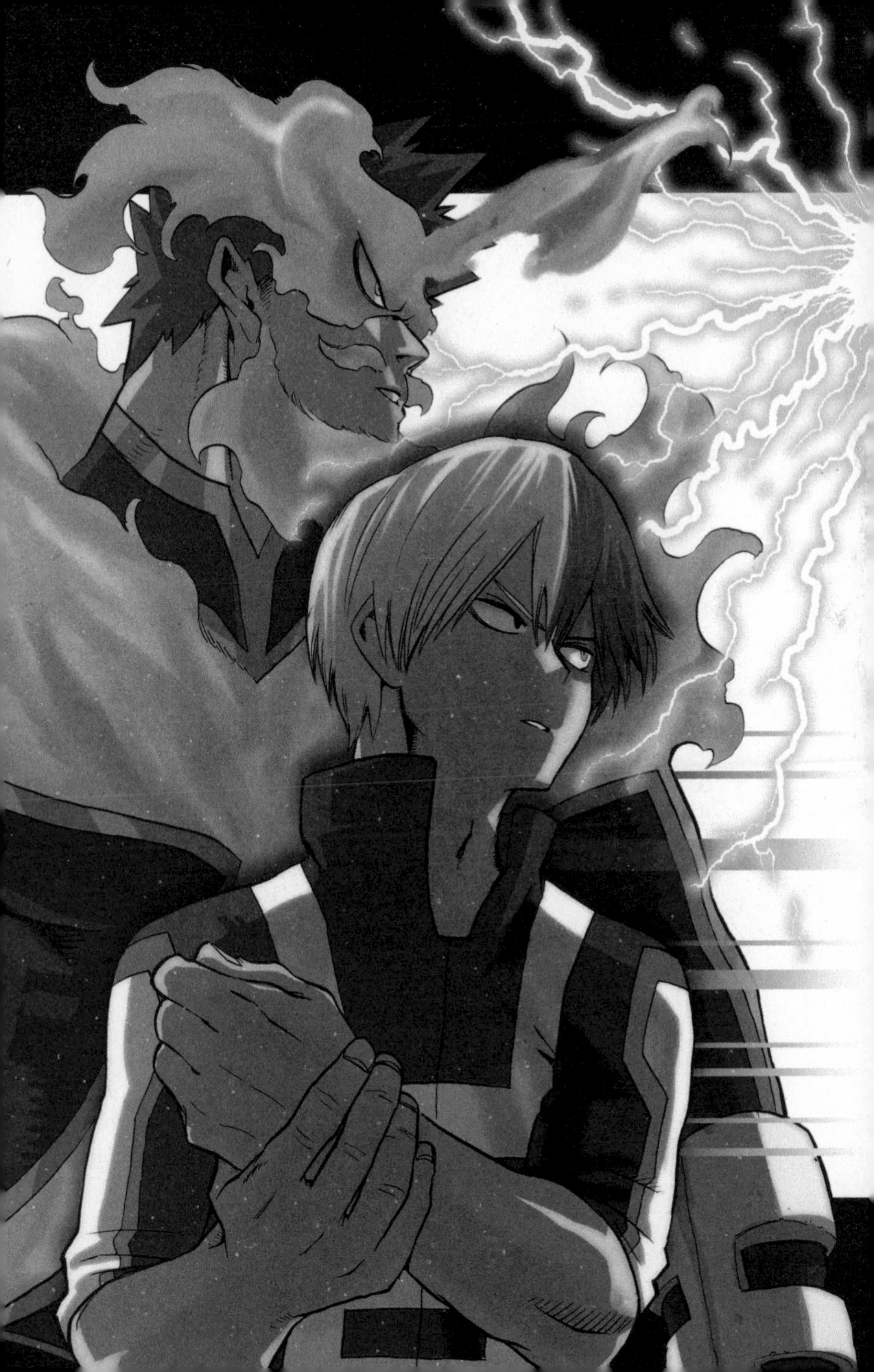

MY HERO ACADEMIA

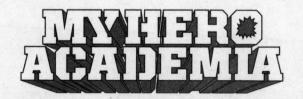

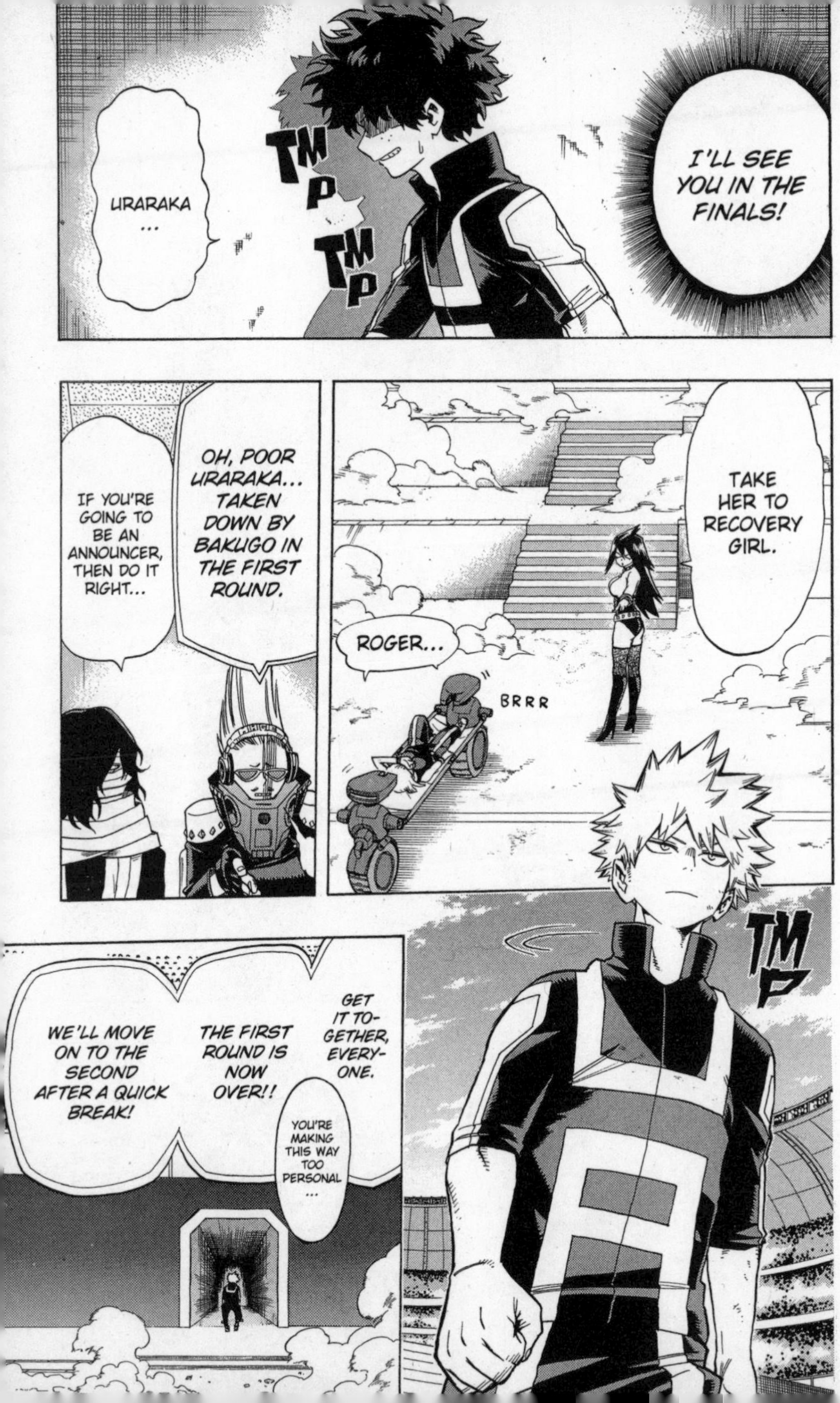
I'LL SEE YOU IN THE FINALS!
TMP
TMP
URARAKA ...
TAKE HER TO RECOVERY GIRL.
ROGER...
BRRR
OH, POOR URARAKA... TAKEN DOWN BY BAKUGO IN THE FIRST ROUND.
IF YOU'RE GOING TO BE AN ANNOUNCER, THEN DO IT RIGHT...
TMP
GET IT TOGETHER, EVERYONE.
THE FIRST ROUND IS NOW OVER!!
WE'LL MOVE ON TO THE SECOND AFTER A QUICK BREAK!
YOU'RE MAKING THIS WAY TOO PERSONAL ...

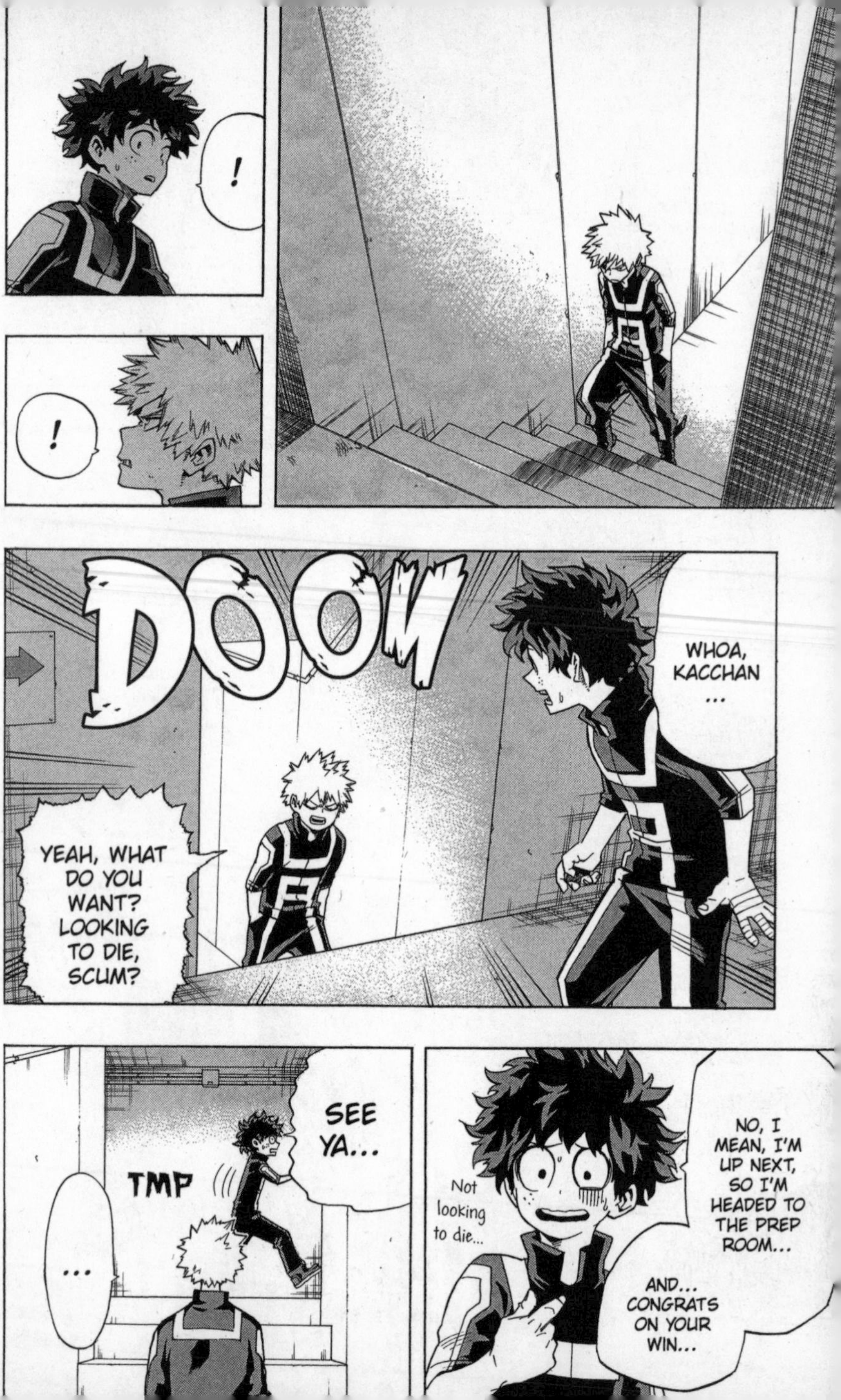
!
!
DOOM
WHOA, KACCHAN ...
YEAH, WHAT DO YOU WANT? LOOKING TO DIE, SCUM?
NO, I MEAN, I'M UP NEXT, SO I'M HEADED TO THE PREP ROOM...
Not looking to die...
AND... CONGRATS ON YOUR WIN...
SEE YA...
TMP
...

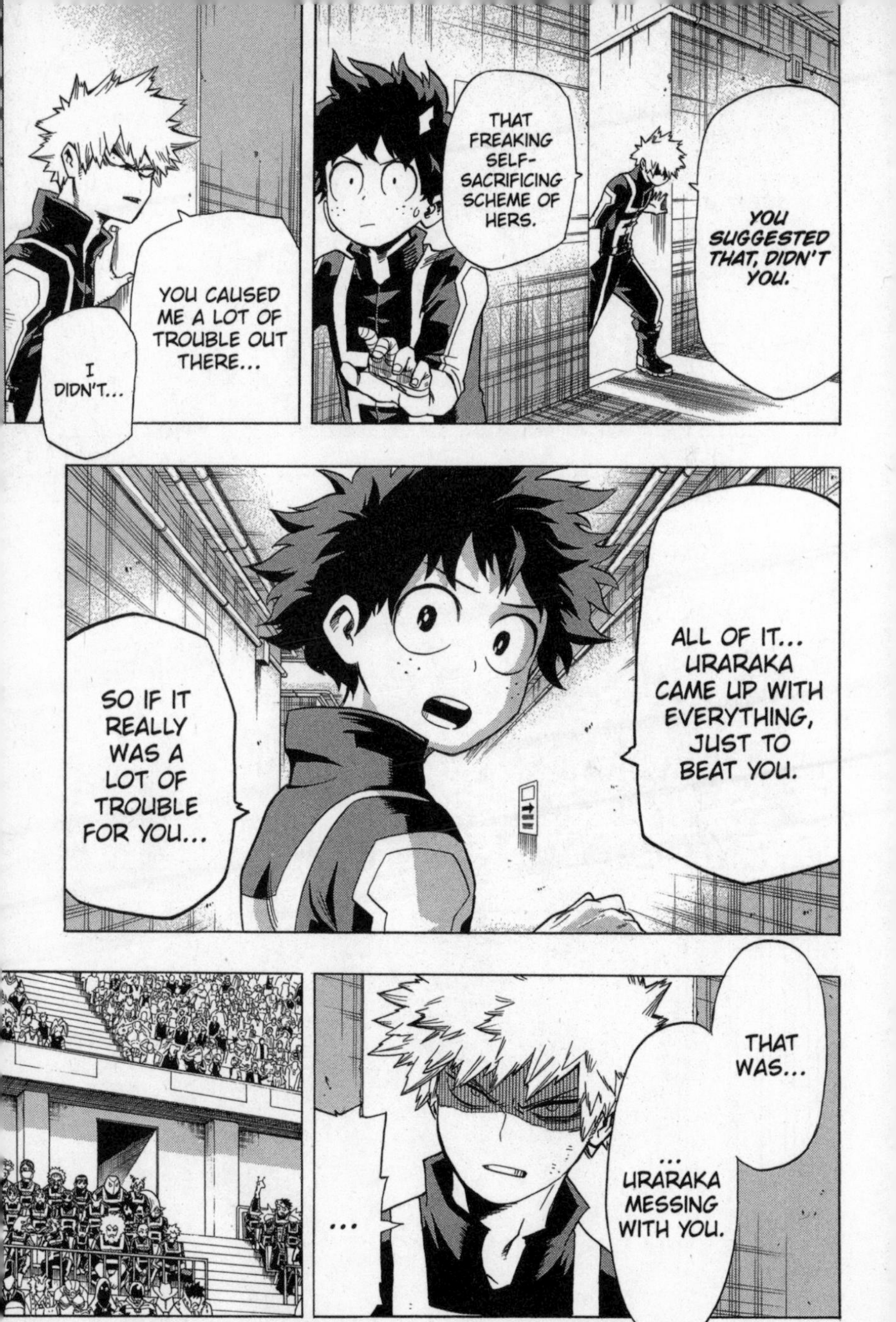
YOU SUGGESTED THAT, DIDN'T YOU.
THAT FREAKING SELF-SACRIFICING SCHEME OF HERS.
YOU CAUSED ME A LOT OF TROUBLE OUT THERE...
I DIDN'T...
ALL OF IT... URARAKA CAME UP WITH EVERYTHING, JUST TO BEAT YOU.
SO IF IT REALLY WAS A LOT OF TROUBLE FOR YOU...
THAT WAS...
... URARAKA MESSING WITH YOU.
...

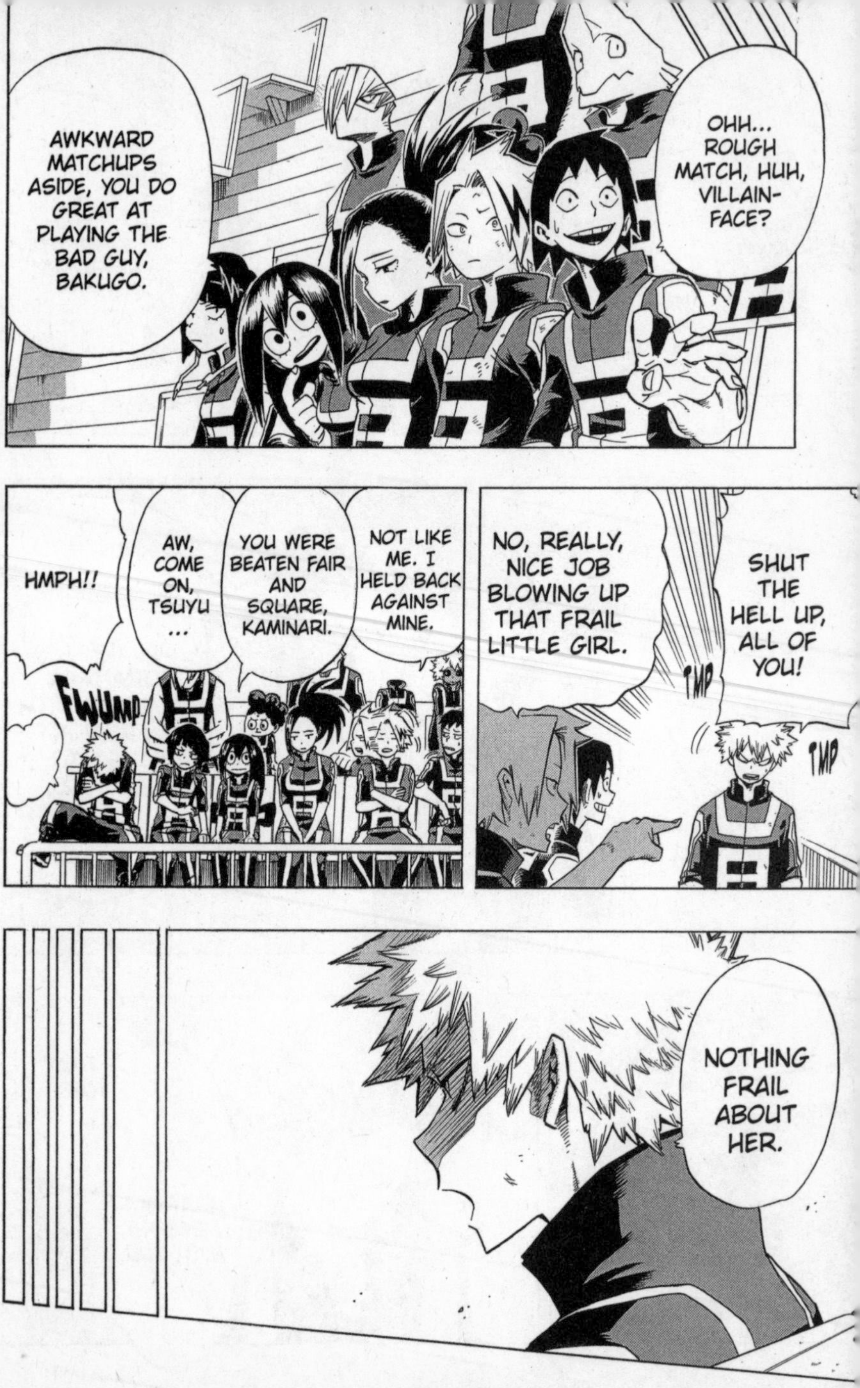
OHH... ROUGH MATCH, HUH, VILLAIN-FACE?
AWKWARD MATCHUPS ASIDE, YOU DO GREAT AT PLAYING THE BAD GUY, BAKUGO.
NO, REALLY, NICE JOB BLOWING UP THAT FRAIL LITTLE GIRL.
SHUT THE HELL UP, ALL OF YOU!
TMP
TMP
NOT LIKE ME. I HELD BACK AGAINST MINE.
YOU WERE BEATEN FAIR AND SQUARE, KAMINARI.
AW, COME ON, TSUYU ...
HMPH!!
FWUMP
NOTHING FRAIL ABOUT HER.

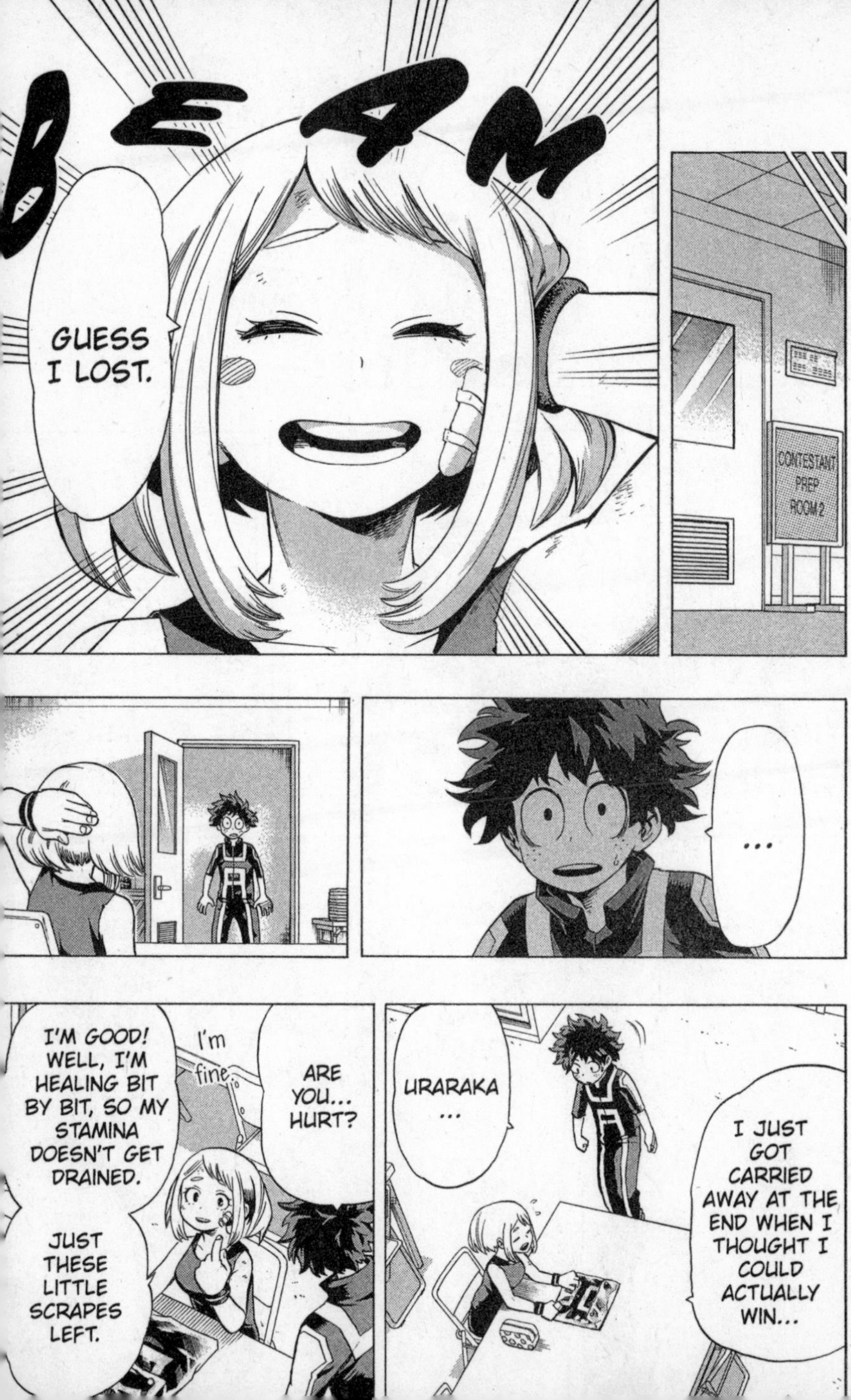
CONTESTANT PREP ROOM 2
BEAM
GUESS I LOST.
...
URARAKA ...
I JUST GOT CARRIED AWAY AT THE END WHEN I THOUGHT I COULD ACTUALLY WIN...
ARE YOU... HURT?
I'm fine.
I'M GOOD! WELL, I'M HEALING BIT BY BIT, SO MY STAMINA DOESN'T GET DRAINED.
JUST THESE LITTLE SCRAPES LEFT.

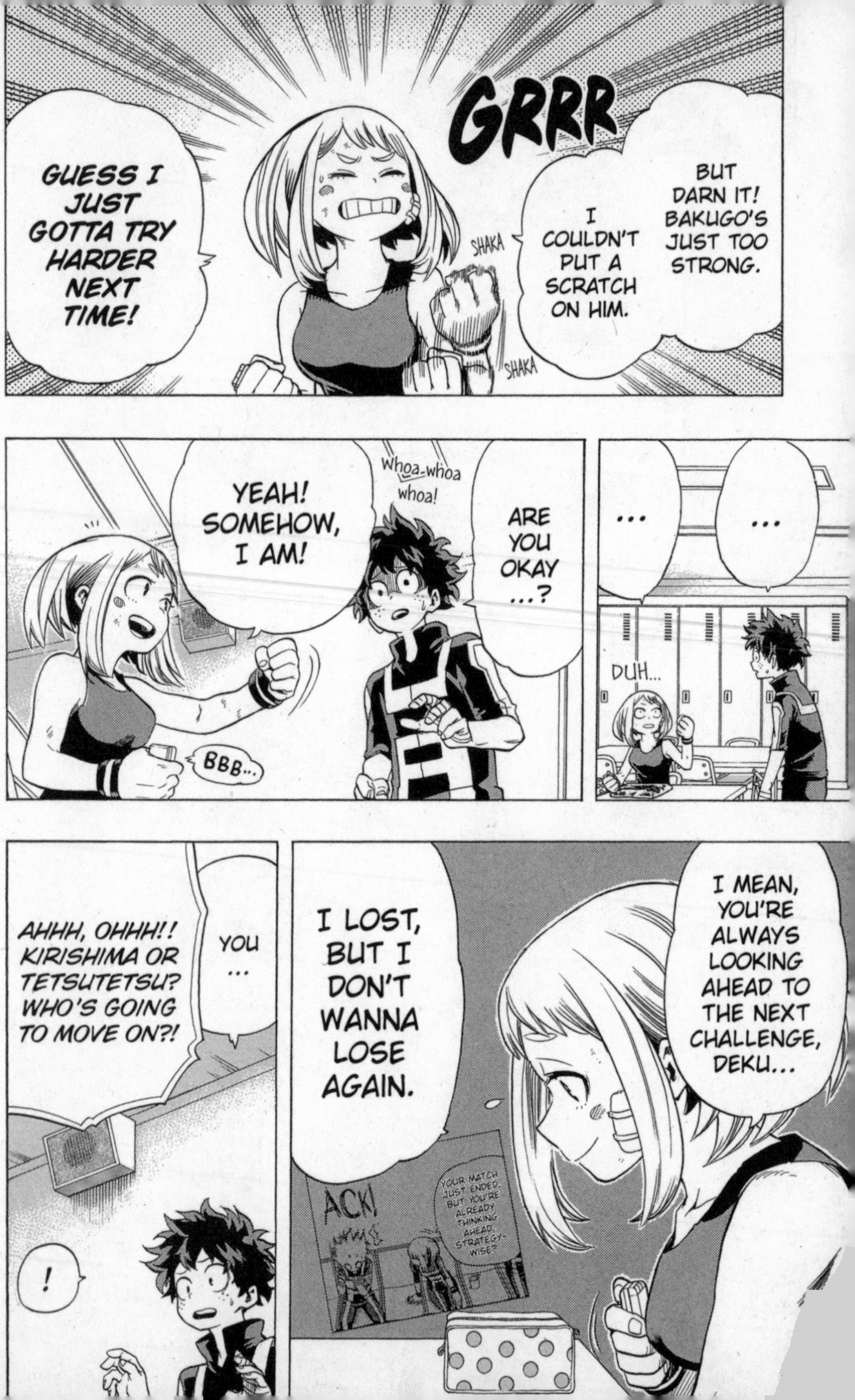
BUT DARN IT! BAKUGO'S JUST TOO STRONG.
I COULDN'T PUT A SCRATCH ON HIM.
GRRR
SHAKA
SHAKA
GUESS I JUST GOTTA TRY HARDER NEXT TIME!
...
...
DUH...
ARE YOU OKAY ...?
Whoa-whoa whoa!
YEAH! SOMEHOW, I AM!
BBB...
I MEAN, YOU'RE ALWAYS LOOKING AHEAD TO THE NEXT CHALLENGE, DEKU...
I LOST, BUT I DON'T WANNA LOSE AGAIN.
ACK!
YOUR MATCH JUST ENDED, BUT YOU'RE ALREADY THINKING AHEAD, STRATEGY-WISE?
YOU ...
AHHH, OHHH!! KIRISHIMA OR TETSUTETSU? WHO'S GOING TO MOVE ON?!
!

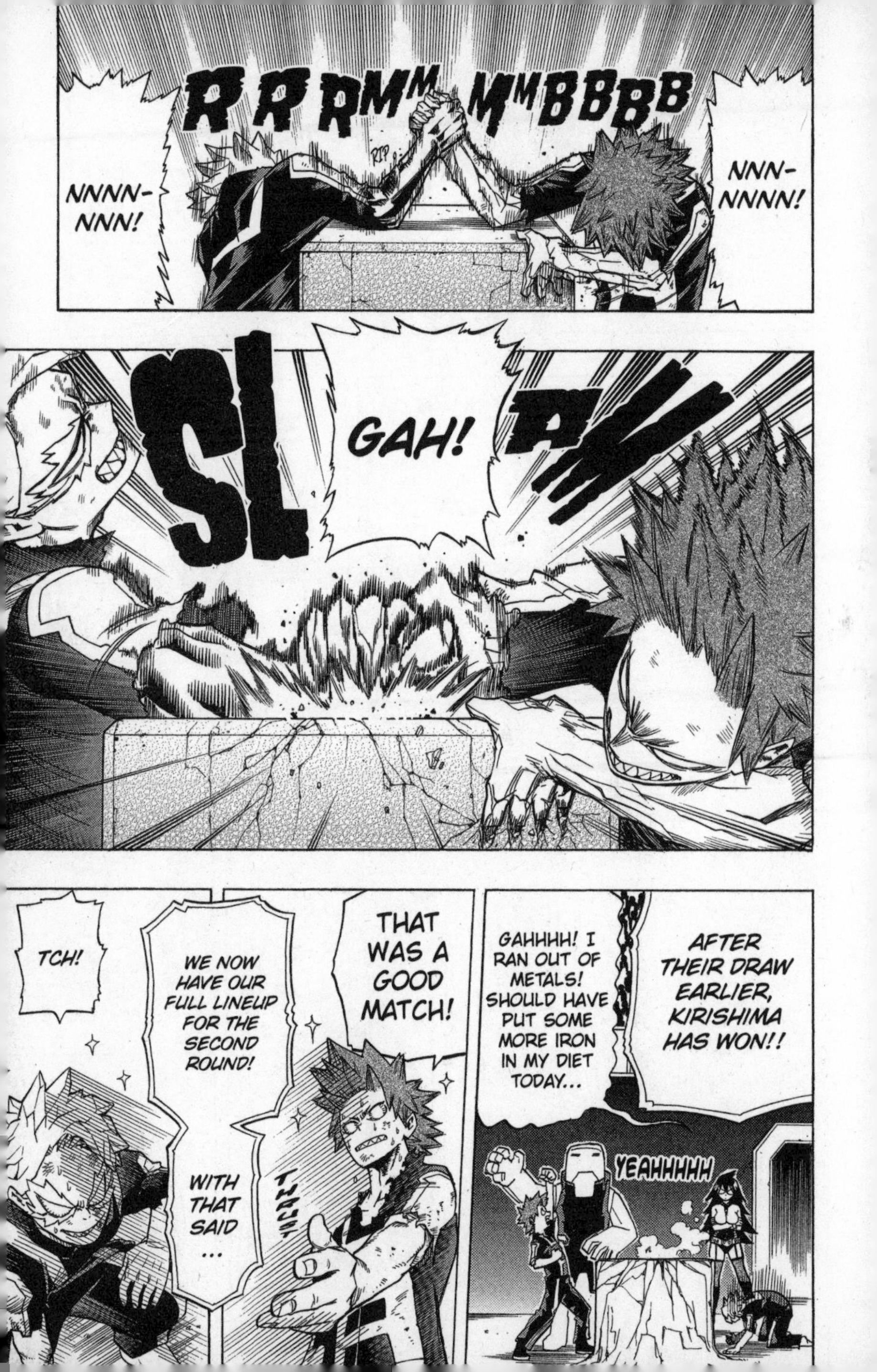
RRRMMM MMBBBB
NNN-NNNNN!
RIP
NNNN-NNN!
SL
AM
GAH!
AFTER THEIR DRAW EARLIER, KIRISHIMA HAS WON!!
GAHHHHH! I RAN OUT OF METALS! SHOULD HAVE PUT SOME MORE IRON IN MY DIET TODAY...
YEAHHHHH
THAT WAS A GOOD MATCH!
WE NOW HAVE OUR FULL LINEUP FOR THE SECOND ROUND!
TCH!
WITH THAT SAID...

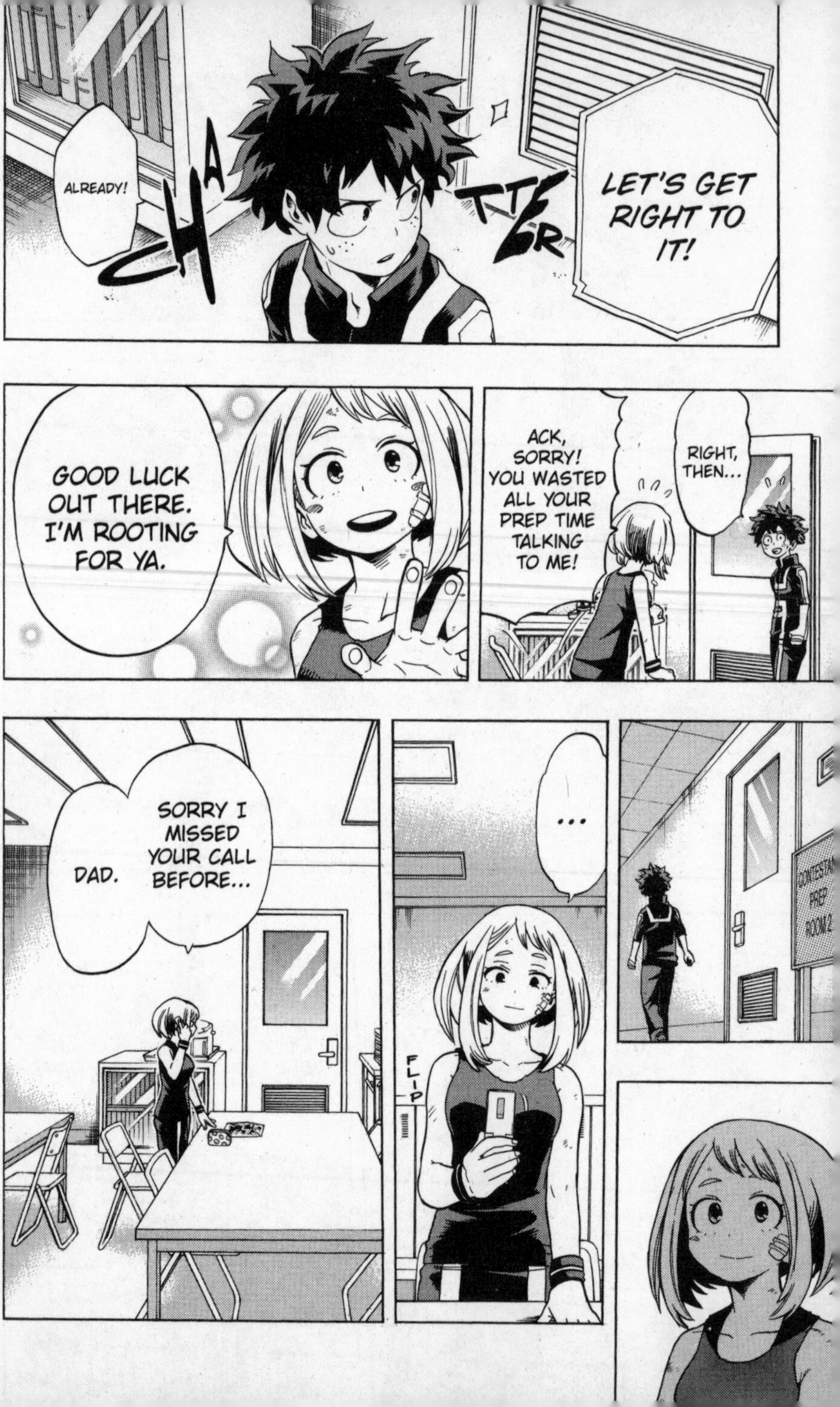
LET'S GET RIGHT TO IT!
CHATTER
ALREADY!
RIGHT, THEN...
ACK, SORRY! YOU WASTED ALL YOUR PREP TIME TALKING TO ME!
GOOD LUCK OUT THERE. I'M ROOTING FOR YA.
PREP ROOM 2
...
FLIP
SORRY I MISSED YOUR CALL BEFORE...
DAD.

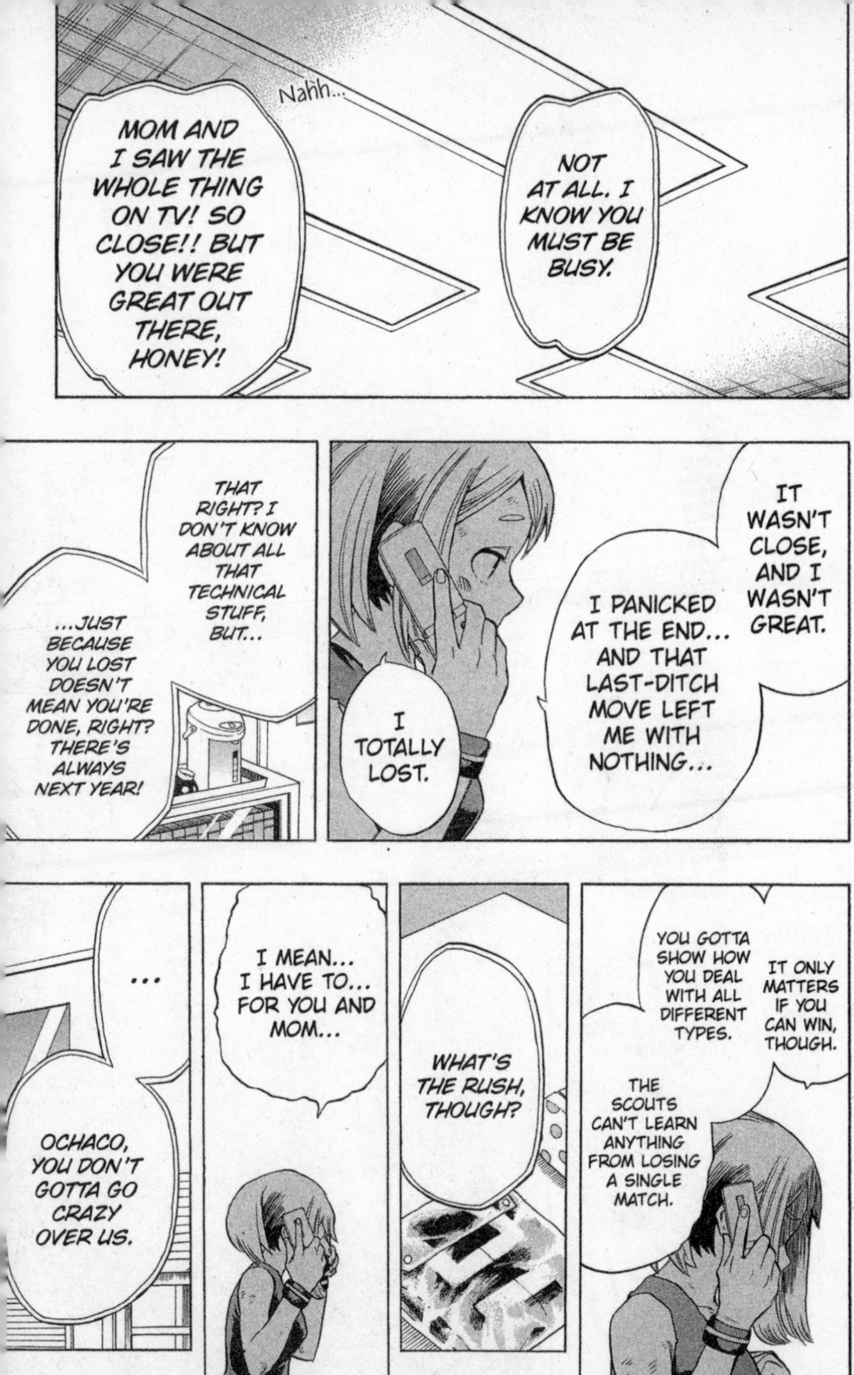
Nahh...
NOT AT ALL. I KNOW YOU MUST BE BUSY.
MOM AND I SAW THE WHOLE THING ON TV! SO CLOSE!! BUT YOU WERE GREAT OUT THERE, HONEY!
IT WASN'T CLOSE, AND I WASN'T GREAT.
I PANICKED AT THE END... AND THAT LAST-DITCH MOVE LEFT ME WITH NOTHING...
I TOTALLY LOST.
THAT RIGHT? I DON'T KNOW ABOUT ALL THAT TECHNICAL STUFF, BUT...
...JUST BECAUSE YOU LOST DOESN'T MEAN YOU'RE DONE, RIGHT? THERE'S ALWAYS NEXT YEAR!
YOU GOTTA SHOW HOW YOU DEAL WITH ALL DIFFERENT TYPES.
IT ONLY MATTERS IF YOU CAN WIN, THOUGH.
THE SCOUTS CAN'T LEARN ANYTHING FROM LOSING A SINGLE MATCH.
WHAT'S THE RUSH, THOUGH?
I MEAN... I HAVE TO... FOR YOU AND MOM...
...
OCHACO, YOU DON'T GOTTA GO CRAZY OVER US.

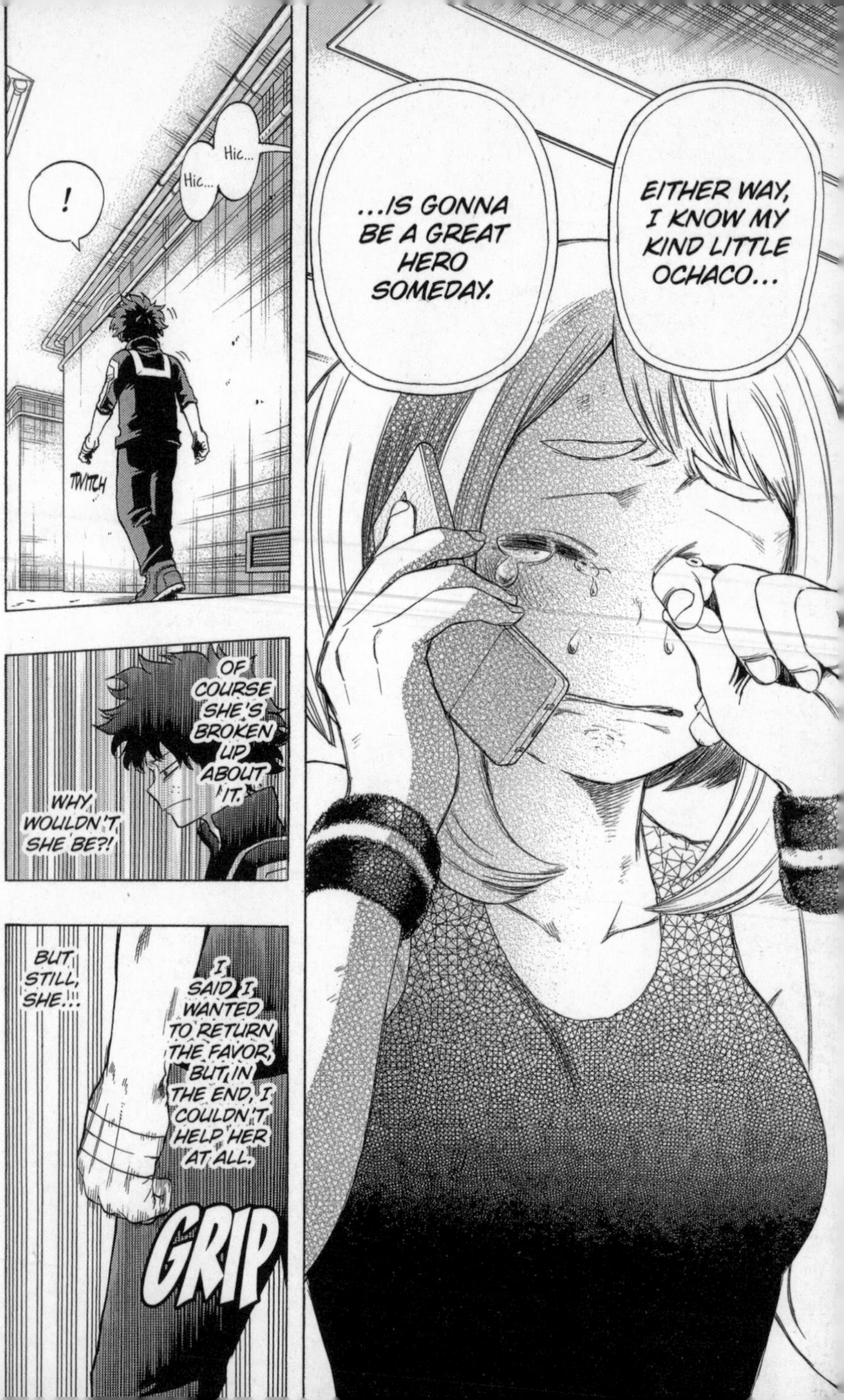
EITHER WAY, I KNOW MY KIND LITTLE OCHACO...
...IS GONNA BE A GREAT HERO SOMEDAY.
Hic...
Hic...
!
TWITCH
OF COURSE SHE'S BROKEN UP ABOUT IT.
WHY WOULDN'T SHE BE?!
I SAID I WANTED TO RETURN THE FAVOR, BUT IN THE END, I COULDN'T HELP HER AT ALL.
BUT STILL, SHE...
GRIP

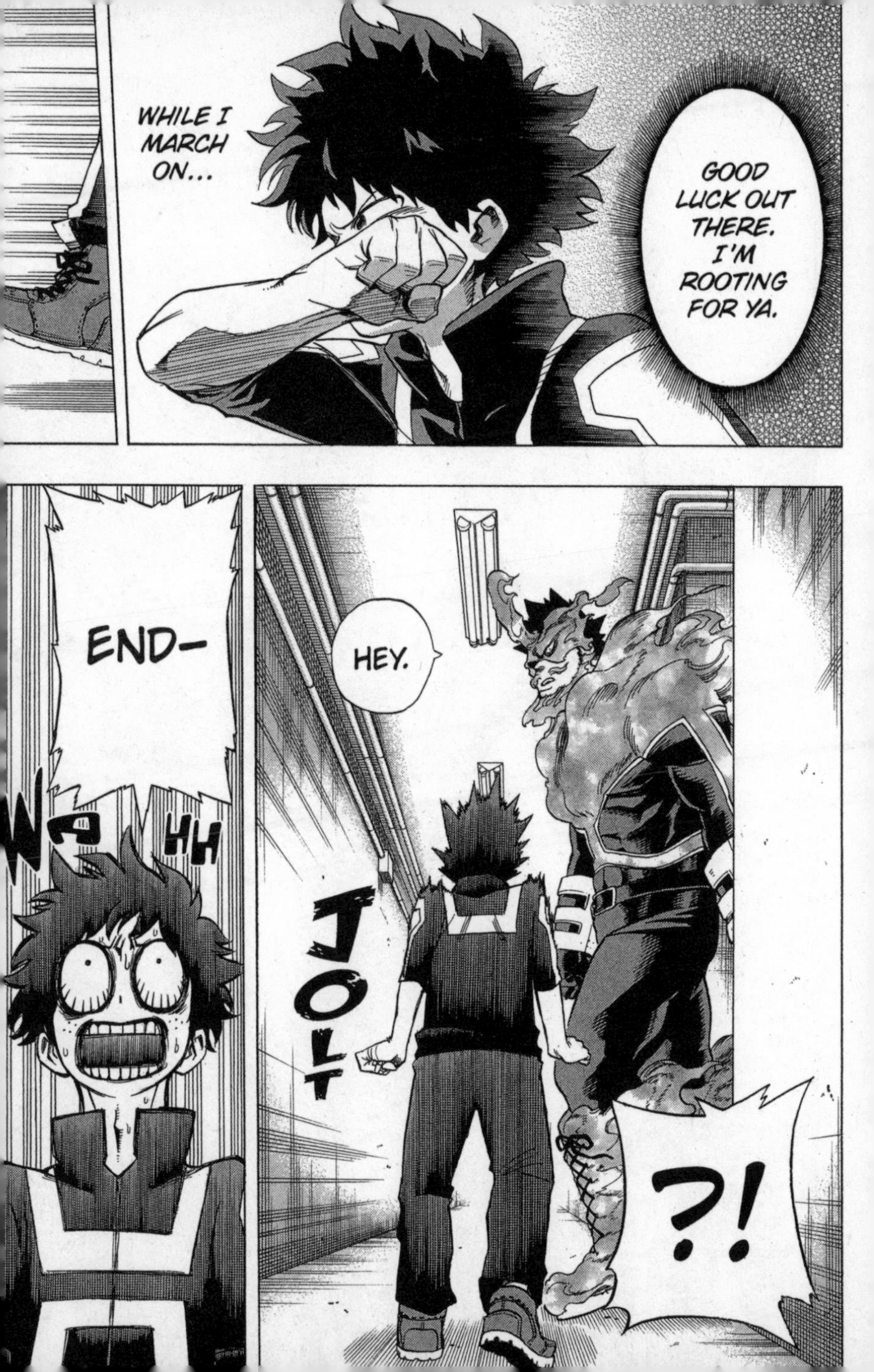
GOOD LUCK OUT THERE. I'M ROOTING FOR YA.
WHILE I MARCH ON...
HEY.
JOLT
?!
END-
WAHH

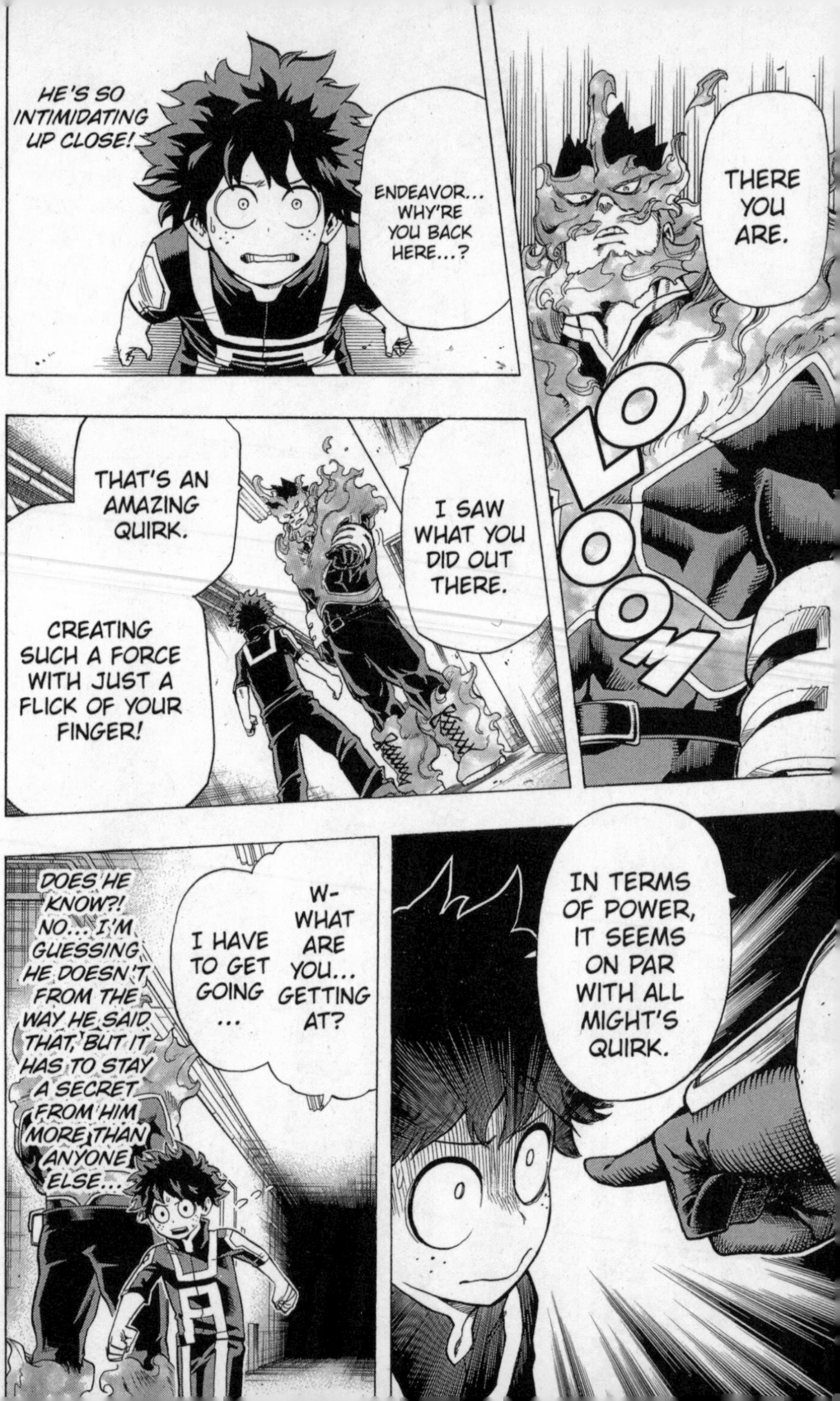
THERE YOU ARE.
LOOOM
ENDEAVOR... WHY'RE YOU BACK HERE...?
HE'S SO INTIMIDATING UP CLOSE!
I SAW WHAT YOU DID OUT THERE.
THAT'S AN AMAZING QUIRK.
CREATING SUCH A FORCE WITH JUST A FLICK OF YOUR FINGER!
IN TERMS OF POWER, IT SEEMS ON PAR WITH ALL MIGHT'S QUIRK.
W-WHAT ARE YOU... GETTING AT?
I HAVE TO GET GOING...
DOES HE KNOW?! NO... I'M GUESSING HE DOESN'T FROM THE WAY HE SAID THAT, BUT IT HAS TO STAY A SECRET FROM HIM MORE THAN ANYONE ELSE...

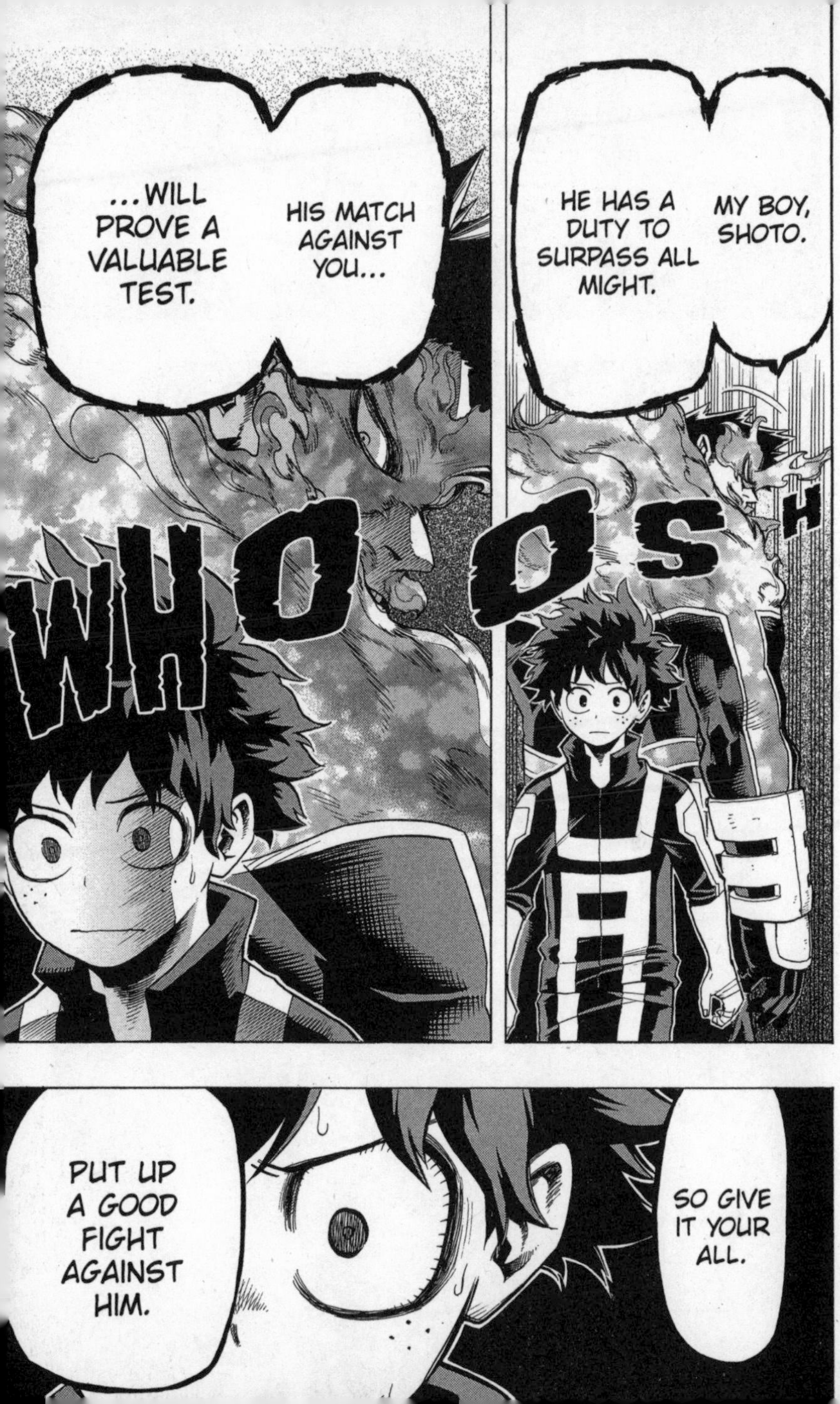
MY BOY, SHOTO.
HE HAS A DUTY TO SURPASS ALL MIGHT.
HIS MATCH AGAINST YOU...
...WILL PROVE A VALUABLE TEST.
WHOOSH
SO GIVE IT YOUR ALL.
PUT UP A GOOD FIGHT AGAINST HIM.

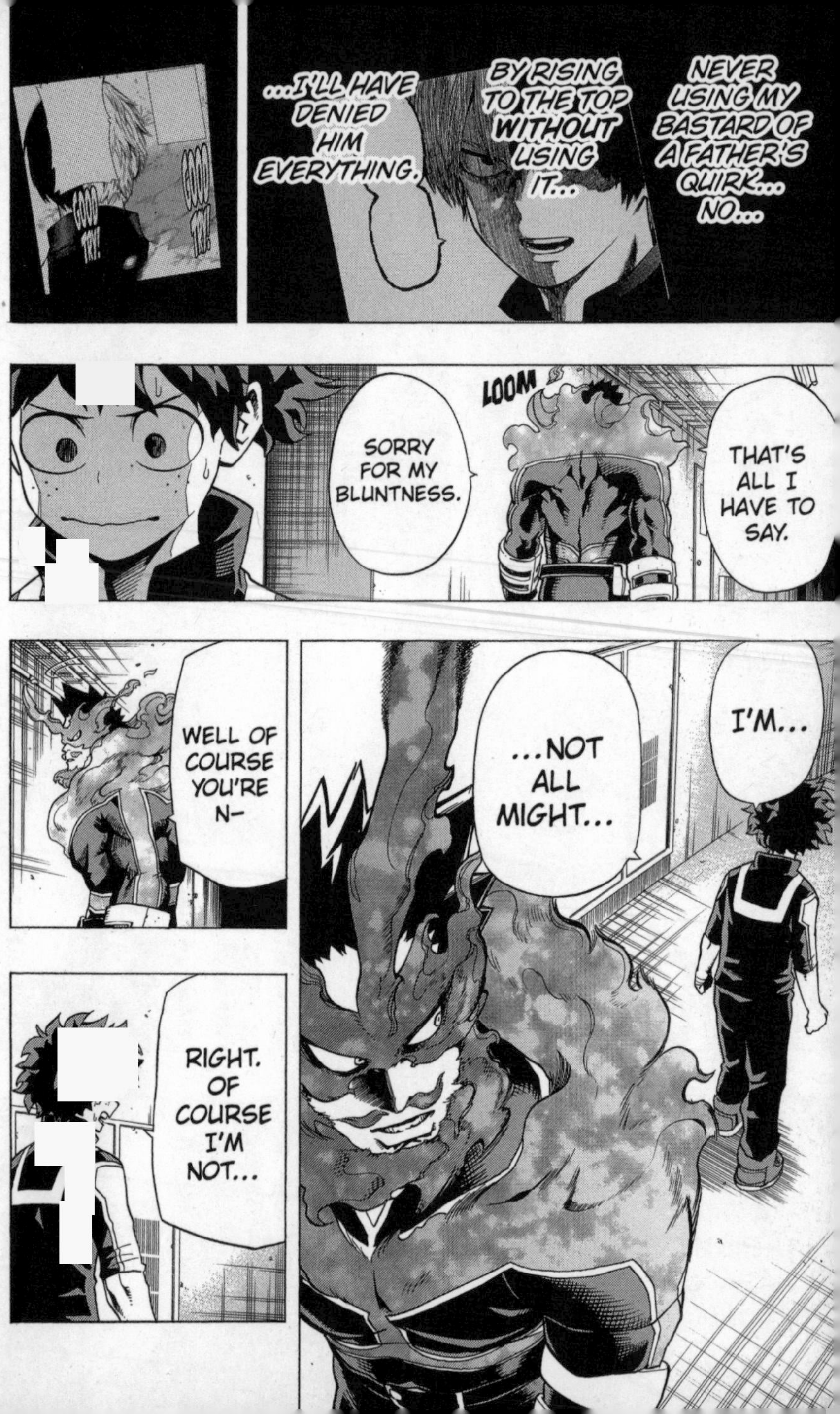
NEVER USING MY BASTARD OF A FATHER'S QUIRK... NO...
BY RISING TO THE TOP WITHOUT USING IT...
...I'LL HAVE DENIED HIM EVERYTHING.
GOOD TRY!
GOOD TRY!
LOOM
THAT'S ALL I HAVE TO SAY.
SORRY FOR MY BLUNTNESS.
I'M...
...NOT ALL MIGHT...
WELL OF COURSE YOU'RE N–
RIGHT. OF COURSE I'M NOT...

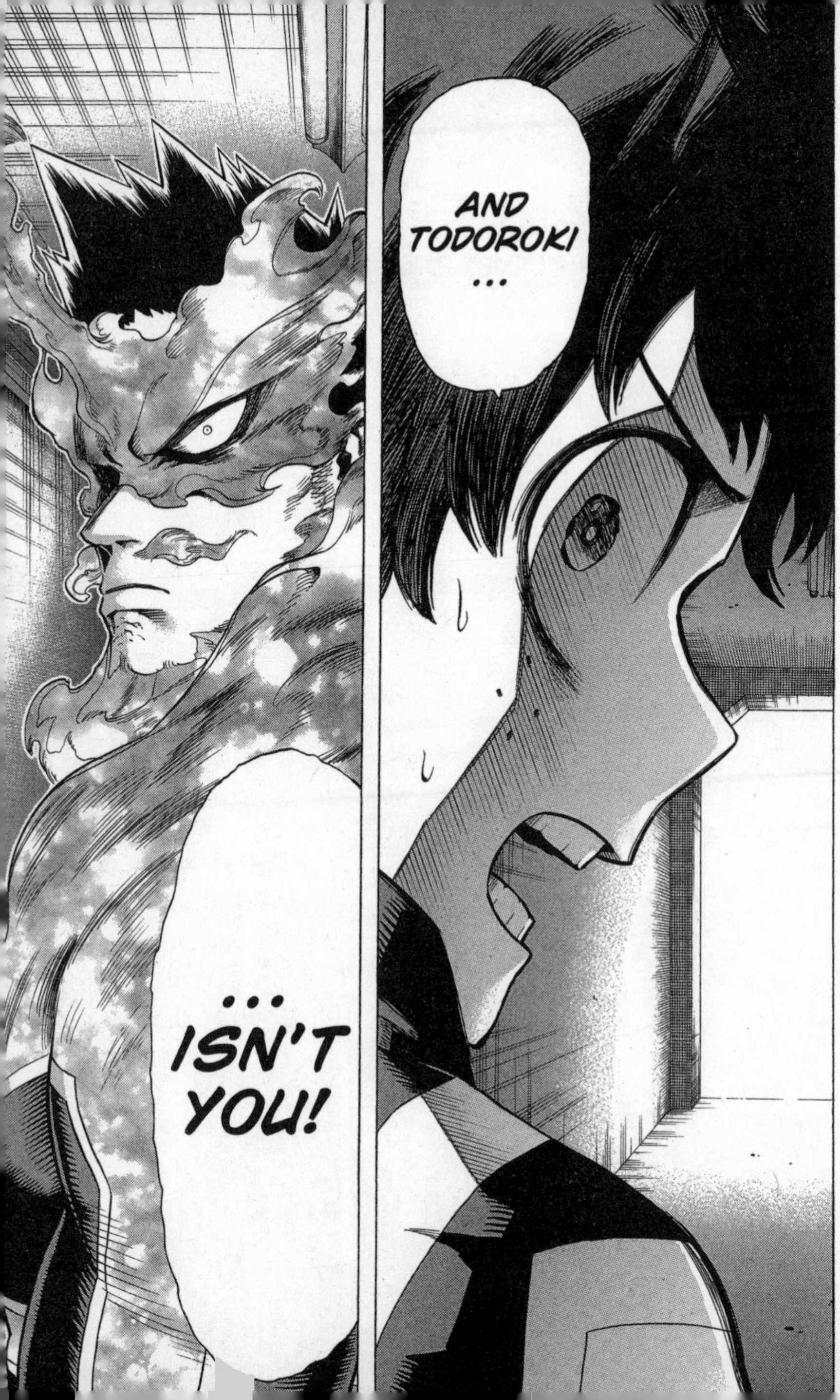
AND TODOROKI ...
... ISN'T YOU!

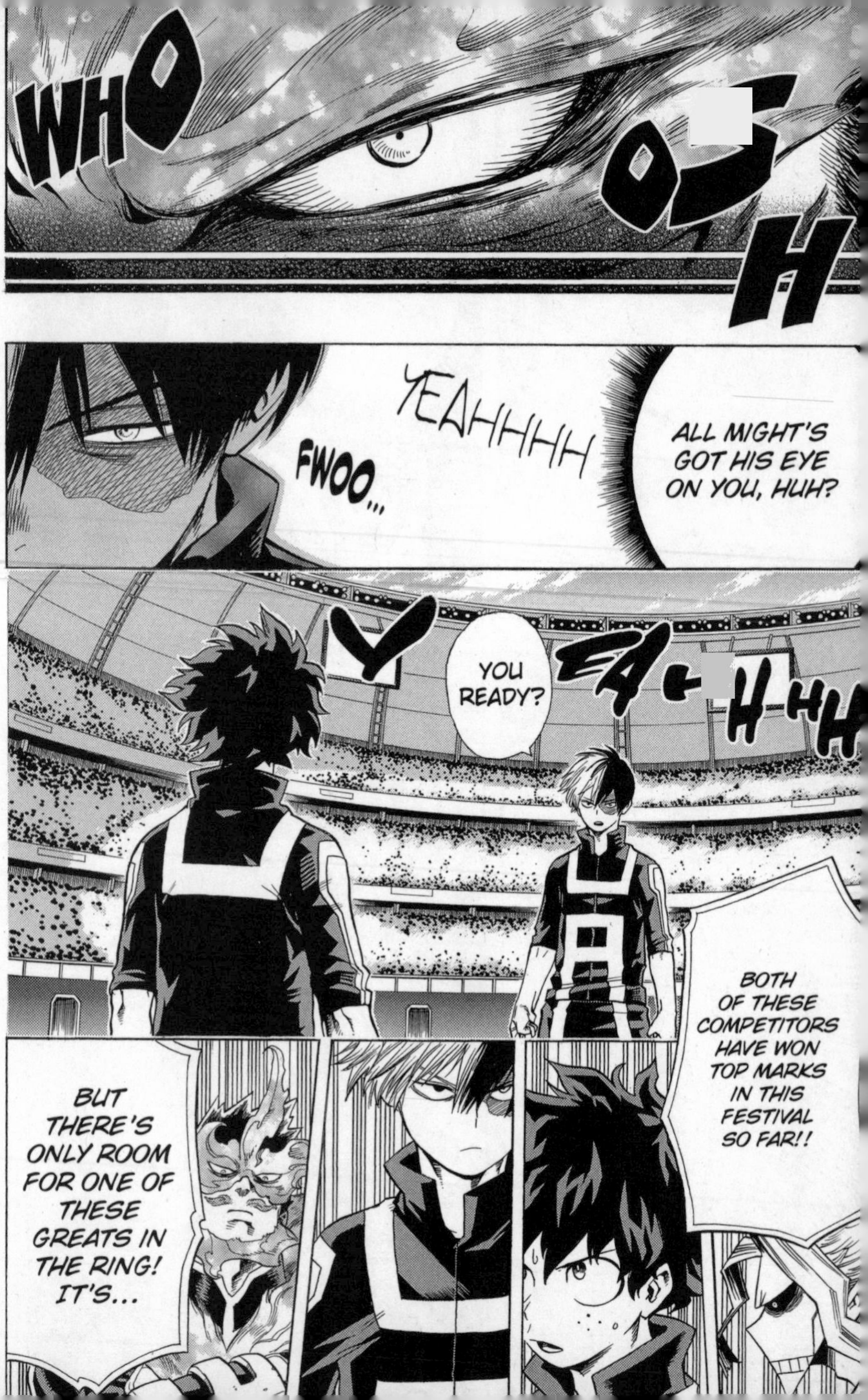
WHOOSH
ALL MIGHT'S GOT HIS EYE ON YOU, HUH?
YEAHHHHH
FWOO...
YEAHHHH
YOU READY?
BOTH OF THESE COMPETITORS HAVE WON TOP MARKS IN THIS FESTIVAL SO FAR!!
BUT THERE'S ONLY ROOM FOR ONE OF THESE GREATS IN THE RING! IT'S...

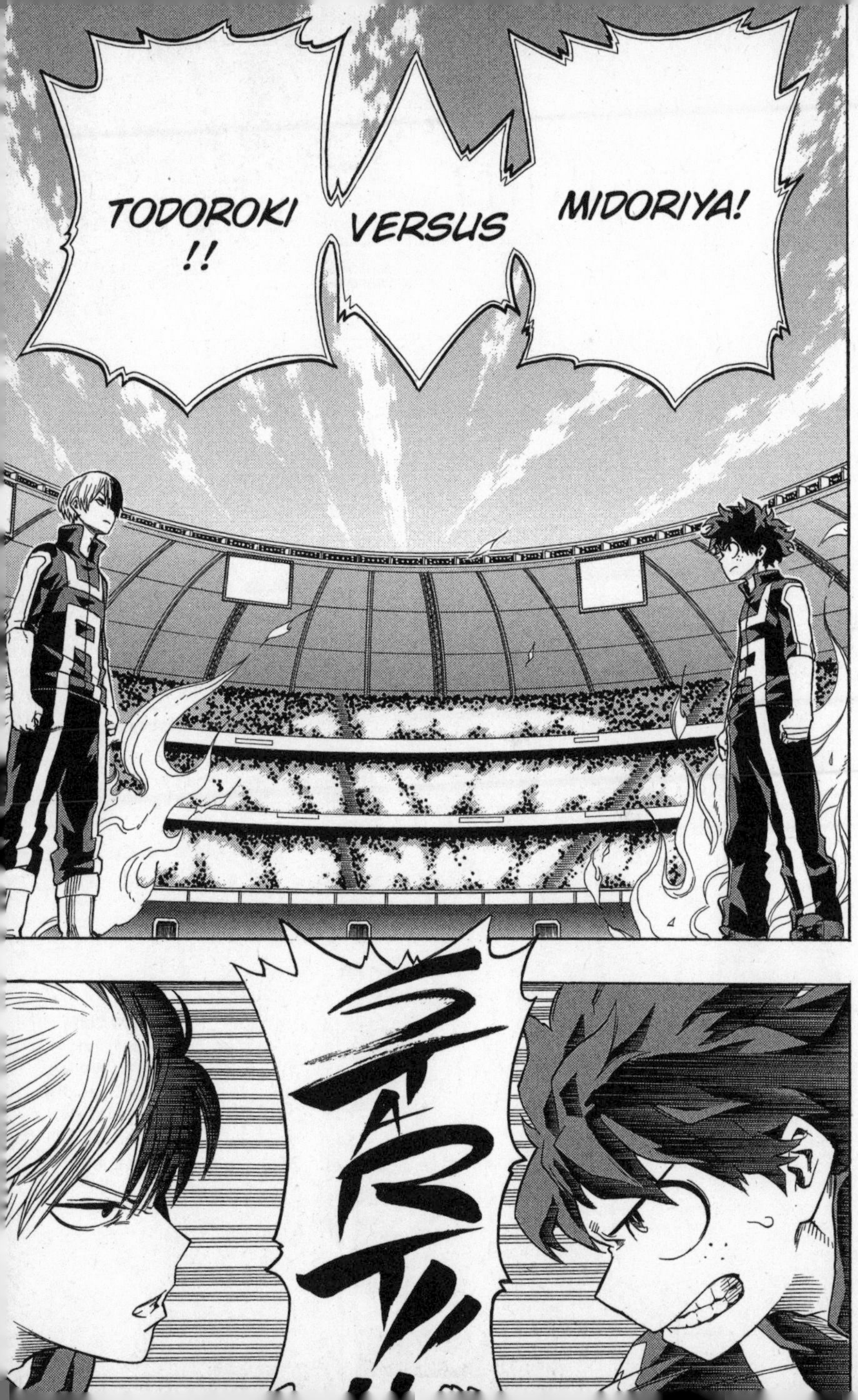
TODOROKI!!
VERSUS
MIDORIYA!

ENDEAVOR [45]
[REAL NAME: ENJI TODOROKI]

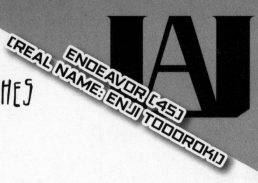

STREET CLOTHES

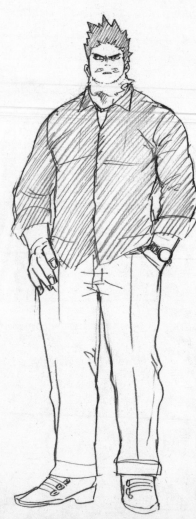

Birthday: 8/8
Height: 195 cm
Favorite Thing: ***Kuzumochi***

BEHIND THE SCENES

He was originally meant to be part of the U.A. faculty, but he ended up being too much of a one-dimensional powerhouse without much else going on, so I decided against that.

Story-wise, he's basically a terrible father, but I hope to eventually portray exactly why that is.

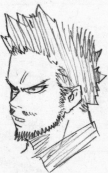

He can switch his beard and mustache flames on and off, but he typically leaves them burning as a flashy show of power.

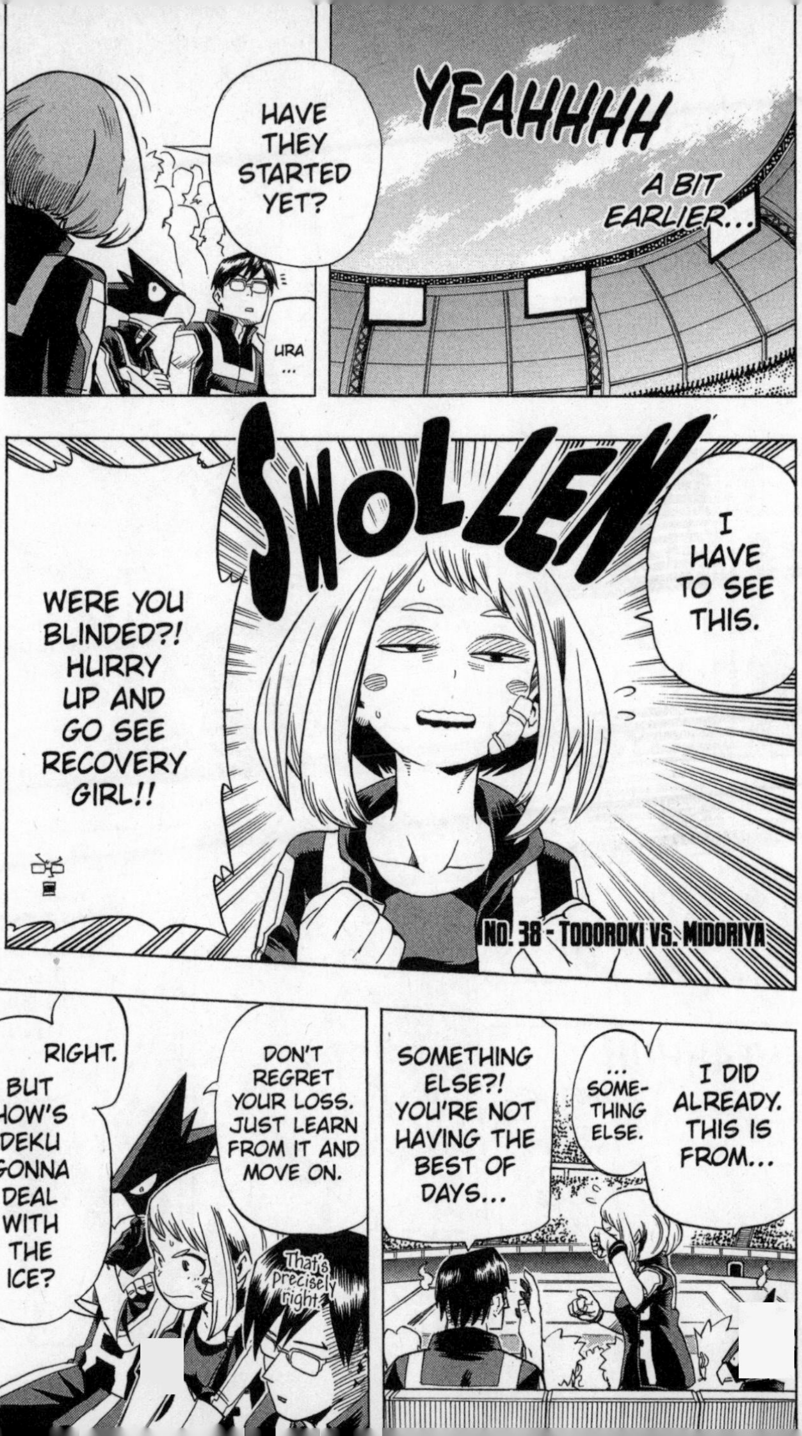
YEAHHHH
A BIT EARLIER...
HAVE THEY STARTED YET?
URA...
I HAVE TO SEE THIS.
SWOLLEN
WERE YOU BLINDED?! HURRY UP AND GO SEE RECOVERY GIRL!!
NO. 38 - TODOROKI VS. MIDORIYA
I DID ALREADY. THIS IS FROM...
... SOME-THING ELSE.
SOMETHING ELSE?! YOU'RE NOT HAVING THE BEST OF DAYS...
DON'T REGRET YOUR LOSS. JUST LEARN FROM IT AND MOVE ON.
That's precisely right.
RIGHT. BUT HOW'S DEKU GONNA DEAL WITH THE ICE?

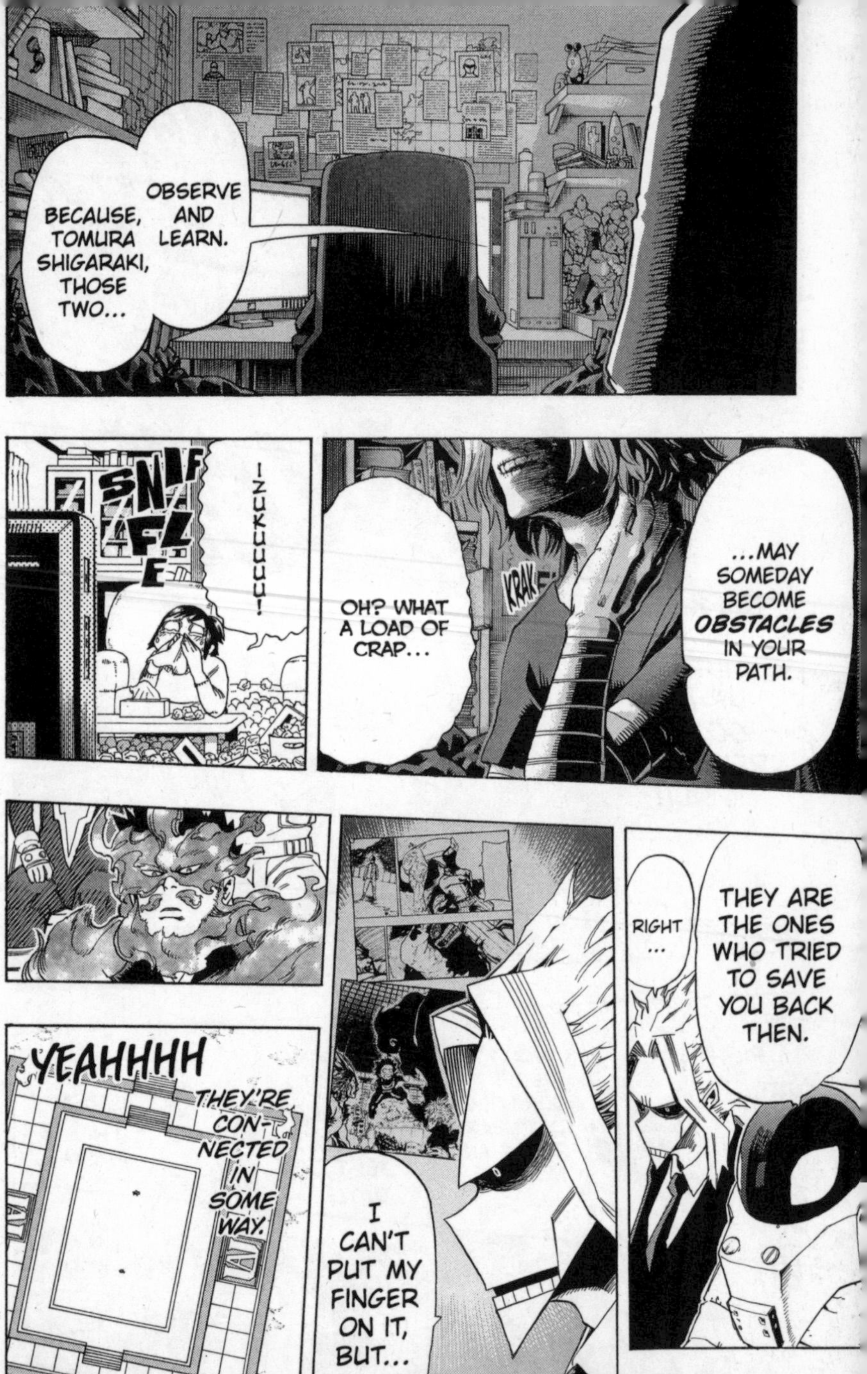
OBSERVE AND LEARN.
BECAUSE, TOMURA SHIGARAKI, THOSE TWO...
...MAY SOMEDAY BECOME OBSTACLES IN YOUR PATH.
KRAK
OH? WHAT A LOAD OF CRAP...
SNIFFLE
IZUKUUUU!
THEY ARE THE ONES WHO TRIED TO SAVE YOU BACK THEN.
RIGHT...
I CAN'T PUT MY FINGER ON IT, BUT...
YEAHHHH
THEY'RE CON-NECTED IN SOME WAY.

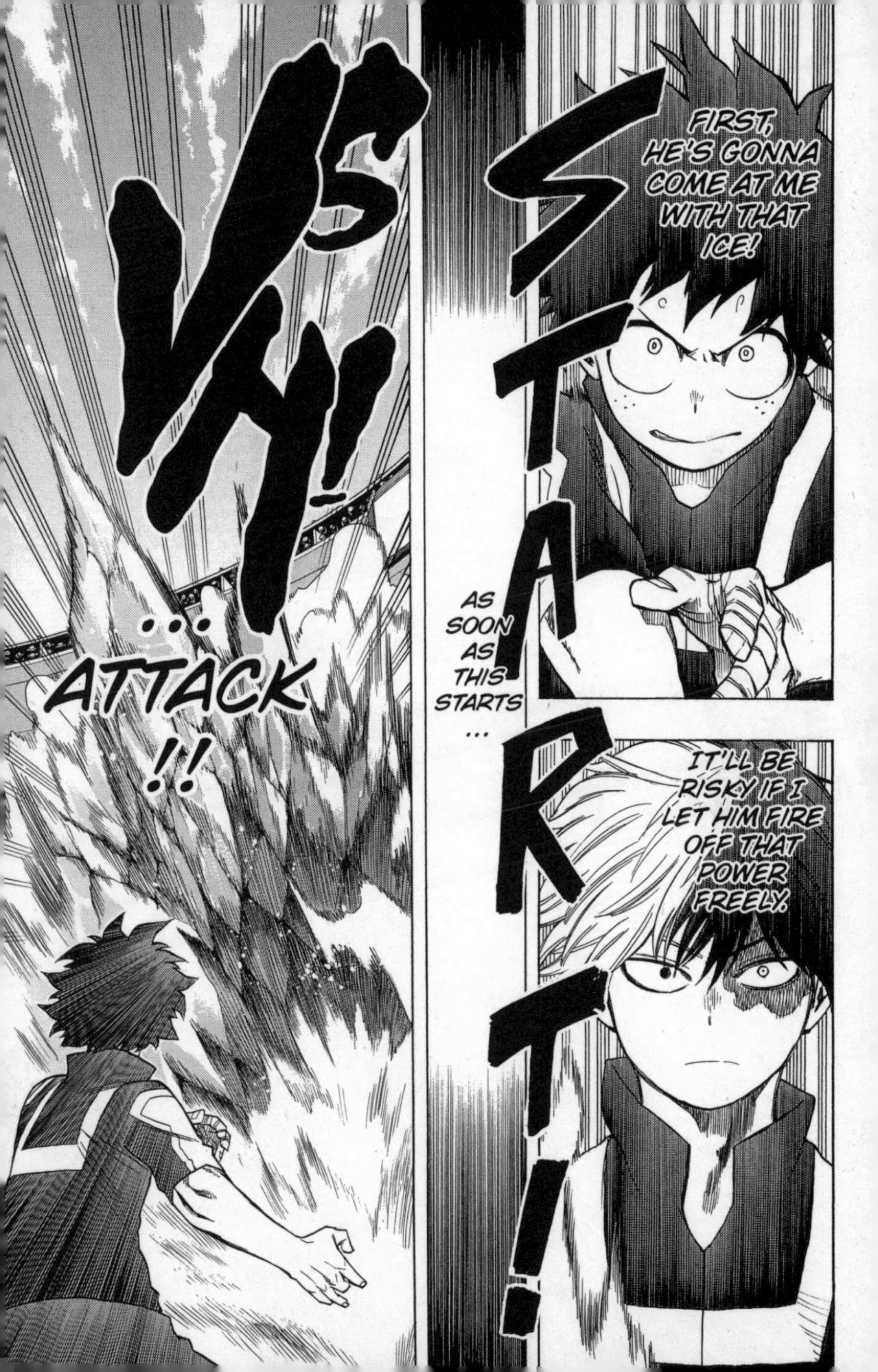
FIRST, HE'S GONNA COME AT ME WITH THAT ICE!
START!
AS SOON AS THIS STARTS...
IT'LL BE RISKY IF I LET HIM FIRE OFF THAT POWER FREELY.
...ATTACK!!

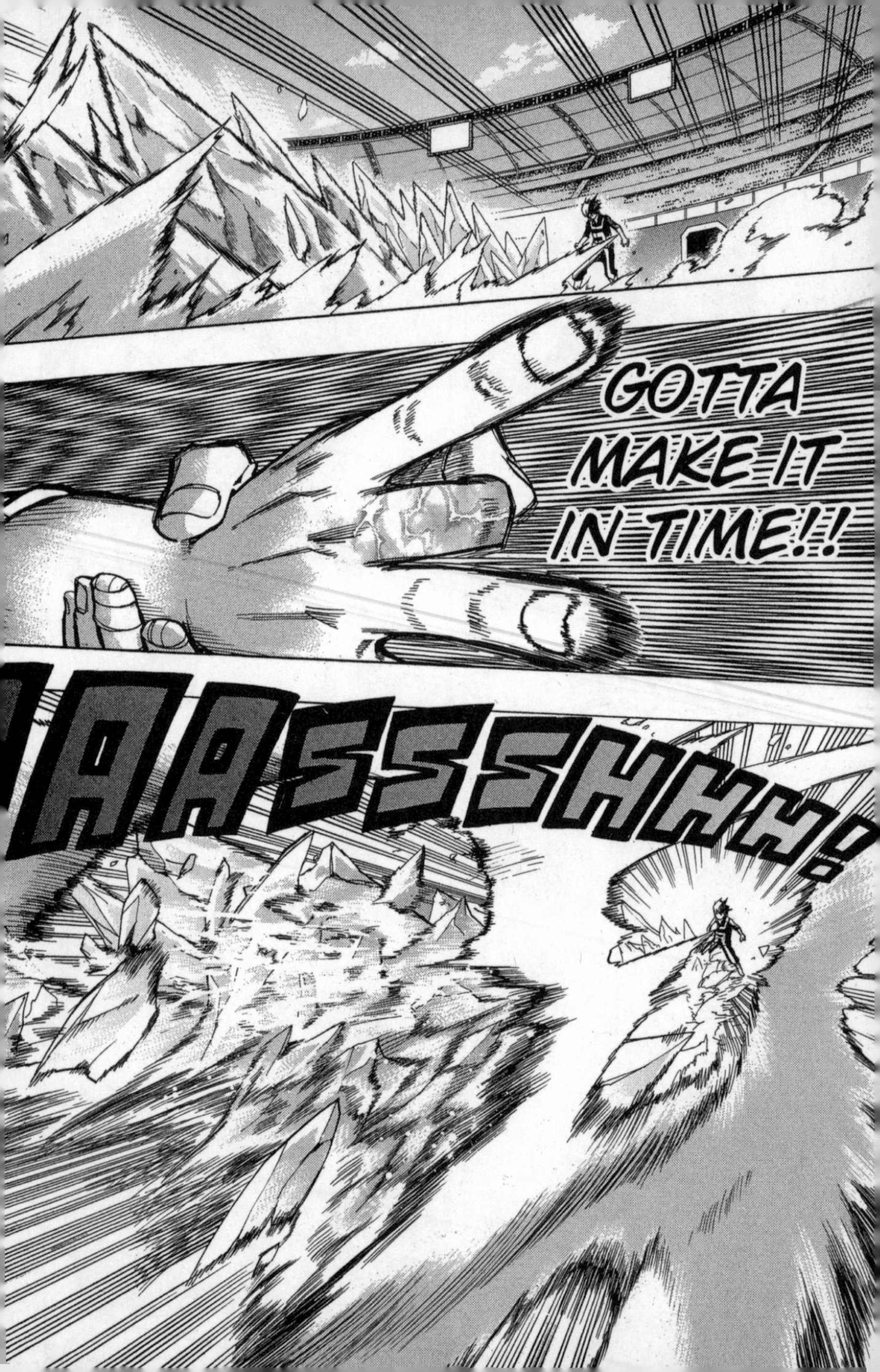
GOTTA MAKE IT IN TIME!!
AASSSHHHH!

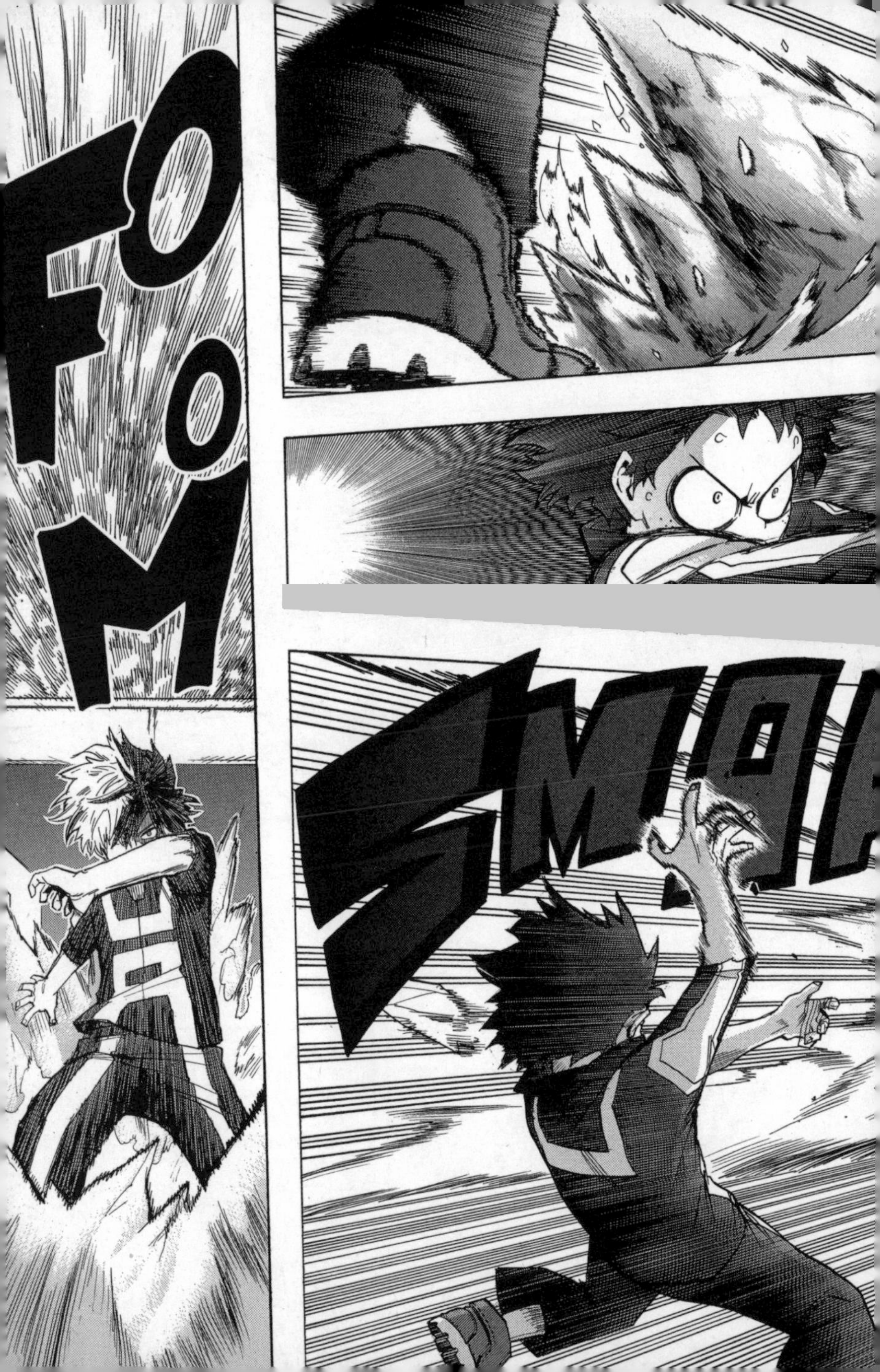
SMA
FOOM

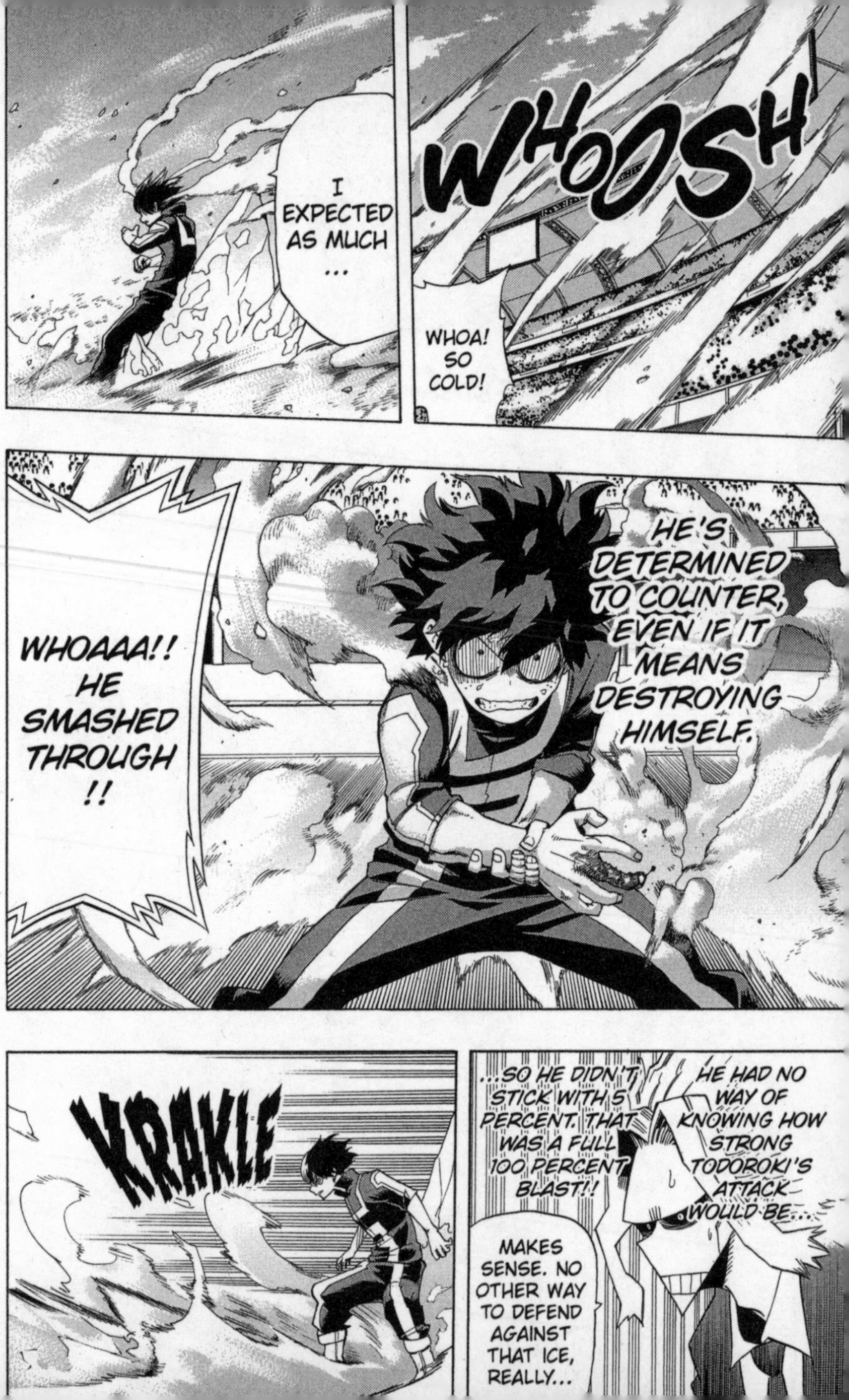
WHOOSH
WHOA! SO COLD!
I EXPECTED AS MUCH...
HE'S DETERMINED TO COUNTER, EVEN IF IT MEANS DESTROYING HIMSELF.
WHOAAA!! HE SMASHED THROUGH!!
HE HAD NO WAY OF KNOWING HOW STRONG TODOROKI'S ATTACK WOULD BE...
...SO HE DIDN'T STICK WITH 5 PERCENT. THAT WAS A FULL 100 PERCENT BLAST!!
MAKES SENSE. NO OTHER WAY TO DEFEND AGAINST THAT ICE, REALLY...
KRAKLE

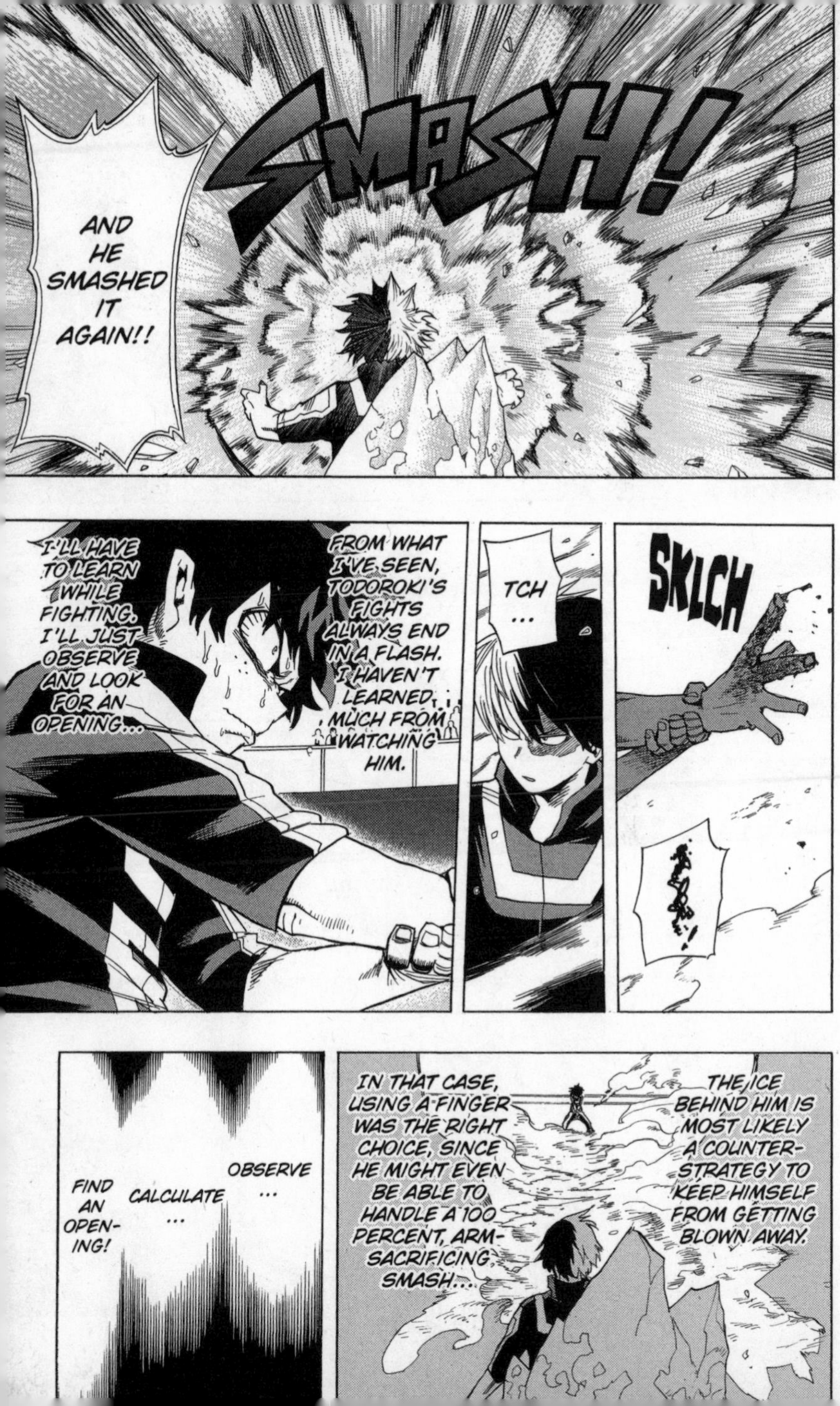
SMASH!
AND HE SMASHED IT AGAIN!!
SKLCH
TCH...
FROM WHAT I'VE SEEN, TODOROKI'S FIGHTS ALWAYS END IN A FLASH. I HAVEN'T LEARNED MUCH FROM WATCHING HIM.
I'LL HAVE TO LEARN WHILE FIGHTING. I'LL JUST OBSERVE AND LOOK FOR AN OPENING...
THE ICE BEHIND HIM IS MOST LIKELY A COUNTER-STRATEGY TO KEEP HIMSELF FROM GETTING BLOWN AWAY.
IN THAT CASE, USING A FINGER WAS THE RIGHT CHOICE, SINCE HE MIGHT EVEN BE ABLE TO HANDLE A 100 PERCENT, ARM-SACRIFICING SMASH...
OBSERVE...
CALCULATE...
FIND AN OPENING!

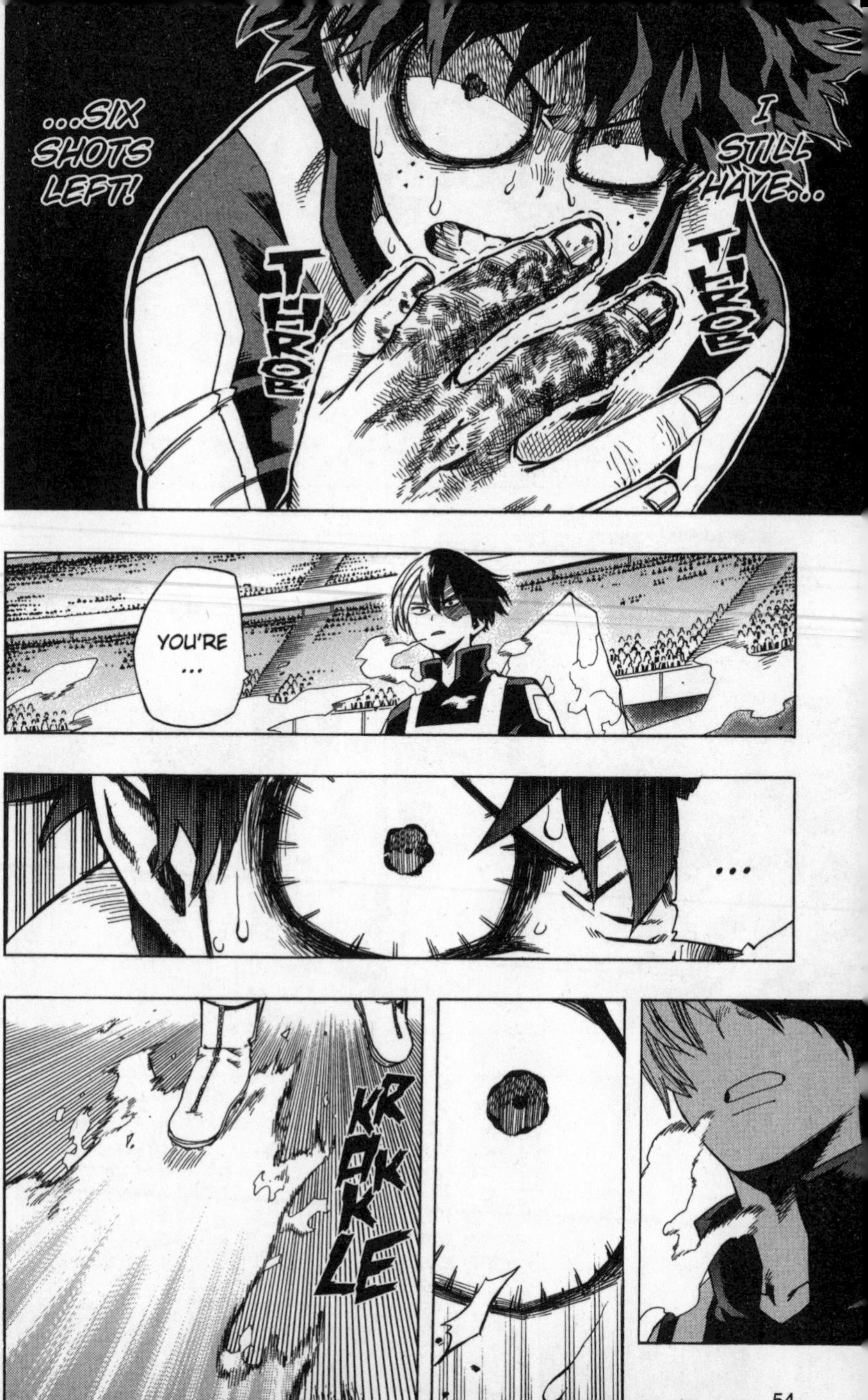
I STILL HAVE...
...SIX SHOTS LEFT!
THROB
THROB
YOU'RE ...
...
KRAKKLE

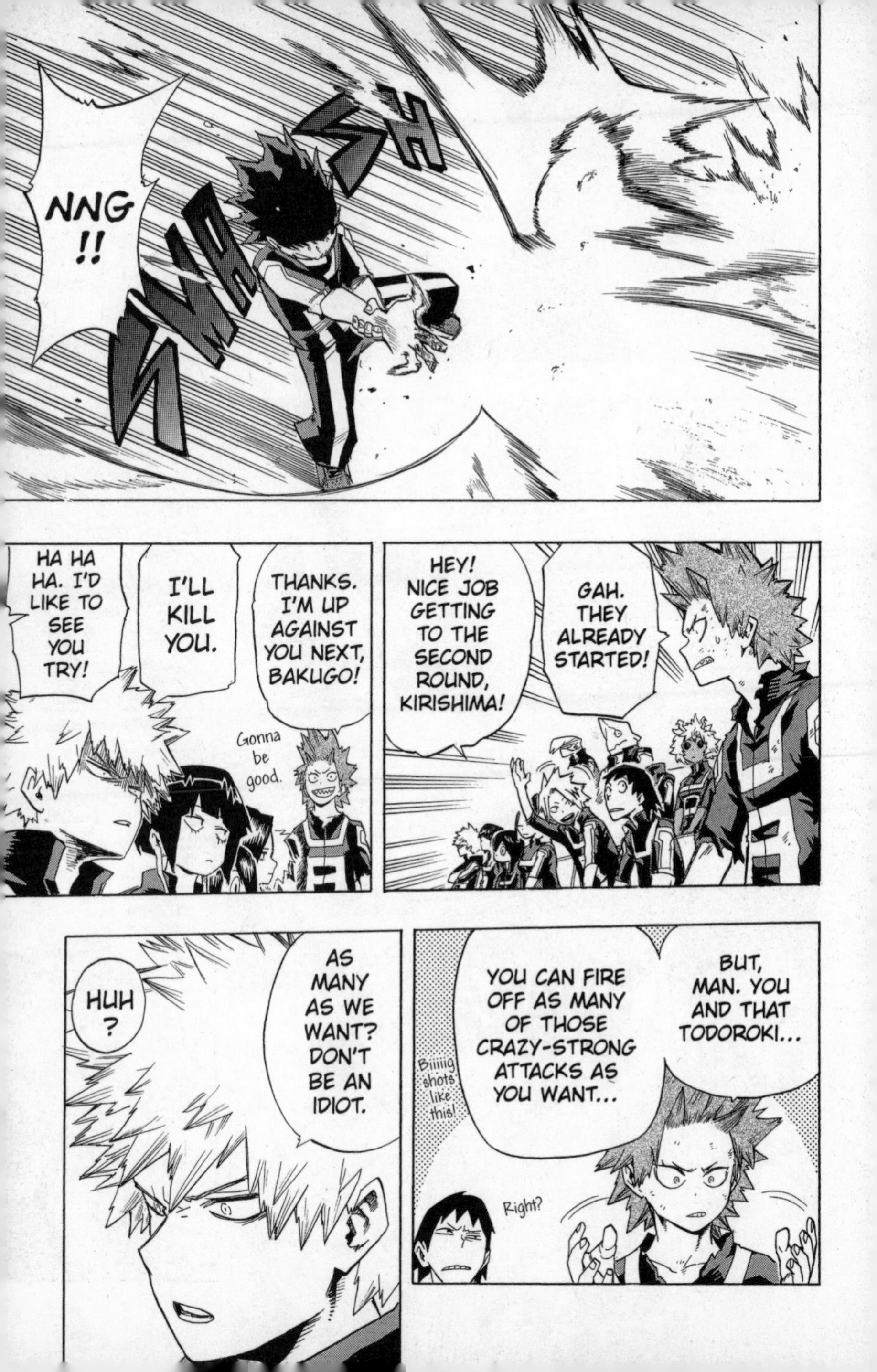
NNG!!
GAH. THEY ALREADY STARTED!
HEY! NICE JOB GETTING TO THE SECOND ROUND, KIRISHIMA!
THANKS. I'M UP AGAINST YOU NEXT, BAKUGO!
Gonna be good.
I'LL KILL YOU.
HA HA HA. I'D LIKE TO SEE YOU TRY!
BUT, MAN. YOU AND THAT TODOROKI...
YOU CAN FIRE OFF AS MANY OF THOSE CRAZY-STRONG ATTACKS AS YOU WANT...
Biiiiig shots like this!
Right?
HUH?
AS MANY AS WE WANT? DON'T BE AN IDIOT.

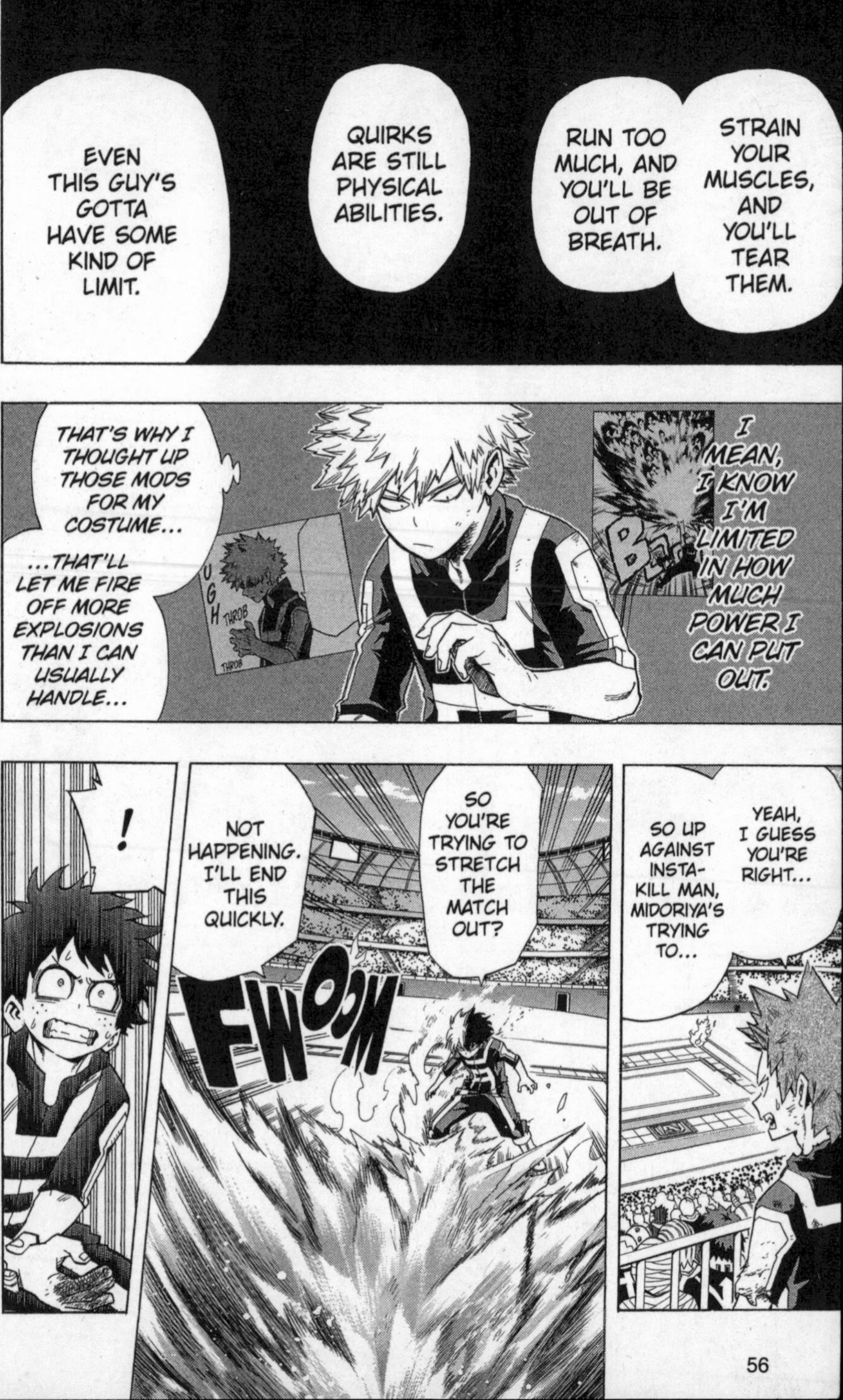
STRAIN YOUR MUSCLES, AND YOU'LL TEAR THEM.
RUN TOO MUCH, AND YOU'LL BE OUT OF BREATH.
QUIRKS ARE STILL PHYSICAL ABILITIES.
EVEN THIS GUY'S GOTTA HAVE SOME KIND OF LIMIT.
I MEAN, I KNOW I'M LIMITED IN HOW MUCH POWER I CAN PUT OUT.
THAT'S WHY I THOUGHT UP THOSE MODS FOR MY COSTUME...
...THAT'LL LET ME FIRE OFF MORE EXPLOSIONS THAN I CAN USUALLY HANDLE...
UGH
THROB
THROB
YEAH, I GUESS YOU'RE RIGHT...
SO UP AGAINST INSTA-KILL MAN, MIDORIYA'S TRYING TO...
SO YOU'RE TRYING TO STRETCH THE MATCH OUT?
NOT HAPPENING. I'LL END THIS QUICKLY.
FWOOM
!

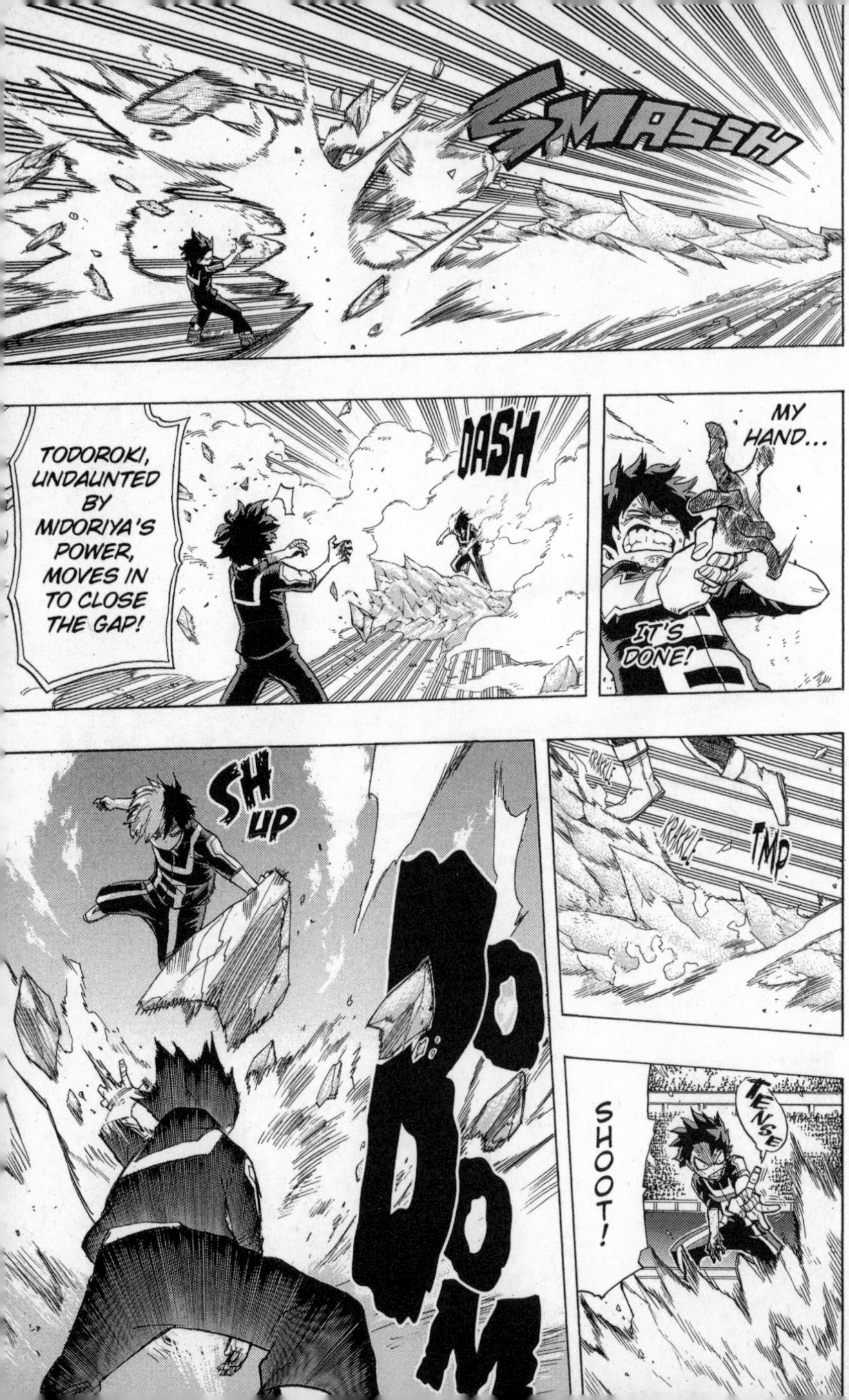
SMASSH
MY HAND...
IT'S DONE!
DASH
TODOROKI, UNDAUNTED BY MIDORIYA'S POWER, MOVES IN TO CLOSE THE GAP!
KRAKLE
KRAKLE!
TMP
TENSE
SHOOT!
SH UP
DOOM

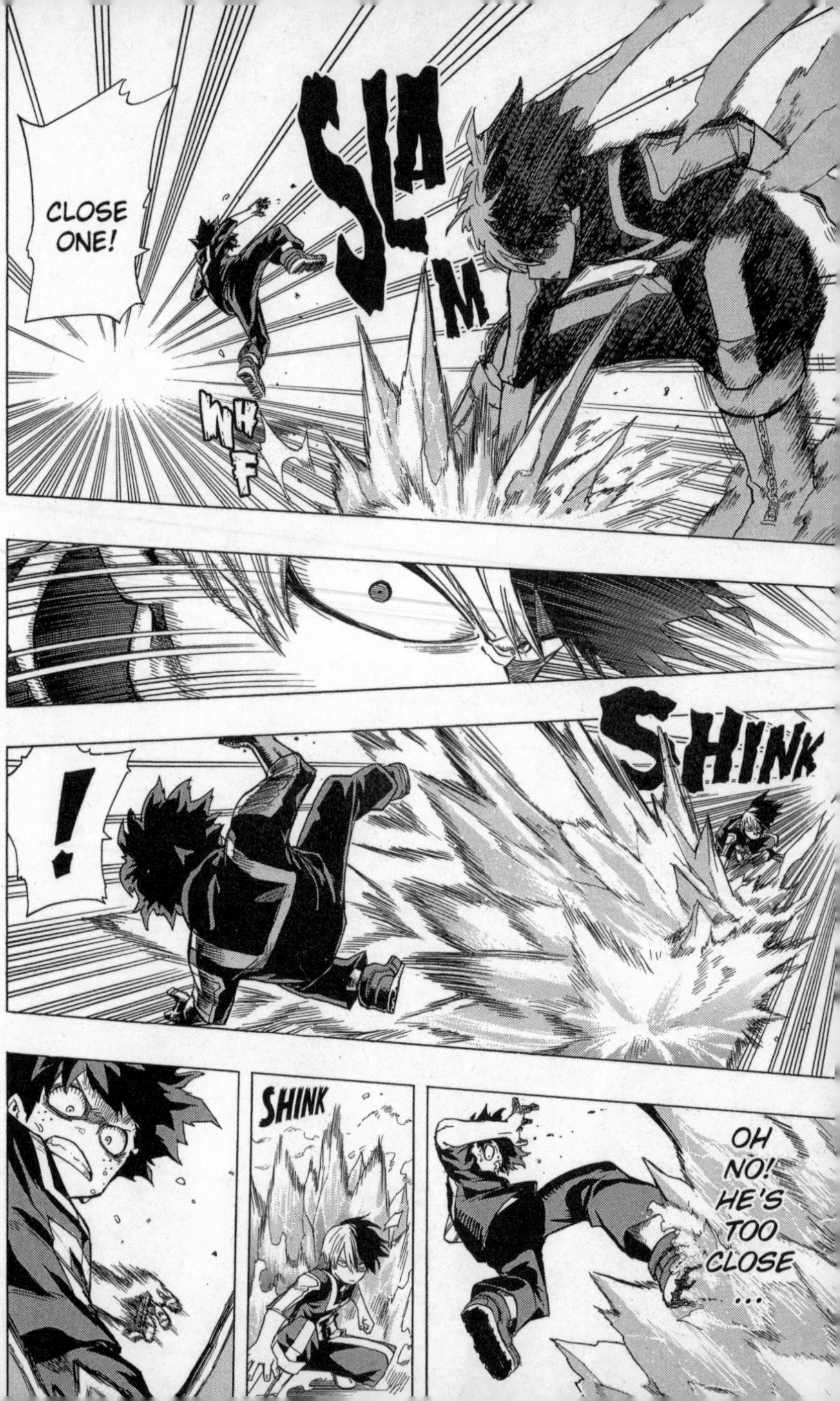
SLAM
CLOSE ONE!
WHF
SHINK
!
OH NO! HE'S TOO CLOSE...
SHINK

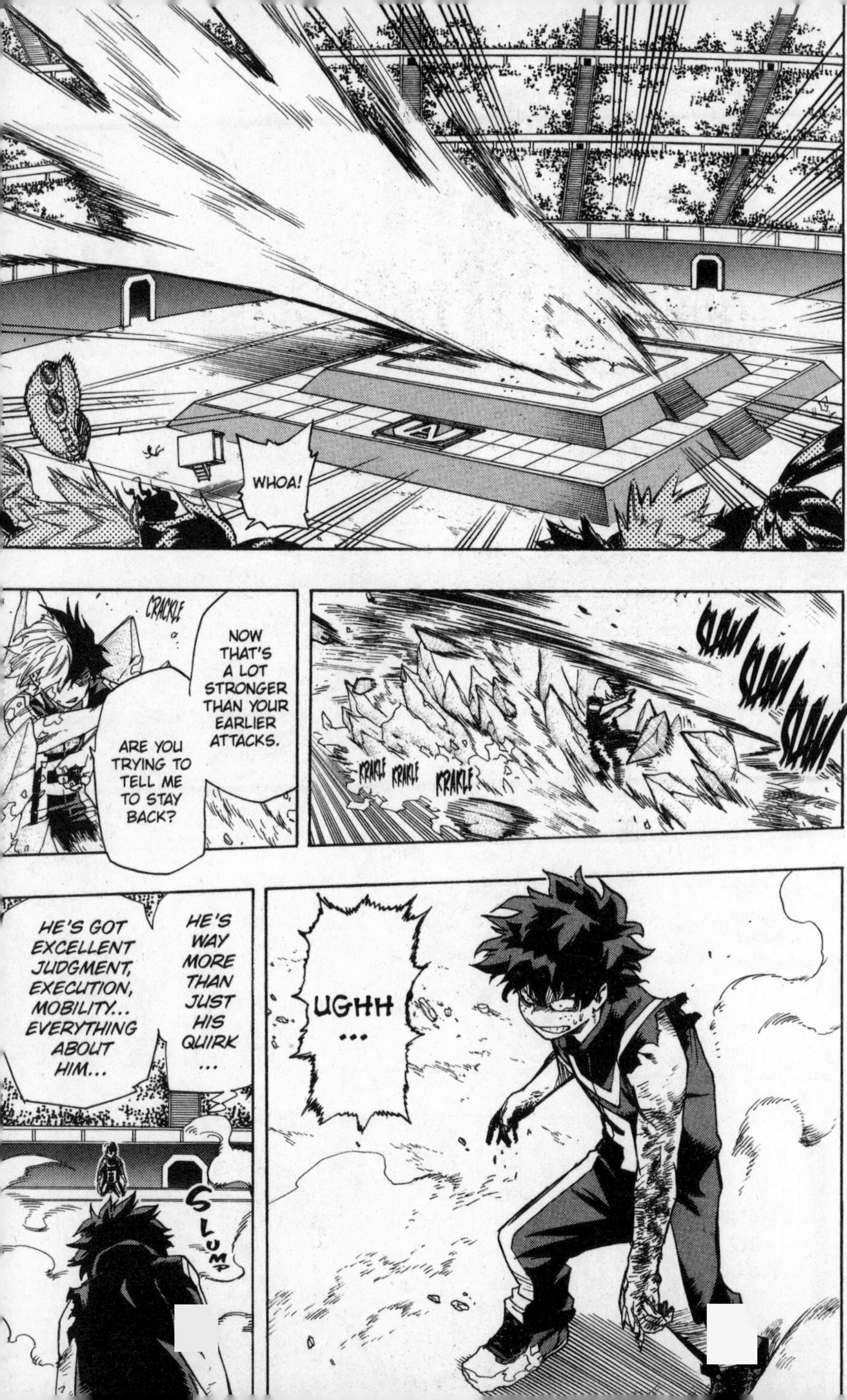
WHOA!
SLAM SLAM SLAM
KRAKLE KRAKLE KRAKLE
CRACKLE
NOW THAT'S A LOT STRONGER THAN YOUR EARLIER ATTACKS.
ARE YOU TRYING TO TELL ME TO STAY BACK?
UGHH...
HE'S WAY MORE THAN JUST HIS QUIRK...
HE'S GOT EXCELLENT JUDGMENT, EXECUTION, MOBILITY... EVERYTHING ABOUT HIM...
SLUMP

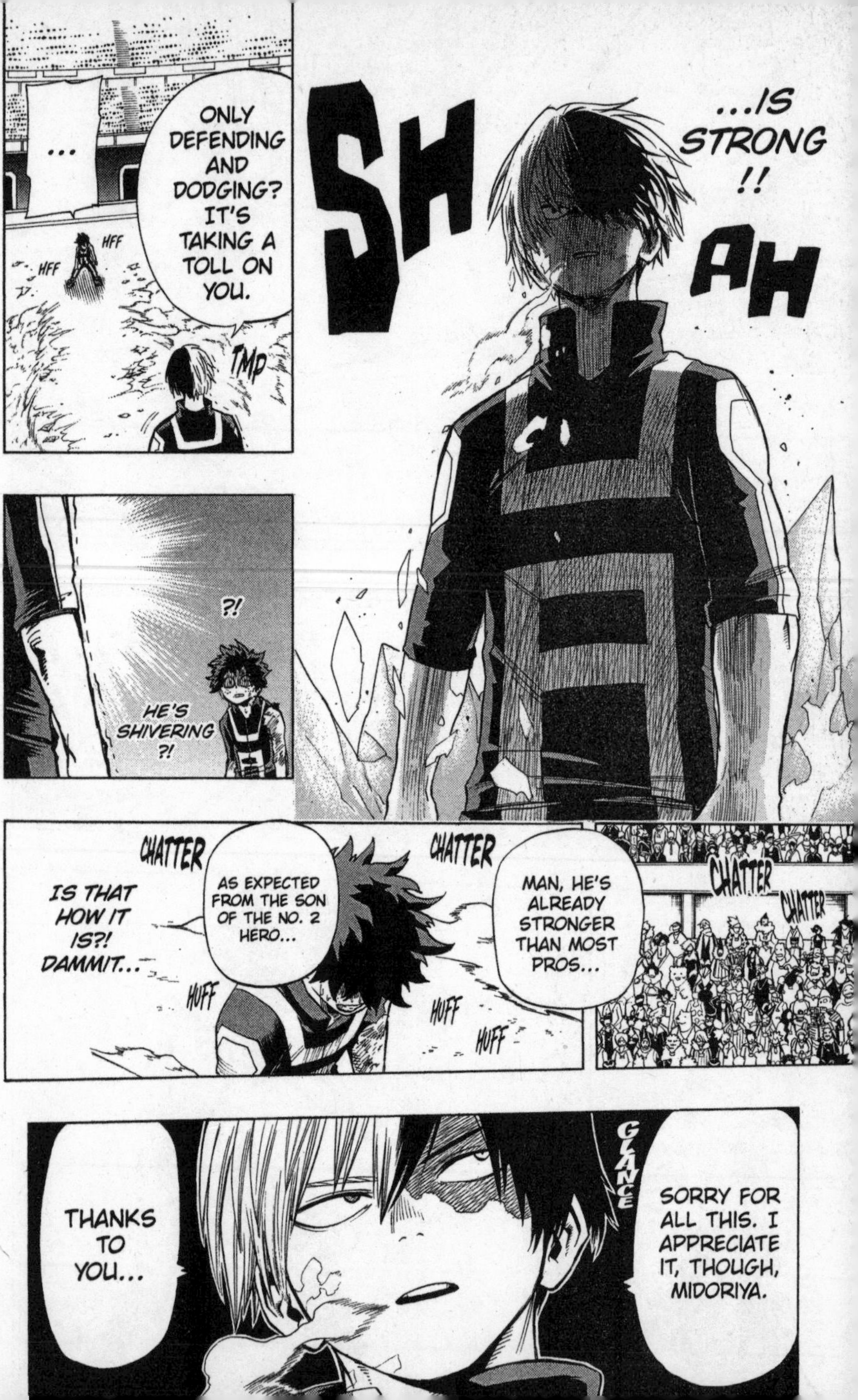
...IS STRONG!!
SHAAH
...
ONLY DEFENDING AND DODGING? IT'S TAKING A TOLL ON YOU.
HFF
HFF
TMP
?!
HE'S SHIVERING?!
CHATTER
CHATTER
MAN, HE'S ALREADY STRONGER THAN MOST PROS...
CHATTER
AS EXPECTED FROM THE SON OF THE NO. 2 HERO...
CHATTER
IS THAT HOW IT IS?! DAMMIT...
HUFF
HUFF
HUFF
SORRY FOR ALL THIS. I APPRECIATE IT, THOUGH, MIDORIYA.
GLANCE
THANKS TO YOU...

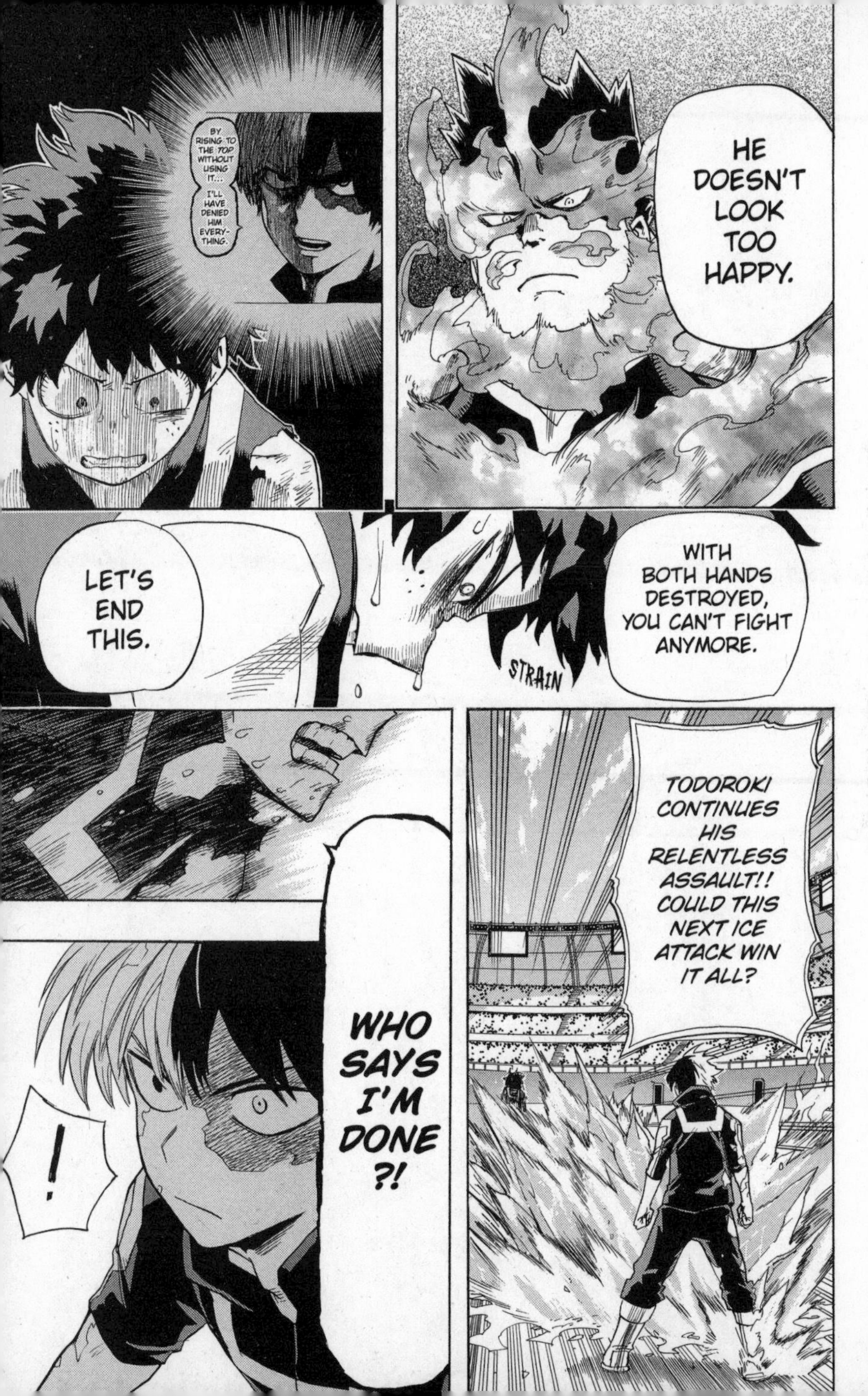
HE DOESN'T LOOK TOO HAPPY.
BY RISING TO THE *TOP* WITHOUT USING IT...
I'LL HAVE DENIED HIM EVERYTHING.
WITH BOTH HANDS DESTROYED, YOU CAN'T FIGHT ANYMORE.
STRAIN
LET'S END THIS.
TODOROKI CONTINUES HIS RELENTLESS ASSAULT!! COULD THIS NEXT ICE ATTACK WIN IT ALL?
WHO SAYS I'M DONE?!
!

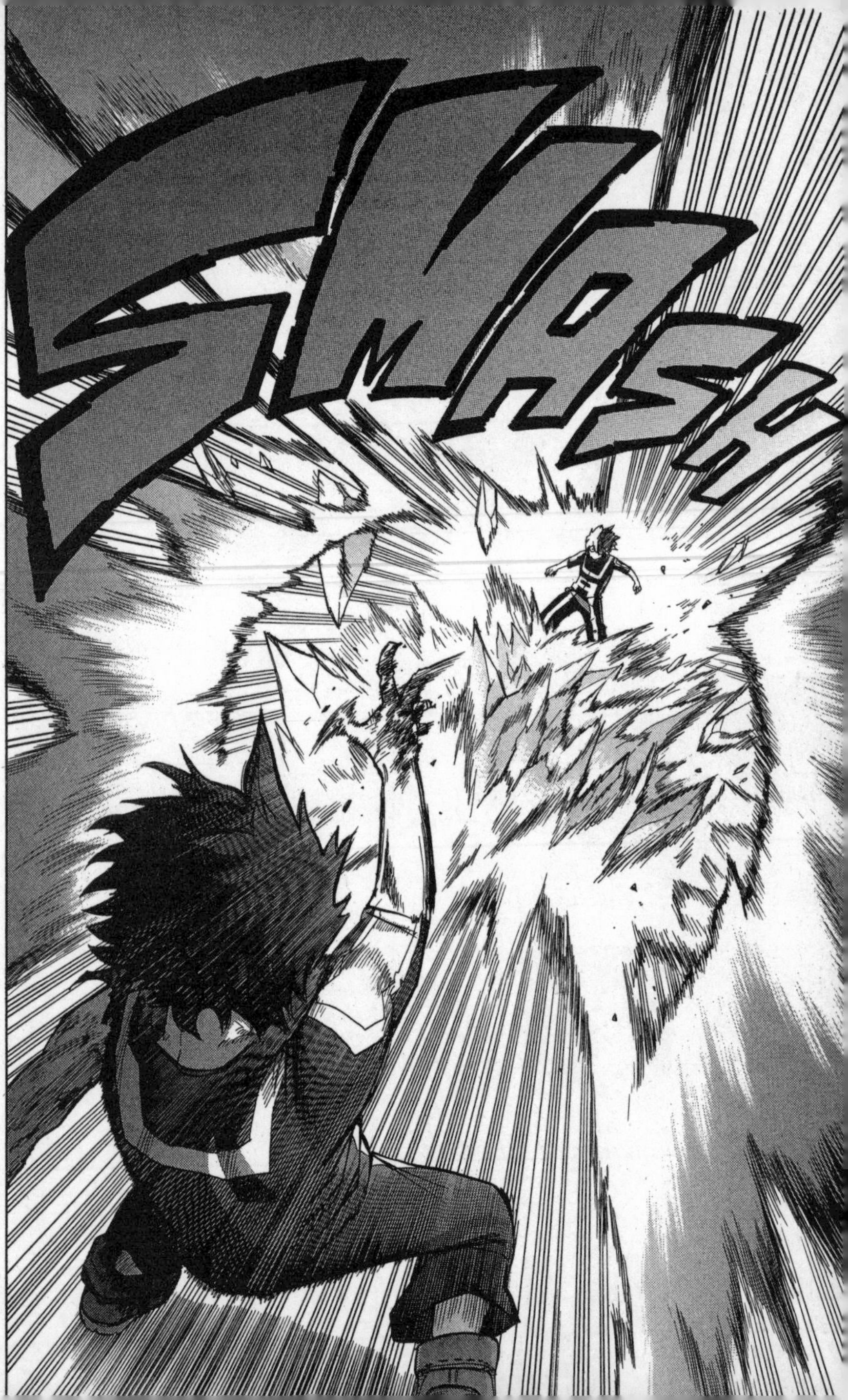
SMASH

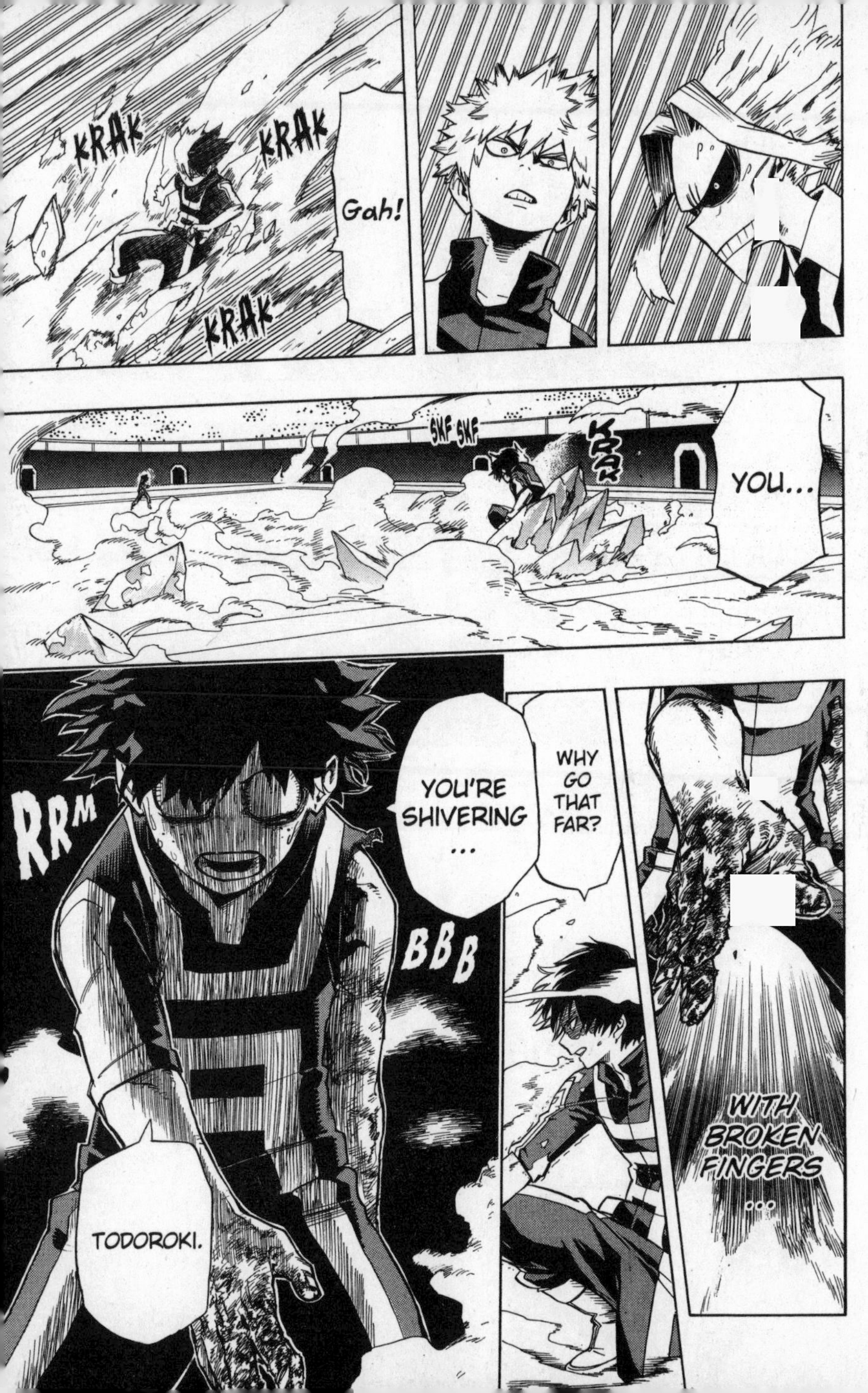
Gah!
KRAK
KRAK
KRAK
YOU...
KRAK
SKF SKF
WITH BROKEN FINGERS...
WHY GO THAT FAR?
YOU'RE SHIVERING...
RRM
BBB
TODOROKI.

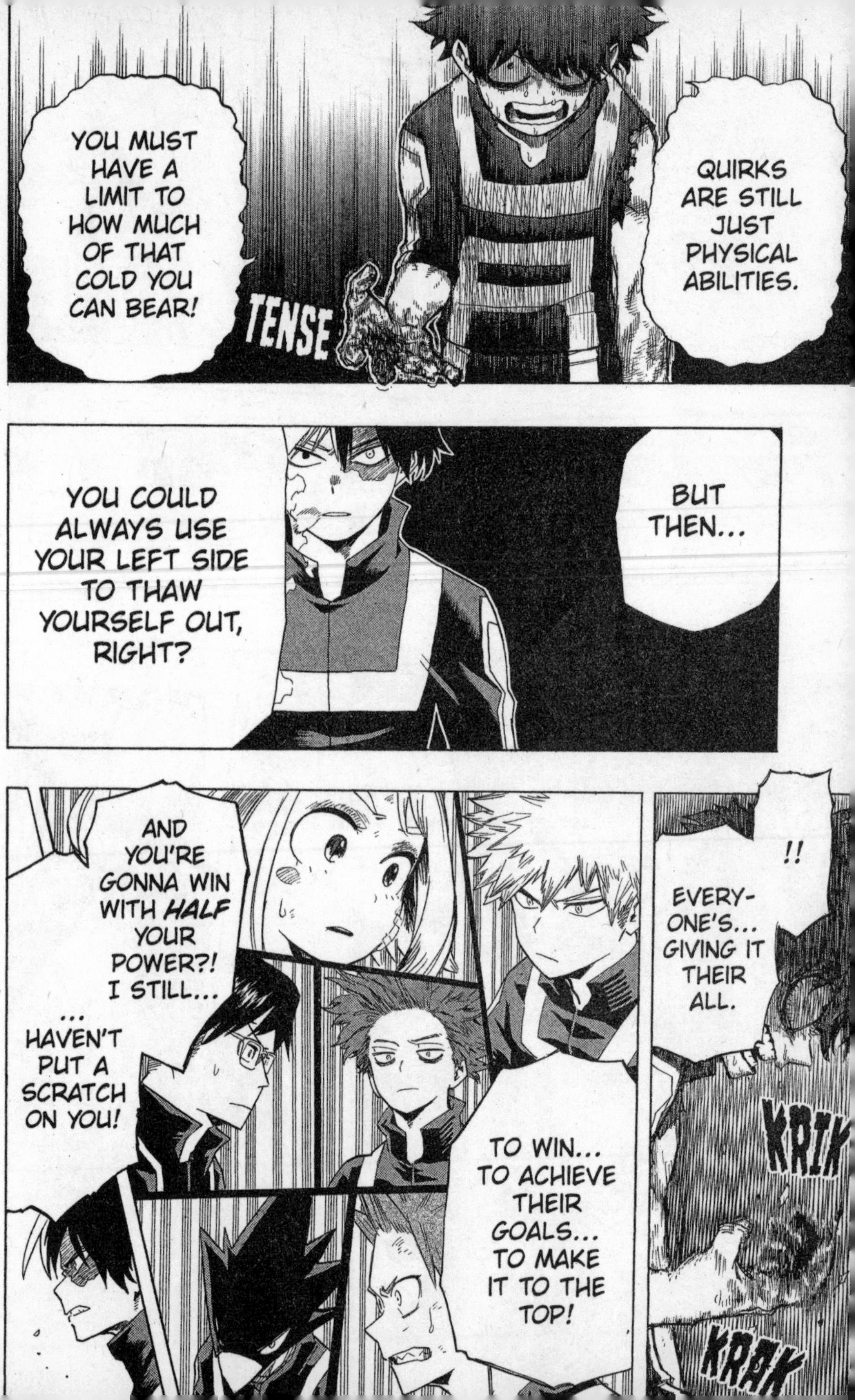
QUIRKS ARE STILL JUST PHYSICAL ABILITIES.
YOU MUST HAVE A LIMIT TO HOW MUCH OF THAT COLD YOU CAN BEAR!
TENSE
BUT THEN...
YOU COULD ALWAYS USE YOUR LEFT SIDE TO THAW YOURSELF OUT, RIGHT?
!!
EVERY-ONE'S... GIVING IT THEIR ALL.
KRIK
KRAK
TO WIN... TO ACHIEVE THEIR GOALS... TO MAKE IT TO THE TOP!
AND YOU'RE GONNA WIN WITH *HALF* YOUR POWER?! I STILL...
... HAVEN'T PUT A SCRATCH ON YOU!

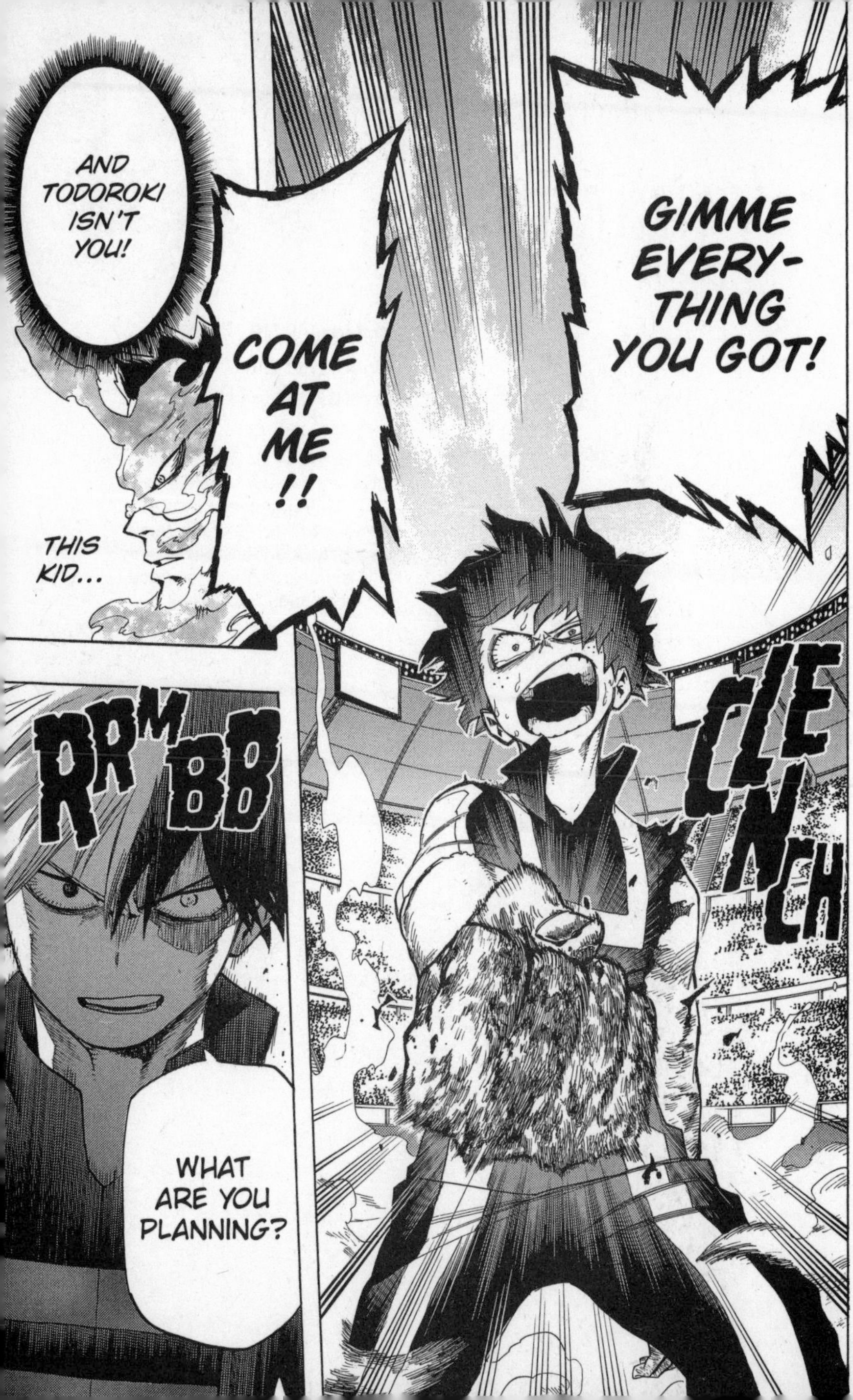
GIMME EVERYTHING YOU GOT!
COME AT ME!!
CLENCH
AND TODOROKI ISN'T YOU!
THIS KID...
RRMBB
WHAT ARE YOU PLANNING?

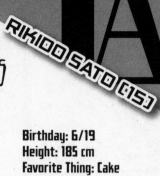

STREET CLOTHES

Birthday: 6/19
Height: 185 cm
Favorite Thing: Cake

BEHIND THE SCENES
I suspect this guy's Quirk is a really strong one, and I want to show it, but I just haven't found the right opportunity. His design kind of reminds me of the good old days, and I really like it.

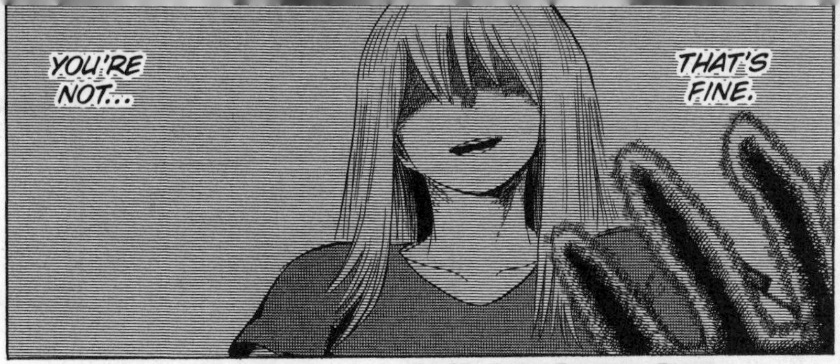
THAT'S FINE.
YOU'RE NOT...

No. 39 - Shoto Todoroki: Origin

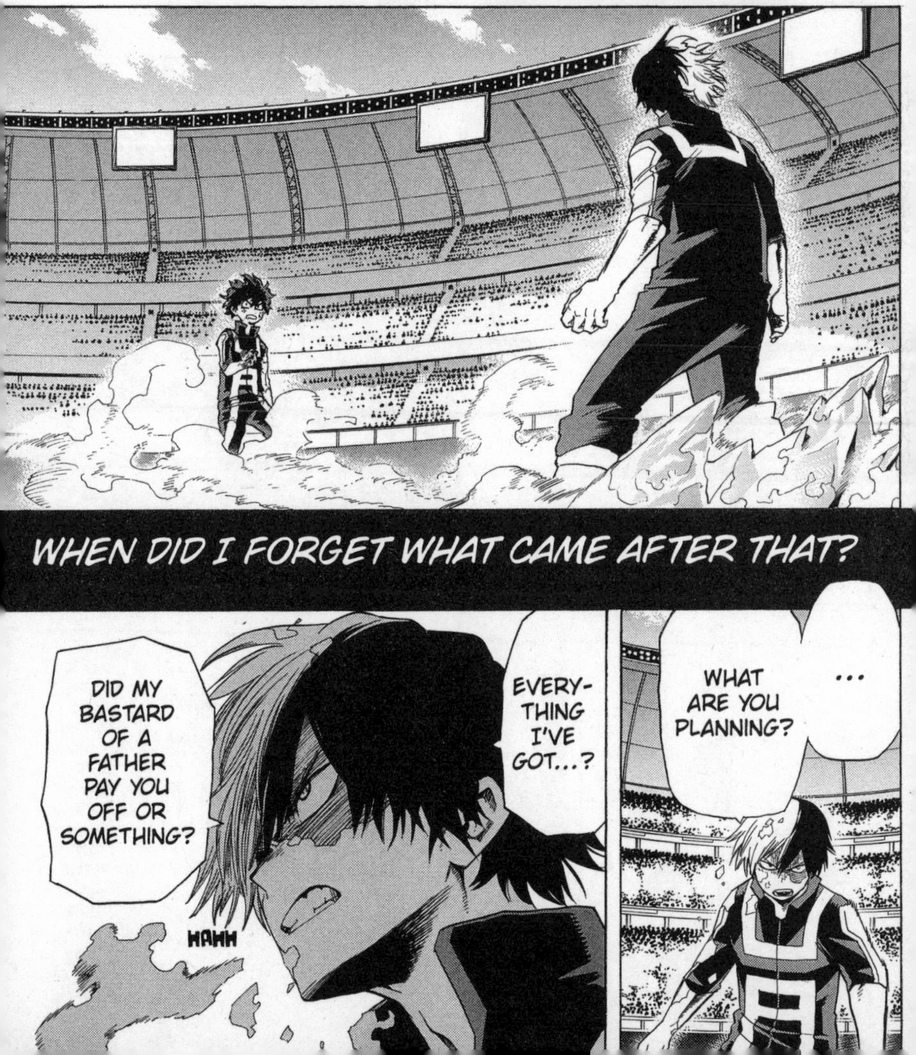
WHEN DID I FORGET WHAT CAME AFTER THAT?
...
WHAT ARE YOU PLANNING?
EVERY-THING I'VE GOT...?
DID MY BASTARD OF A FATHER PAY YOU OFF OR SOMETHING?
HAHH

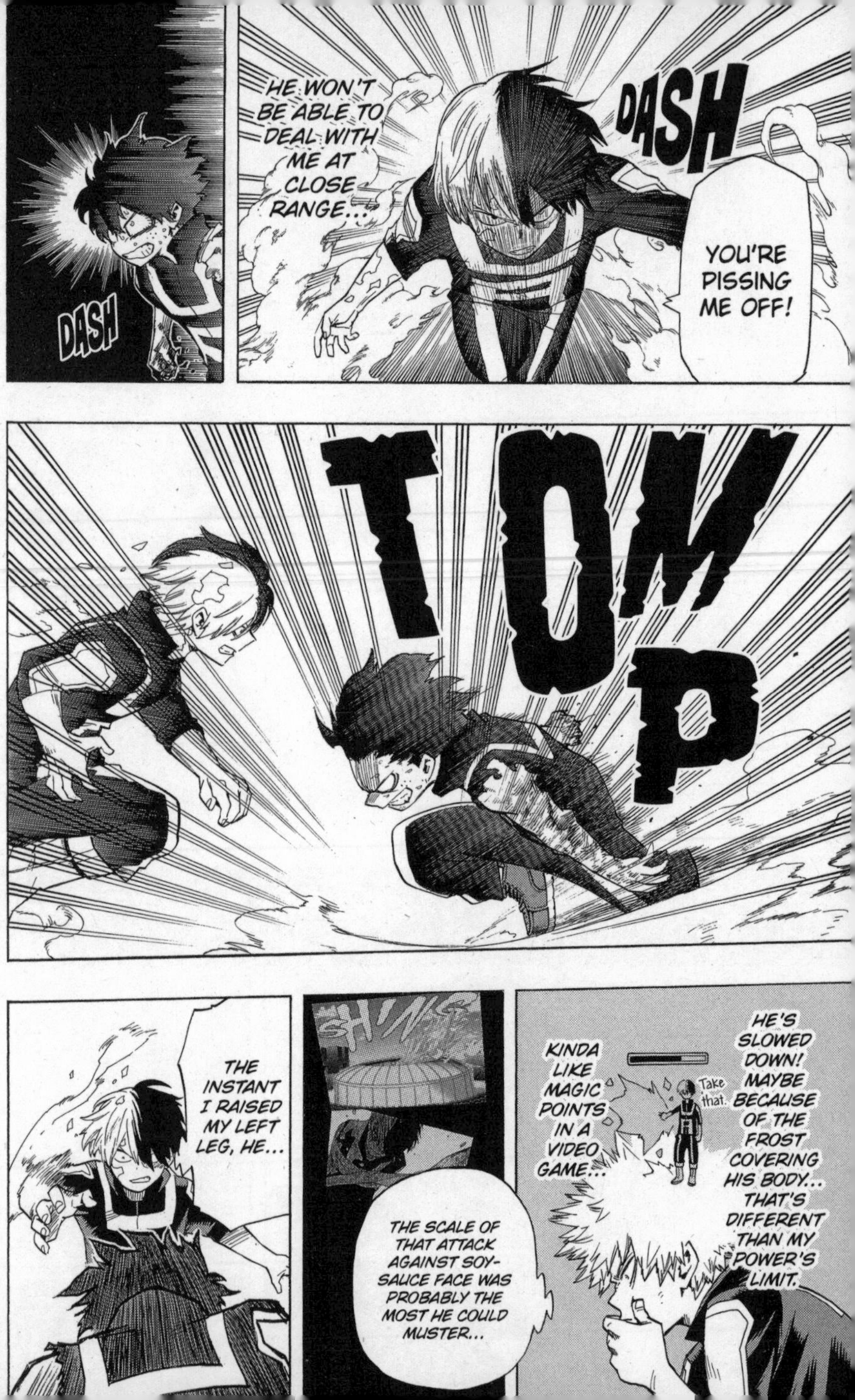
DASH
HE WON'T BE ABLE TO DEAL WITH ME AT CLOSE RANGE...
YOU'RE PISSING ME OFF!
DASH
TOMP
HE'S SLOWED DOWN! MAYBE BECAUSE OF THE FROST COVERING HIS BODY... THAT'S DIFFERENT THAN MY POWER'S LIMIT.
KINDA LIKE MAGIC POINTS IN A VIDEO GAME...
Take that.
THE SCALE OF THAT ATTACK AGAINST SOY-SAUCE FACE WAS PROBABLY THE MOST HE COULD MUSTER...
SHING
THE INSTANT I RAISED MY LEFT LEG, HE...

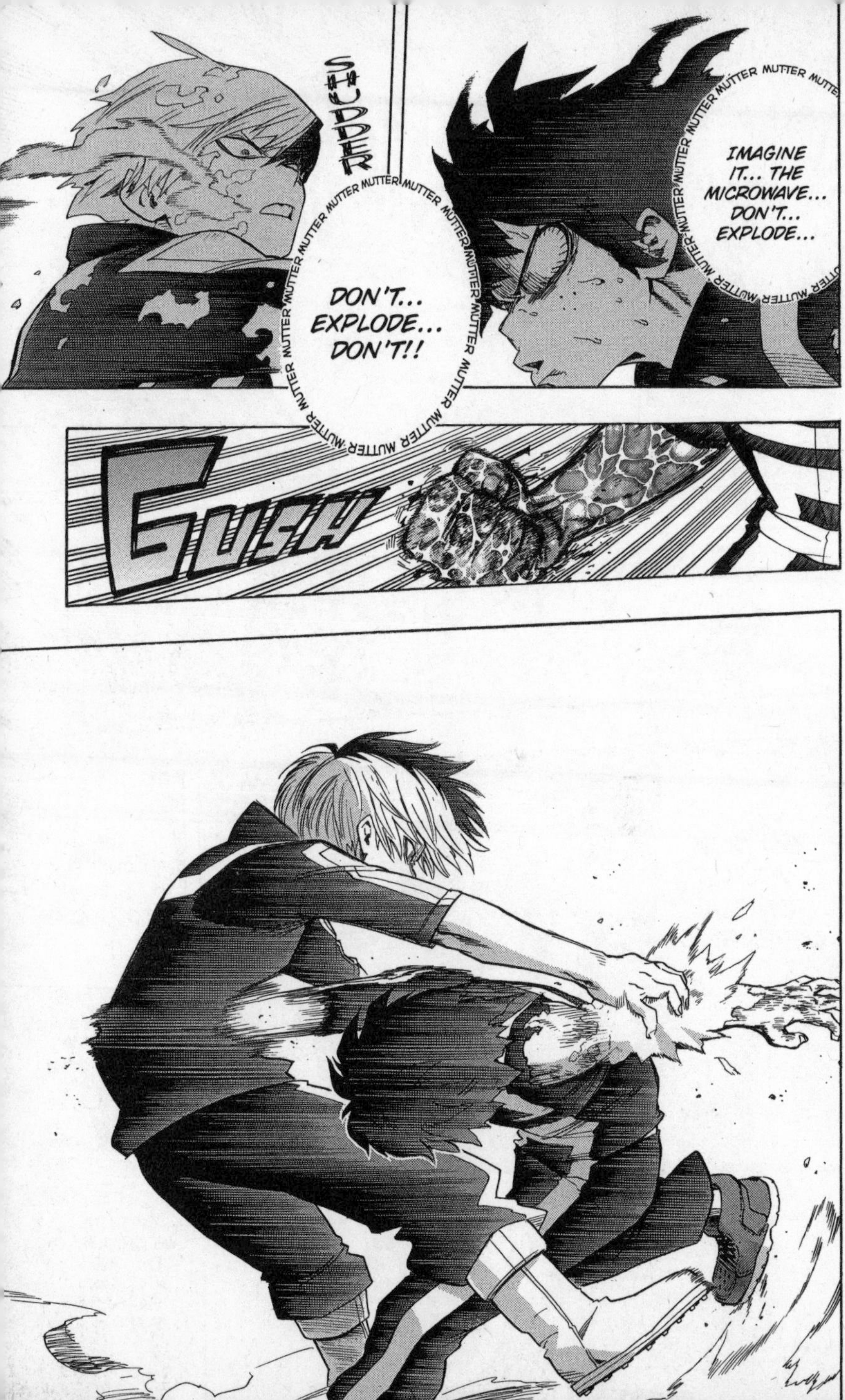
MUTTER MUTTER MUTTER MUTTER MUTTER MUTTER
IMAGINE IT... THE MICROWAVE... DON'T... EXPLODE...
SHUDDER
MUTTER MUTTER MUTTER MUTTER MUTTER MUTTER MUTTER
DON'T... EXPLODE... DON'T!!
GUSH

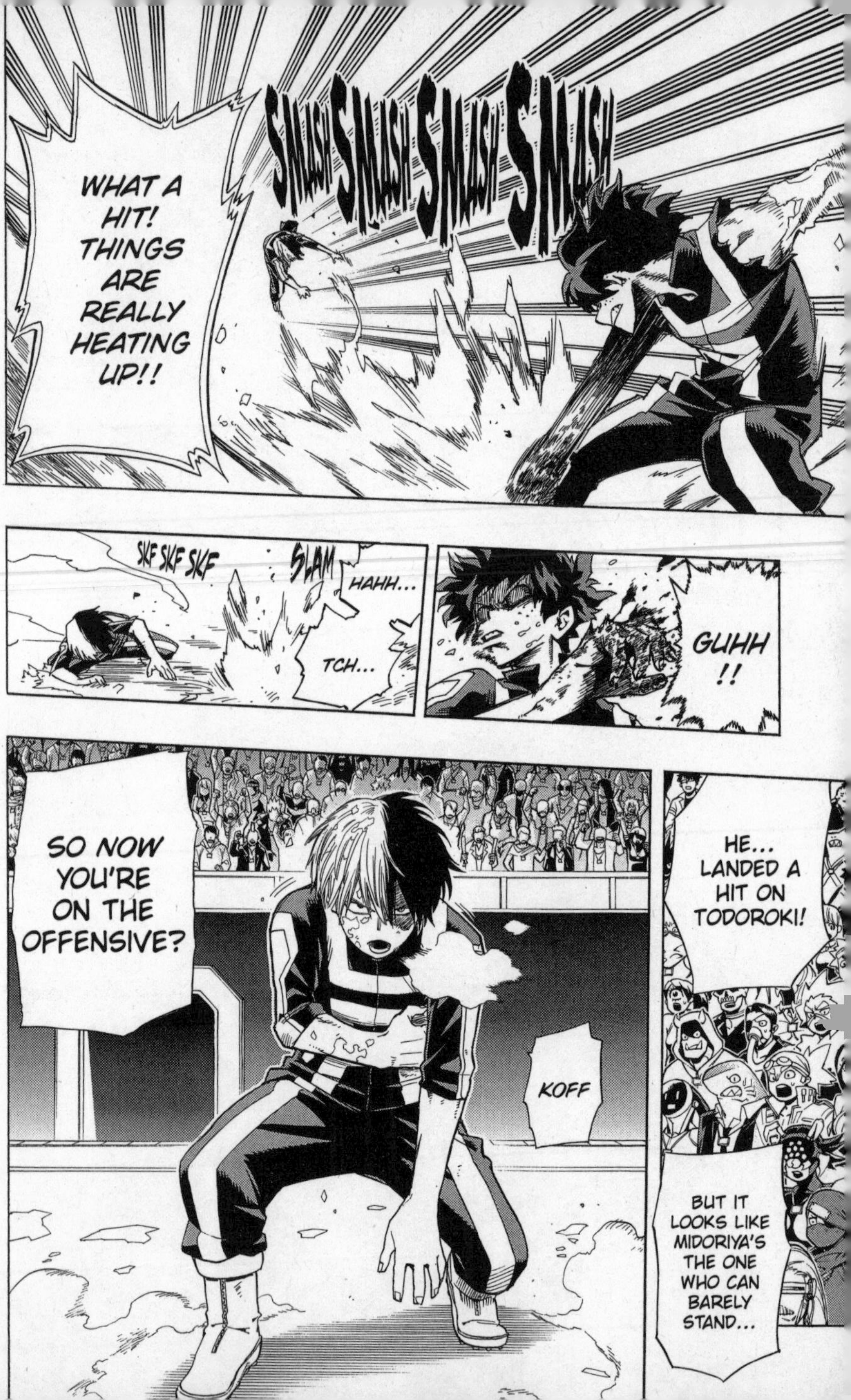
SMASH SMASH SMASH SMASH
WHAT A HIT! THINGS ARE REALLY HEATING UP!!
GUHH!!
HAHH...
SLAM
SKF SKF SKF
TCH...
HE... LANDED A HIT ON TODOROKI!
BUT IT LOOKS LIKE MIDORIYA'S THE ONE WHO CAN BARELY STAND...
SO NOW YOU'RE ON THE OFFENSIVE?
KOFF

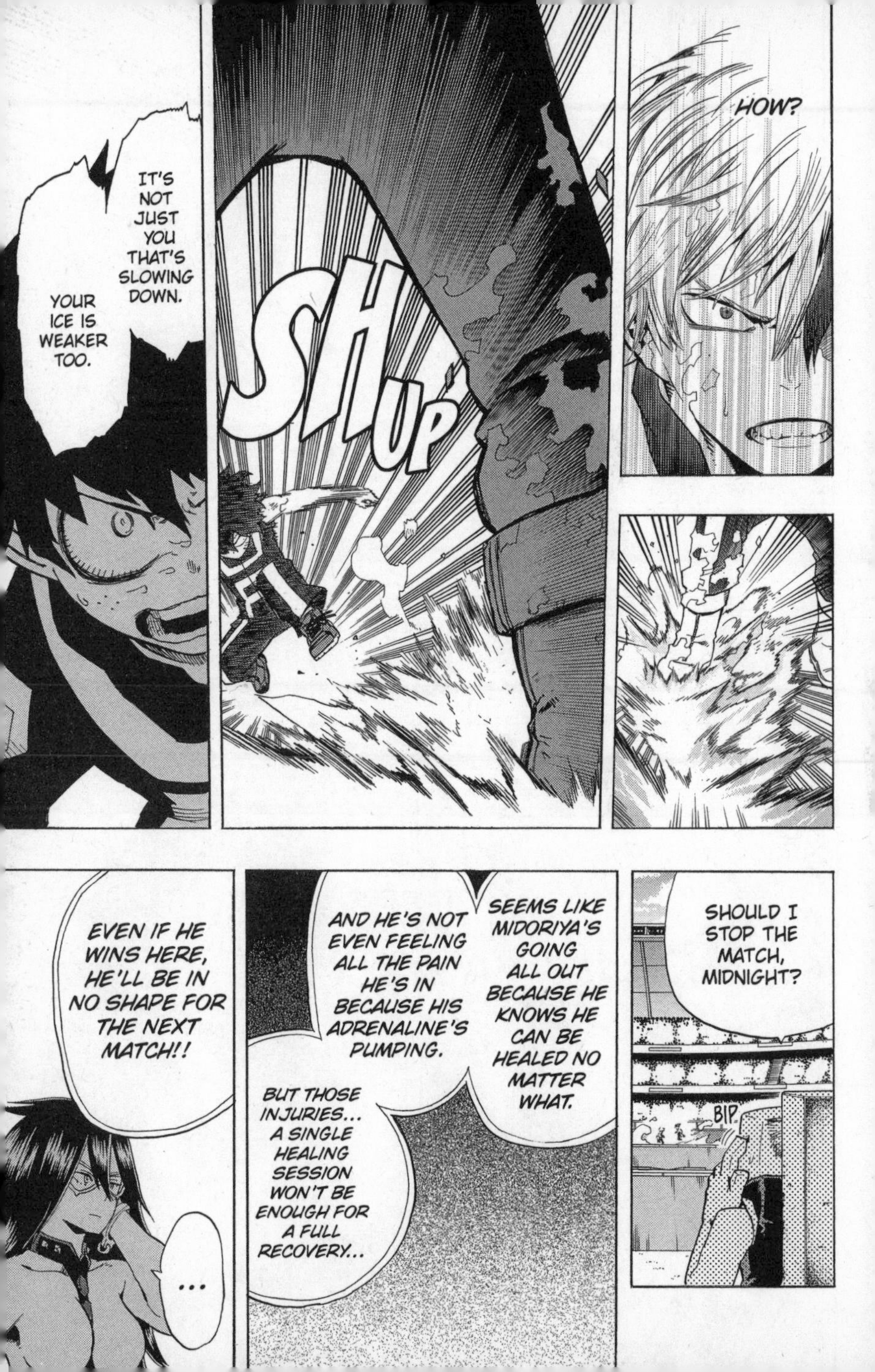
HOW?
SHUP
IT'S NOT JUST YOU THAT'S SLOWING DOWN.
YOUR ICE IS WEAKER TOO.
SHOULD I STOP THE MATCH, MIDNIGHT?
BIP
SEEMS LIKE MIDORIYA'S GOING ALL OUT BECAUSE HE KNOWS HE CAN BE HEALED NO MATTER WHAT.
AND HE'S NOT EVEN FEELING ALL THE PAIN HE'S IN BECAUSE HIS ADRENALINE'S PUMPING.
BUT THOSE INJURIES... A SINGLE HEALING SESSION WON'T BE ENOUGH FOR A FULL RECOVERY...
EVEN IF HE WINS HERE, HE'LL BE IN NO SHAPE FOR THE NEXT MATCH!!
...

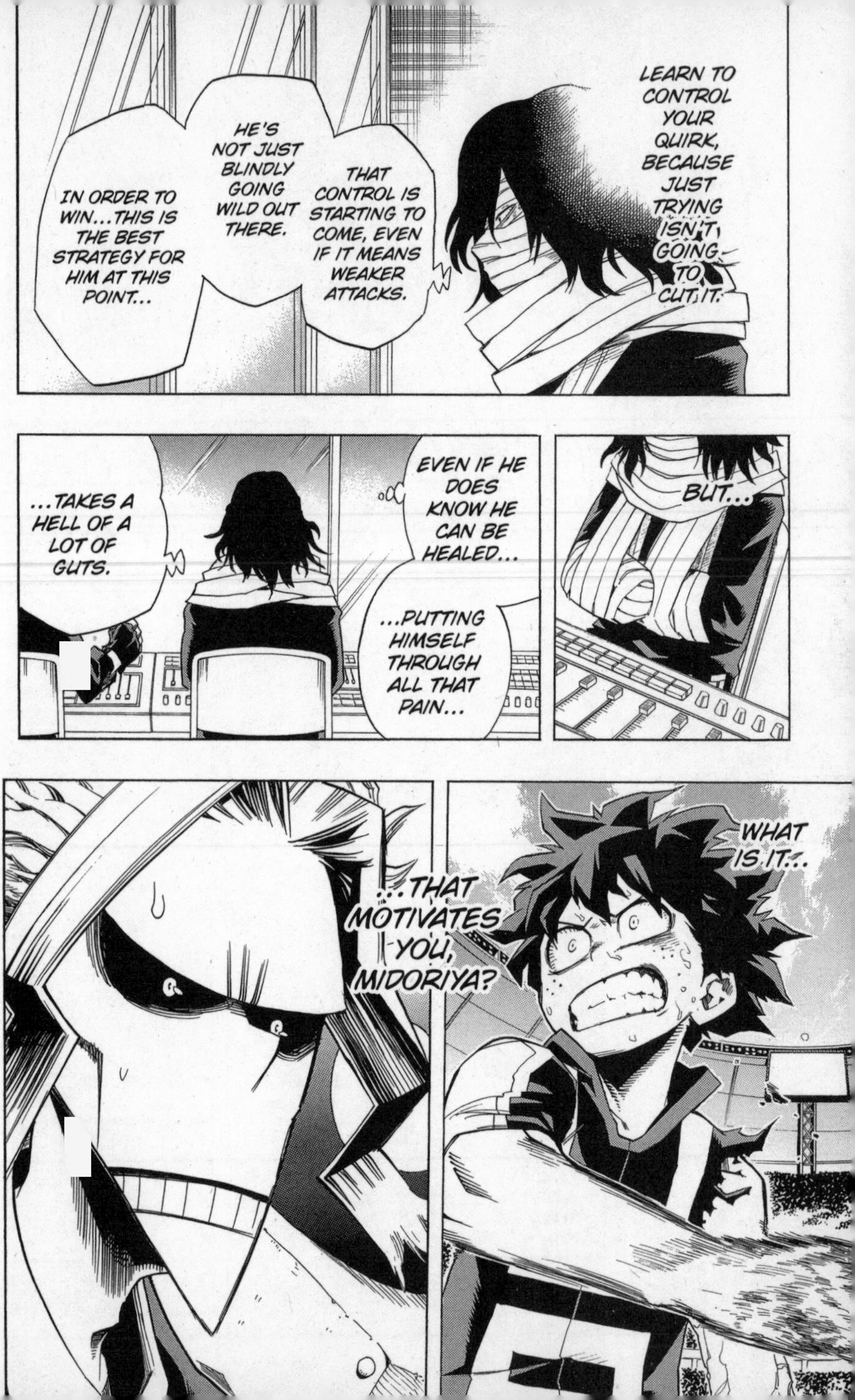
LEARN TO CONTROL YOUR QUIRK, BECAUSE JUST TRYING ISN'T GOING TO CUT IT.
THAT CONTROL IS STARTING TO COME, EVEN IF IT MEANS WEAKER ATTACKS.
HE'S NOT JUST BLINDLY GOING WILD OUT THERE.
IN ORDER TO WIN...THIS IS THE BEST STRATEGY FOR HIM AT THIS POINT...
BUT...
EVEN IF HE DOES KNOW HE CAN BE HEALED...
...PUTTING HIMSELF THROUGH ALL THAT PAIN...
...TAKES A HELL OF A LOT OF GUTS.
WHAT IS IT...
...THAT MOTIVATES YOU, MIDORIYA?

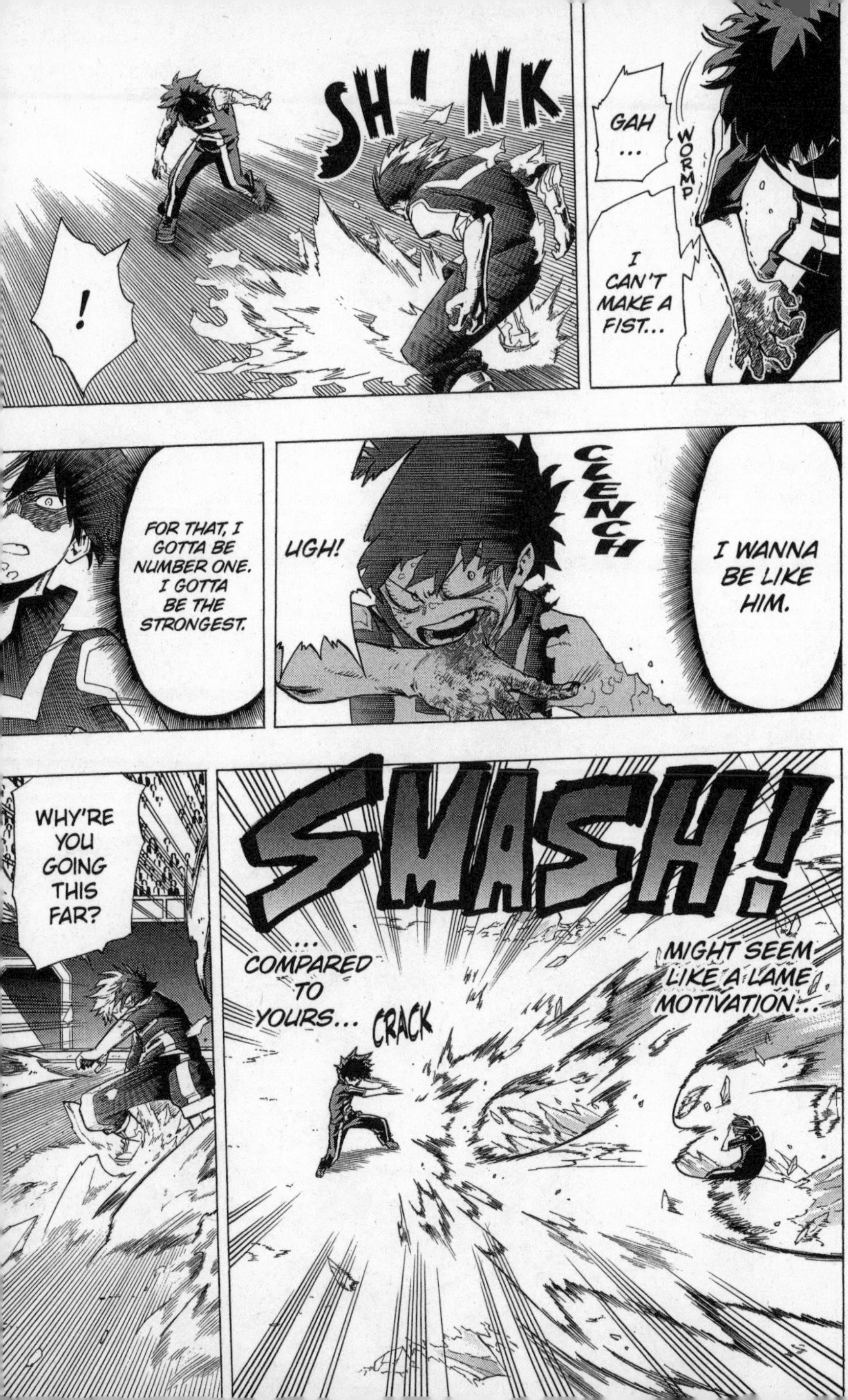
GAH ...
WORMP
I CAN'T MAKE A FIST...
SHINK
!
I WANNA BE LIKE HIM.
CLENCH
UGH!
FOR THAT, I GOTTA BE NUMBER ONE. I GOTTA BE THE STRONGEST.
SMASH!
MIGHT SEEM LIKE A LAME MOTIVATION...
... COMPARED TO YOURS...
CRACK
WHY'RE YOU GOING THIS FAR?

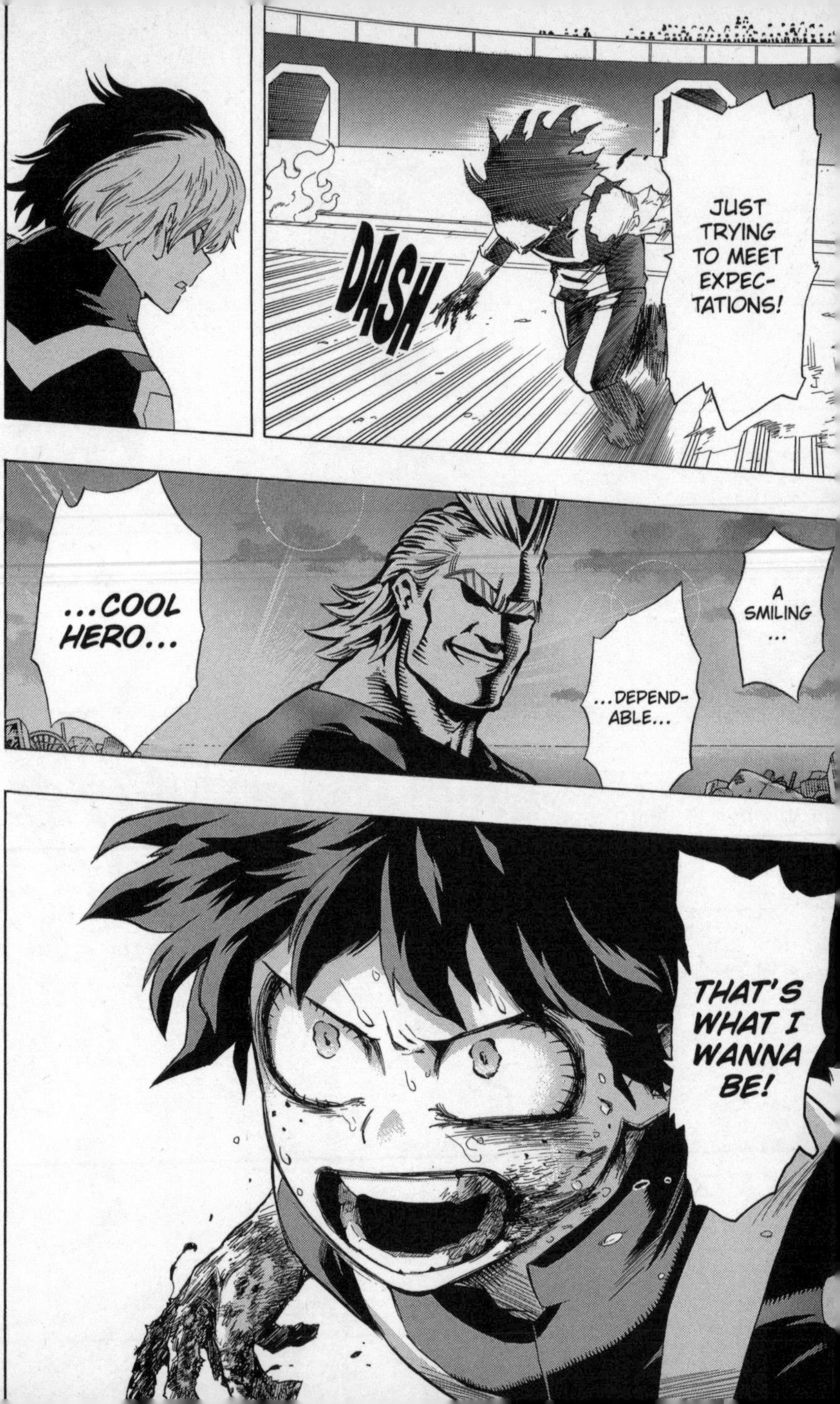
JUST TRYING TO MEET EXPECTATIONS!
DASH
A SMILING...
...DEPENDABLE...
...COOL HERO...
THAT'S WHAT I WANNA BE!

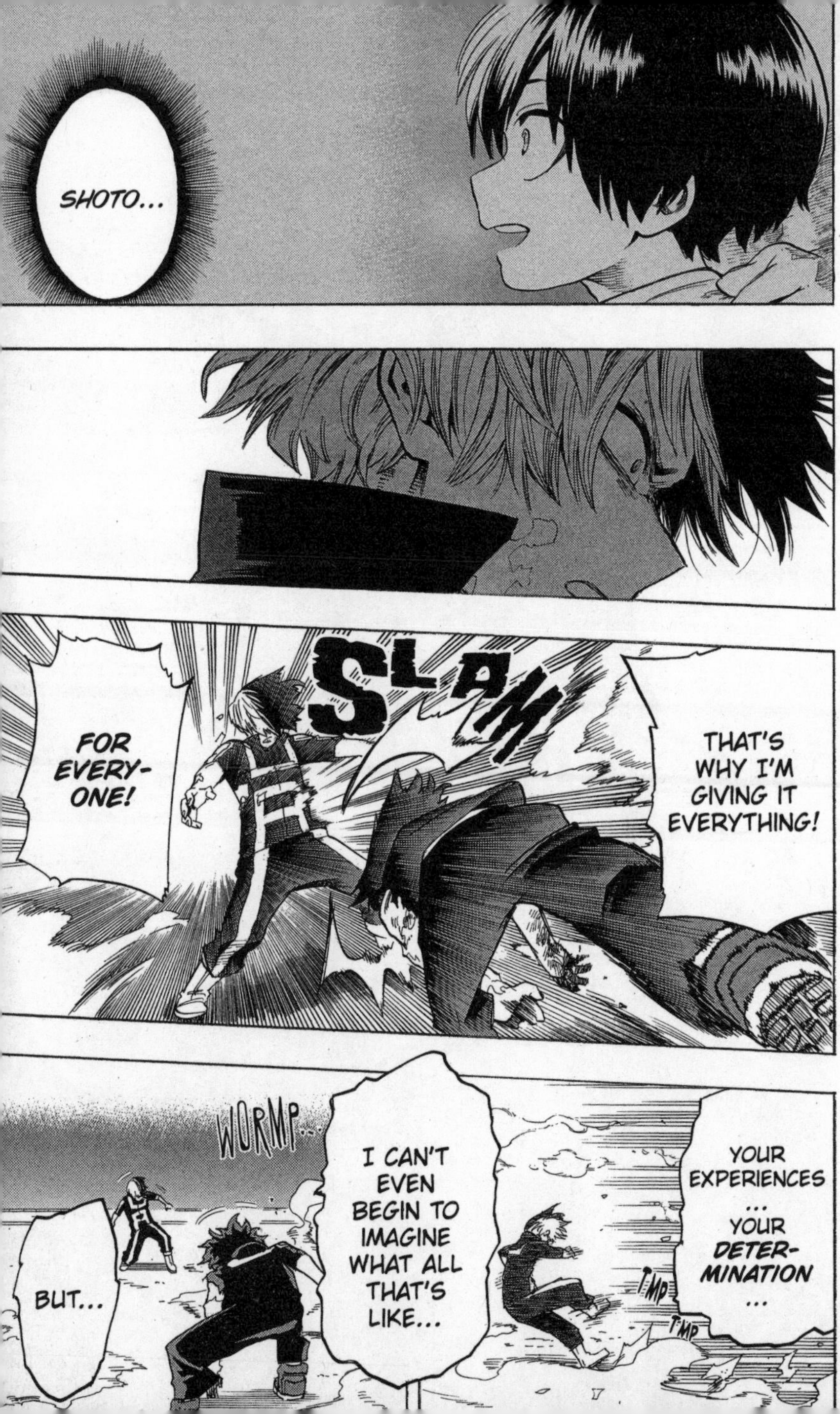
SHOTO...
SLAM
THAT'S WHY I'M GIVING IT EVERYTHING!
FOR EVERY-ONE!
YOUR EXPERIENCES ... YOUR DETER-MINATION ...
T'MP
T'MP
I CAN'T EVEN BEGIN TO IMAGINE WHAT ALL THAT'S LIKE...
WORMP..
BUT...

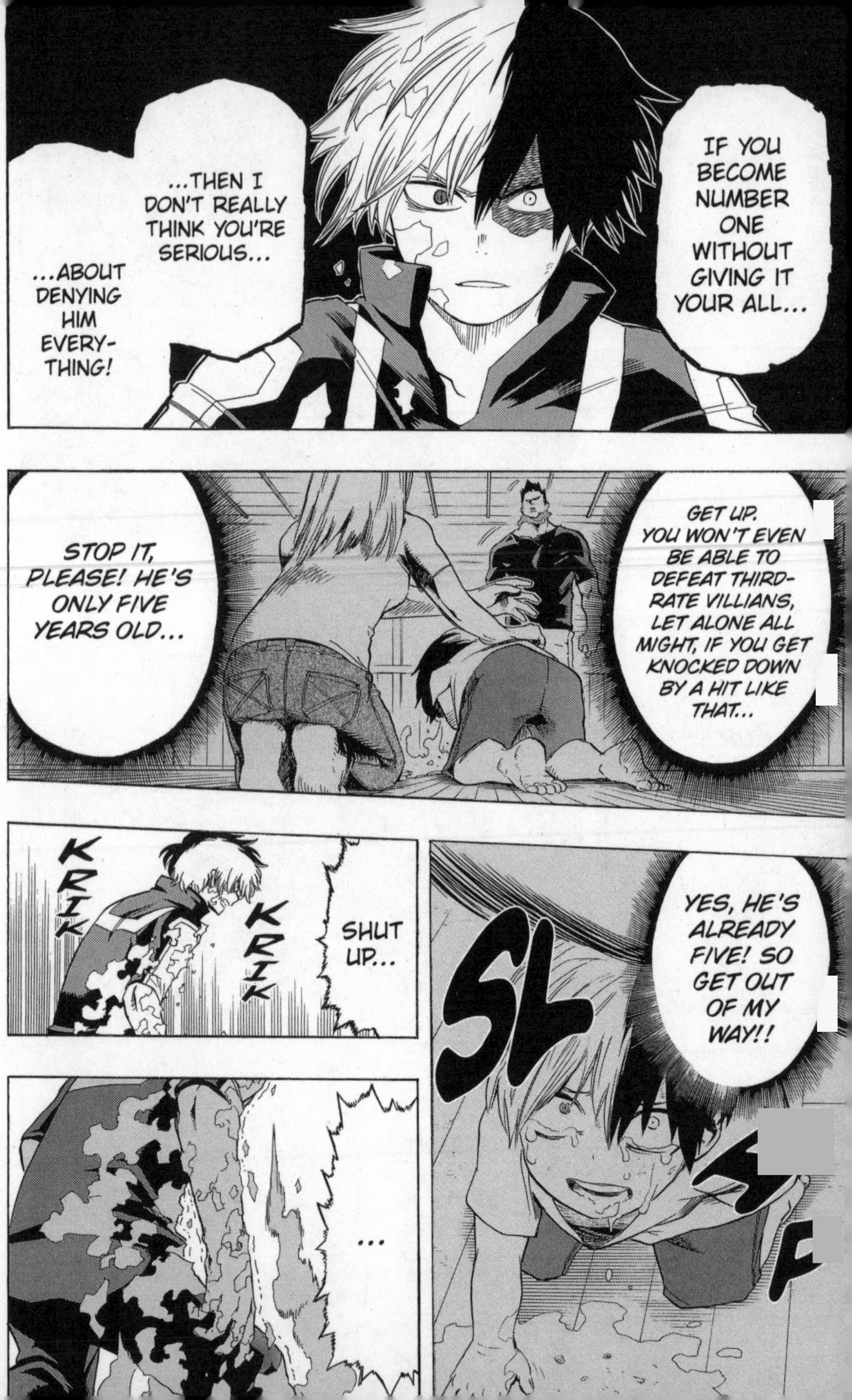
IF YOU BECOME NUMBER ONE WITHOUT GIVING IT YOUR ALL...
...THEN I DON'T REALLY THINK YOU'RE SERIOUS...
...ABOUT DENYING HIM EVERYTHING!
GET UP. YOU WON'T EVEN BE ABLE TO DEFEAT THIRD-RATE VILLIANS, LET ALONE ALL MIGHT, IF YOU GET KNOCKED DOWN BY A HIT LIKE THAT...
STOP IT, PLEASE! HE'S ONLY FIVE YEARS OLD...
YES, HE'S ALREADY FIVE! SO GET OUT OF MY WAY!!
SL
KRIK
KRIK
SHUT UP...
...

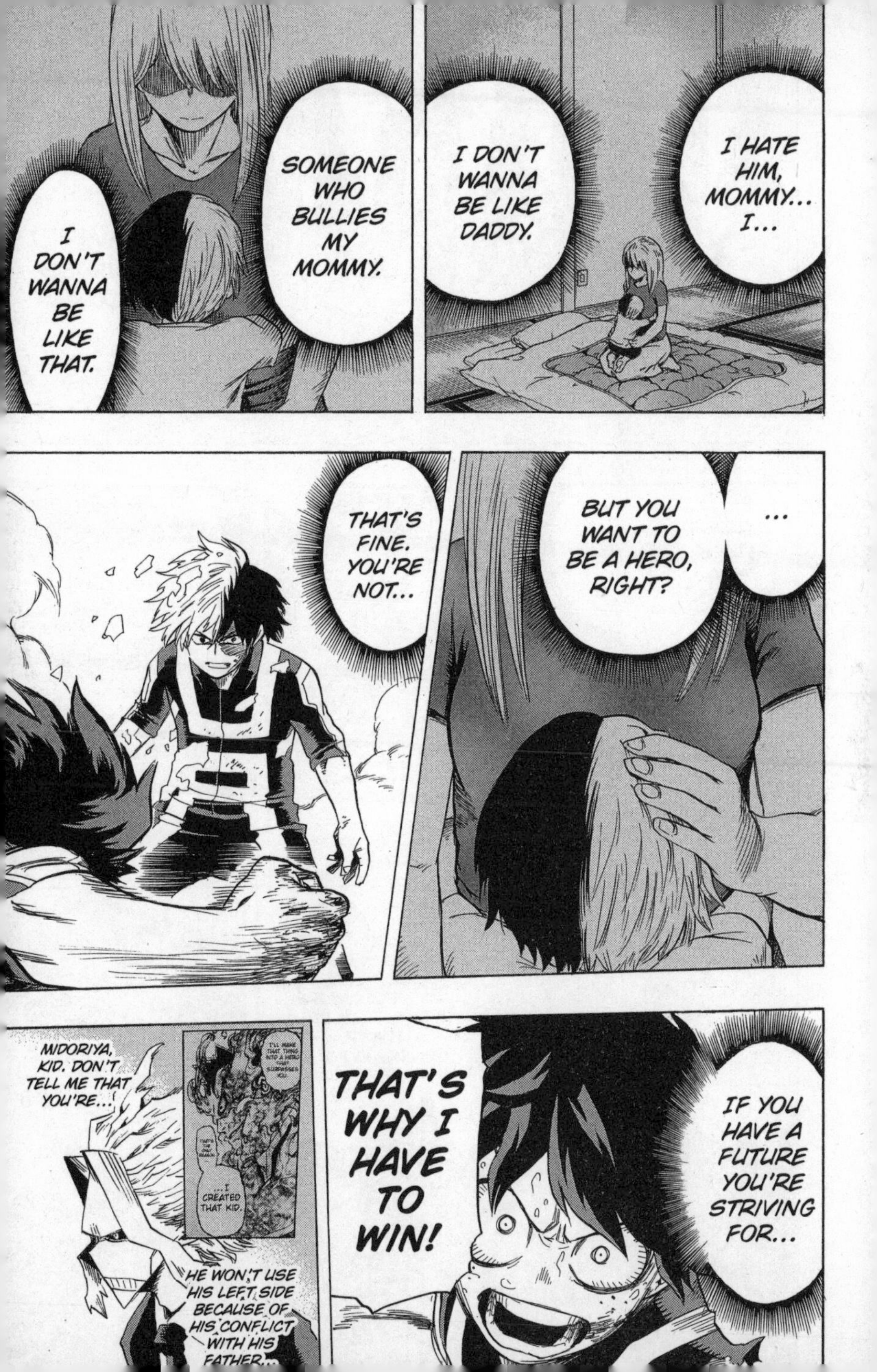
I HATE HIM, MOMMY... I...
I DON'T WANNA BE LIKE DADDY.
SOMEONE WHO BULLIES MY MOMMY.
I DON'T WANNA BE LIKE THAT.
...
BUT YOU WANT TO BE A HERO, RIGHT?
THAT'S FINE. YOU'RE NOT...
IF YOU HAVE A FUTURE YOU'RE STRIVING FOR...
THAT'S WHY I HAVE TO WIN!
MIDORIYA, KID. DON'T TELL ME THAT YOU'RE...
I'LL MAKE THAT THING INTO A HERO THAT SURPASSES YOU.
...I CREATED THAT KID.
HE WON'T USE HIS LEFT SIDE BECAUSE OF HIS CONFLICT WITH HIS FATHER...

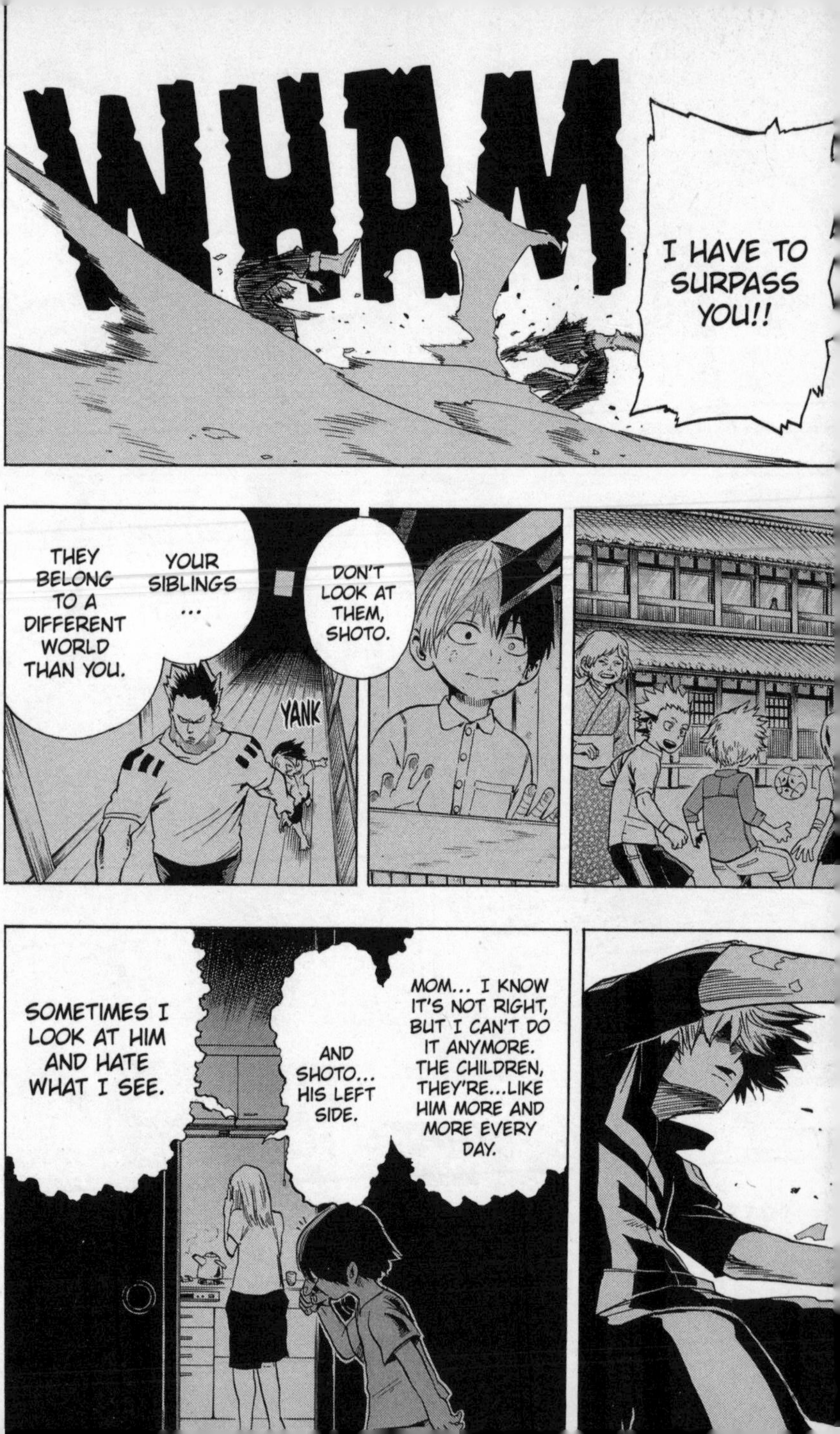
I HAVE TO SURPASS YOU!!
WHAM
DON'T LOOK AT THEM, SHOTO.
YOUR SIBLINGS ...
THEY BELONG TO A DIFFERENT WORLD THAN YOU.
YANK
MOM... I KNOW IT'S NOT RIGHT, BUT I CAN'T DO IT ANYMORE. THE CHILDREN, THEY'RE...LIKE HIM MORE AND MORE EVERY DAY.
AND SHOTO... HIS LEFT SIDE.
SOMETIMES I LOOK AT HIM AND HATE WHAT I SEE.

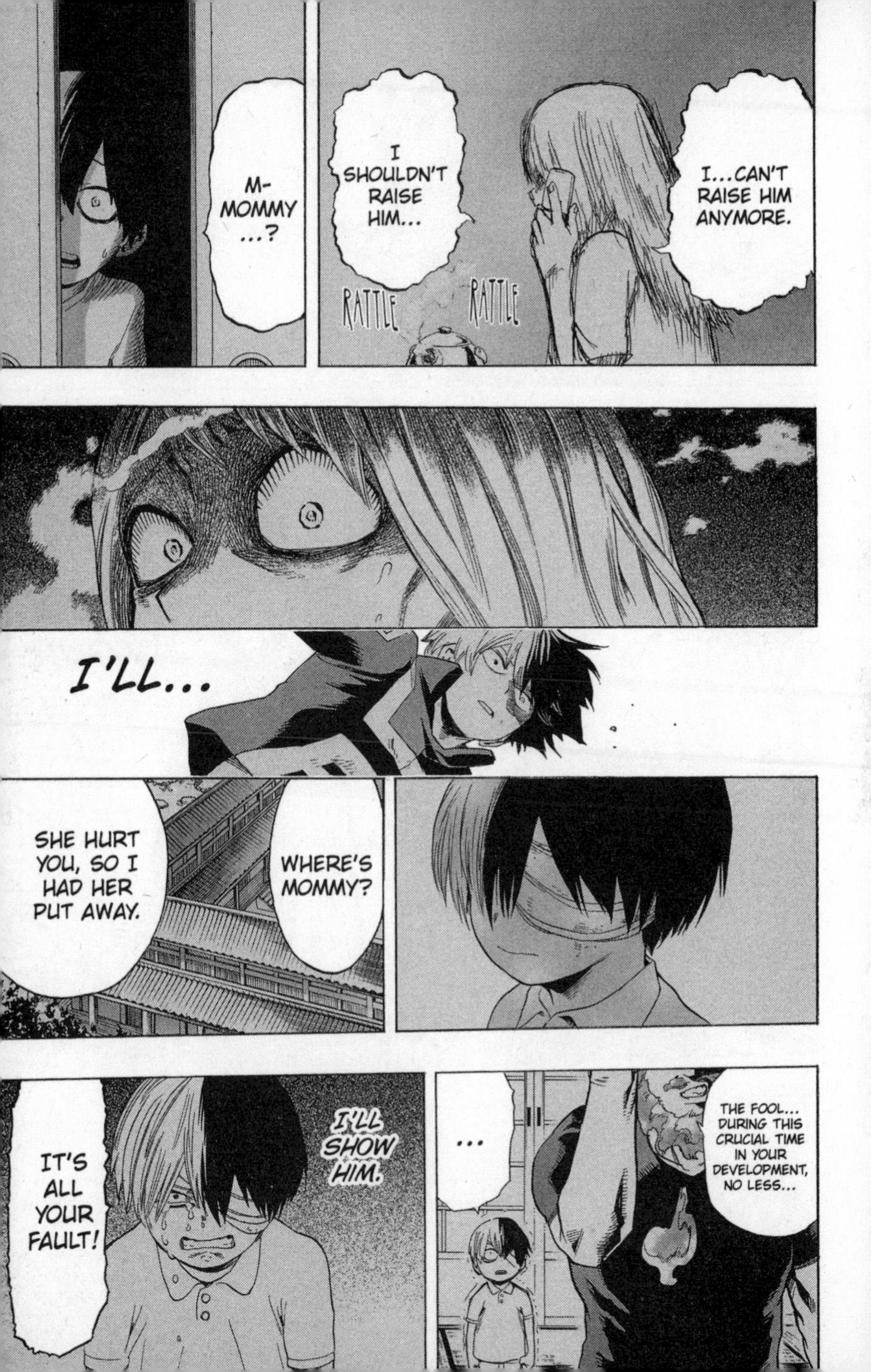
I...CAN'T RAISE HIM ANYMORE.
I SHOULDN'T RAISE HIM...
RATTLE
RATTLE
M-MOMMY...?
I'LL...
WHERE'S MOMMY?
SHE HURT YOU, SO I HAD HER PUT AWAY.
THE FOOL... DURING THIS CRUCIAL TIME IN YOUR DEVELOPMENT, NO LESS...
...
I'LL SHOW HIM.
IT'S ALL YOUR FAULT!

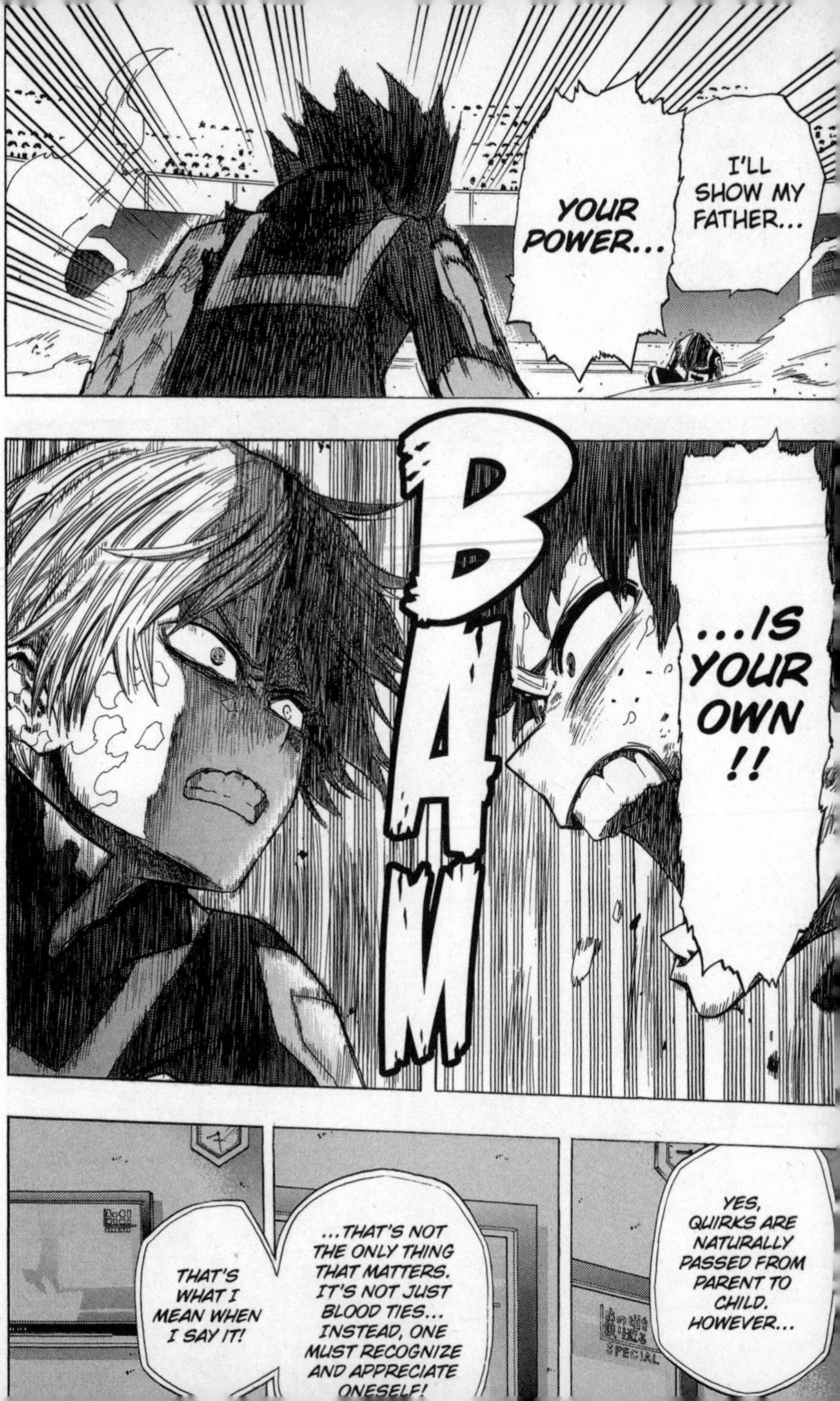
I'LL SHOW MY FATHER...
YOUR POWER...
...IS YOUR OWN !!
BAM
YES, QUIRKS ARE NATURALLY PASSED FROM PARENT TO CHILD. HOWEVER...
...THAT'S NOT THE ONLY THING THAT MATTERS. IT'S NOT JUST BLOOD TIES... INSTEAD, ONE MUST RECOGNIZE AND APPRECIATE ONESELF!
THAT'S WHAT I MEAN WHEN I SAY IT!

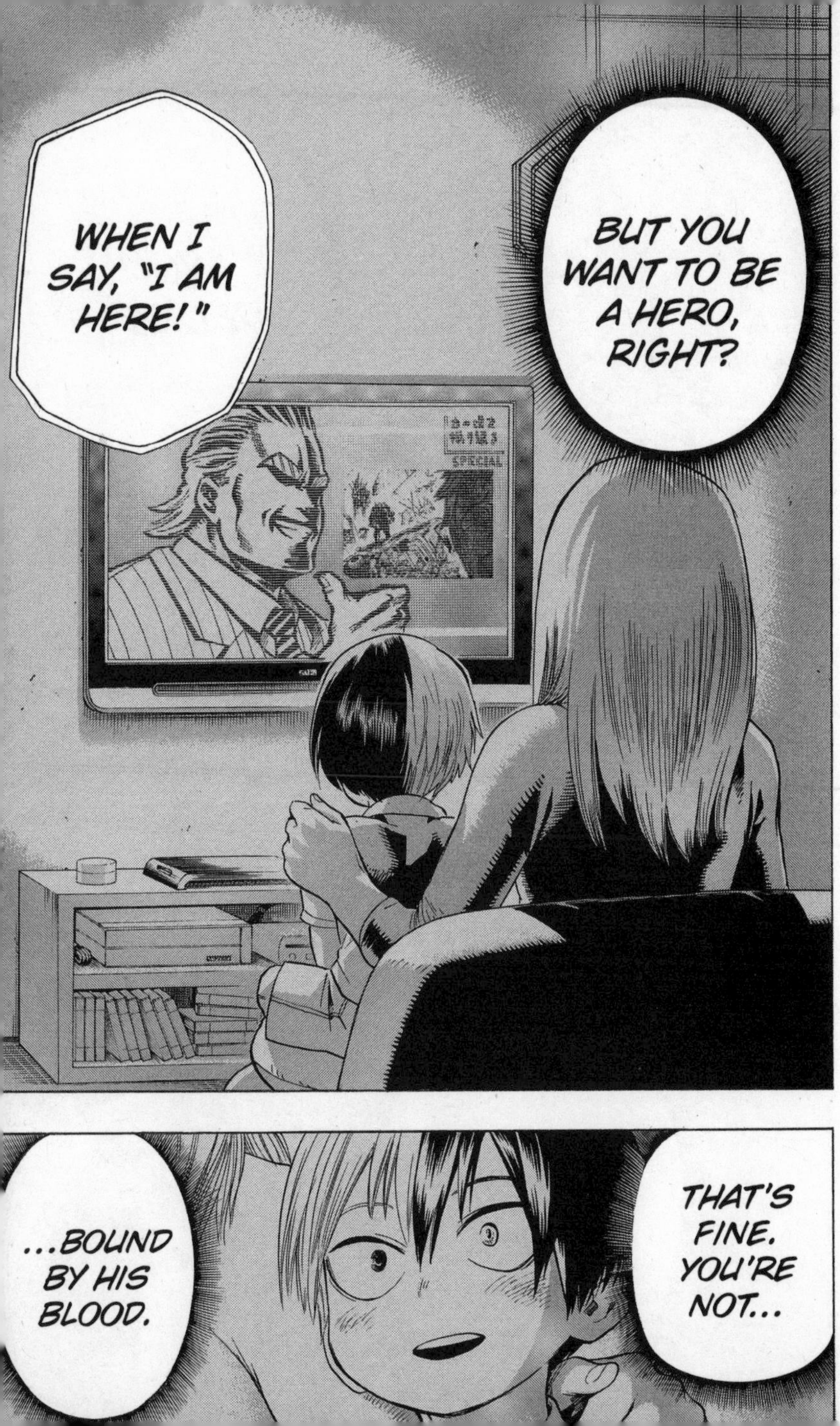
BUT YOU WANT TO BE A HERO, RIGHT?
WHEN I SAY, "I AM HERE!"
SPECIAL
THAT'S FINE. YOU'RE NOT...
...BOUND BY HIS BLOOD.

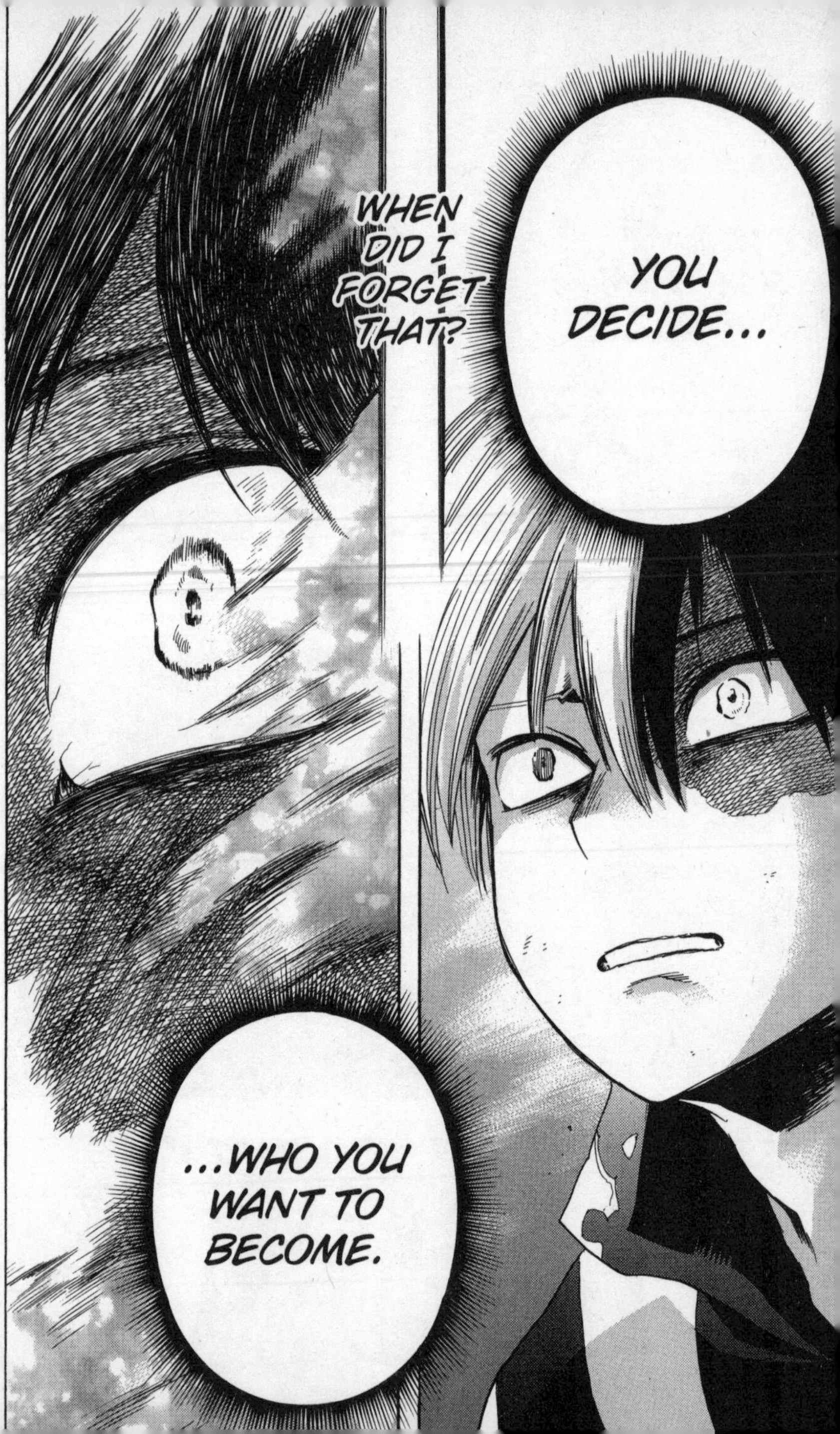
YOU DECIDE...
WHEN DID I FORGET THAT?
...WHO YOU WANT TO BECOME.

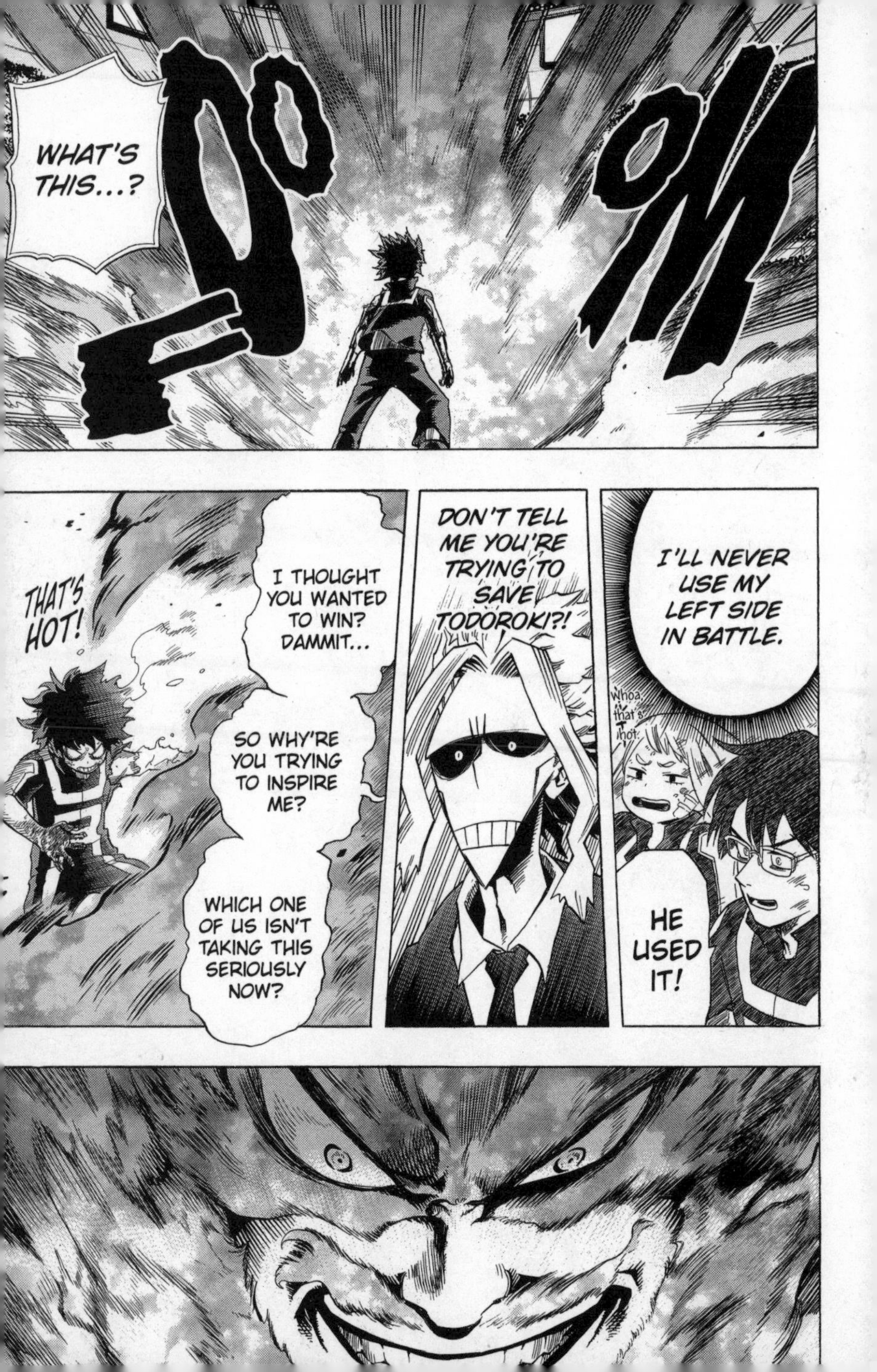
WHAT'S THIS...?
DOOM
I'LL NEVER USE MY LEFT SIDE IN BATTLE.
Whoa, that's hot.
HE USED IT!
DON'T TELL ME YOU'RE TRYING TO SAVE TODOROKI?!
I THOUGHT YOU WANTED TO WIN? DAMMIT...
THAT'S HOT!
SO WHY'RE YOU TRYING TO INSPIRE ME?
WHICH ONE OF US ISN'T TAKING THIS SERIOUSLY NOW?

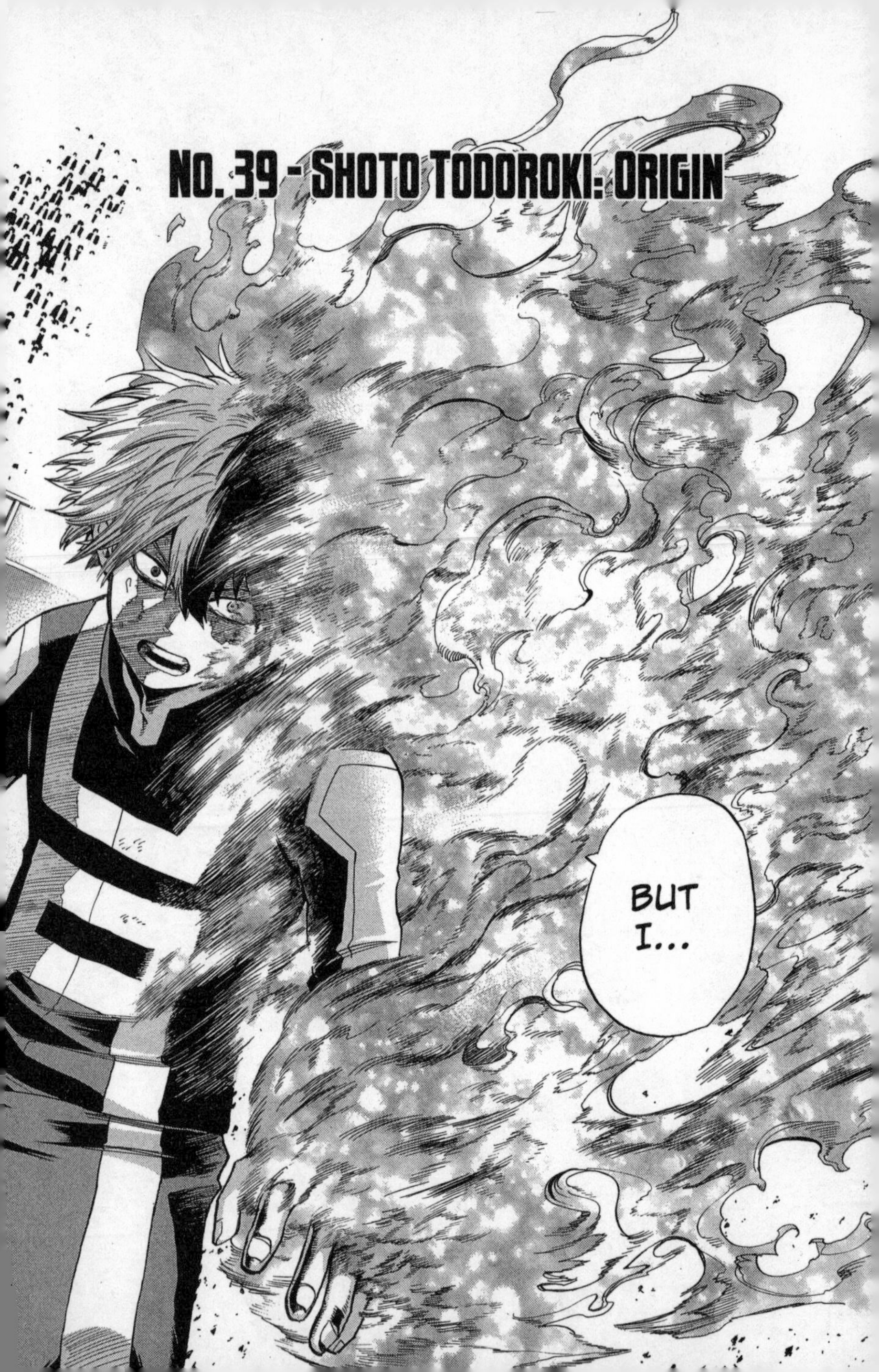
No. 39 - Shoto Todoroki: Origin
BUT I...

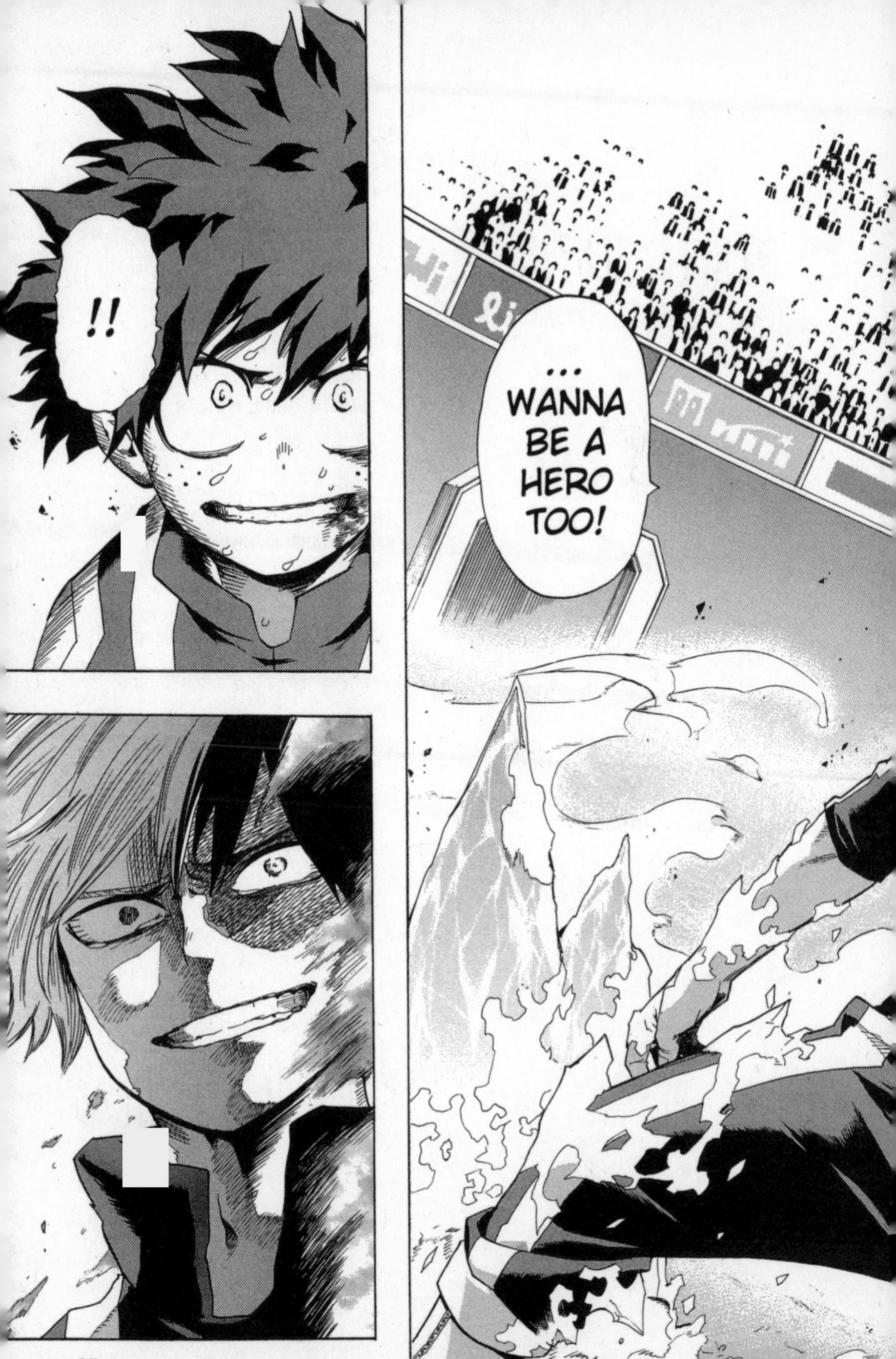
...WANNA BE A HERO TOO!
!!

STREET CLOTHES
(HE WAS BORN IN THE TOHOKU REGION)

Birthday: 2/1
Height: 186 cm
Favorite Thing: Nature

BEHIND THE SCENES
He's another one who hasn't gotten much exposure yet. Will I ever even give him a line to say?! Stay tuned!!! (No promises.)

It's no secret that I like making not-quite-human characters, so I'm fond of this guy's design, too.

BACK OF THE HEAD

He's got this weird, fluttery-looking thing back there. It's probably hair.

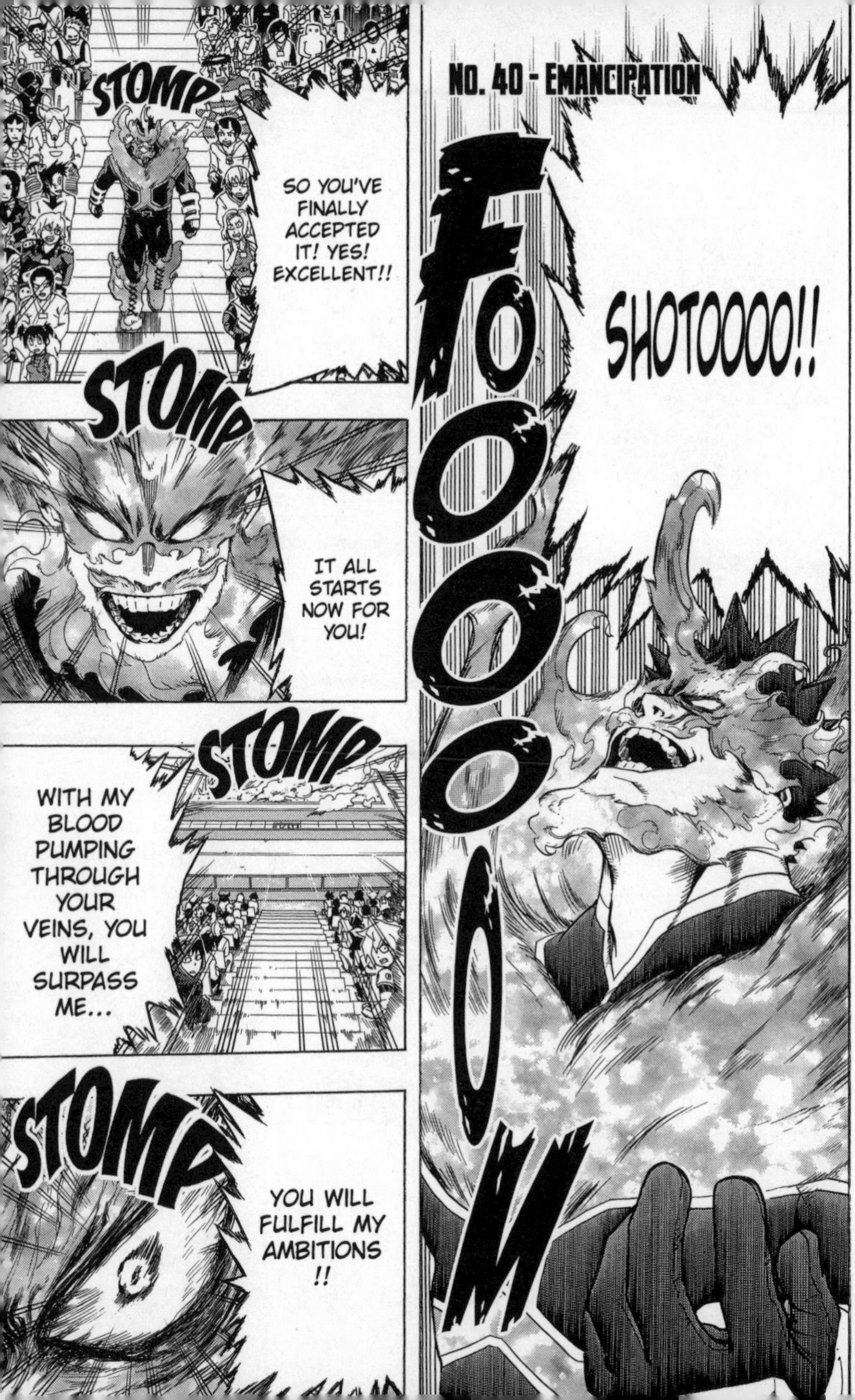

No. 40 - Emancipation
FOOOOOM
SHOTOOOO!!
STOMP
SO YOU'VE FINALLY ACCEPTED IT! YES! EXCELLENT!!
STOMP
IT ALL STARTS NOW FOR YOU!
STOMP
WITH MY BLOOD PUMPING THROUGH YOUR VEINS, YOU WILL SURPASS ME...
STOMP
YOU WILL FULFILL MY AMBITIONS!!

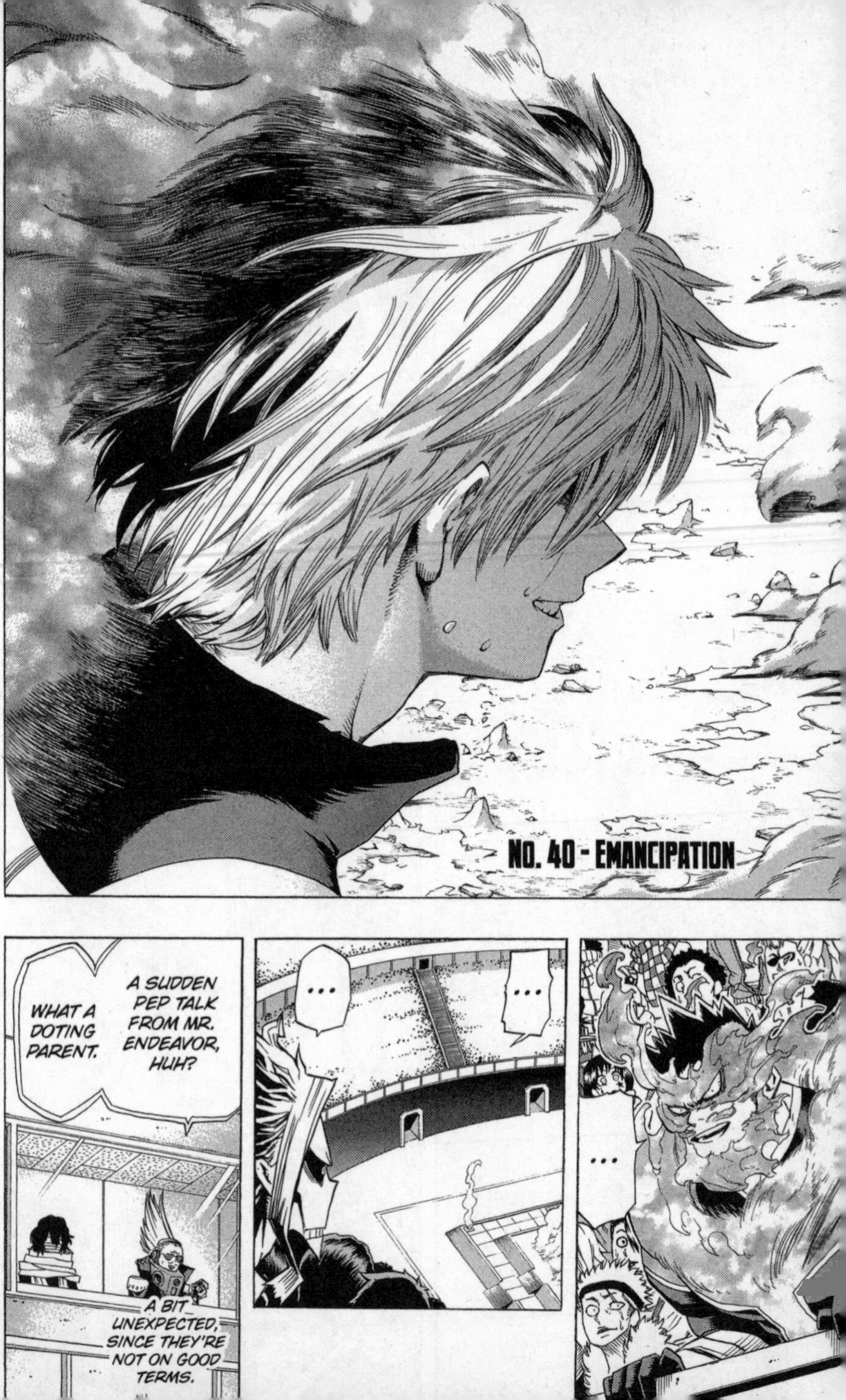
NO. 40 - EMANCIPATION
...
...
...
A SUDDEN PEP TALK FROM MR. ENDEAVOR, HUH?
WHAT A DOTING PARENT.
A BIT UNEXPECTED, SINCE THEY'RE NOT ON GOOD TERMS.

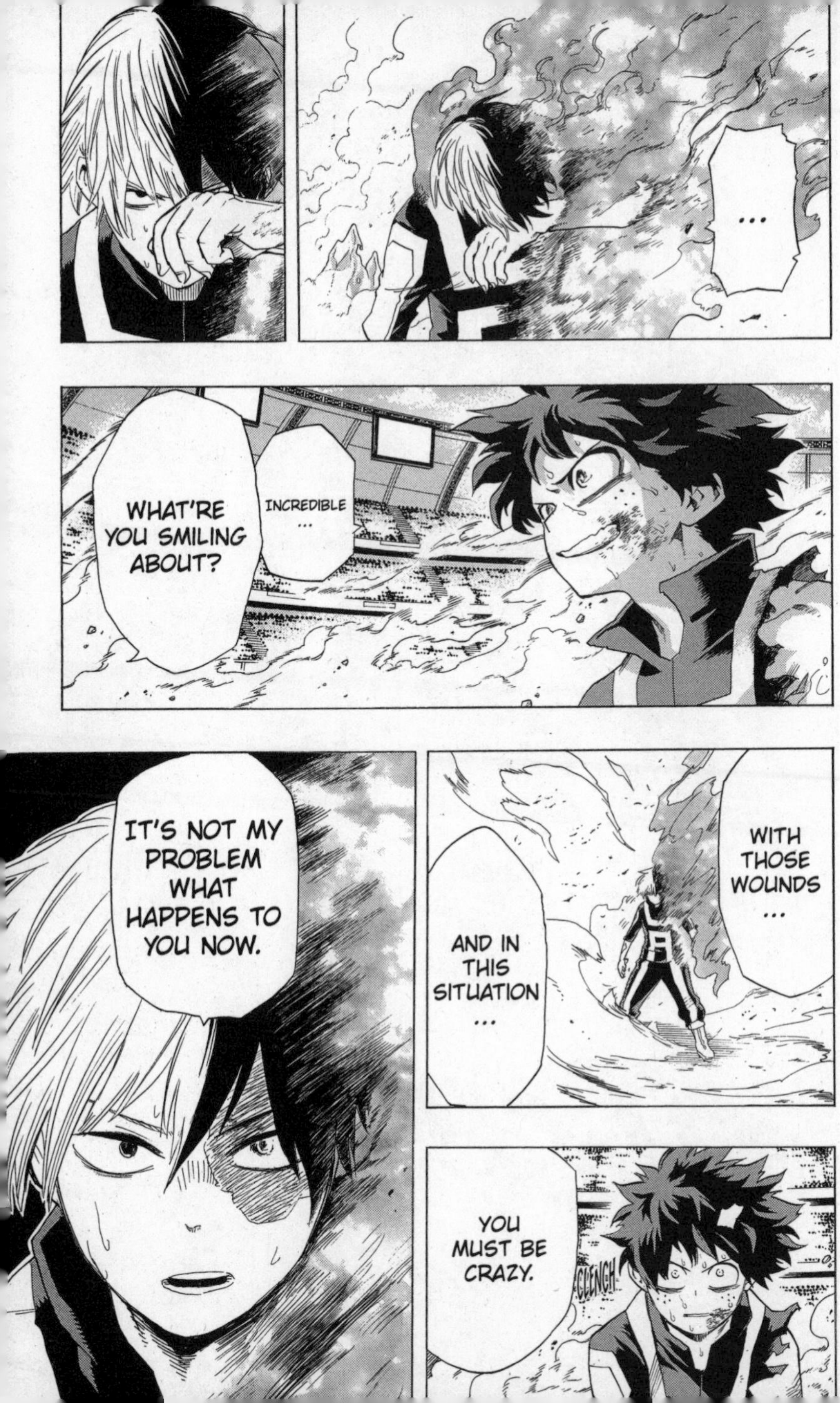
...
INCREDIBLE ...
WHAT'RE YOU SMILING ABOUT?
WITH THOSE WOUNDS ...
AND IN THIS SITUATION ...
YOU MUST BE CRAZY.
CLENCH
IT'S NOT MY PROBLEM WHAT HAPPENS TO YOU NOW.

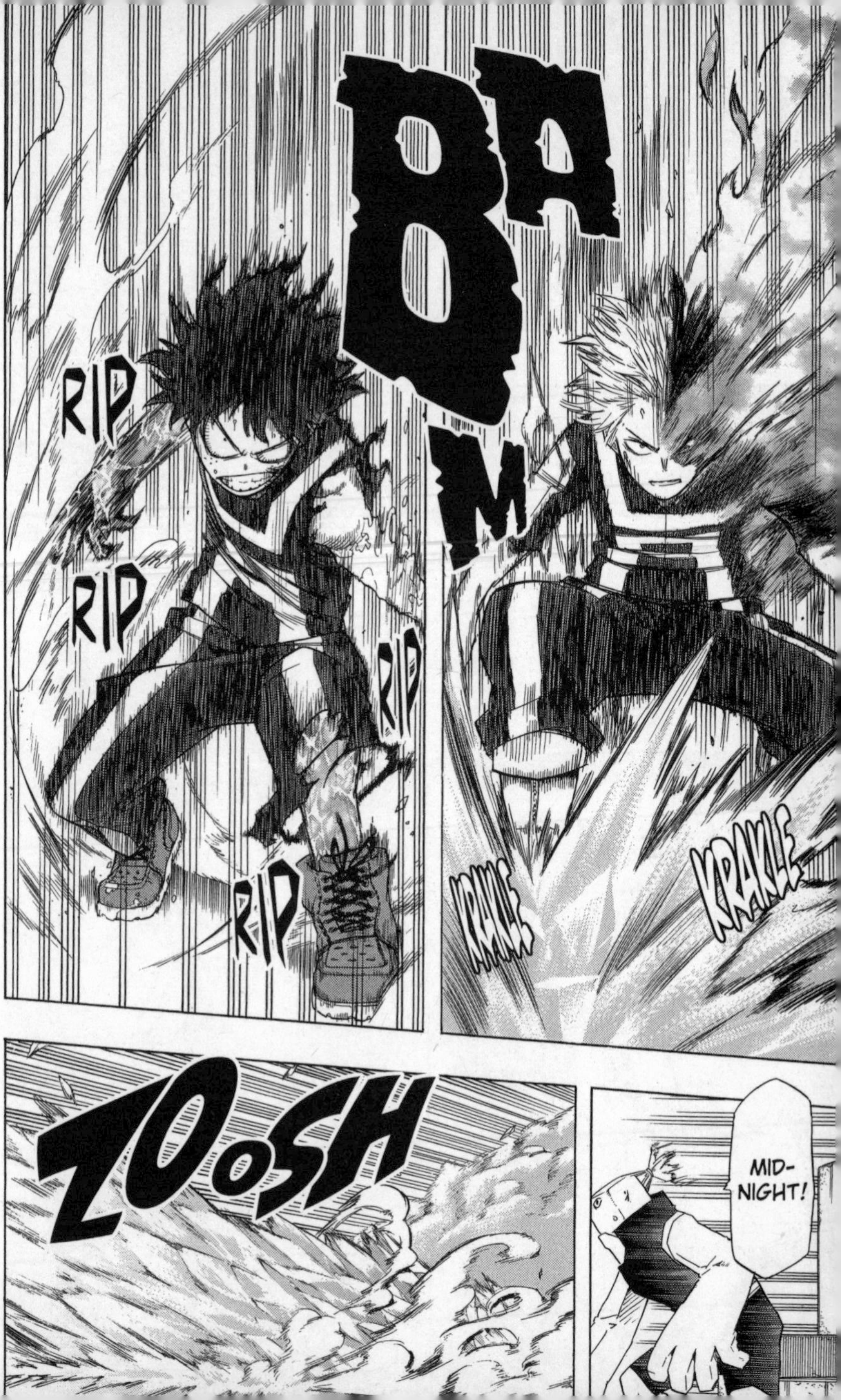
BAM
KRAKLE
KRAKLE
RIP
RIP
RIP
RIP
MID-NIGHT!
ZOOSH

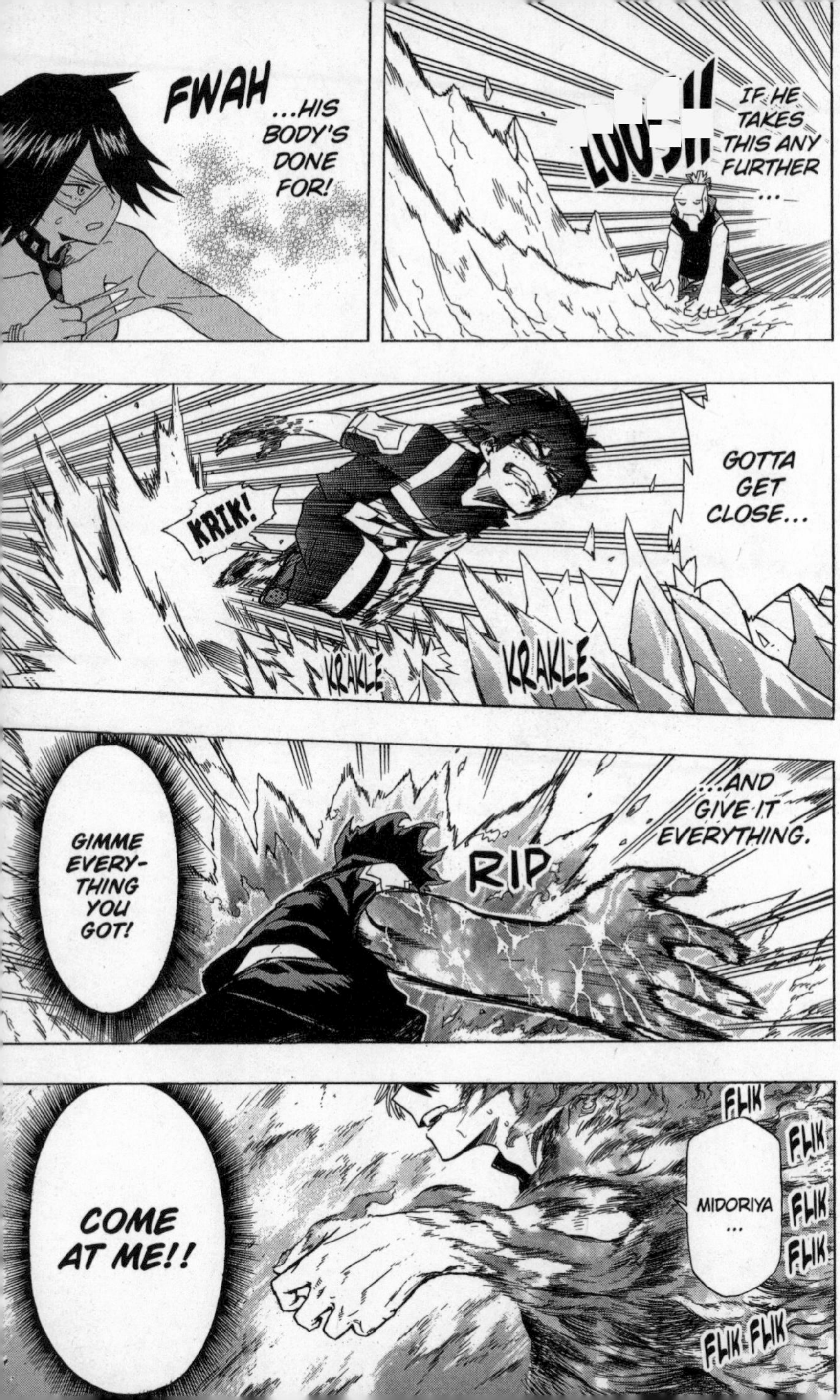
IF HE TAKES THIS ANY FURTHER...
FWAH
...HIS BODY'S DONE FOR!
GOTTA GET CLOSE...
KRIK!
KRAKLE
KRAKLE
...AND GIVE IT EVERYTHING.
RIP
GIMME EVERYTHING YOU GOT!
FLIK FLIK FLIK FLIK
MIDORIYA...
FLIK FLIK
COME AT ME!!

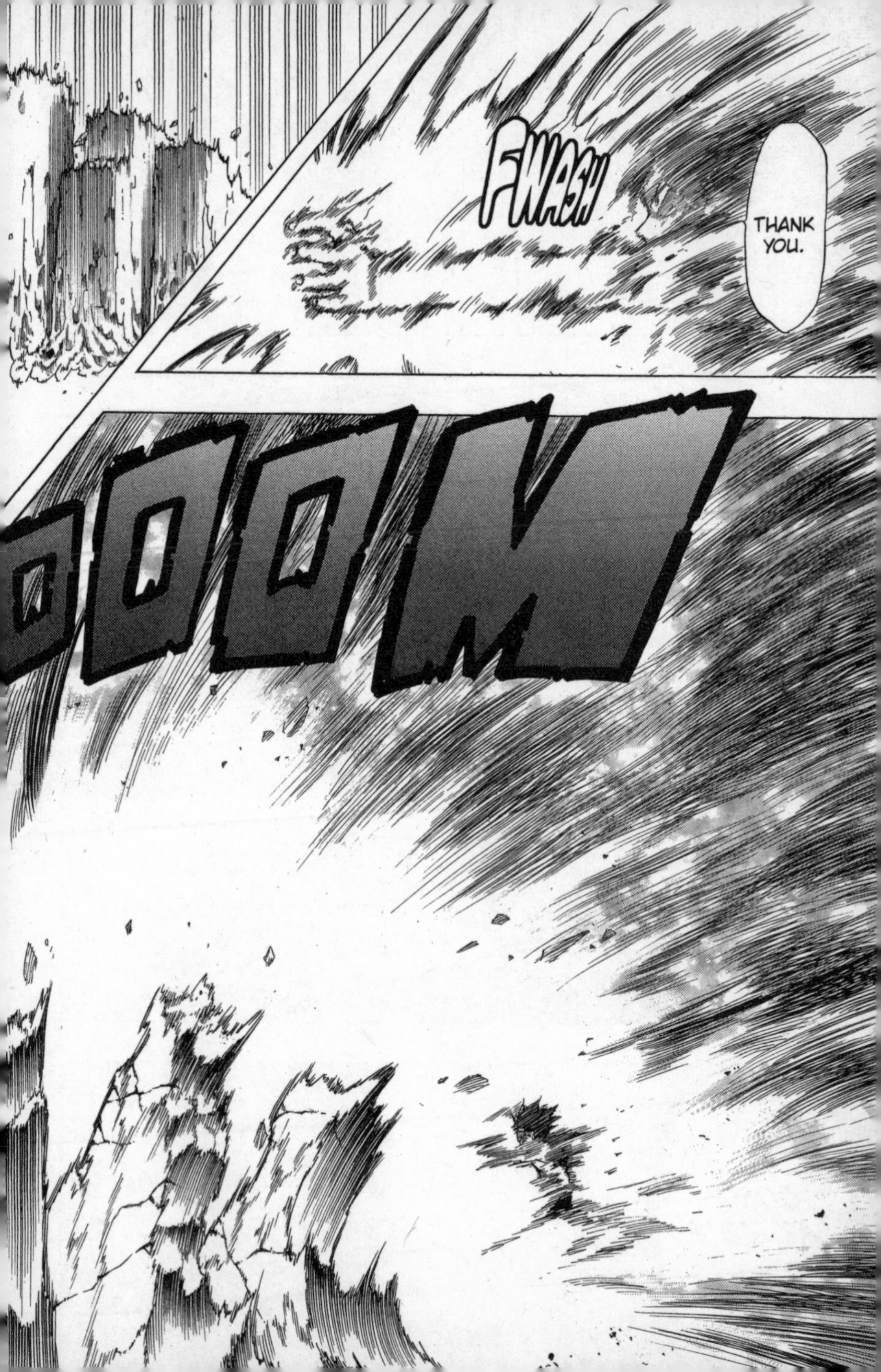
THANK YOU.
FWASH
OOOM

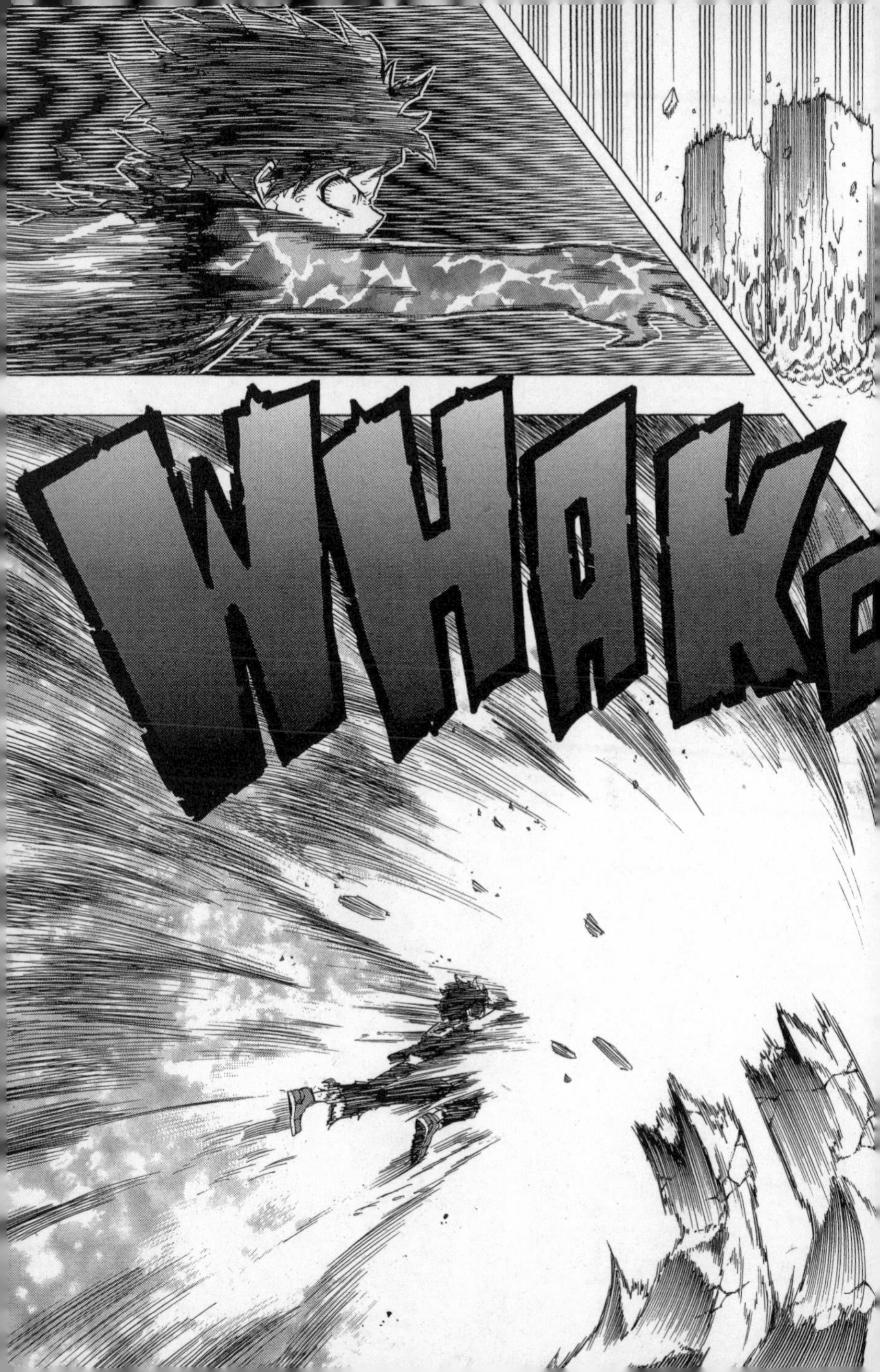
WHAK

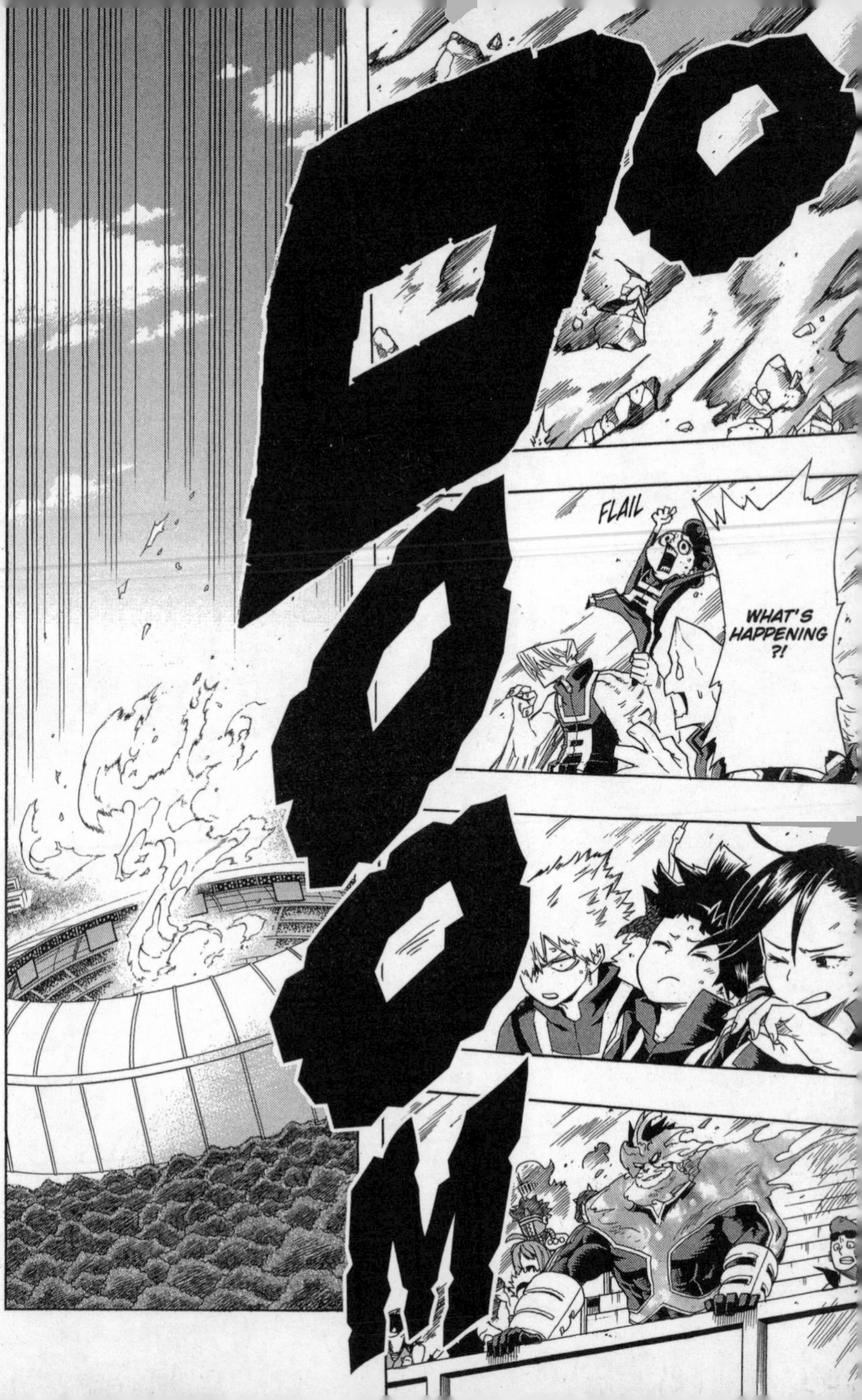
FLAIL
WHAT'S HAPPENING ?!

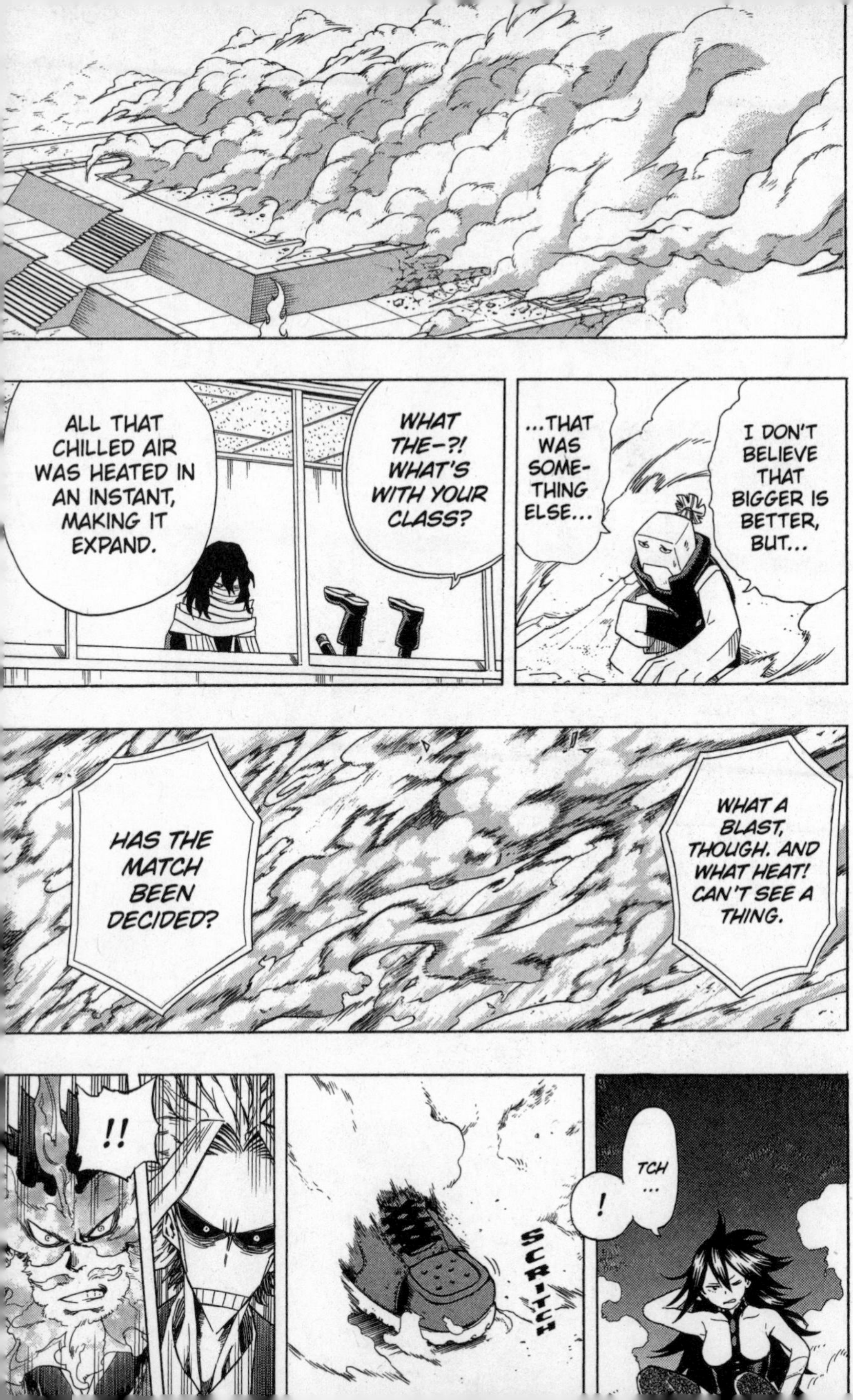
I DON'T BELIEVE THAT BIGGER IS BETTER, BUT...
...THAT WAS SOME-THING ELSE...
WHAT THE-?! WHAT'S WITH YOUR CLASS?
ALL THAT CHILLED AIR WAS HEATED IN AN INSTANT, MAKING IT EXPAND.
WHAT A BLAST, THOUGH. AND WHAT HEAT! CAN'T SEE A THING.
HAS THE MATCH BEEN DECIDED?
TCH ...
!
SCRITCH
!!

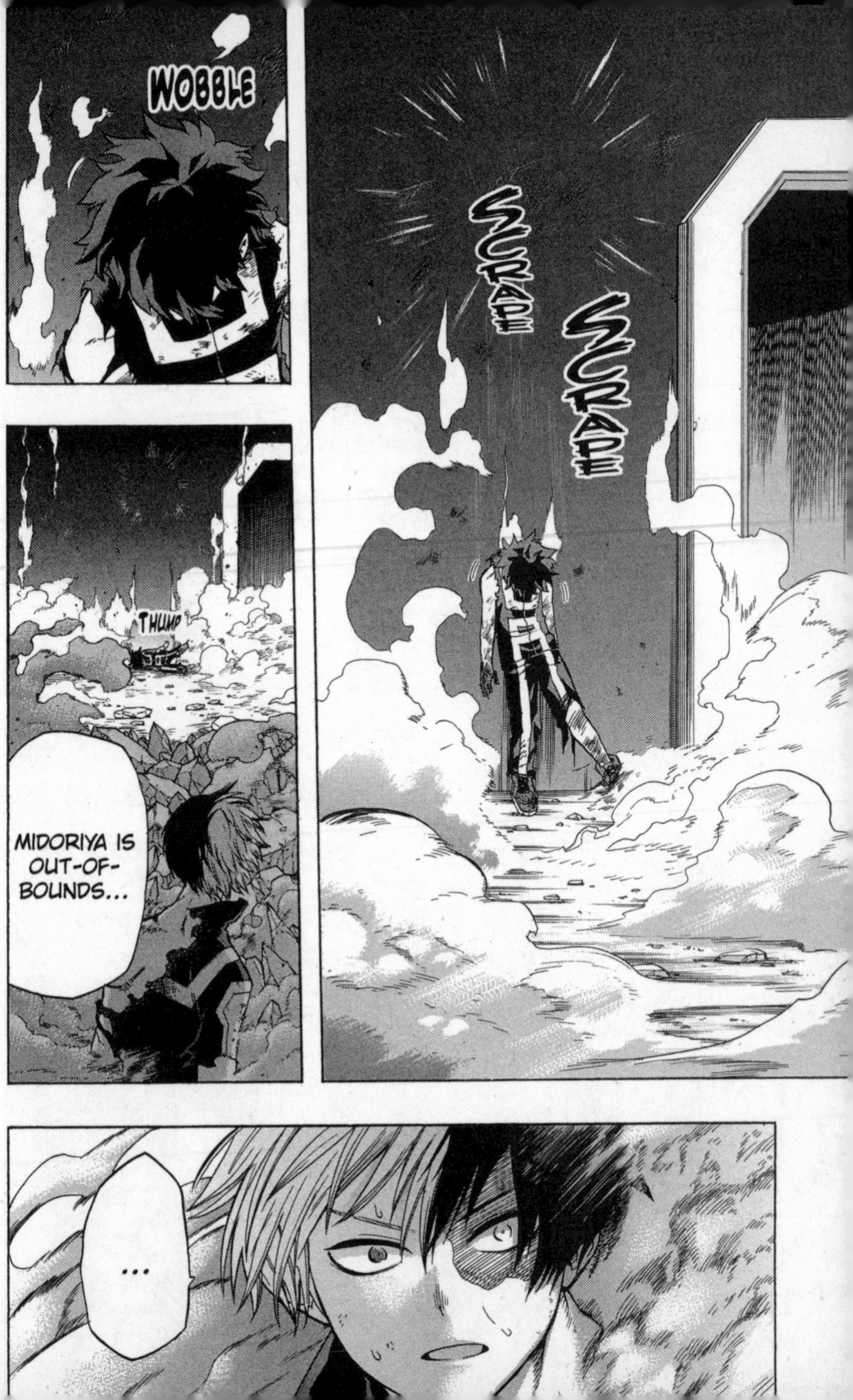
SCRAPE
SCRAPE
WOBBLE
THUMP
MIDORIYA IS OUT-OF-BOUNDS...
...

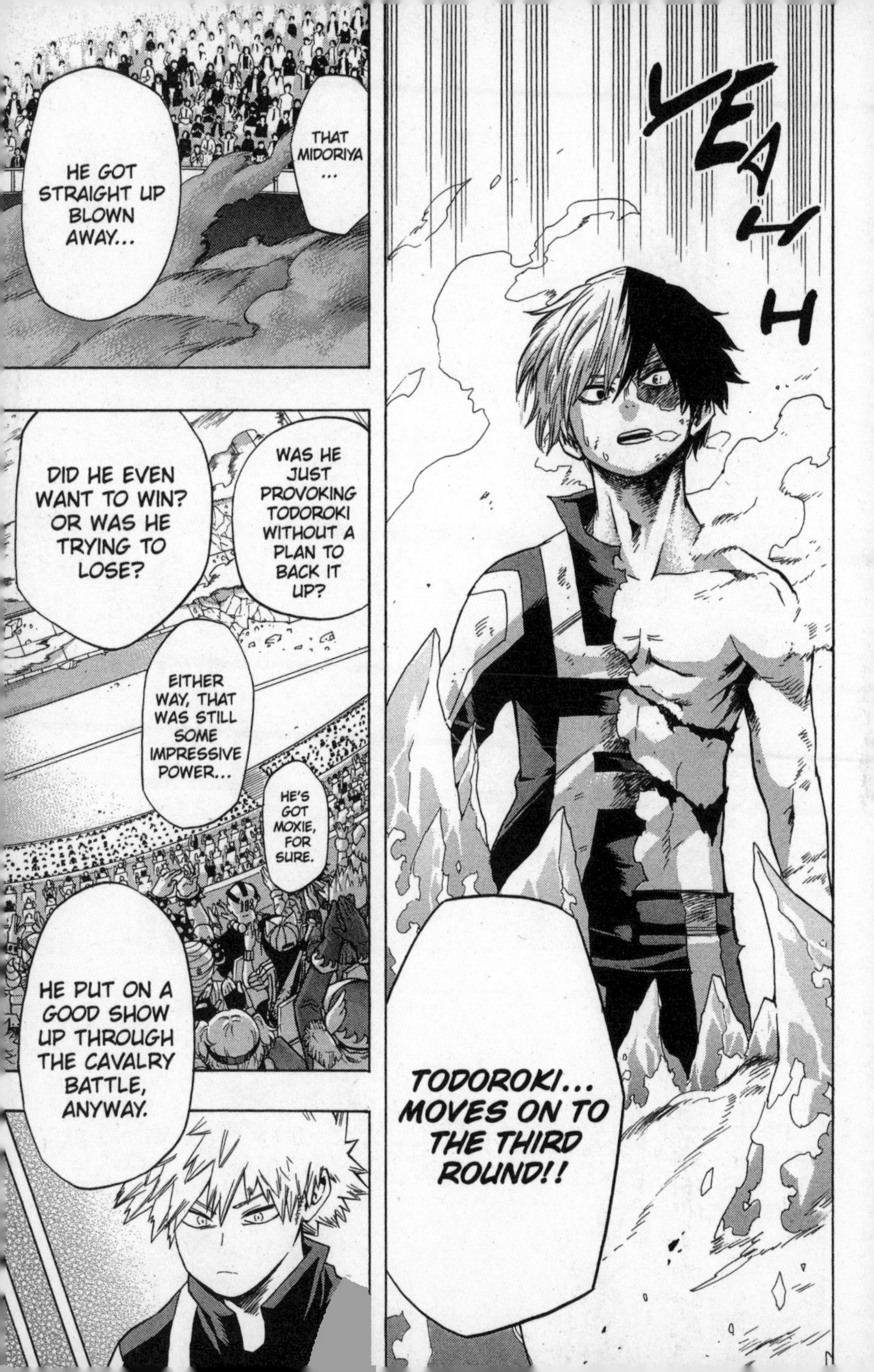
YEAHHH
TODOROKI... MOVES ON TO THE THIRD ROUND!!
THAT MIDORIYA...
HE GOT STRAIGHT UP BLOWN AWAY...
WAS HE JUST PROVOKING TODOROKI WITHOUT A PLAN TO BACK IT UP?
DID HE EVEN WANT TO WIN? OR WAS HE TRYING TO LOSE?
EITHER WAY, THAT WAS STILL SOME IMPRESSIVE POWER...
HE'S GOT MOXIE, FOR SURE.
HE PUT ON A GOOD SHOW UP THROUGH THE CAVALRY BATTLE, ANYWAY.

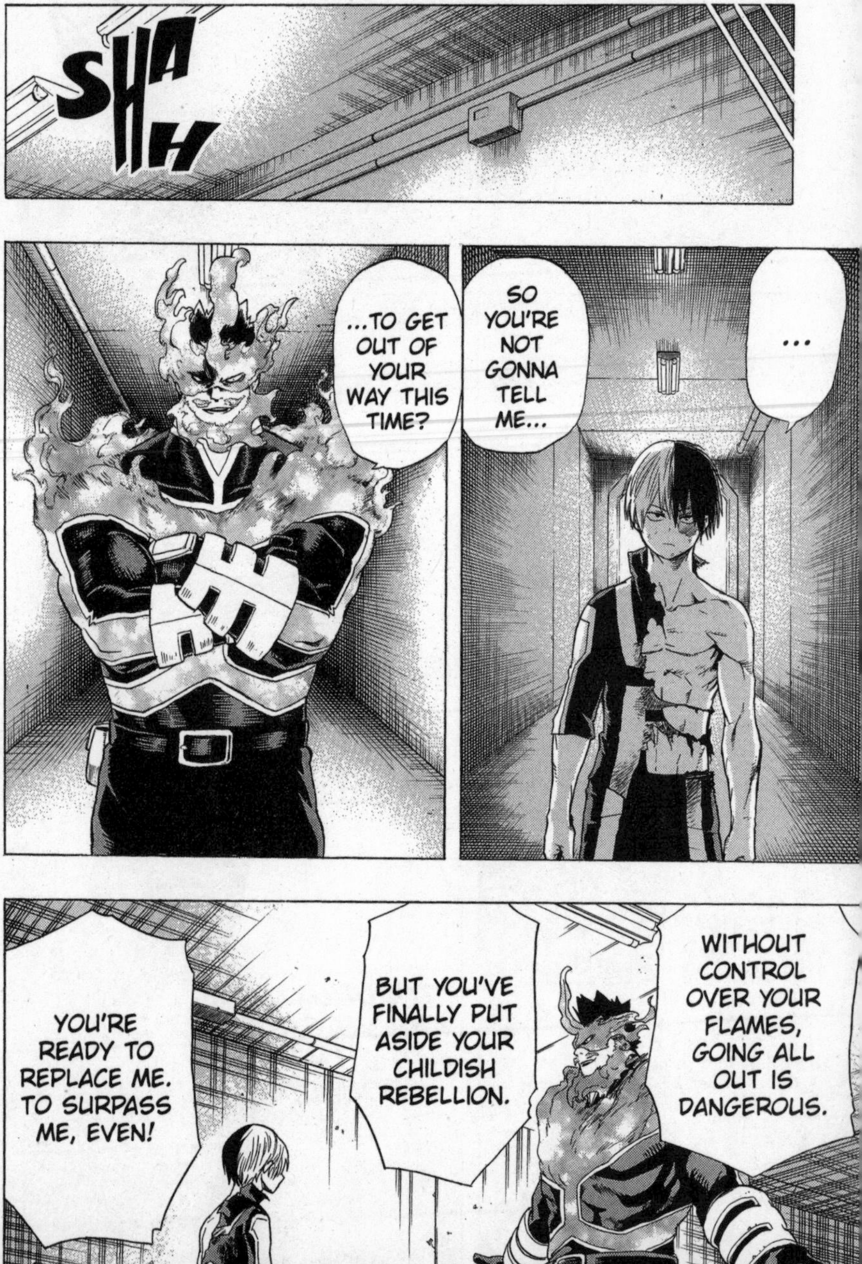
SHAHH
...
SO YOU'RE NOT GONNA TELL ME...
...TO GET OUT OF YOUR WAY THIS TIME?
WITHOUT CONTROL OVER YOUR FLAMES, GOING ALL OUT IS DANGEROUS.
BUT YOU'VE FINALLY PUT ASIDE YOUR CHILDISH REBELLION.
YOU'RE READY TO REPLACE ME. TO SURPASS ME, EVEN!

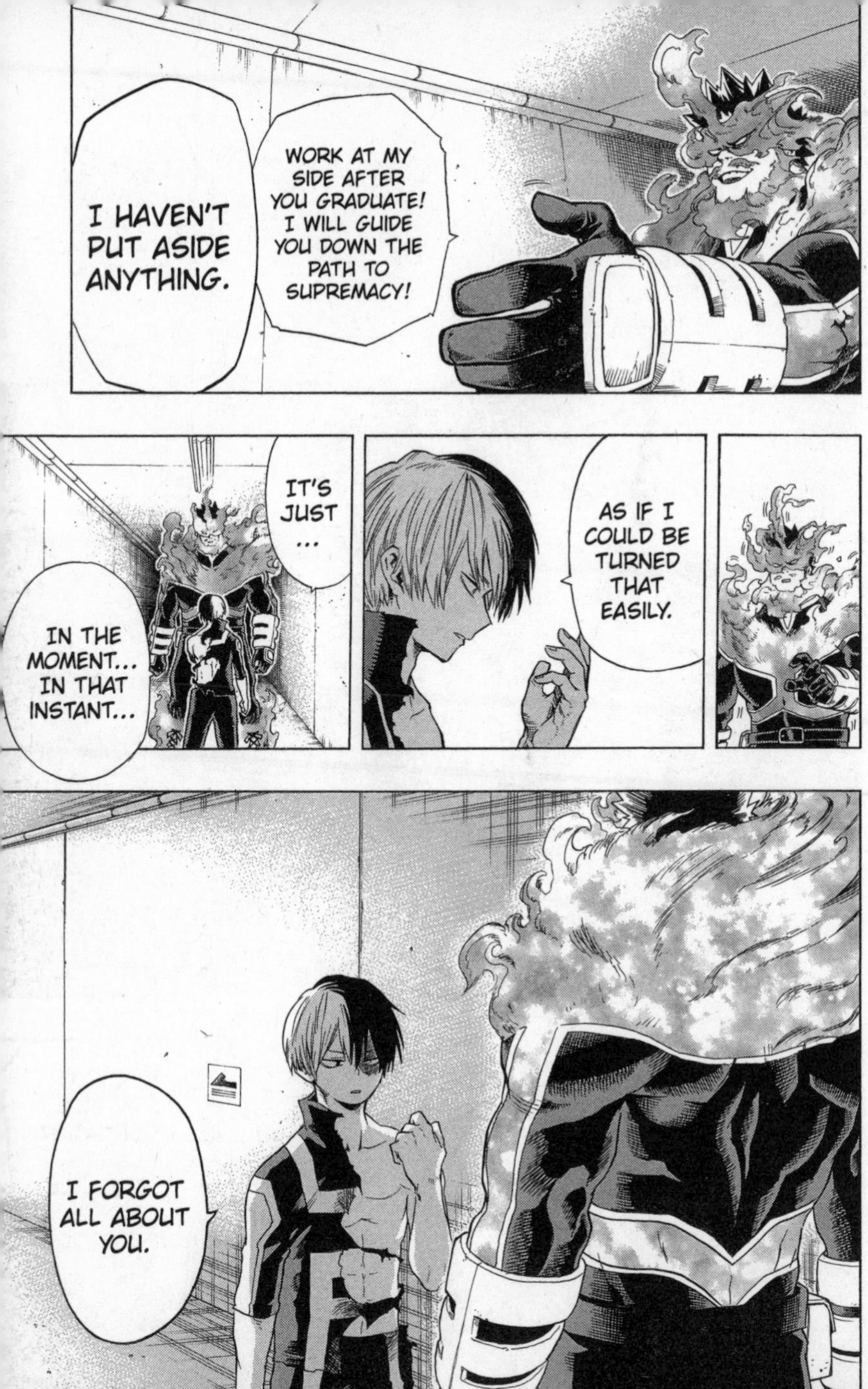
WORK AT MY SIDE AFTER YOU GRADUATE! I WILL GUIDE YOU DOWN THE PATH TO SUPREMACY!
I HAVEN'T PUT ASIDE ANYTHING.
AS IF I COULD BE TURNED THAT EASILY.
IT'S JUST ...
IN THE MOMENT... IN THAT INSTANT...
I FORGOT ALL ABOUT YOU.

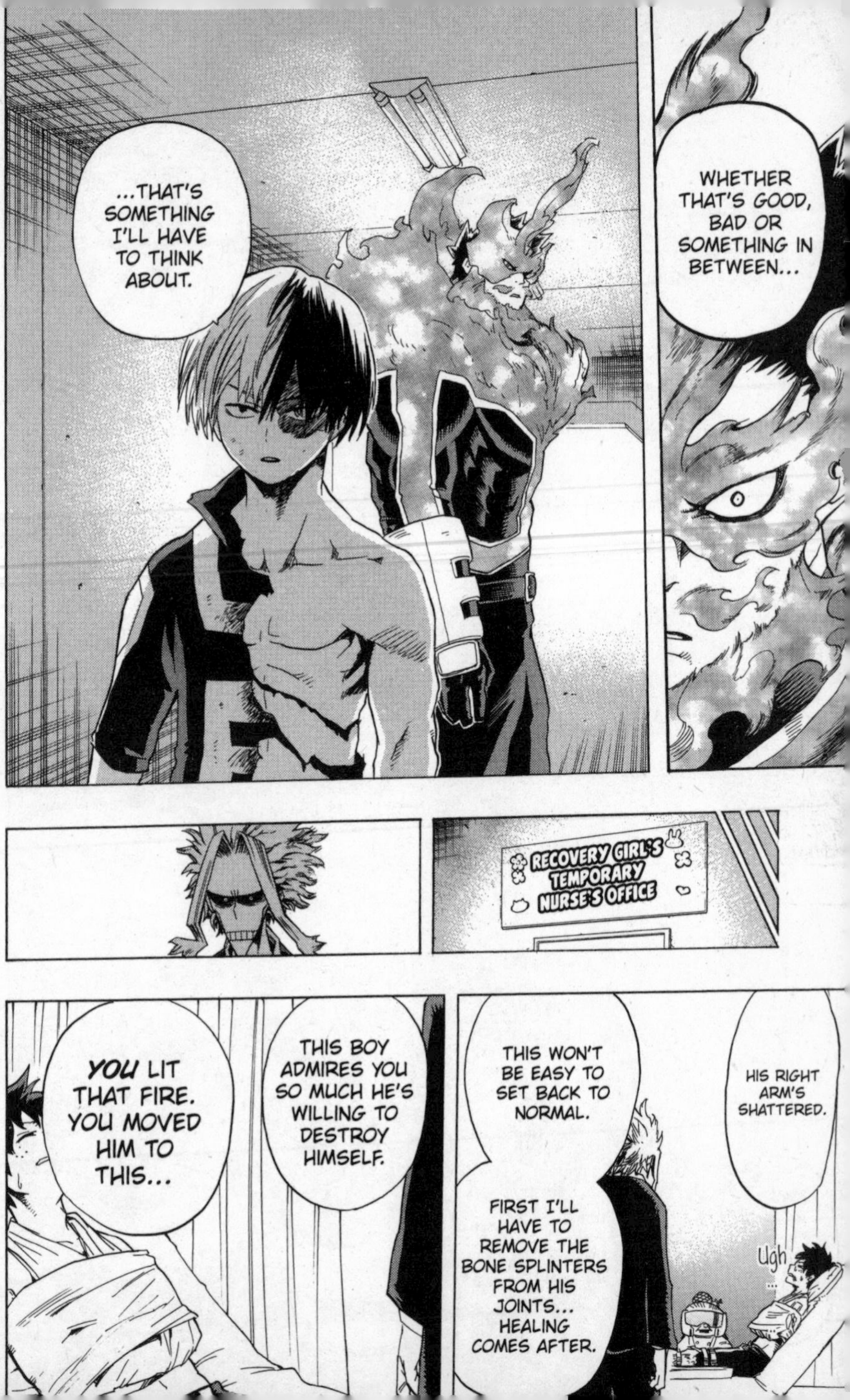
WHETHER THAT'S GOOD, BAD OR SOMETHING IN BETWEEN...
...THAT'S SOMETHING I'LL HAVE TO THINK ABOUT.
RECOVERY GIRL'S TEMPORARY NURSE'S OFFICE
HIS RIGHT ARM'S SHATTERED.
Ugh...
THIS WON'T BE EASY TO SET BACK TO NORMAL.
FIRST I'LL HAVE TO REMOVE THE BONE SPLINTERS FROM HIS JOINTS... HEALING COMES AFTER.
THIS BOY ADMIRES YOU SO MUCH HE'S WILLING TO DESTROY HIMSELF.
YOU LIT THAT FIRE. YOU MOVED HIM TO THIS...

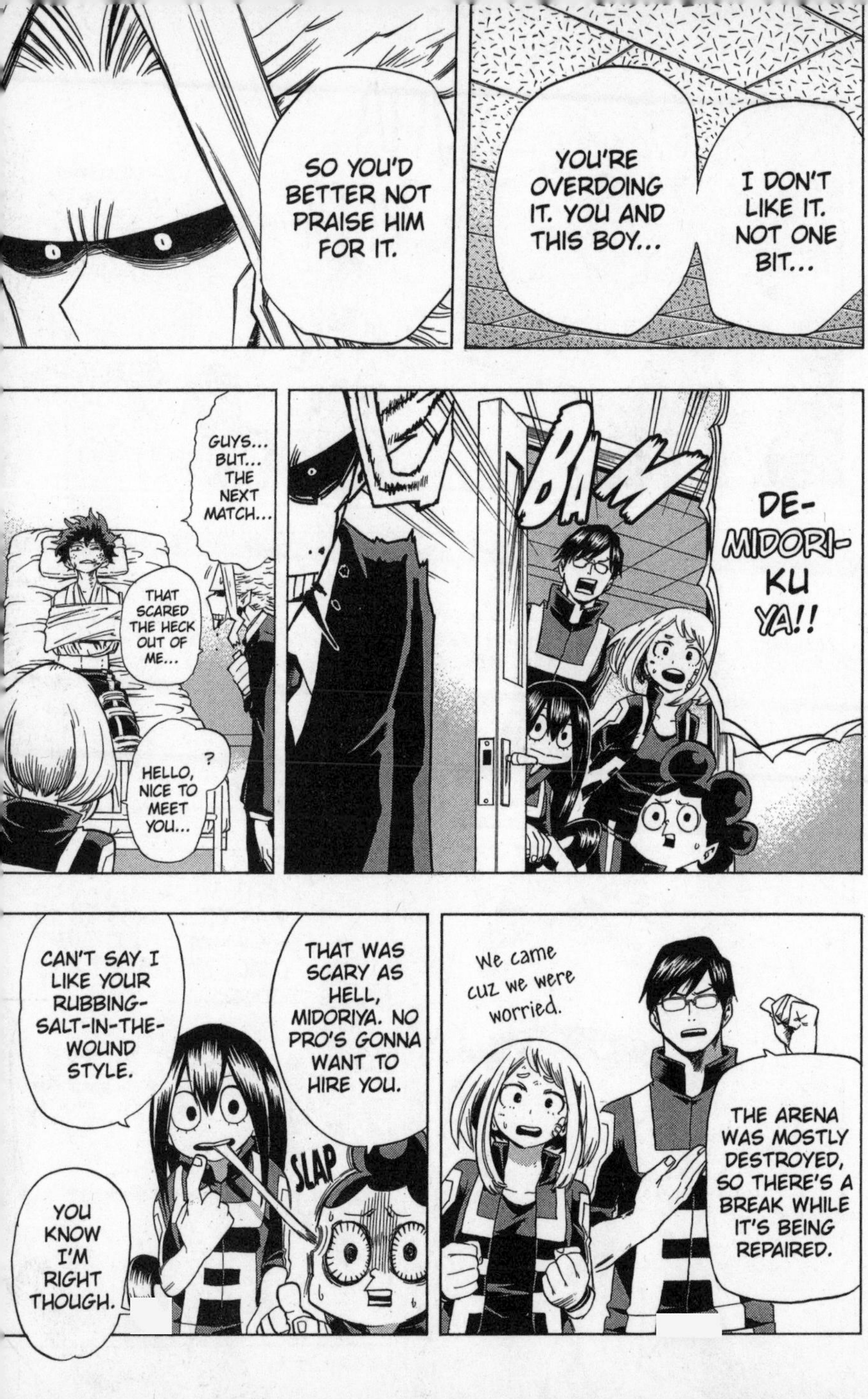
I DON'T LIKE IT. NOT ONE BIT...
YOU'RE OVERDOING IT. YOU AND THIS BOY...
SO YOU'D BETTER NOT PRAISE HIM FOR IT.
BAM
DE-MIDORIKU YA!!
GUYS... BUT... THE NEXT MATCH...
THAT SCARED THE HECK OUT OF ME...
?
HELLO, NICE TO MEET YOU...
We came cuz we were worried.
THE ARENA WAS MOSTLY DESTROYED, SO THERE'S A BREAK WHILE IT'S BEING REPAIRED.
THAT WAS SCARY AS HELL, MIDORIYA. NO PRO'S GONNA WANT TO HIRE YOU.
CAN'T SAY I LIKE YOUR RUBBING-SALT-IN-THE-WOUND STYLE.
SLAP
YOU KNOW I'M RIGHT THOUGH.

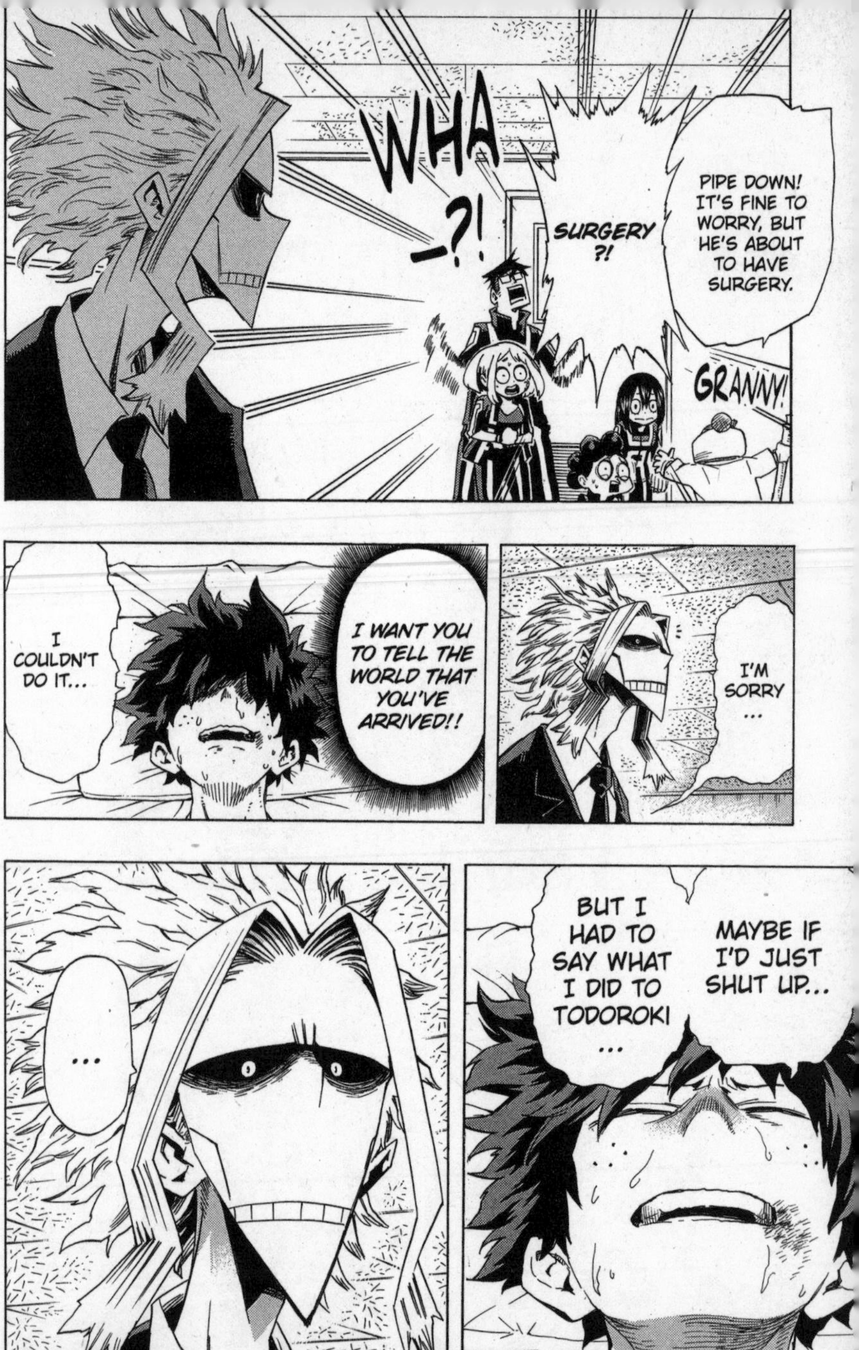

PIPE DOWN! IT'S FINE TO WORRY, BUT HE'S ABOUT TO HAVE SURGERY.
SURGERY ?!
WHA —?!
GRANNY!
I'M SORRY ...
I WANT YOU TO TELL THE WORLD THAT YOU'VE ARRIVED!!
I COULDN'T DO IT...
MAYBE IF I'D JUST SHUT UP...
BUT I HAD TO SAY WHAT I DID TO TODOROKI ...
...

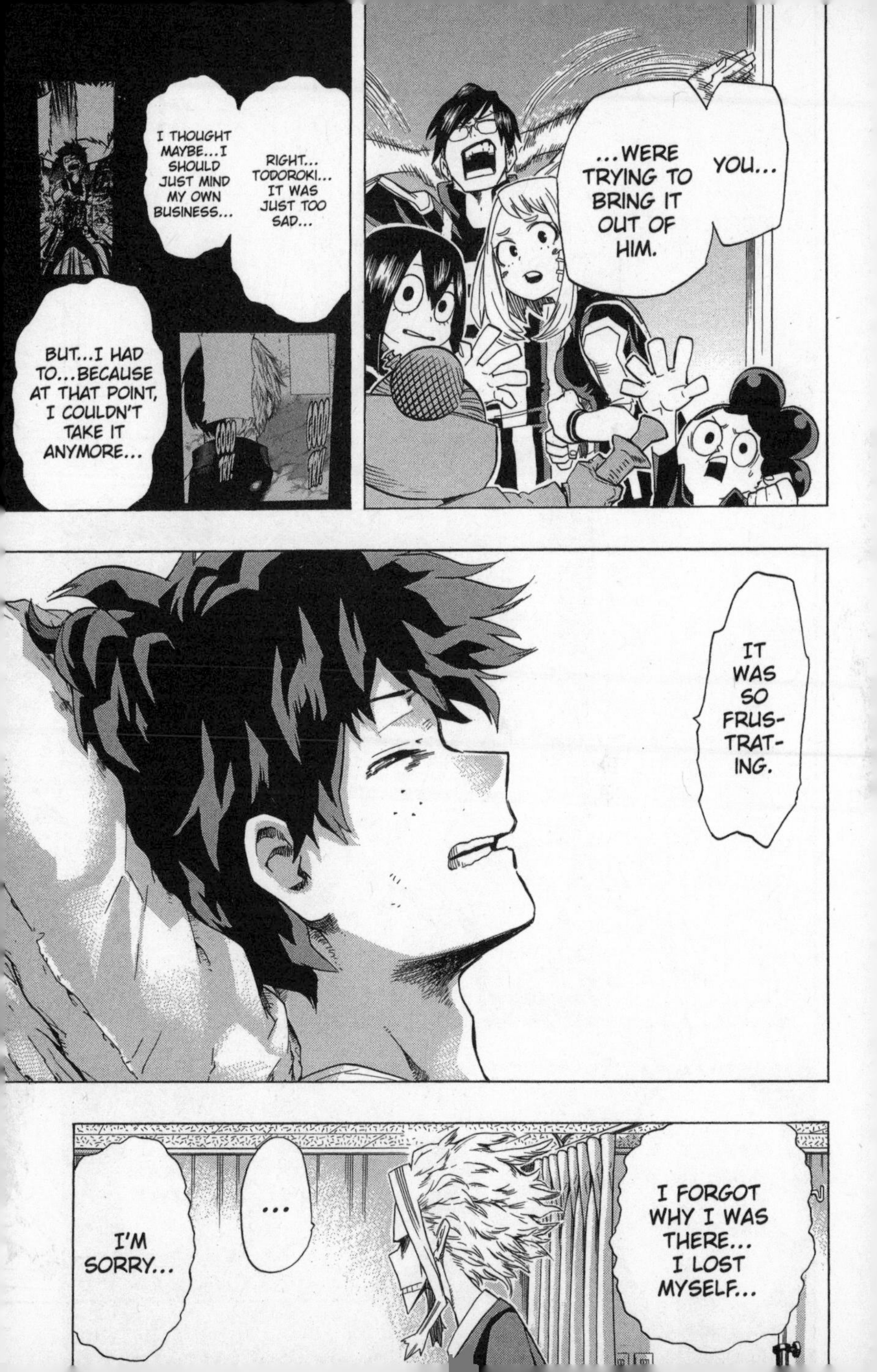
YOU...
...WERE TRYING TO BRING IT OUT OF HIM.
RIGHT... TODOROKI... IT WAS JUST TOO SAD...
I THOUGHT MAYBE...I SHOULD JUST MIND MY OWN BUSINESS...
BUT...I HAD TO...BECAUSE AT THAT POINT, I COULDN'T TAKE IT ANYMORE...
IT WAS SO FRUS-TRAT-ING.
I FORGOT WHY I WAS THERE... I LOST MYSELF...
...
I'M SORRY...

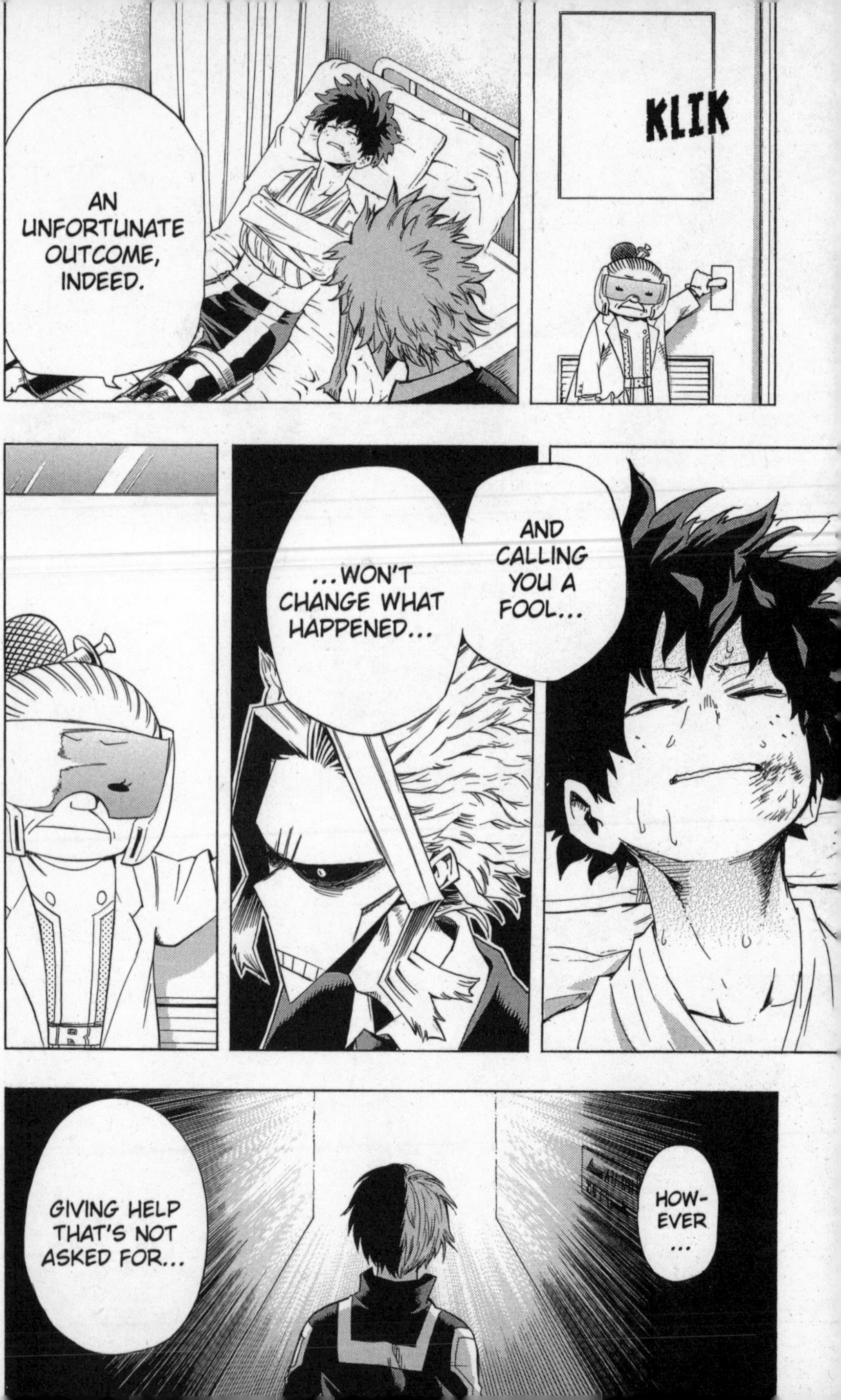
KLIK
AN UNFORTUNATE OUTCOME, INDEED.
AND CALLING YOU A FOOL...
...WON'T CHANGE WHAT HAPPENED...
HOW-EVER...
GIVING HELP THAT'S NOT ASKED FOR...

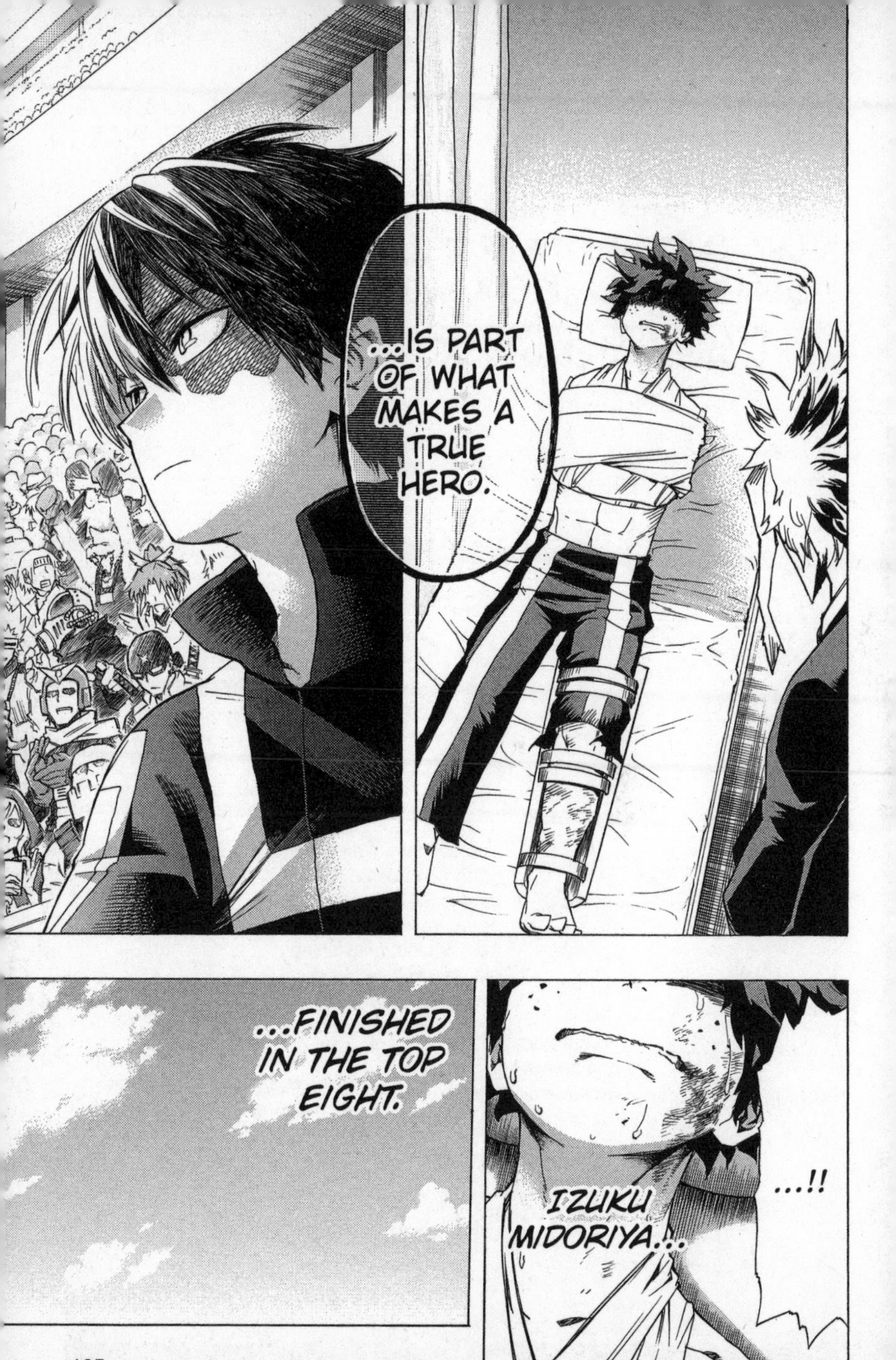
...IS PART OF WHAT MAKES A TRUE HERO.
...!!
IZUKU MIDORIYA...
...FINISHED IN THE TOP EIGHT.

THE "I CAN'T THINK OF ANY MORE CHARACTERS TO PROFILE, SO HERE'S SOME COSTUME COMMENTARY" CORNER

KATSUKI BAKUGO'S COSTUME

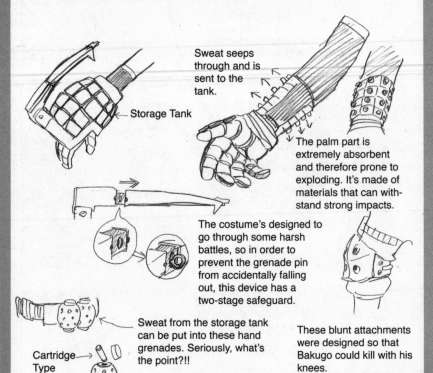

Sweat seeps through and is sent to the tank.

Storage Tank

The palm part is extremely absorbent and therefore prone to exploding. It's made of materials that can withstand strong impacts.

The costume's designed to go through some harsh battles, so in order to prevent the grenade pin from accidentally falling out, this device has a two-stage safeguard.

Sweat from the storage tank can be put into these hand grenades. Seriously, what's the point?!!

Cartridge Type

These blunt attachments were designed so that Bakugo could kill with his knees.

ALL IN ALL: HEARTLESS

No. 41 - Fight On, Ida

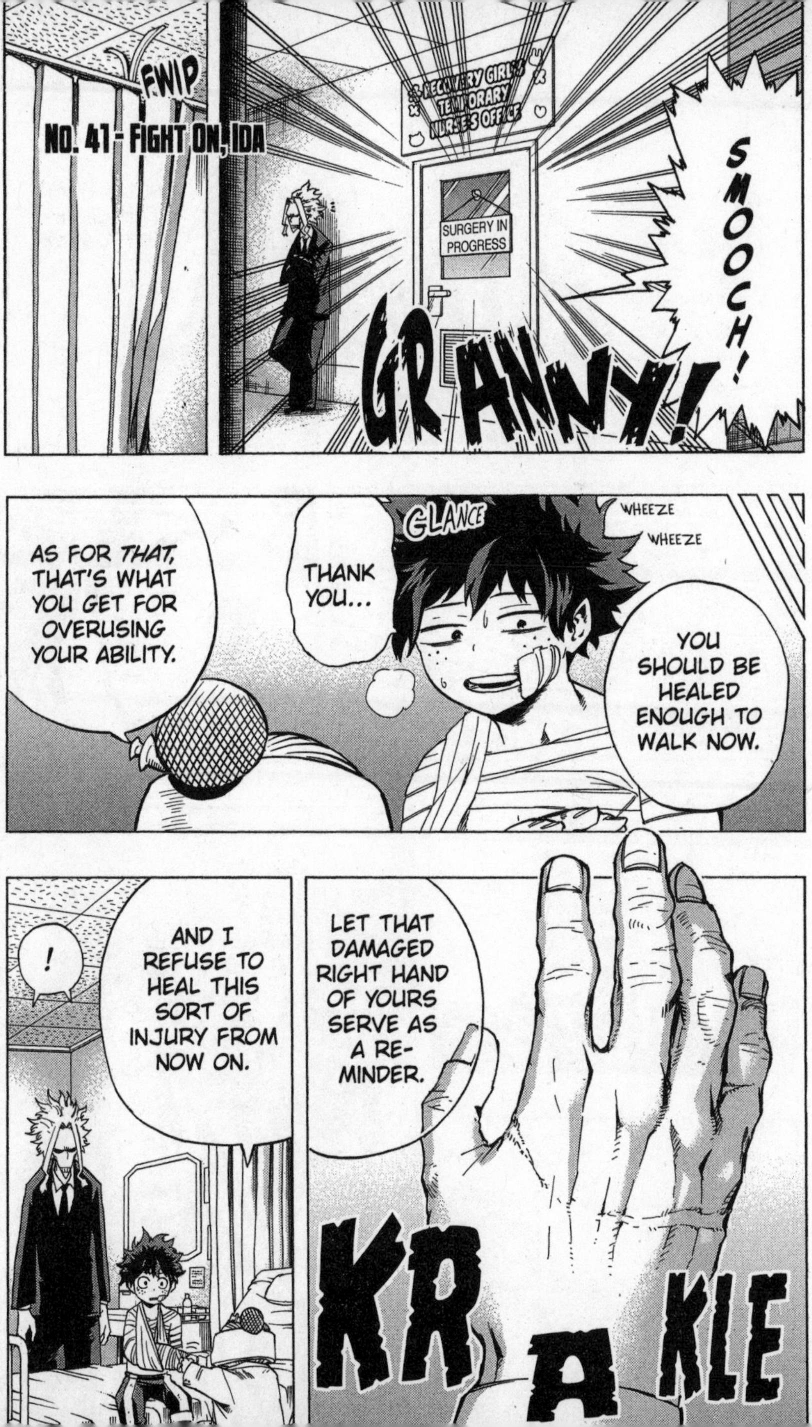
RECOVERY GIRL'S TEMPORARY NURSE'S OFFICE
SURGERY IN PROGRESS
SMOOCH!
GRANNY!
FWIP
WHEEZE
WHEEZE
GLANCE
YOU SHOULD BE HEALED ENOUGH TO WALK NOW.
THANK YOU...
AS FOR *THAT*, THAT'S WHAT YOU GET FOR OVERUSING YOUR ABILITY.
LET THAT DAMAGED RIGHT HAND OF YOURS SERVE AS A RE-MINDER.
KRAKLE
AND I REFUSE TO HEAL THIS SORT OF INJURY FROM NOW ON.
!

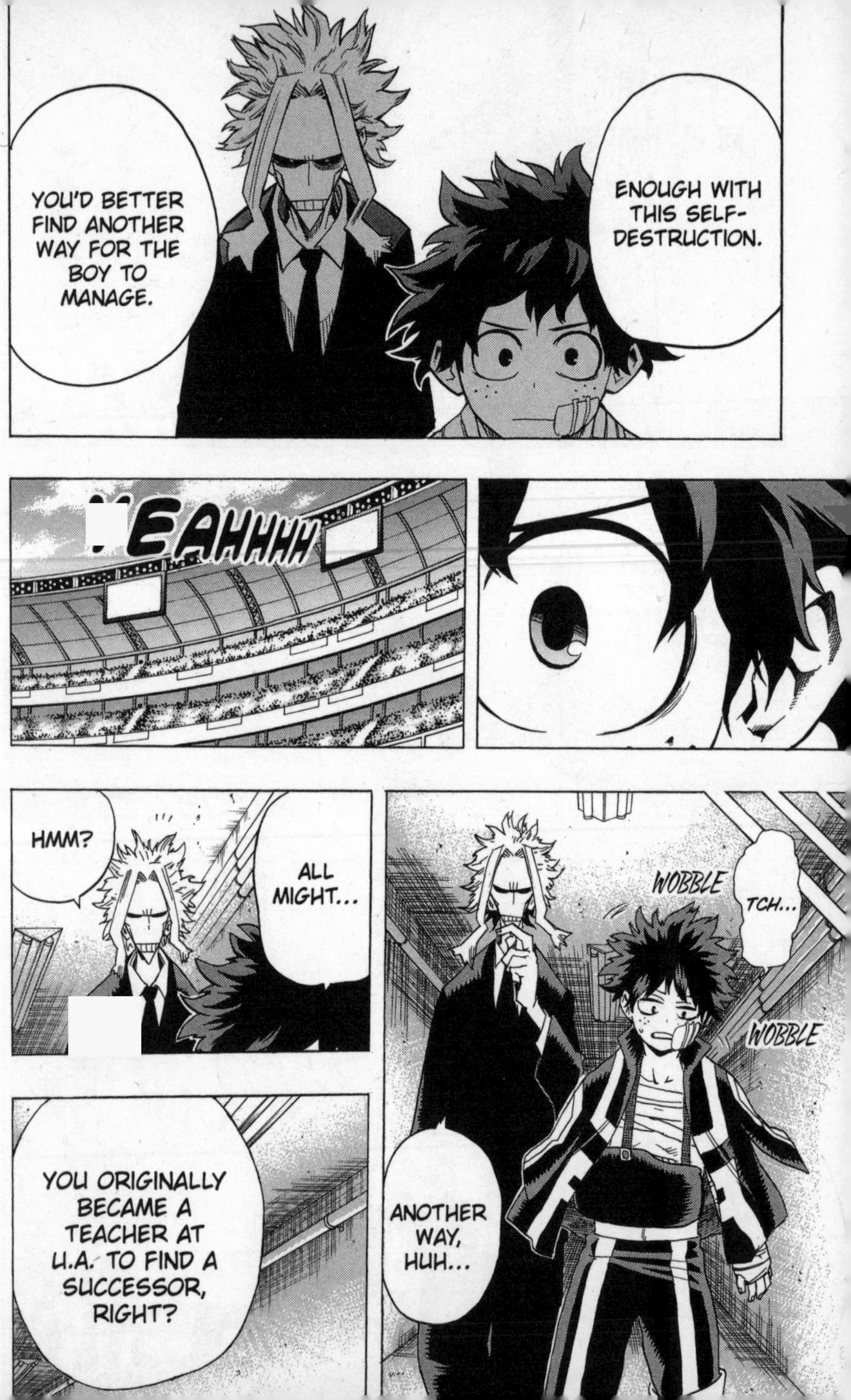
ENOUGH WITH THIS SELF-DESTRUCTION.
YOU'D BETTER FIND ANOTHER WAY FOR THE BOY TO MANAGE.
EAHHHH
TCH...
WOBBLE
WOBBLE
ANOTHER WAY, HUH...
ALL MIGHT...
HMM?
YOU ORIGINALLY BECAME A TEACHER AT U.A. TO FIND A SUCCESSOR, RIGHT?

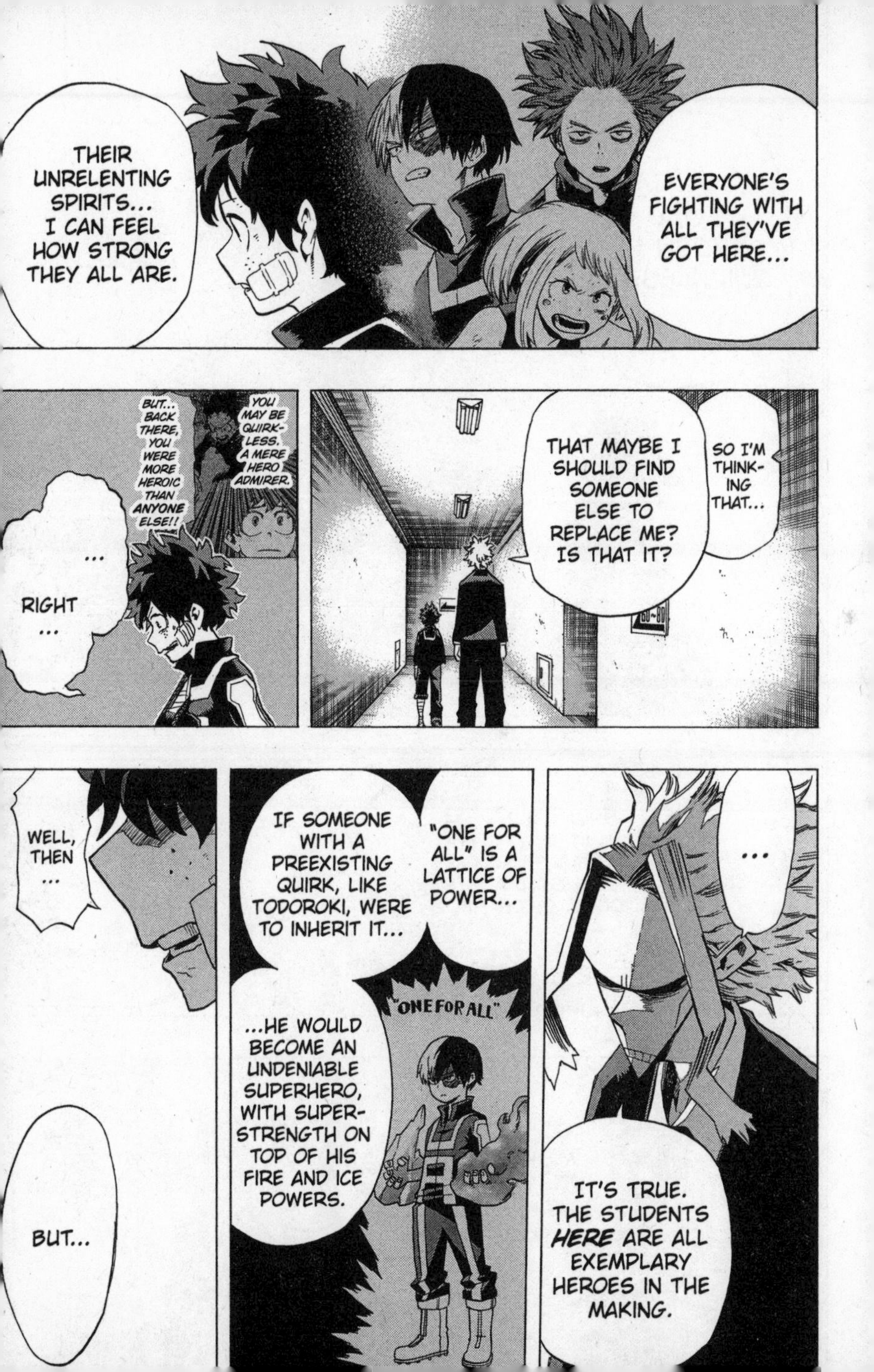
EVERYONE'S FIGHTING WITH ALL THEY'VE GOT HERE...
THEIR UNRELENTING SPIRITS... I CAN FEEL HOW STRONG THEY ALL ARE.
SO I'M THINKING THAT...
THAT MAYBE I SHOULD FIND SOMEONE ELSE TO REPLACE ME? IS THAT IT?
YOU MAY BE QUIRKLESS. A MERE HERO ADMIRER.
BUT... BACK THERE, YOU WERE MORE HEROIC THAN ANYONE ELSE!!
...
RIGHT ...
...
IT'S TRUE. THE STUDENTS *HERE* ARE ALL EXEMPLARY HEROES IN THE MAKING.
"ONE FOR ALL" IS A LATTICE OF POWER...
IF SOMEONE WITH A PREEXISTING QUIRK, LIKE TODOROKI, WERE TO INHERIT IT...
"ONE FOR ALL"
...HE WOULD BECOME AN UNDENIABLE SUPERHERO, WITH SUPER-STRENGTH ON TOP OF HIS FIRE AND ICE POWERS.
WELL, THEN ...
BUT...

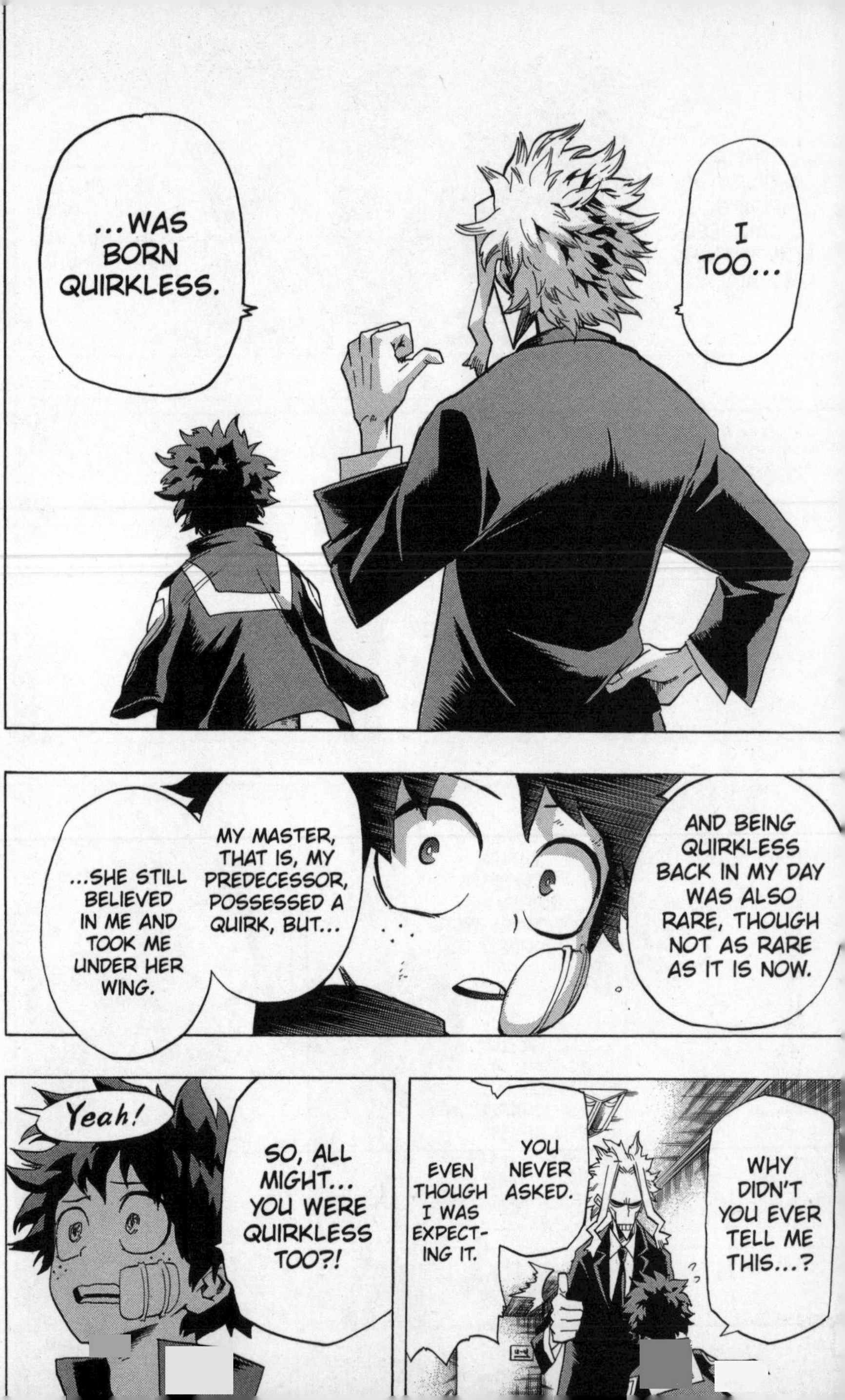
I TOO...
...WAS BORN QUIRKLESS.
AND BEING QUIRKLESS BACK IN MY DAY WAS ALSO RARE, THOUGH NOT AS RARE AS IT IS NOW.
MY MASTER, THAT IS, MY PREDECESSOR, POSSESSED A QUIRK, BUT...
...SHE STILL BELIEVED IN ME AND TOOK ME UNDER HER WING.
WHY DIDN'T YOU EVER TELL ME THIS...?
YOU NEVER ASKED.
EVEN THOUGH I WAS EXPECTING IT.
SO, ALL MIGHT... YOU WERE QUIRKLESS TOO?!
Yeah!

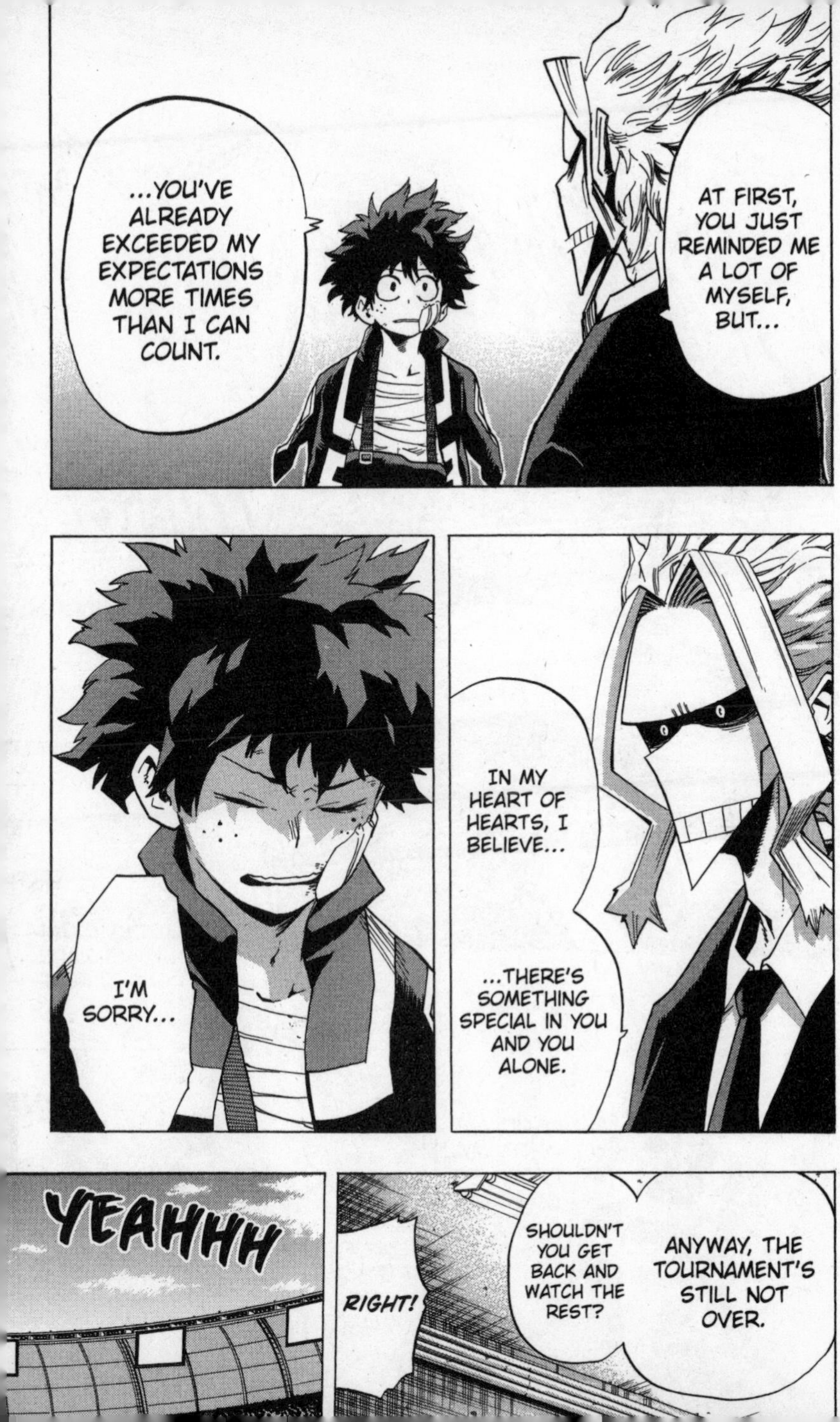
AT FIRST, YOU JUST REMINDED ME A LOT OF MYSELF, BUT...
...YOU'VE ALREADY EXCEEDED MY EXPECTATIONS MORE TIMES THAN I CAN COUNT.
IN MY HEART OF HEARTS, I BELIEVE...
...THERE'S SOMETHING SPECIAL IN YOU AND YOU ALONE.
I'M SORRY...
ANYWAY, THE TOURNAMENT'S STILL NOT OVER.
SHOULDN'T YOU GET BACK AND WATCH THE REST?
RIGHT!
YEAHHH

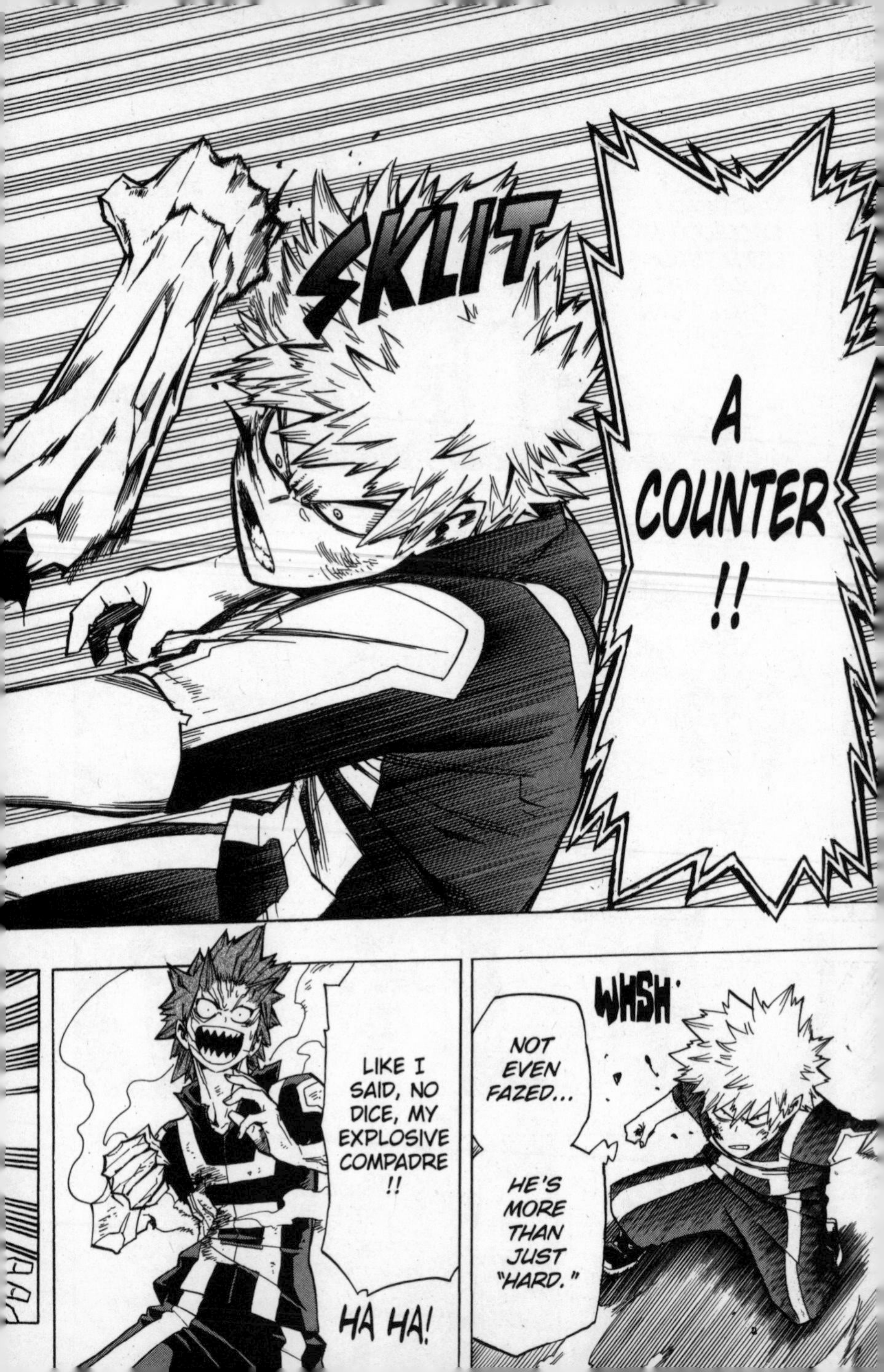
A COUNTER !!
SKLIT
WHSH
NOT EVEN FAZED...
HE'S MORE THAN JUST "HARD."
LIKE I SAID, NO DICE, MY EXPLOSIVE COMPADRE !!
HA HA!

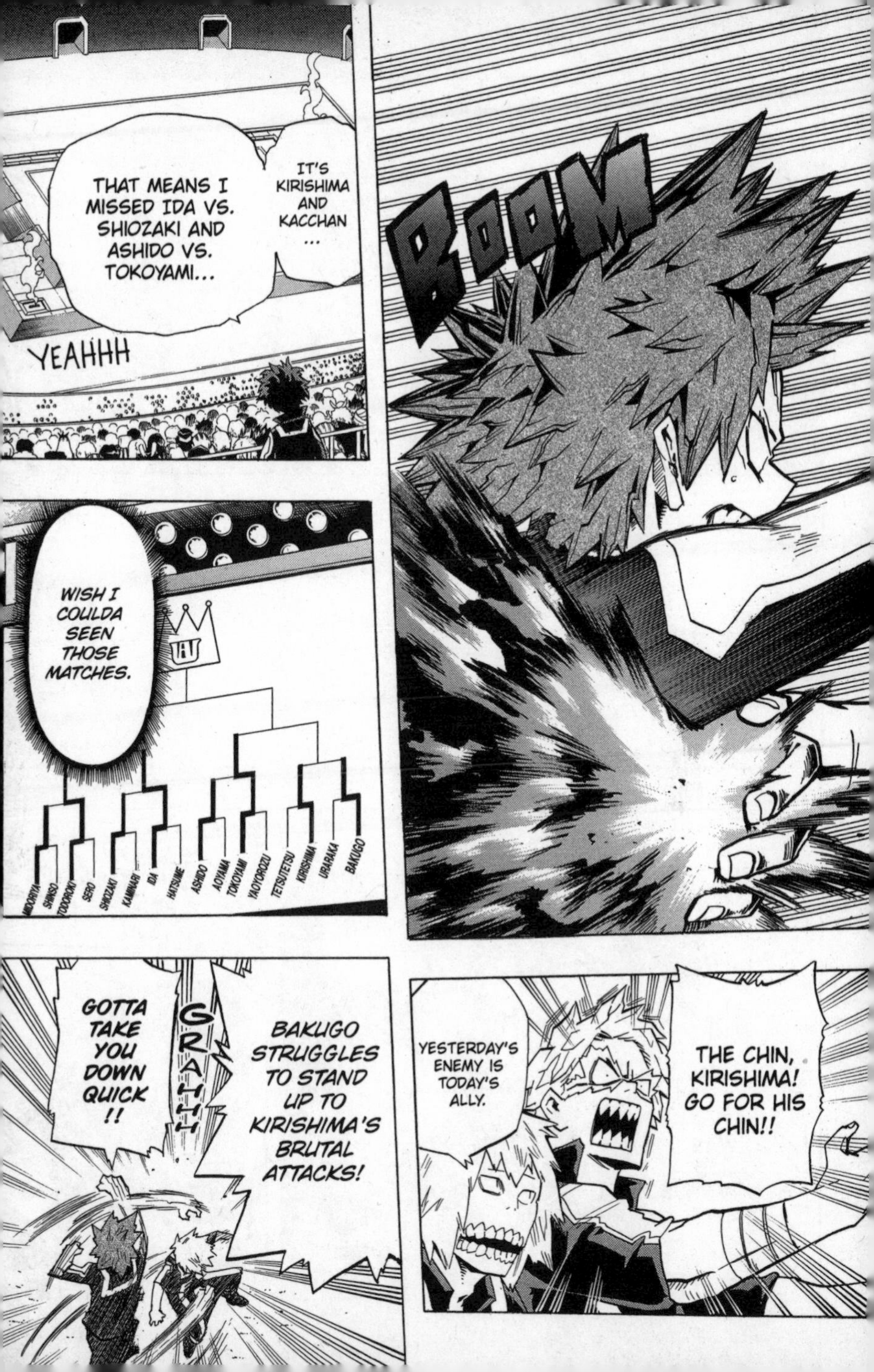
BOOM
IT'S KIRISHIMA AND KACCHAN...
THAT MEANS I MISSED IDA VS. SHIOZAKI AND ASHIDO VS. TOKOYAMI...
YEAHHH
WISH I COULDA SEEN THOSE MATCHES.
MIDORIYA SHINSO TODOROKI SERO SHIOZAKI KAMINARI IDA HATSUME ASHIDO AOYAMA TOKOYAMI YAOYOROZU TETSUTETSU KIRISHIMA URARAKA BAKUGO
THE CHIN, KIRISHIMA! GO FOR HIS CHIN!!
YESTERDAY'S ENEMY IS TODAY'S ALLY.
BAKUGO STRUGGLES TO STAND UP TO KIRISHIMA'S BRUTAL ATTACKS!
GRAHHH
GOTTA TAKE YOU DOWN QUICK!!

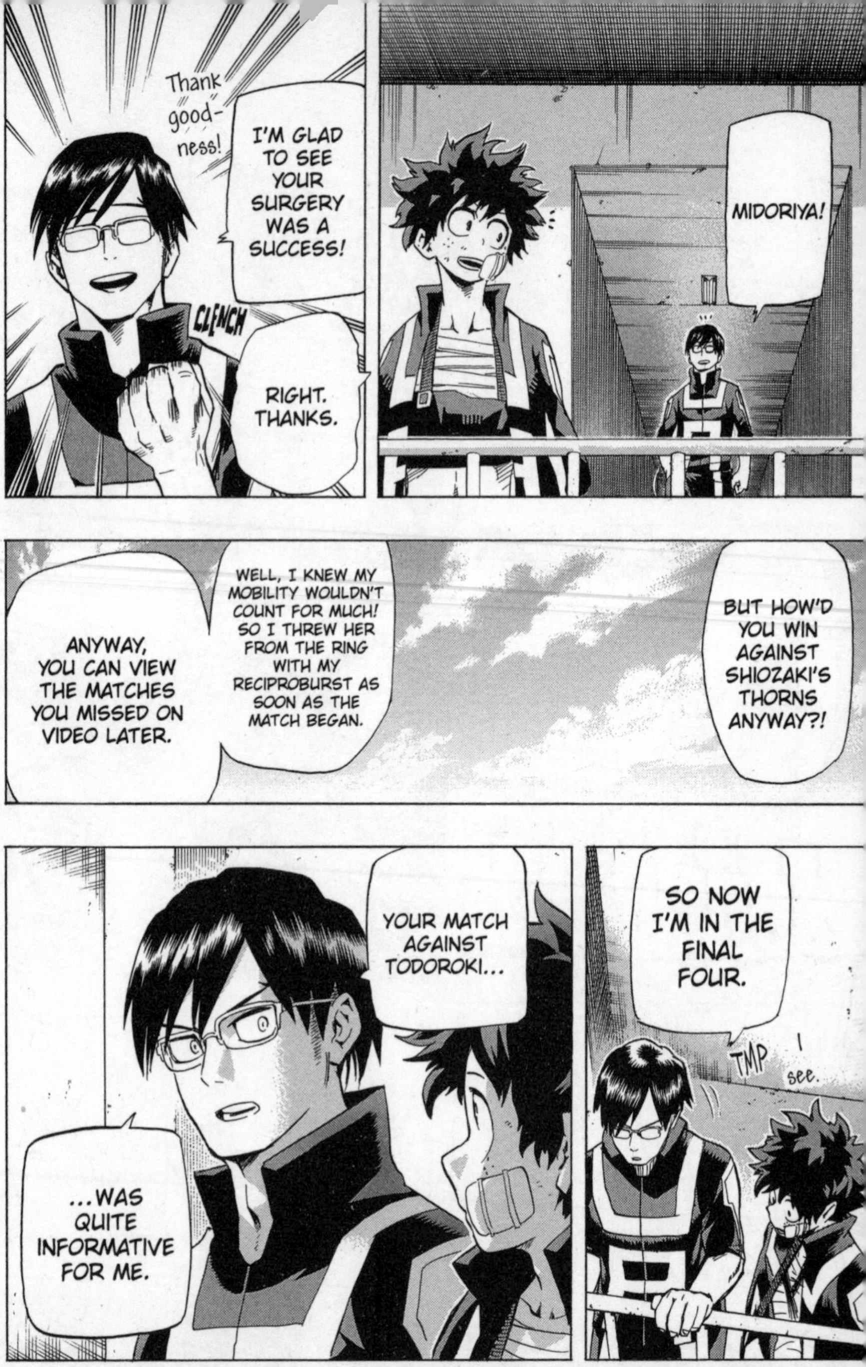
MIDORIYA!
Thank goodness!
I'M GLAD TO SEE YOUR SURGERY WAS A SUCCESS!
CLENCH
RIGHT. THANKS.
BUT HOW'D YOU WIN AGAINST SHIOZAKI'S THORNS ANYWAY?!
WELL, I KNEW MY MOBILITY WOULDN'T COUNT FOR MUCH! SO I THREW HER FROM THE RING WITH MY RECIPROBURST AS SOON AS THE MATCH BEGAN.
ANYWAY, YOU CAN VIEW THE MATCHES YOU MISSED ON VIDEO LATER.
SO NOW I'M IN THE FINAL FOUR.
TMP
I see.
YOUR MATCH AGAINST TODOROKI...
...WAS QUITE INFORMATIVE FOR ME.

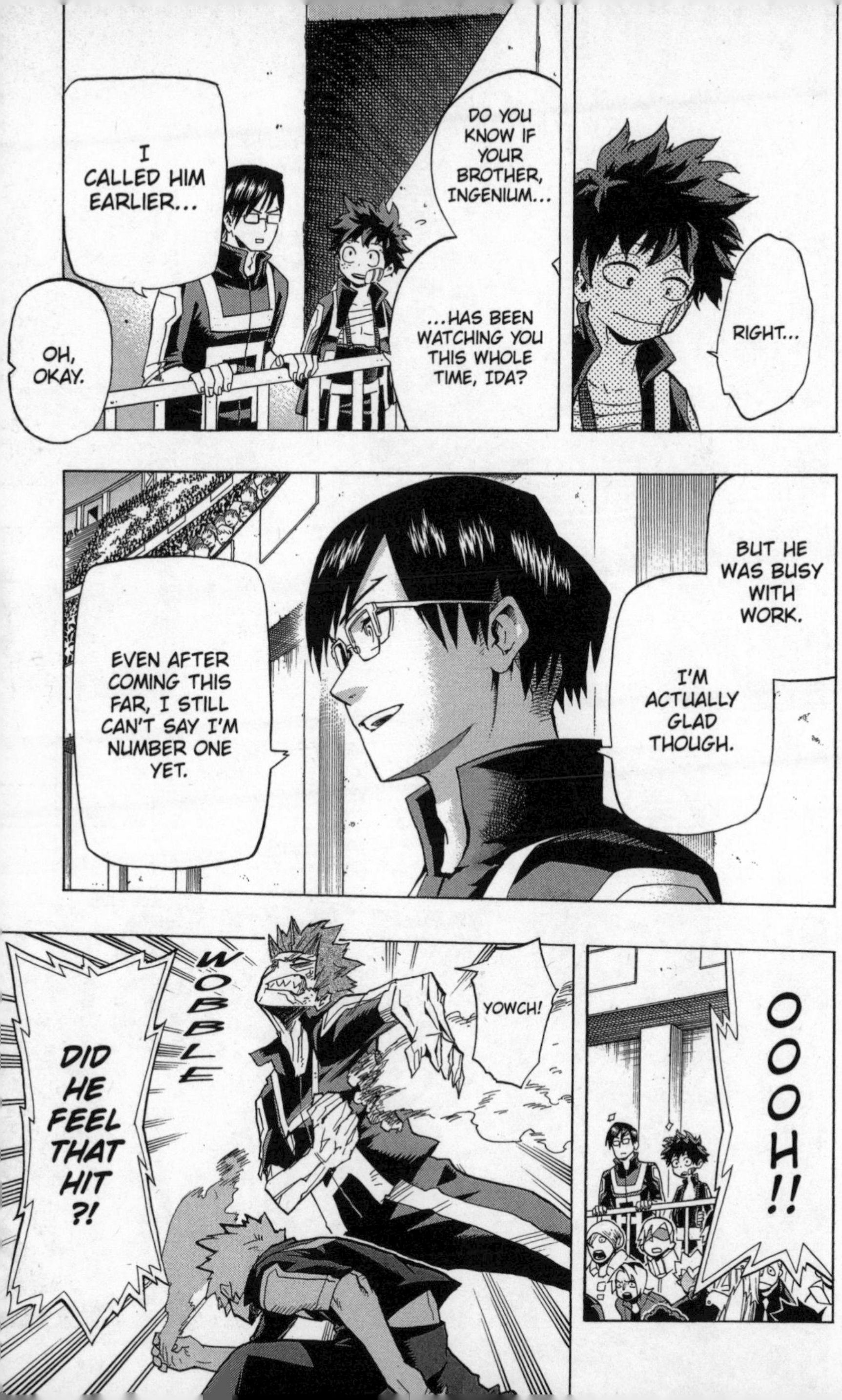
RIGHT...
DO YOU KNOW IF YOUR BROTHER, INGENIUM...
...HAS BEEN WATCHING YOU THIS WHOLE TIME, IDA?
I CALLED HIM EARLIER...
OH, OKAY.
BUT HE WAS BUSY WITH WORK.
I'M ACTUALLY GLAD THOUGH.
EVEN AFTER COMING THIS FAR, I STILL CAN'T SAY I'M NUMBER ONE YET.
OOOH!!
YOWCH!
WOBBLE
DID HE FEEL THAT HIT?!

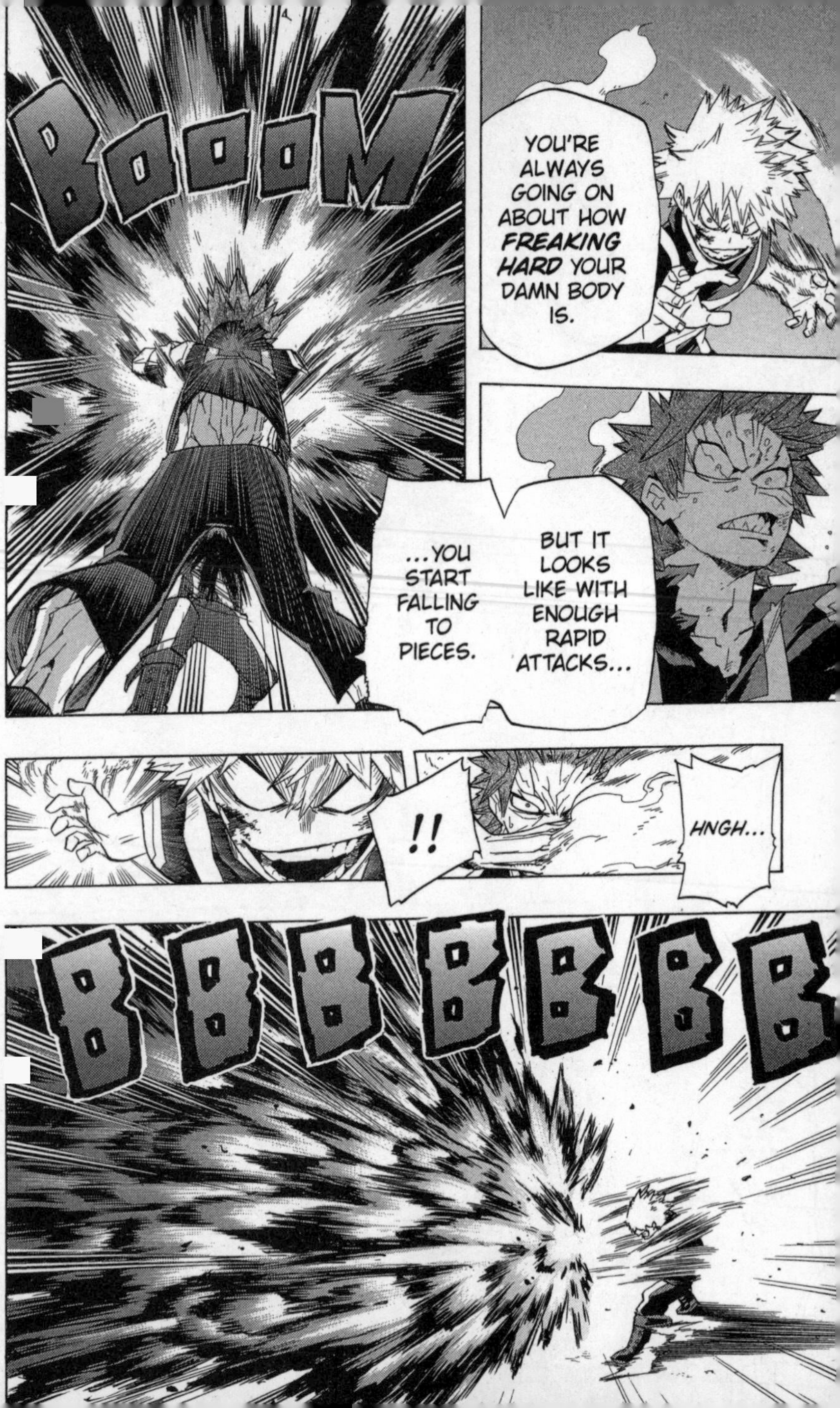
YOU'RE ALWAYS GOING ON ABOUT HOW ***FREAKING HARD*** YOUR DAMN BODY IS.
BUT IT LOOKS LIKE WITH ENOUGH RAPID ATTACKS...
...YOU START FALLING TO PIECES.
BOOOM
HNGH...
!!
BBBBBBB

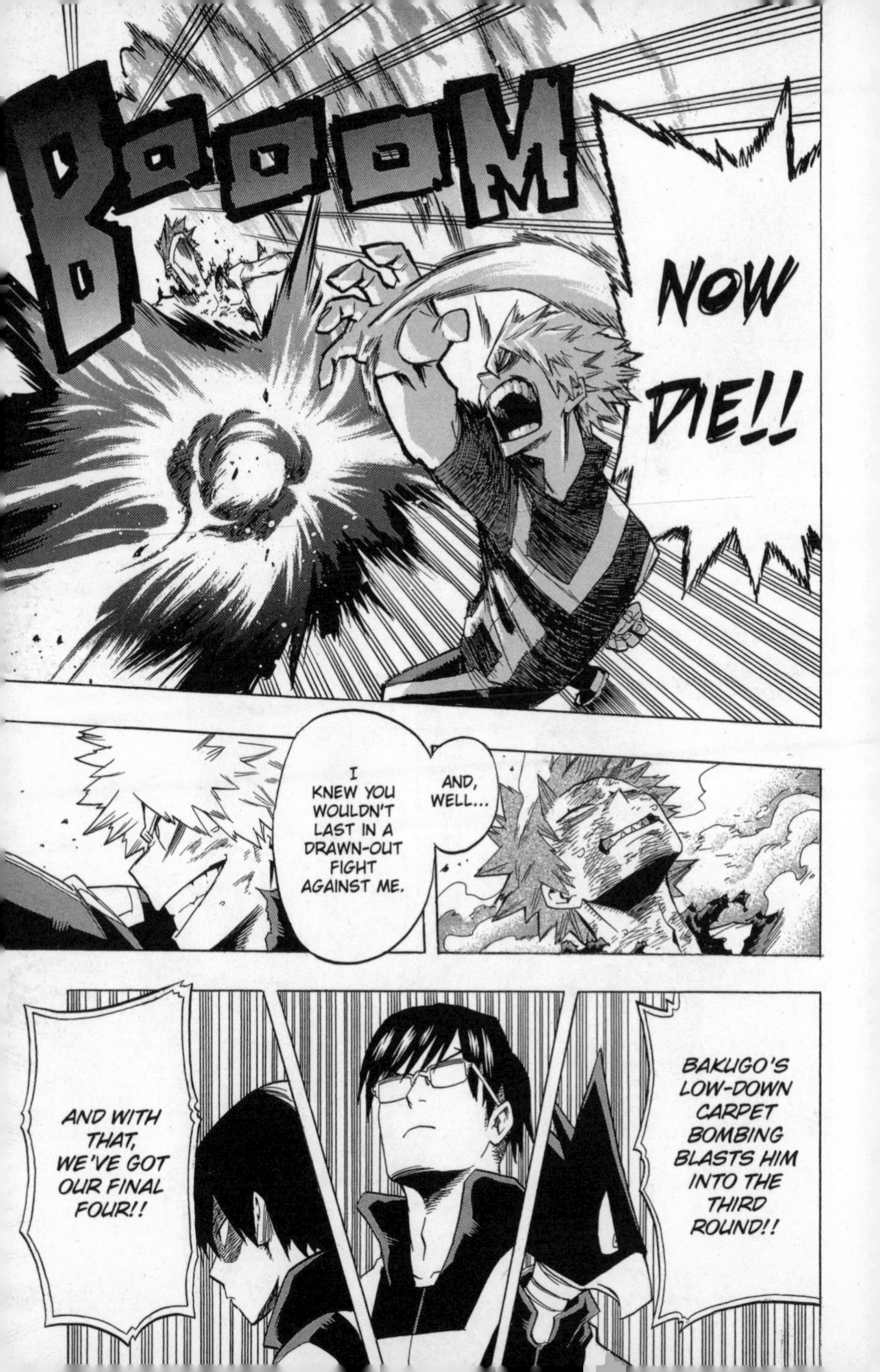
BOOOOM
NOW DIE!!
AND, WELL...
I KNEW YOU WOULDN'T LAST IN A DRAWN-OUT FIGHT AGAINST ME.
BAKUGO'S LOW-DOWN CARPET BOMBING BLASTS HIM INTO THE THIRD ROUND!!
AND WITH THAT, WE'VE GOT OUR FINAL FOUR!!

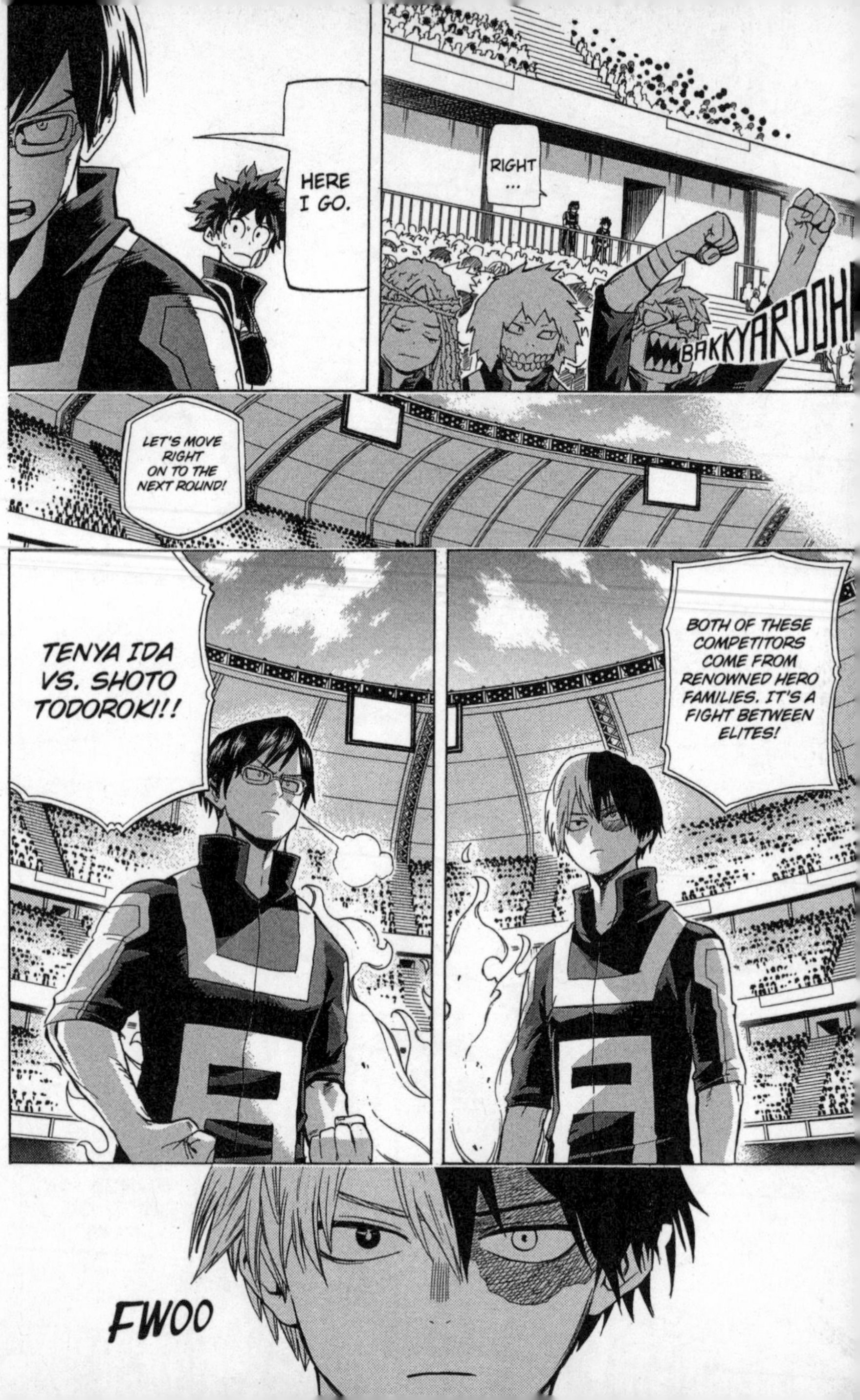
RIGHT ...
BAKKYAROOH
HERE I GO.
LET'S MOVE RIGHT ON TO THE NEXT ROUND!
BOTH OF THESE COMPETITORS COME FROM RENOWNED HERO FAMILIES. IT'S A FIGHT BETWEEN ELITES!
TENYA IDA VS. SHOTO TODOROKI!!
FWOO

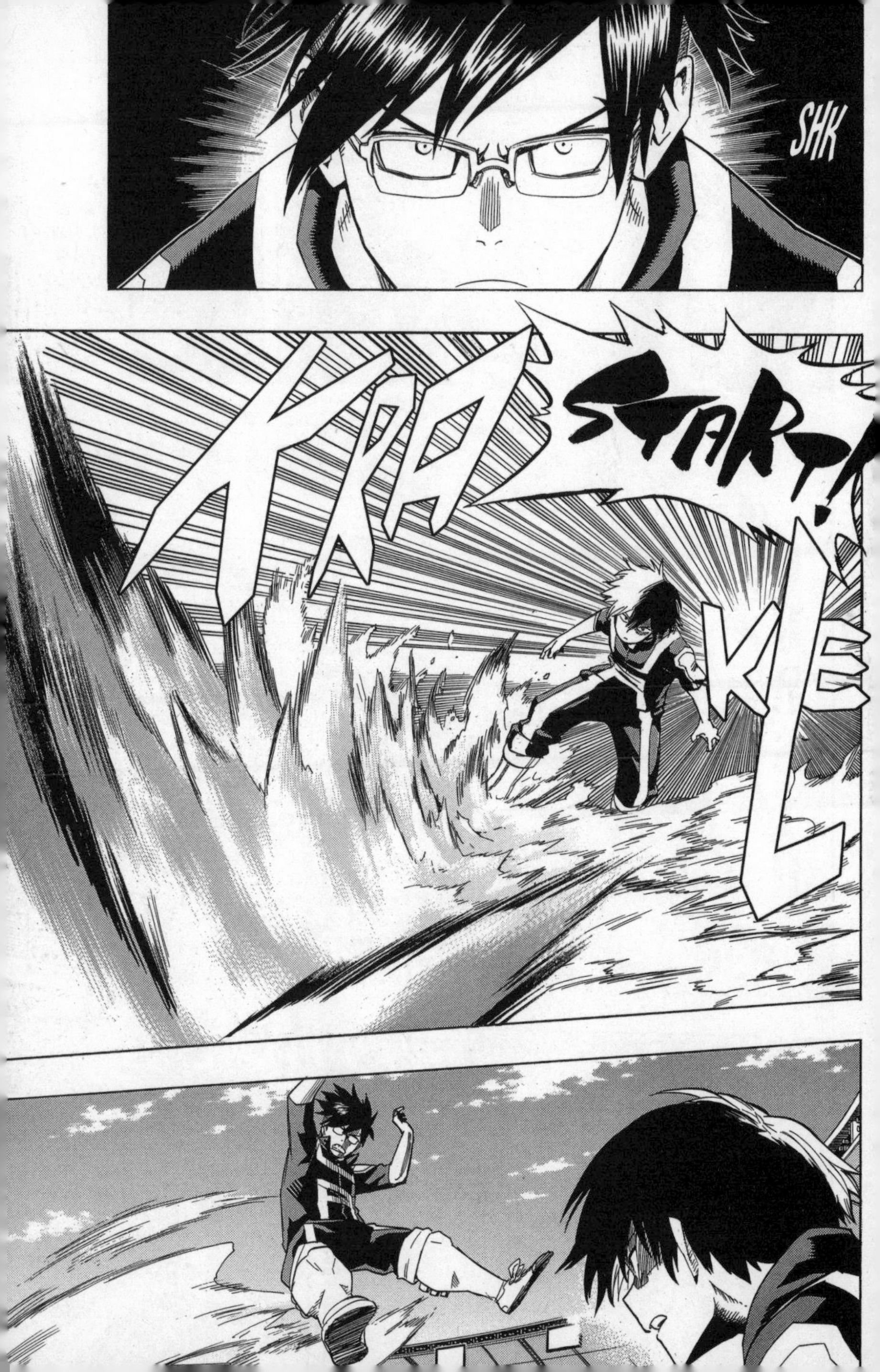
SHK
START!
KRAA
KLE

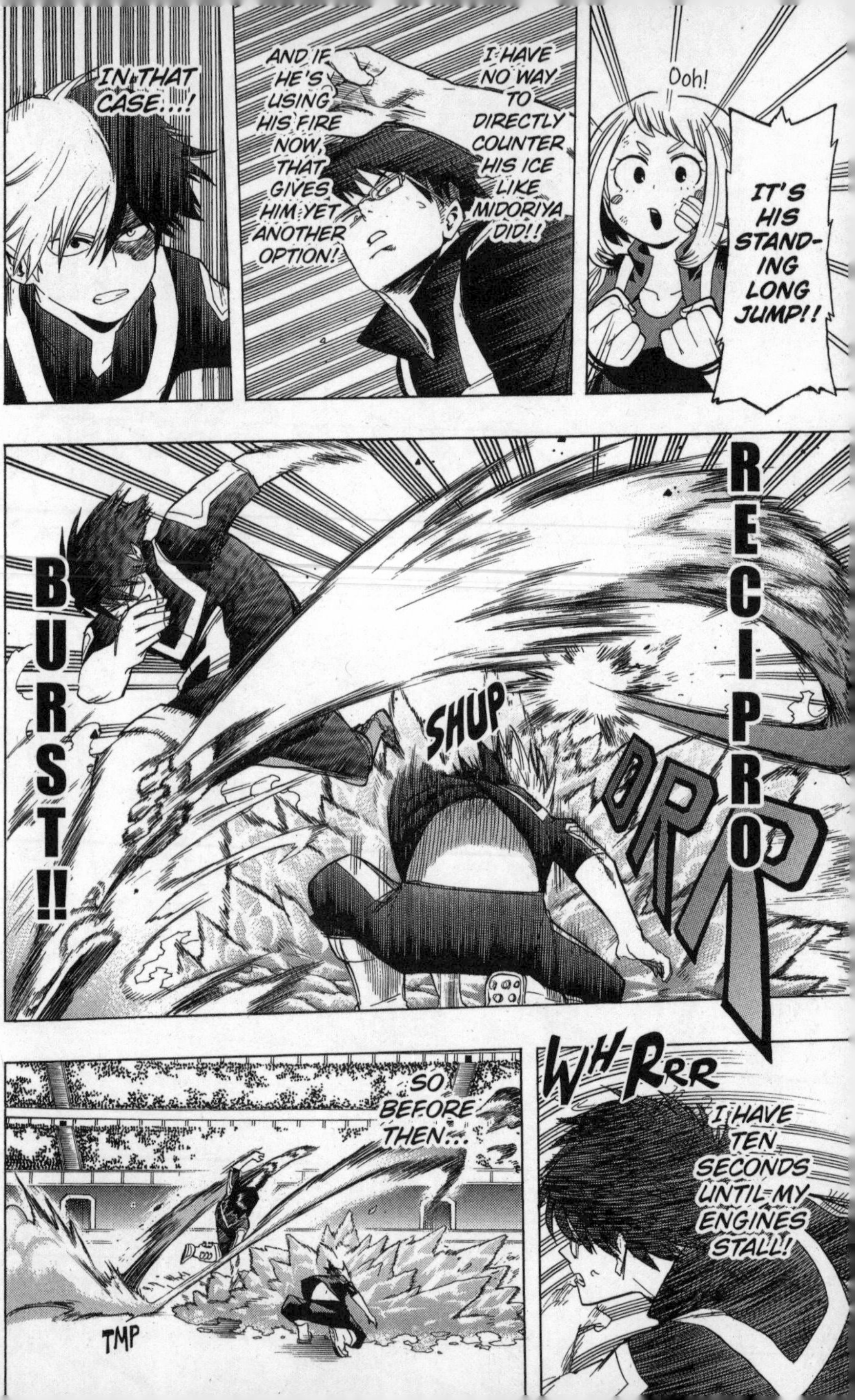
Ooh!
IT'S HIS STANDING-LONG JUMP!!
I HAVE NO WAY TO DIRECTLY COUNTER HIS ICE LIKE MIDORIYA DID!!
AND IF HE'S USING HIS FIRE NOW, THAT GIVES HIM YET ANOTHER OPTION!
IN THAT CASE...!
RECIPRO
SHUP
BURST!!
WHRrr
I HAVE TEN SECONDS UNTIL MY ENGINES STALL!
SO BEFORE THEN...
TMP

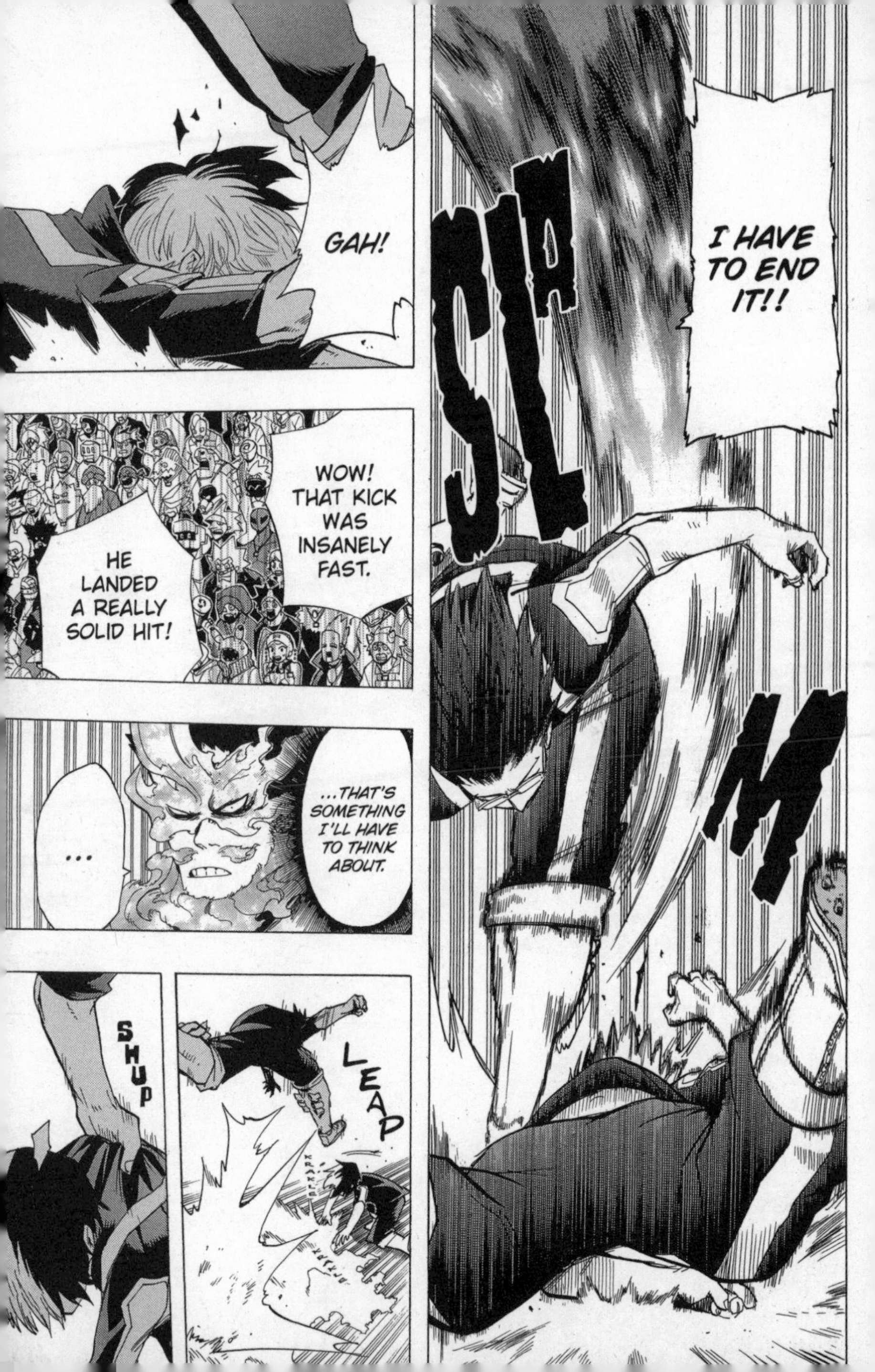
I HAVE TO END IT!!
SLAM
GAH!
WOW! THAT KICK WAS INSANELY FAST.
HE LANDED A REALLY SOLID HIT!
...THAT'S SOMETHING I'LL HAVE TO THINK ABOUT.
...
LEAP
SHUP

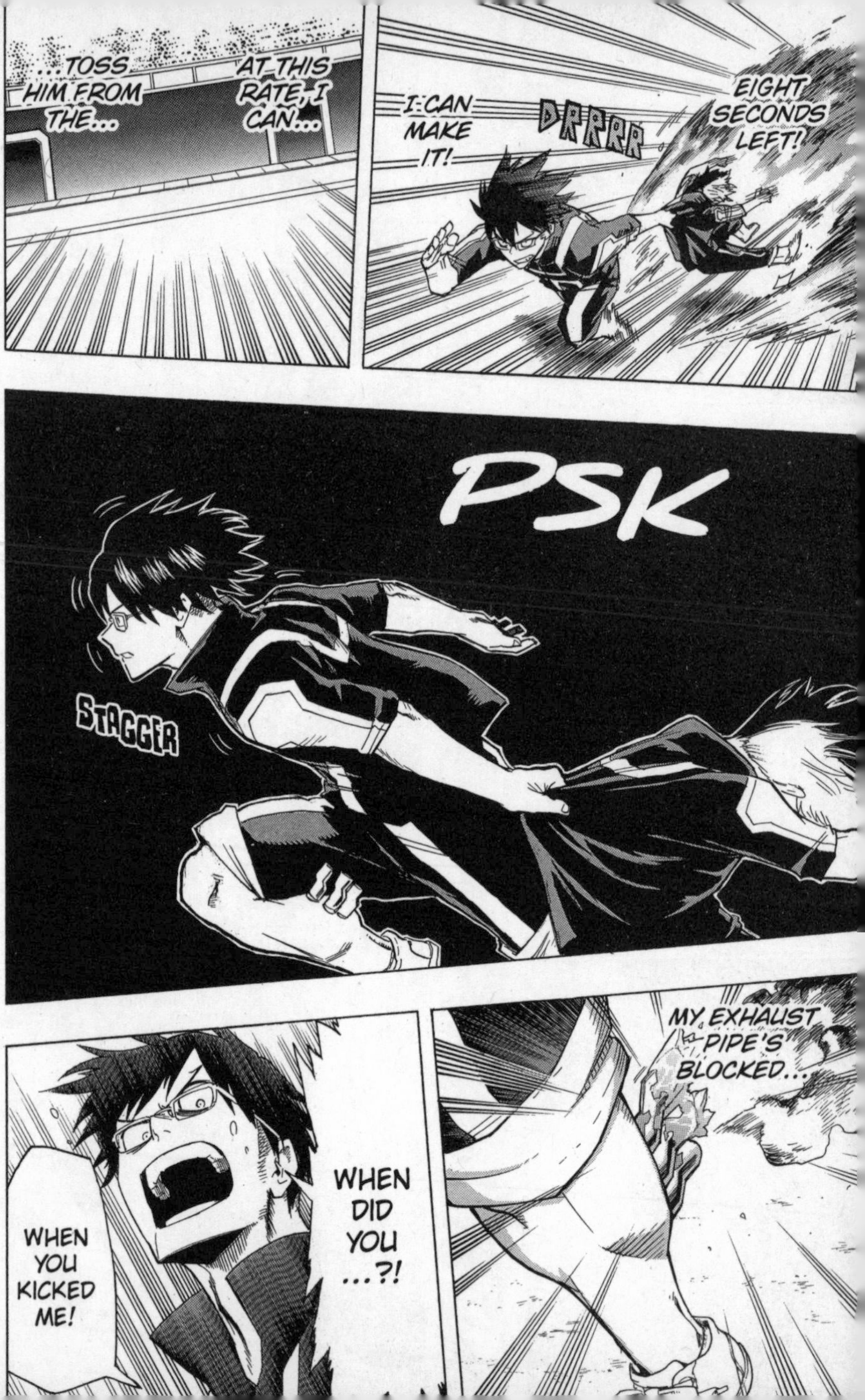

EIGHT SECONDS LEFT!
DRRRR
I CAN MAKE IT!
AT THIS RATE, I CAN...
...TOSS HIM FROM THE...
PSK
STAGGER
MY EXHAUST PIPE'S BLOCKED...
WHEN DID YOU ...?!
WHEN YOU KICKED ME!

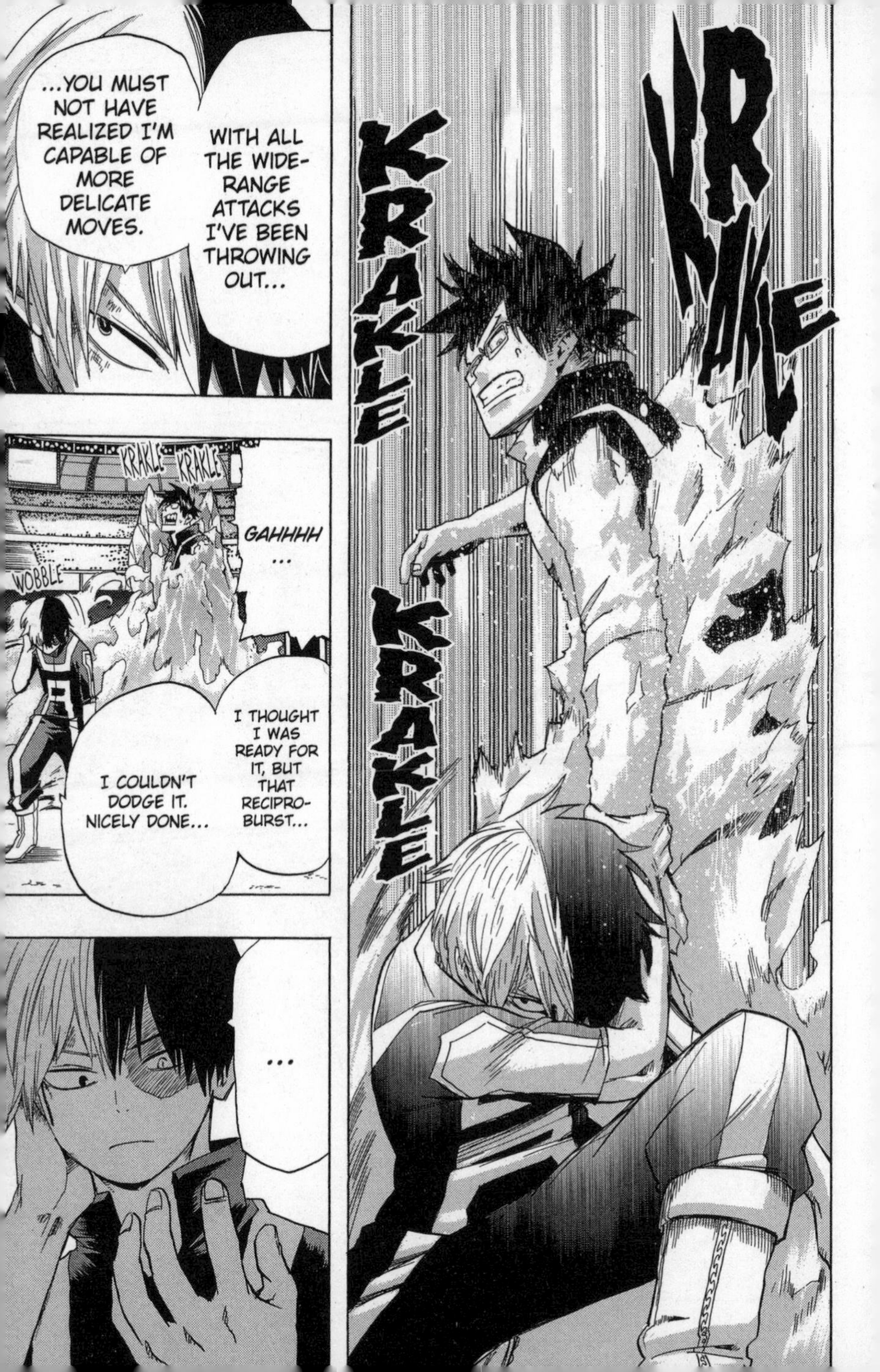

KRAKLE
KRAKLE
...YOU MUST NOT HAVE REALIZED I'M CAPABLE OF MORE DELICATE MOVES.
WITH ALL THE WIDE-RANGE ATTACKS I'VE BEEN THROWING OUT...
KRAKLE KRAKLE
GAHHHH ...
WOBBLE
I THOUGHT I WAS READY FOR IT, BUT THAT RECIPRO-BURST...
I COULDN'T DODGE IT. NICELY DONE...
...

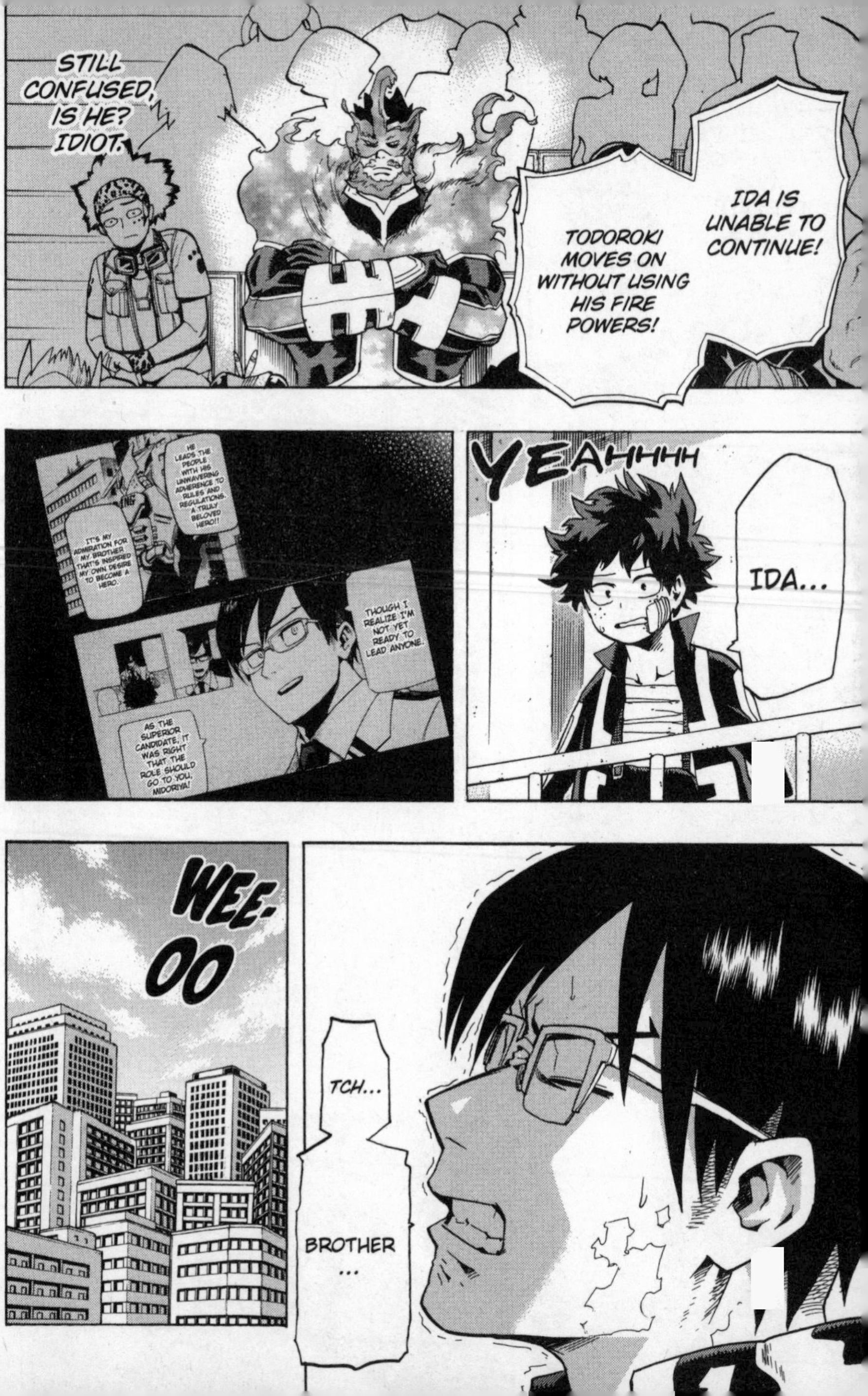
IDA IS UNABLE TO CONTINUE!
TODOROKI MOVES ON WITHOUT USING HIS FIRE POWERS!
STILL CONFUSED, IS HE? IDIOT.
YEAHHHH
IDA...
HE LEADS THE PEOPLE WITH HIS UNWAVERING ADHERENCE TO RULES AND REGULATIONS. A TRULY BELOVED HERO!!
IT'S MY ADMIRATION FOR MY BROTHER THAT'S INSPIRED MY OWN DESIRE TO BECOME A HERO.
THOUGH I REALIZE I'M NOT YET READY TO LEAD ANYONE.
AS THE SUPERIOR CANDIDATE, IT WAS RIGHT THAT THE ROLE SHOULD GO TO YOU, MIDORIYA!
TCH...
BROTHER...
WEE-OO

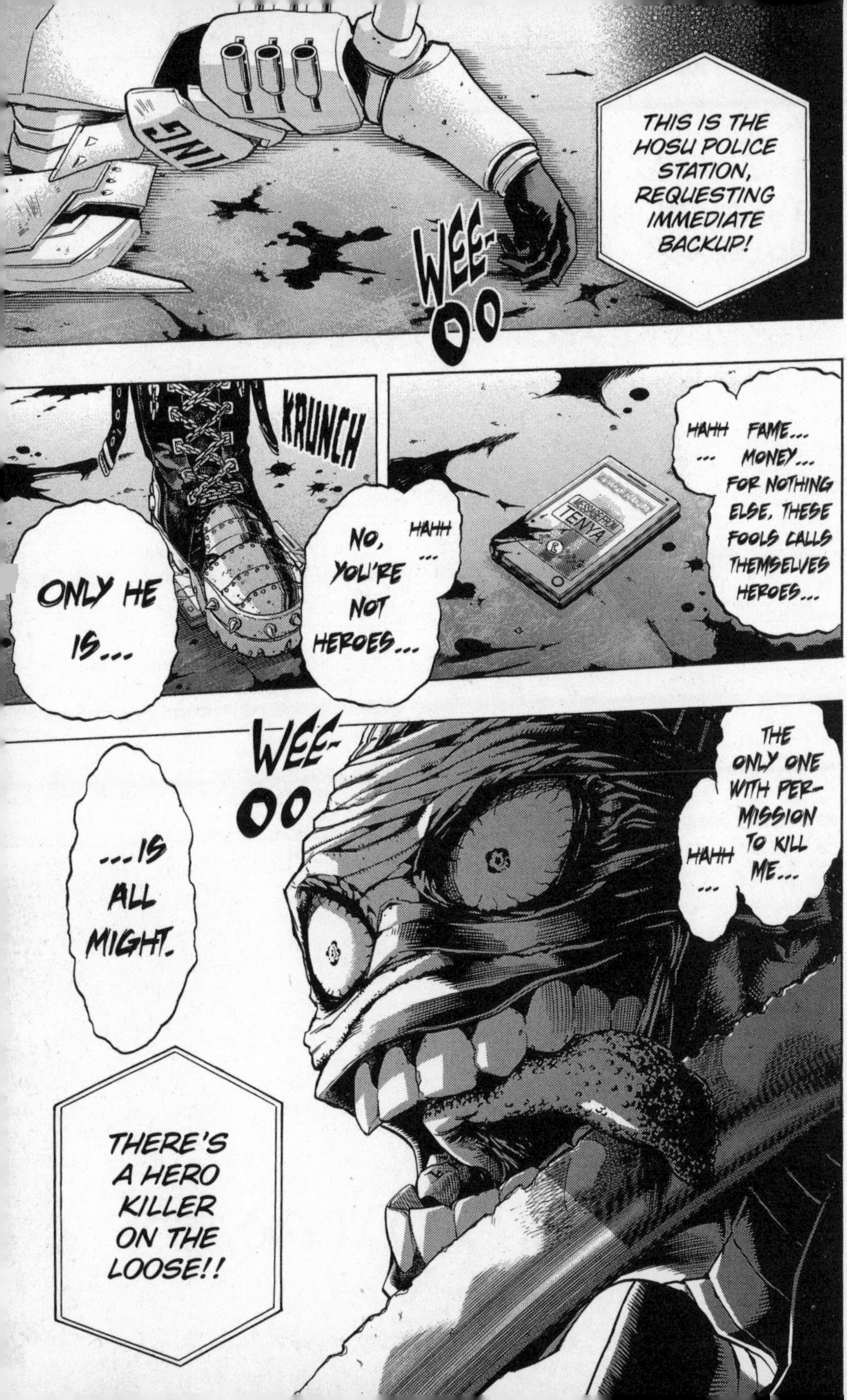
WEE-OO
THIS IS THE HOSU POLICE STATION, REQUESTING IMMEDIATE BACKUP!
HAHH...
FAME... MONEY... FOR NOTHING ELSE, THESE FOOLS CALLS THEMSELVES HEROES...
MESSAGE FROM TENYA
KRUNCH
HAHH...
NO, YOU'RE NOT HEROES...
ONLY HE IS...
THE ONLY ONE WITH PER-MISSION TO KILL ME...
HAHH...
WEE-OO
...IS ALL MIGHT.
THERE'S A HERO KILLER ON THE LOOSE!!

THE "WHAT THE HECK DO I DO WITH THESE BLANK PAGES STARTING NEXT VOLUME?!" CORNER

IZUKU MIDORIYA'S COSTUME

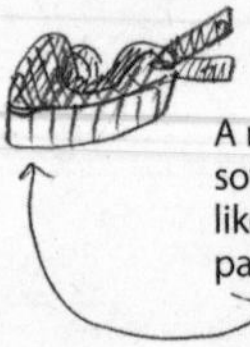

¥4,980 at a military surplus shop.

A mask used in airsoft games and the like. The bottom part is painted cloth.

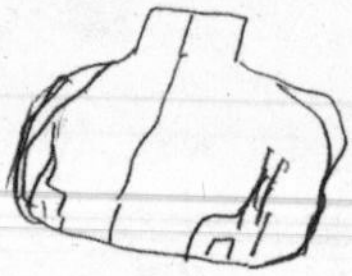

An ordinary jumpsuit. ¥12,800 at a sporting goods store.

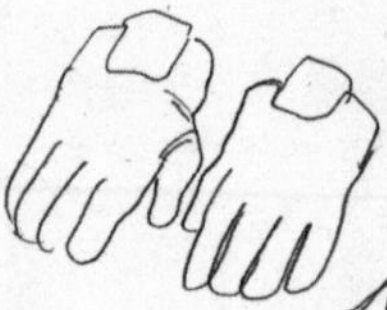

Ordinary gloves. ¥2,600 at a home improvement store.

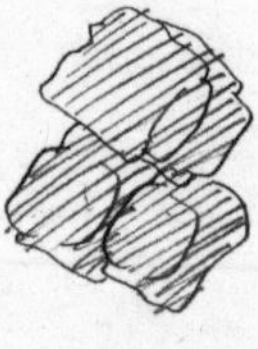

Elbow and knee pads. ¥11,500 for a pair of each at a sporting goods store.

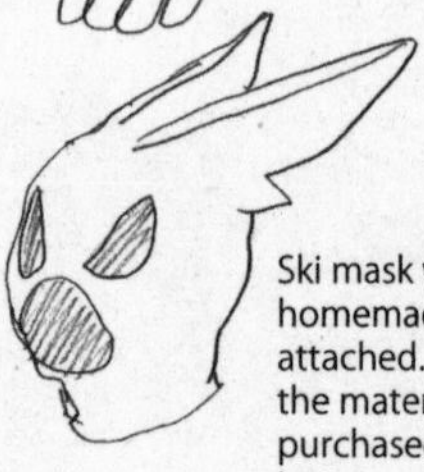

Ski mask with homemade horns attached. ¥4,700 for the materials, purchased at a home improvement store.

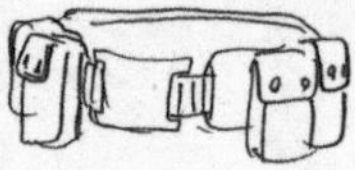

Belt. ¥3,800 at a military shop.

ALL IN ALL: ¥40,380

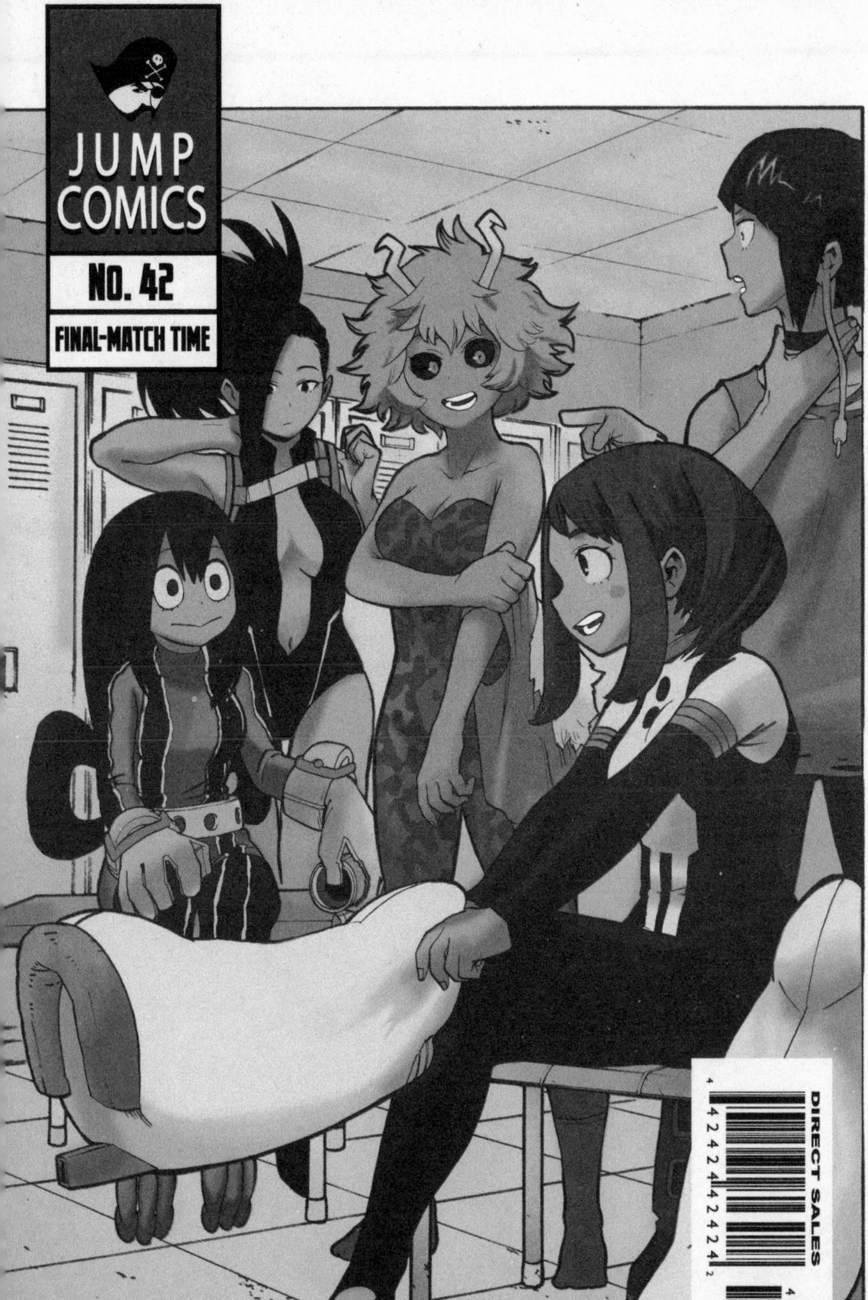
JUMP COMICS
NO. 42
FINAL-MATCH TIME
DIRECT SALES

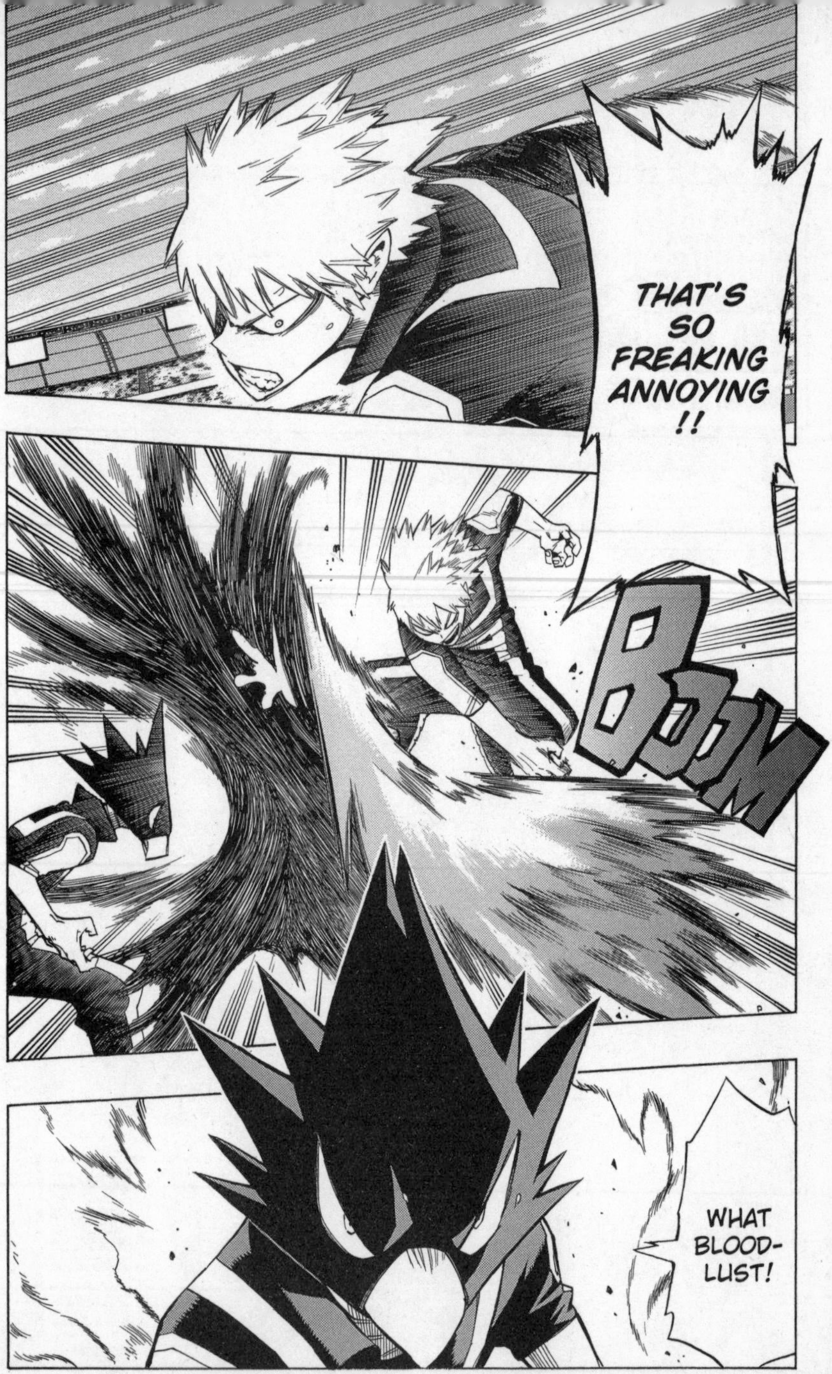
THAT'S SO FREAKING ANNOYING !!
BOOM
WHAT BLOOD-LUST!

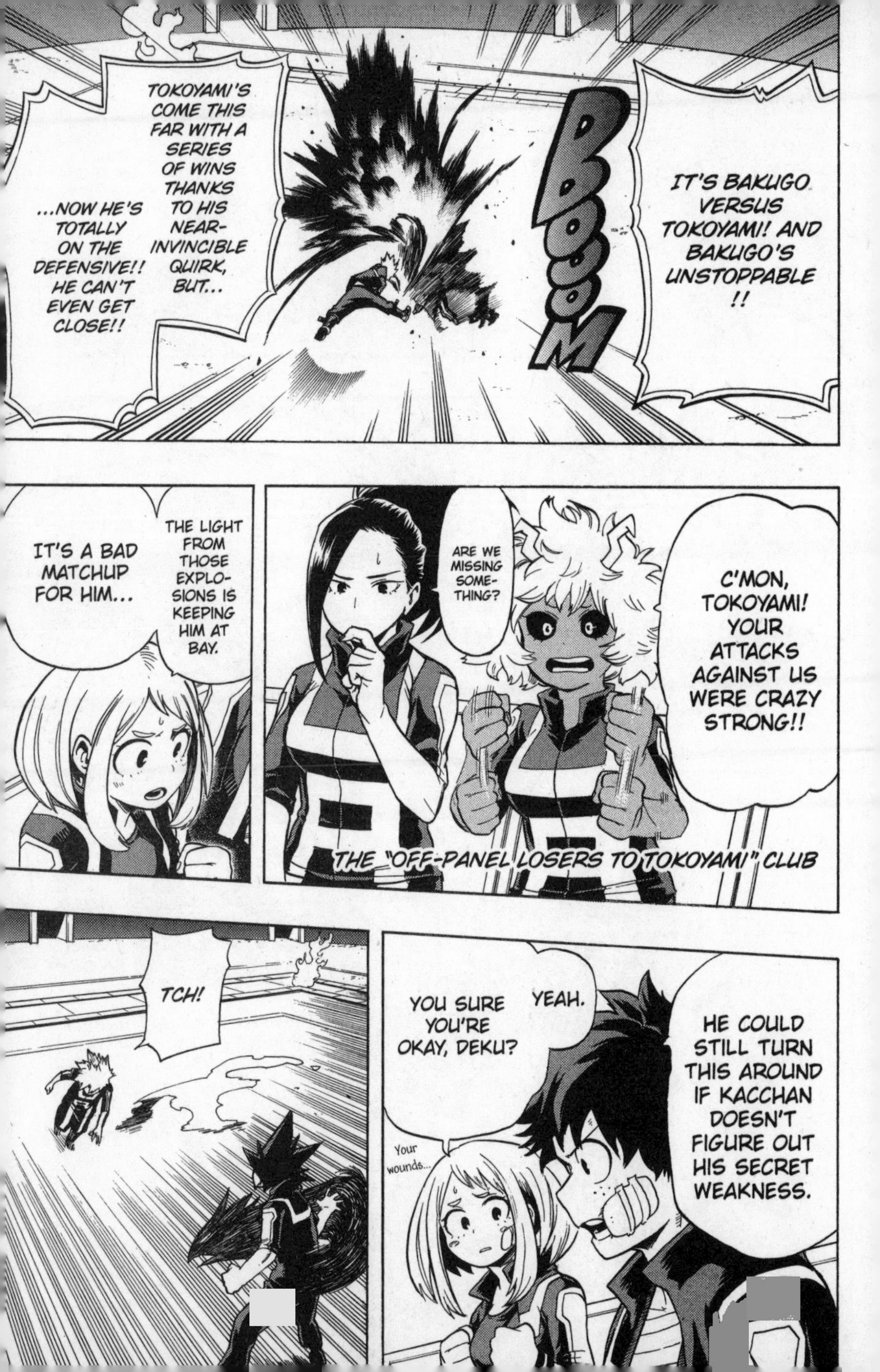
IT'S BAKUGO VERSUS TOKOYAMI! AND BAKUGO'S UNSTOPPABLE !!
BOOOOM
TOKOYAMI'S COME THIS FAR WITH A SERIES OF WINS THANKS TO HIS NEAR-INVINCIBLE QUIRK, BUT...
...NOW HE'S TOTALLY ON THE DEFENSIVE!! HE CAN'T EVEN GET CLOSE!!
C'MON, TOKOYAMI! YOUR ATTACKS AGAINST US WERE CRAZY STRONG!!
ARE WE MISSING SOMETHING?
THE "OFF-PANEL LOSERS TO TOKOYAMI" CLUB
THE LIGHT FROM THOSE EXPLOSIONS IS KEEPING HIM AT BAY.
IT'S A BAD MATCHUP FOR HIM...
HE COULD STILL TURN THIS AROUND IF KACCHAN DOESN'T FIGURE OUT HIS SECRET WEAKNESS.
YEAH.
YOU SURE YOU'RE OKAY, DEKU?
Your wounds...
TCH!

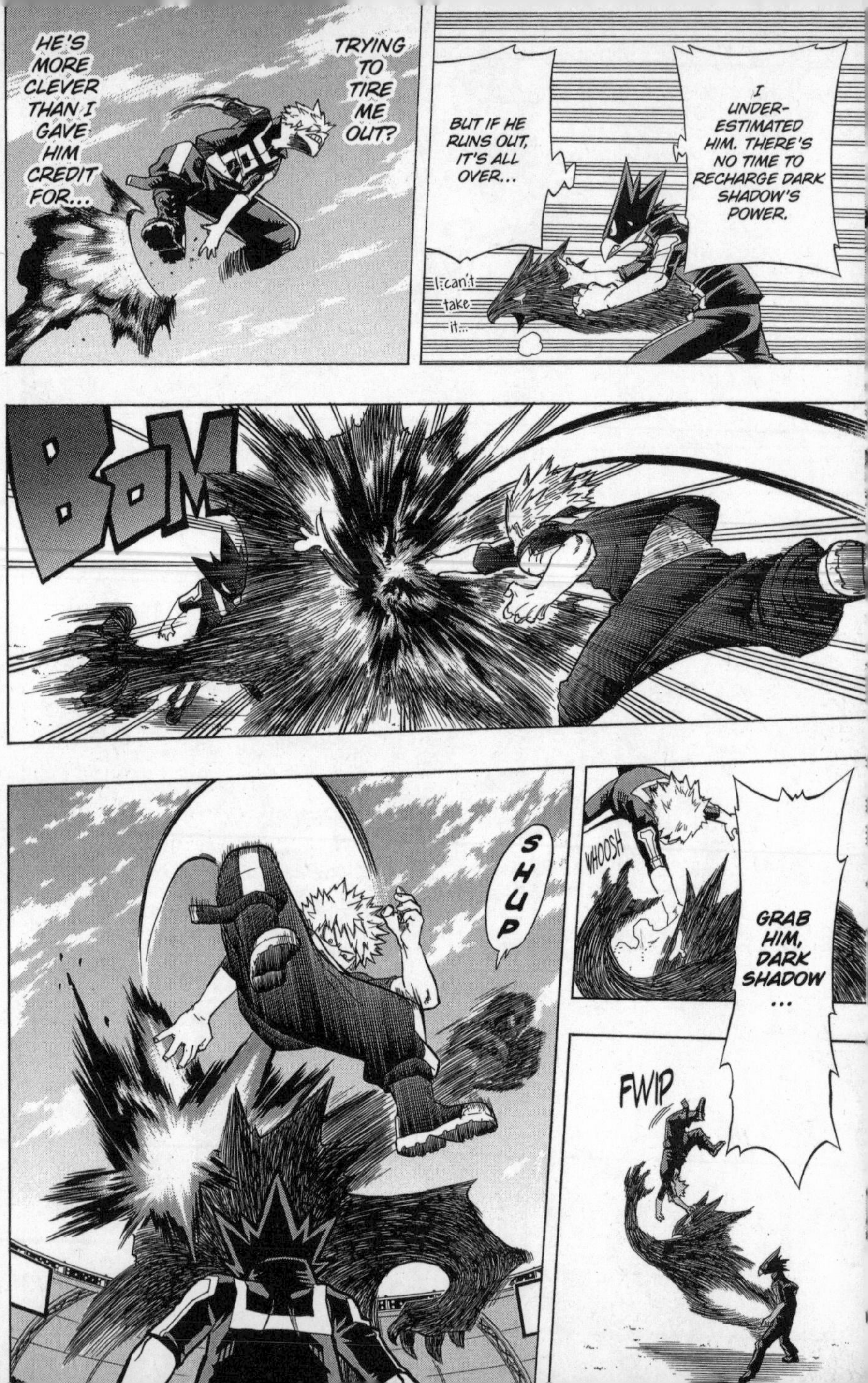
I UNDER-ESTIMATED HIM. THERE'S NO TIME TO RECHARGE DARK SHADOW'S POWER.
BUT IF HE RUNS OUT, IT'S ALL OVER...
I can't take it...
TRYING TO TIRE ME OUT?
HE'S MORE CLEVER THAN I GAVE HIM CREDIT FOR...
BOM
WHOOSH
GRAB HIM, DARK SHADOW...
FWIP
SHUP

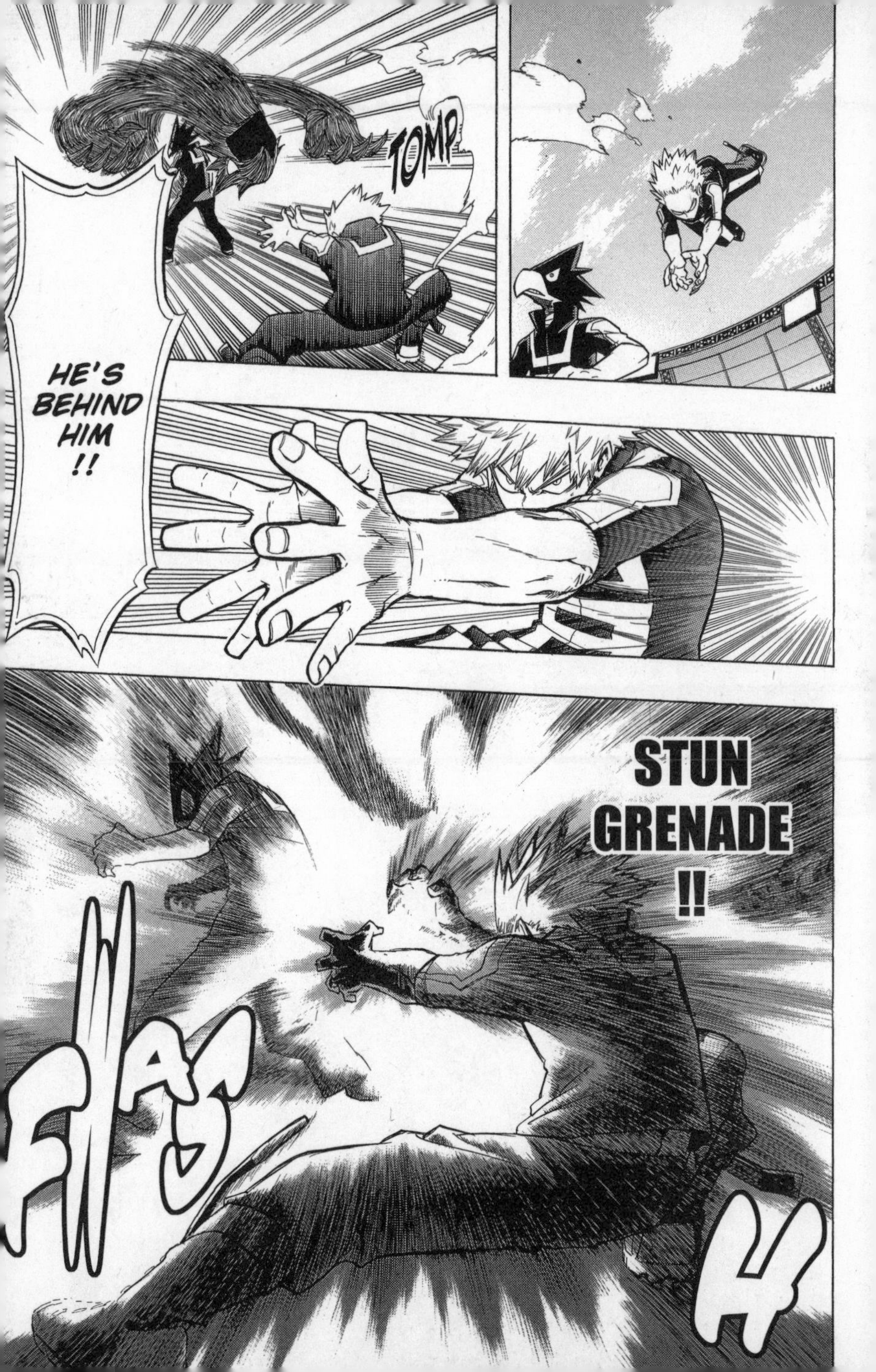
TOMP
HE'S BEHIND HIM!!
STUN GRENADE!!
FLASH

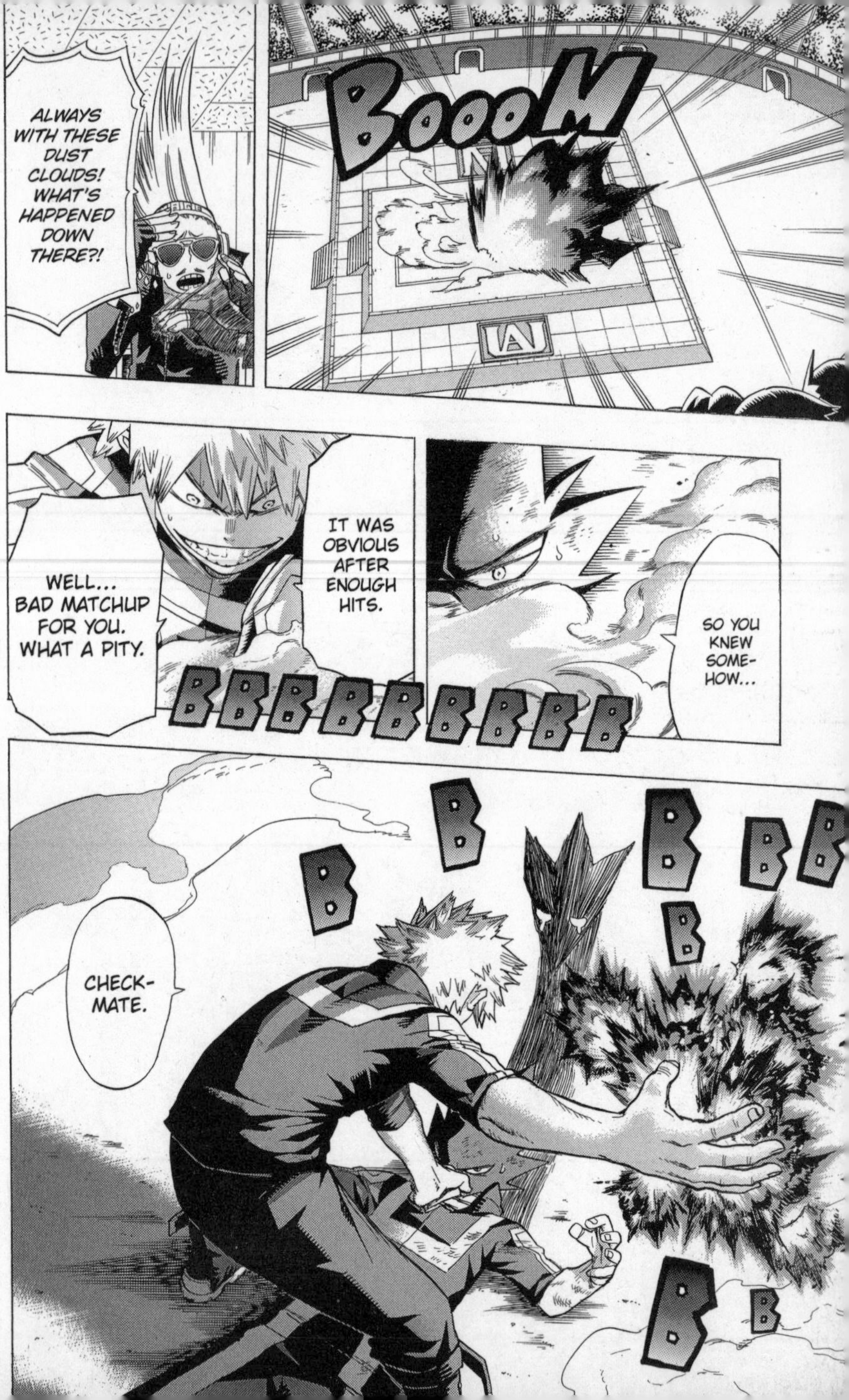
BOOOM
ALWAYS WITH THESE DUST CLOUDS! WHAT'S HAPPENED DOWN THERE?!
SO YOU KNEW SOME-HOW...
IT WAS OBVIOUS AFTER ENOUGH HITS.
WELL... BAD MATCHUP FOR YOU. WHAT A PITY.
BBBBBBBBB
B B B BB B
CHECK-MATE.
B B

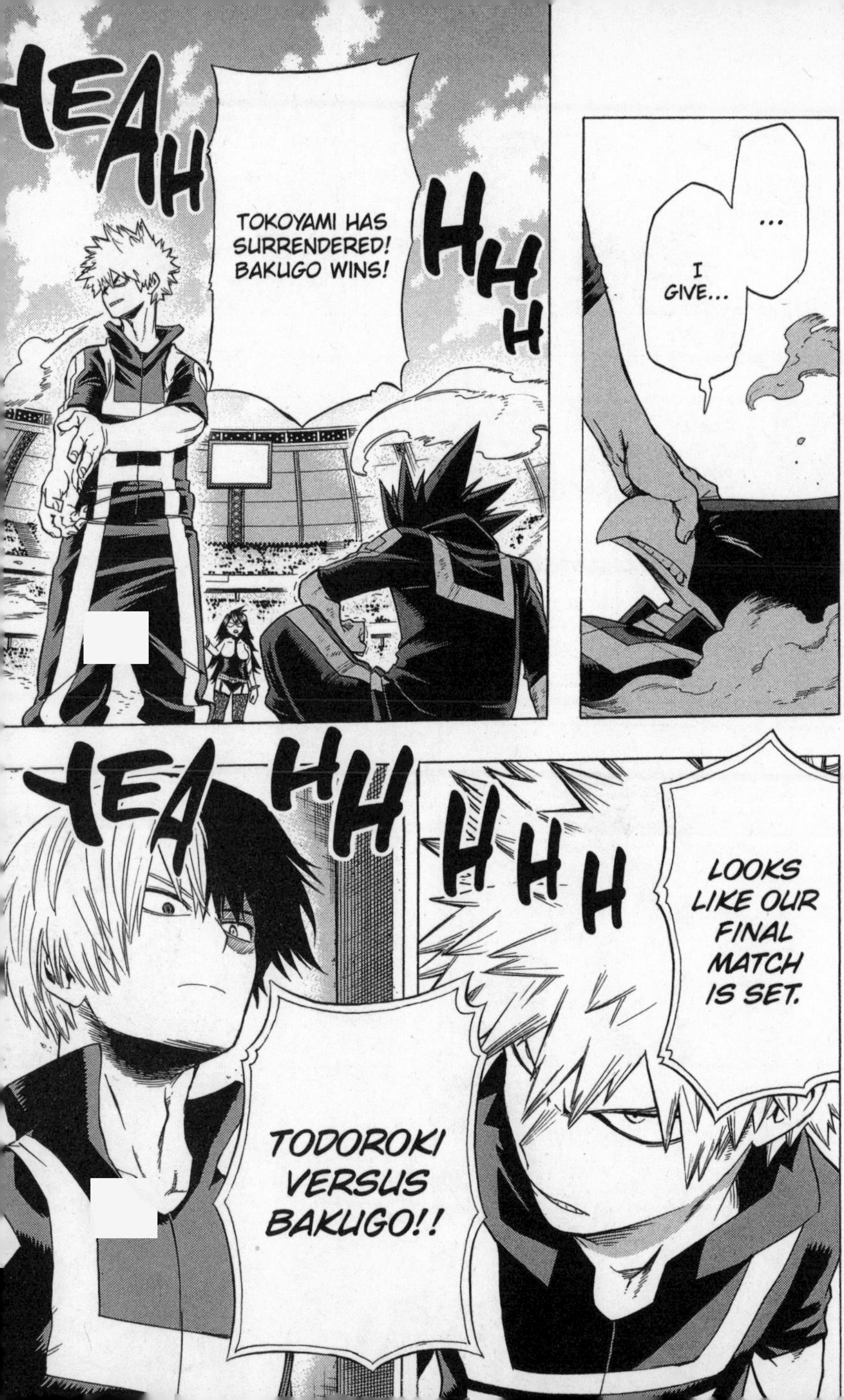
...
I GIVE...
YEAHHHH
TOKOYAMI HAS SURRENDERED! BAKUGO WINS!
LOOKS LIKE OUR FINAL MATCH IS SET.
YEAHHHHHHH
TODOROKI VERSUS BAKUGO!!

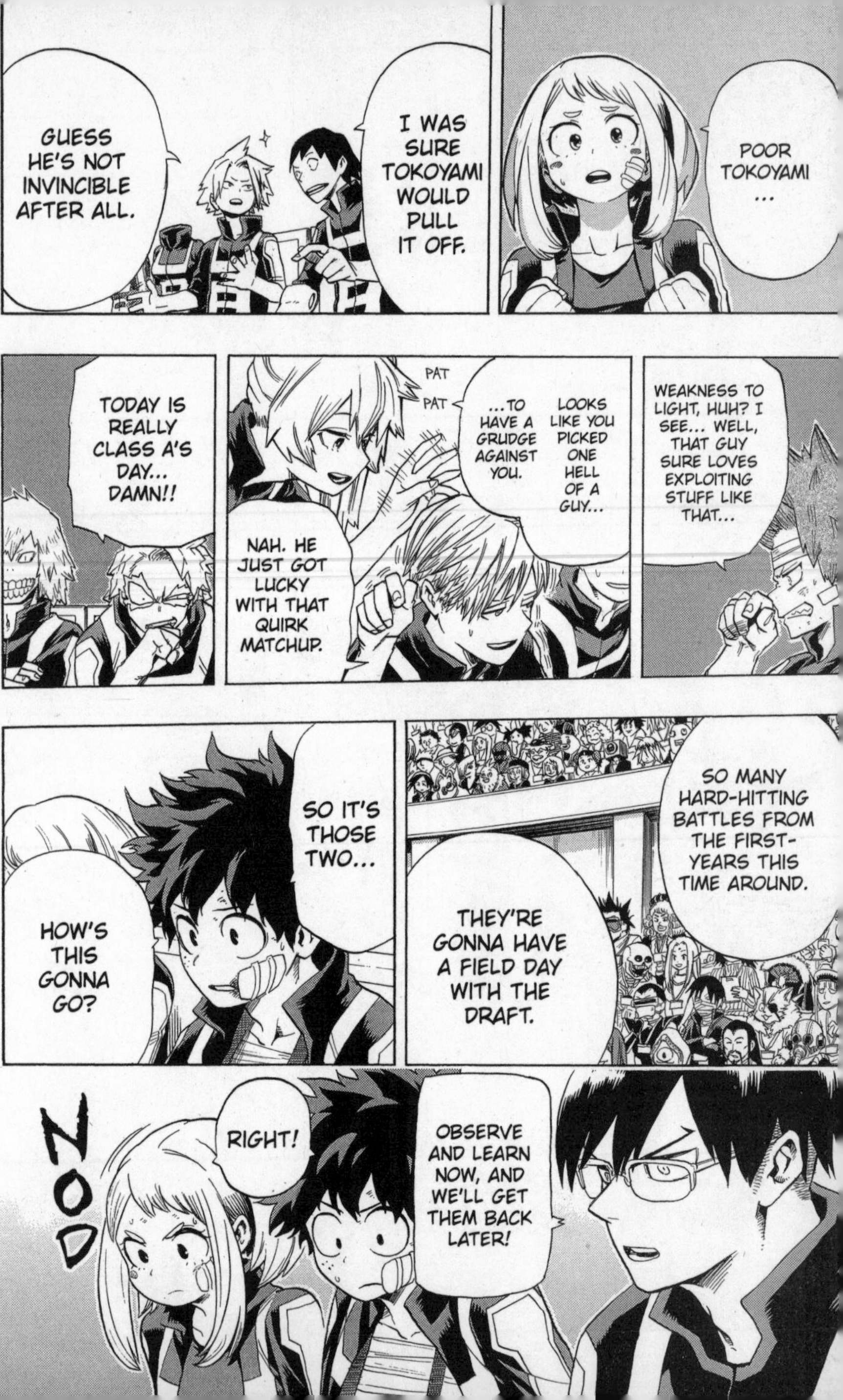
POOR TOKOYAMI ...
I WAS SURE TOKOYAMI WOULD PULL IT OFF.
GUESS HE'S NOT INVINCIBLE AFTER ALL.
WEAKNESS TO LIGHT, HUH? I SEE... WELL, THAT GUY SURE LOVES EXPLOITING STUFF LIKE THAT...
LOOKS LIKE YOU PICKED ONE HELL OF A GUY...
...TO HAVE A GRUDGE AGAINST YOU.
PAT
PAT
NAH. HE JUST GOT LUCKY WITH THAT QUIRK MATCHUP.
TODAY IS REALLY CLASS A'S DAY... DAMN!!
SO MANY HARD-HITTING BATTLES FROM THE FIRST-YEARS THIS TIME AROUND.
THEY'RE GONNA HAVE A FIELD DAY WITH THE DRAFT.
SO IT'S THOSE TWO...
HOW'S THIS GONNA GO?
OBSERVE AND LEARN NOW, AND WE'LL GET THEM BACK LATER!
RIGHT!
NOD

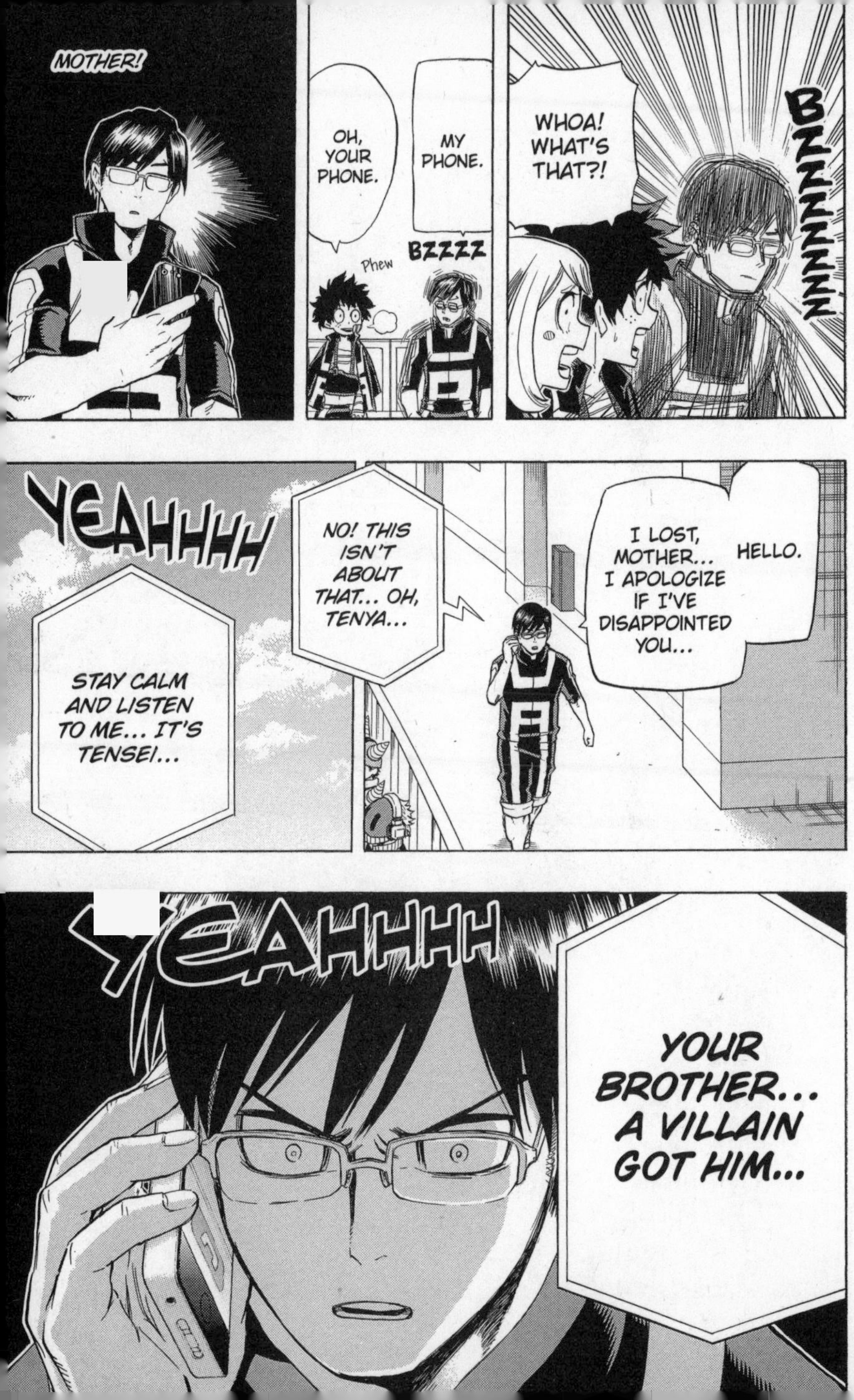
BZZZZZZZ
WHOA! WHAT'S THAT?!
MY PHONE.
BZZZZ
OH, YOUR PHONE.
Phew
MOTHER!
HELLO.
I LOST, MOTHER... I APOLOGIZE IF I'VE DISAPPOINTED YOU...
NO! THIS ISN'T ABOUT THAT... OH, TENYA...
YEAHHHH
STAY CALM AND LISTEN TO ME... IT'S TENSEI...
YOUR BROTHER... A VILLAIN GOT HIM...
YEAHHHH

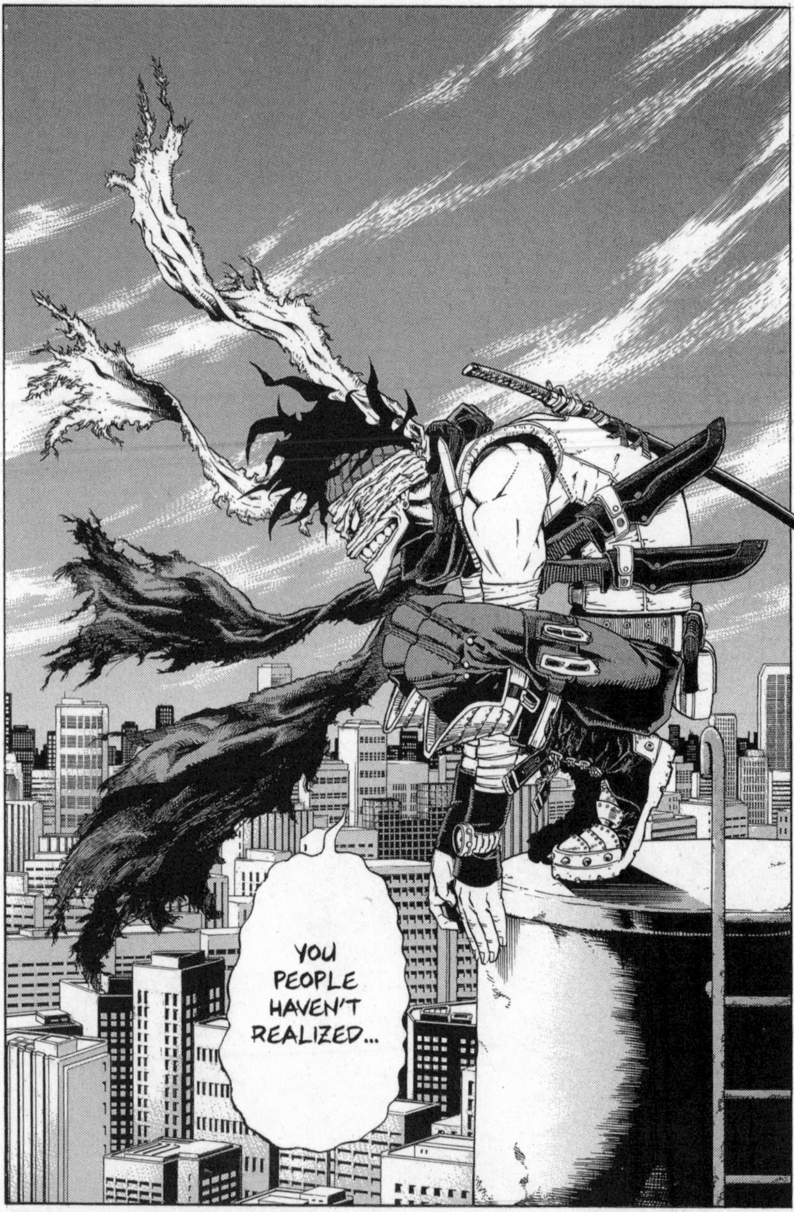
YOU PEOPLE HAVEN'T REALIZED...

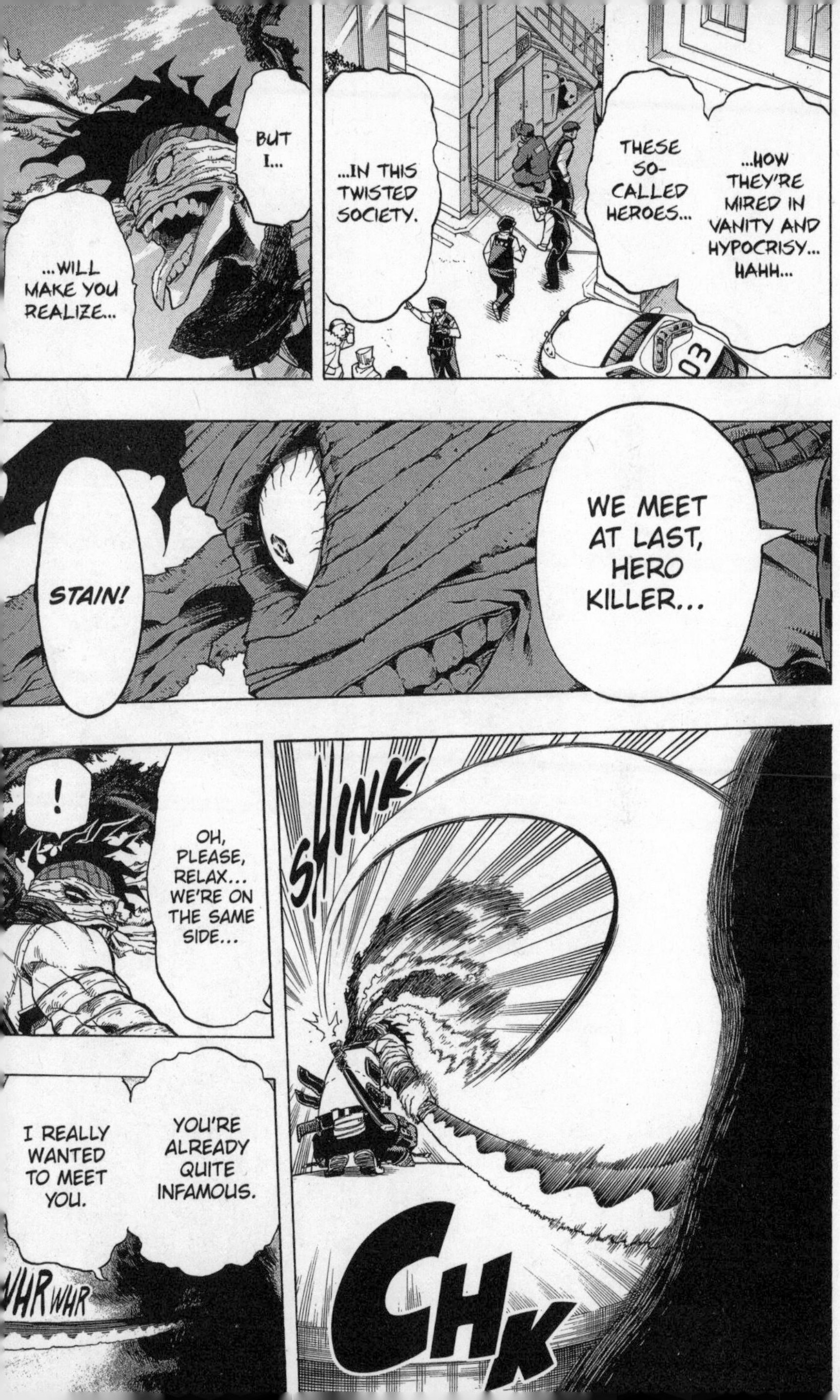
...HOW THEY'RE MIRED IN VANITY AND HYPOCRISY... HAHH...
THESE SO-CALLED HEROES...
03
...IN THIS TWISTED SOCIETY.
BUT I...
...WILL MAKE YOU REALIZE...
WE MEET AT LAST, HERO KILLER...
STAIN!
SHINK
CHK
!
OH, PLEASE, RELAX... WE'RE ON THE SAME SIDE...
YOU'RE ALREADY QUITE INFAMOUS.
I REALLY WANTED TO MEET YOU.
WHR WHR

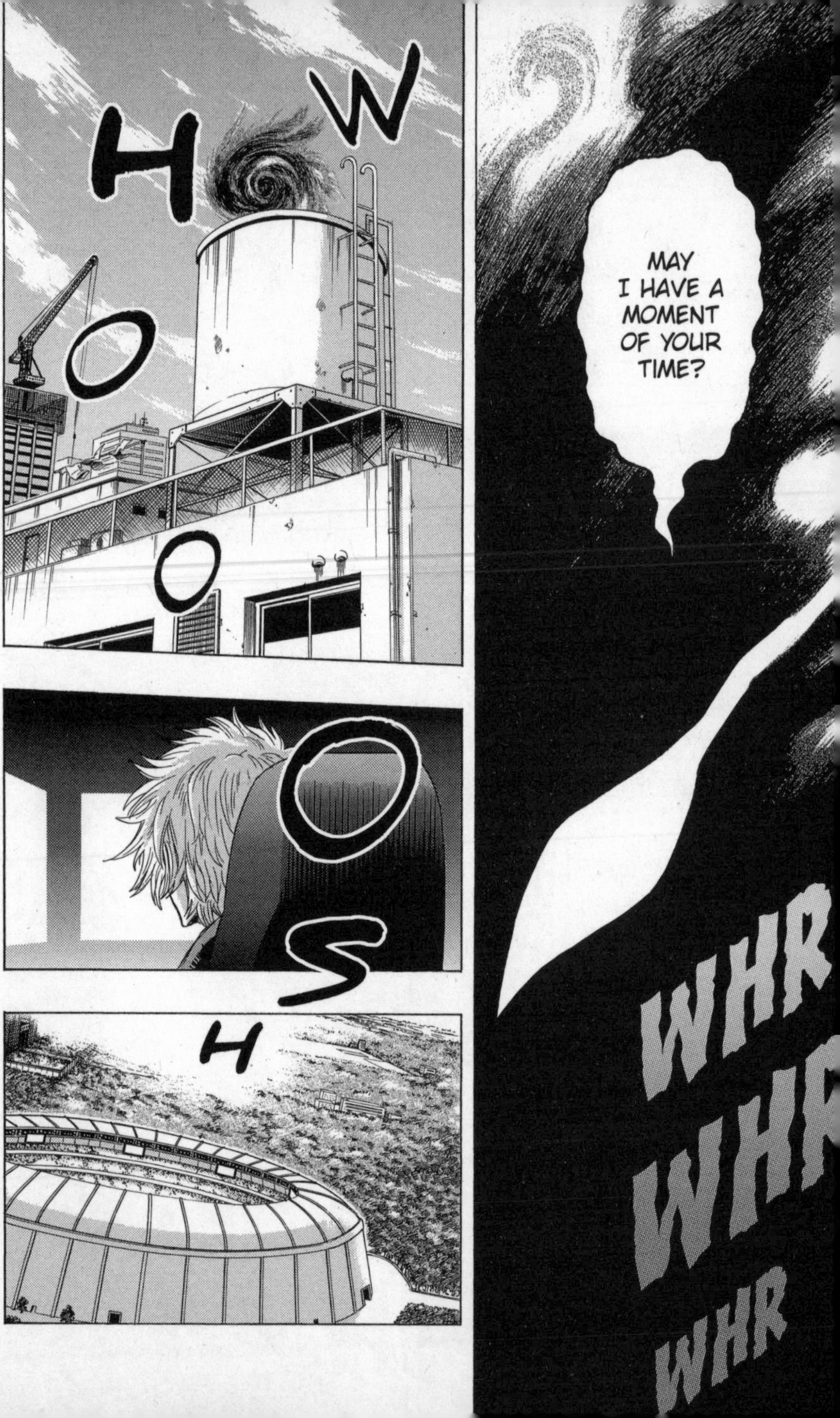
MAY I HAVE A MOMENT OF YOUR TIME?
WHR
WHR
WHR

CONTESTANT
PREP
ROOM 2

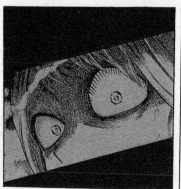

YOUR POWER IS YOUR OWN!!

!

BAM

MOTHER, I...

BEFORE MY FIGHT WITH HIM, I NEVER... I NEVER THOUGHT ABOUT IT.

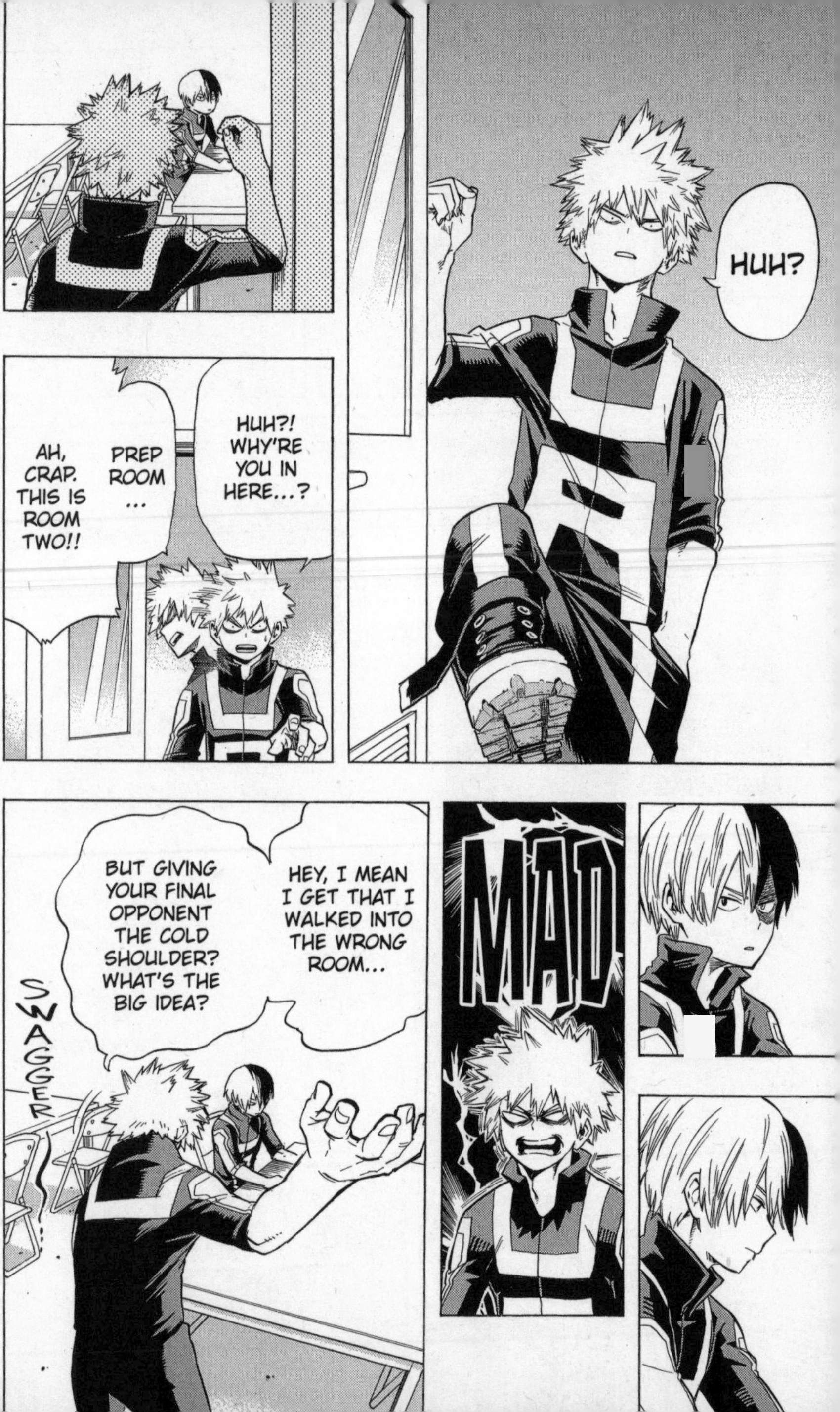
HUH?
HUH?! WHY'RE YOU IN HERE...?
PREP ROOM ...
AH, CRAP. THIS IS ROOM TWO!!
MAD
HEY, I MEAN I GET THAT I WALKED INTO THE WRONG ROOM...
BUT GIVING YOUR FINAL OPPONENT THE COLD SHOULDER? WHAT'S THE BIG IDEA?
SWAGGER

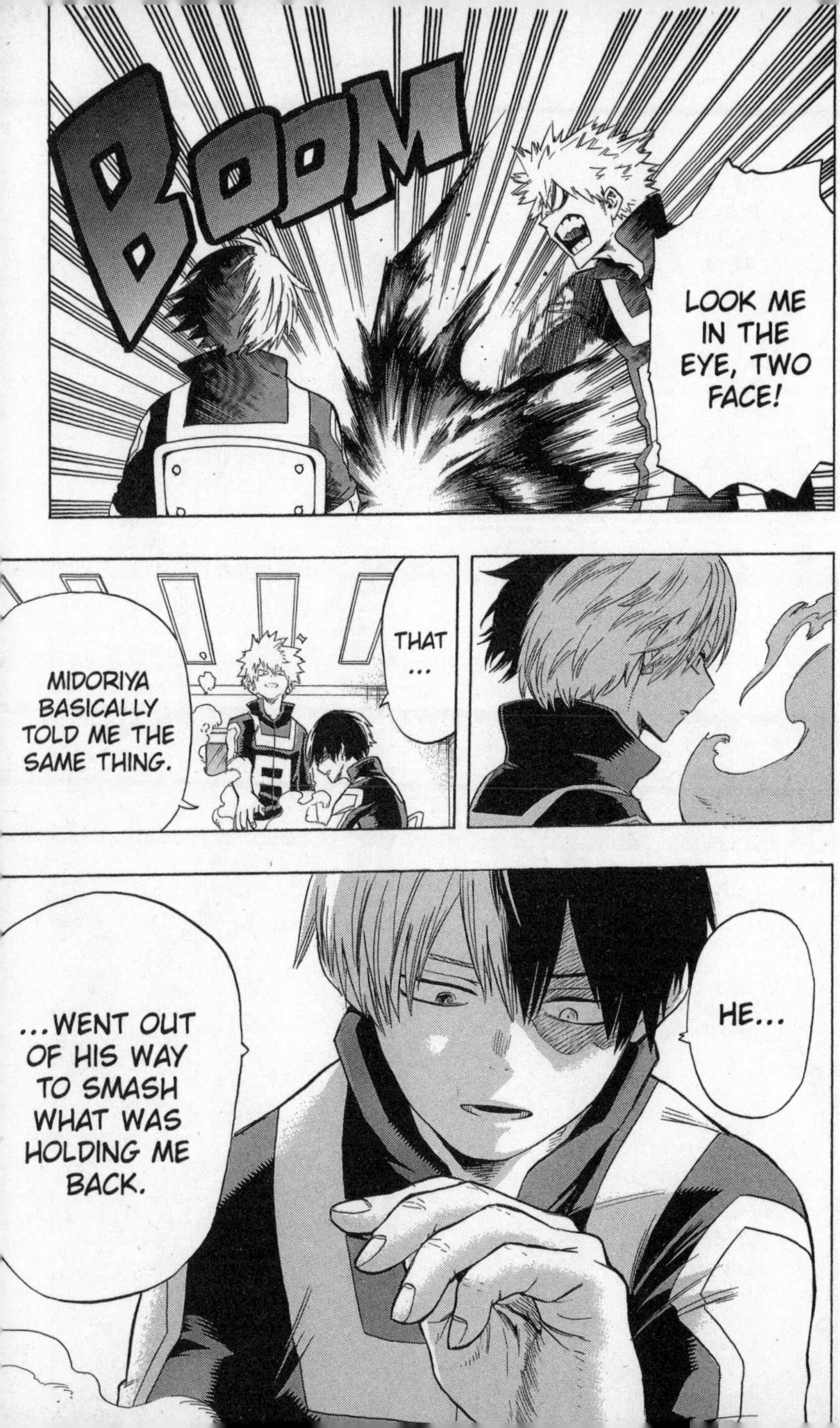
BOOM
LOOK ME IN THE EYE, TWO FACE!
THAT ...
MIDORIYA BASICALLY TOLD ME THE SAME THING.
HE...
...WENT OUT OF HIS WAY TO SMASH WHAT WAS HOLDING ME BACK.

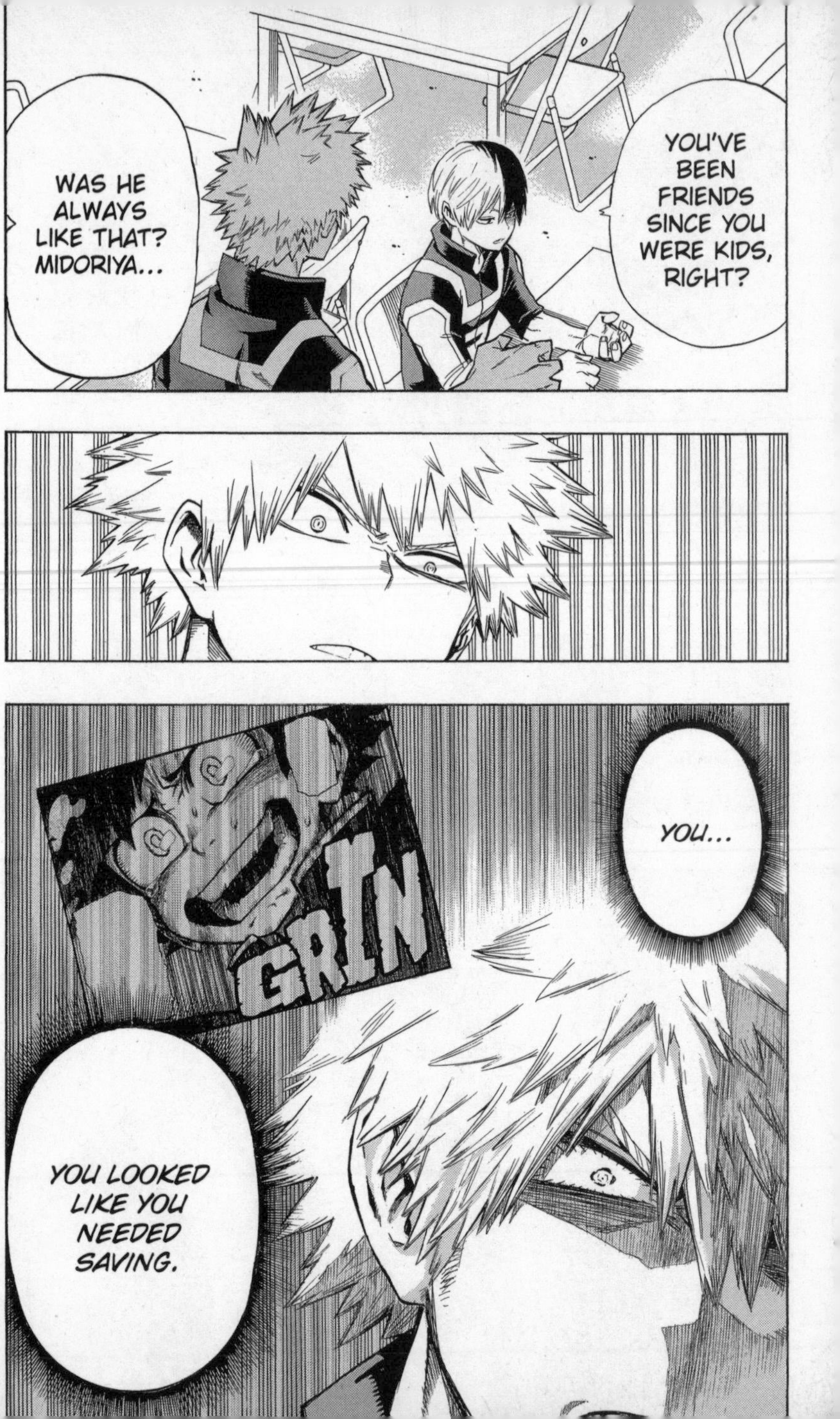
YOU'VE BEEN FRIENDS SINCE YOU WERE KIDS, RIGHT?
WAS HE ALWAYS LIKE THAT? MIDORIYA...
YOU...
GRIN
YOU LOOKED LIKE YOU NEEDED SAVING.

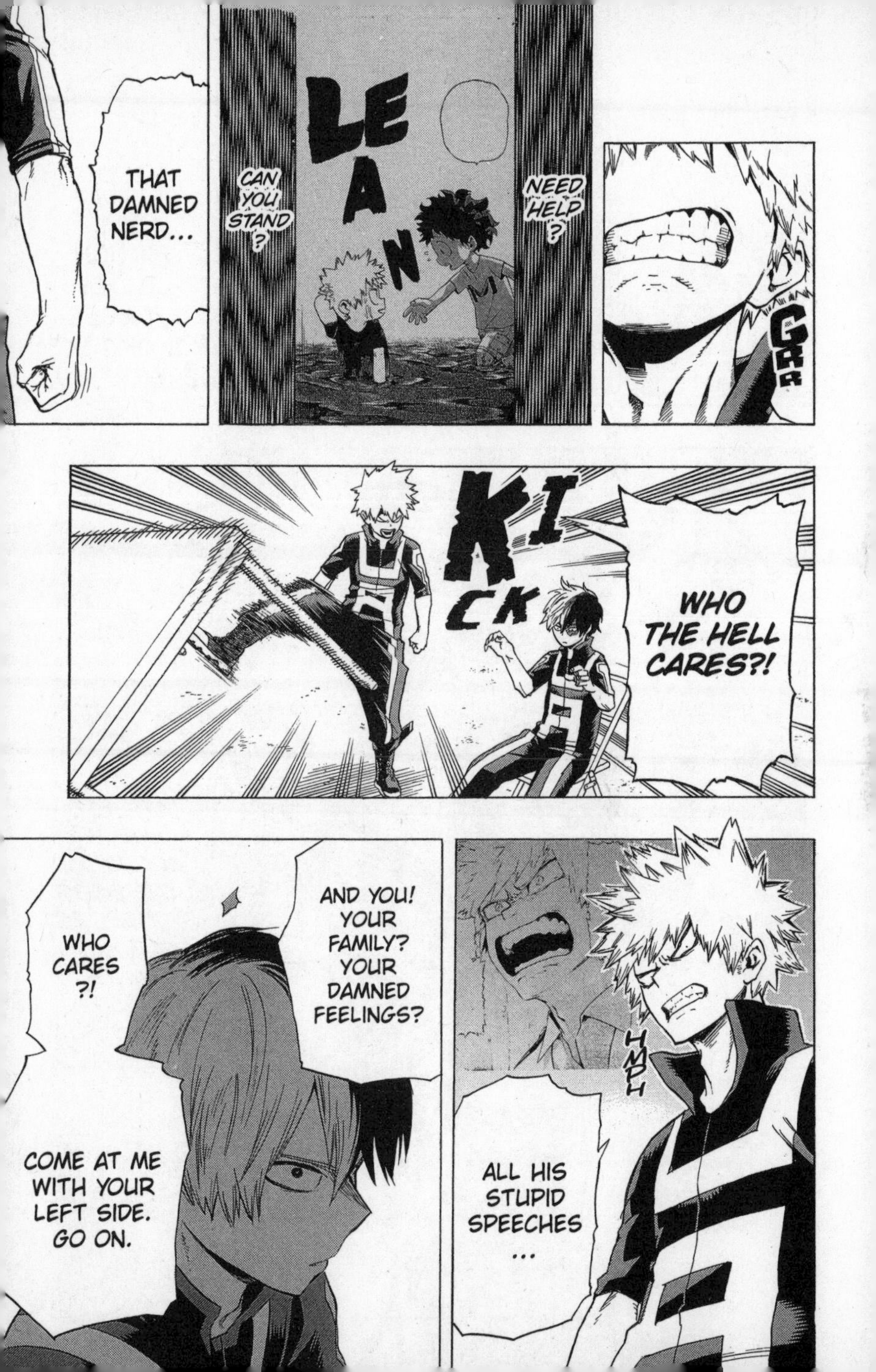
GRR
NEED HELP?
LEAN
CAN YOU STAND?
THAT DAMNED NERD...
WHO THE HELL CARES?!
KICK
HMPH
ALL HIS STUPID SPEECHES...
AND YOU! YOUR FAMILY? YOUR DAMNED FEELINGS?
WHO CARES?!
COME AT ME WITH YOUR LEFT SIDE. GO ON.

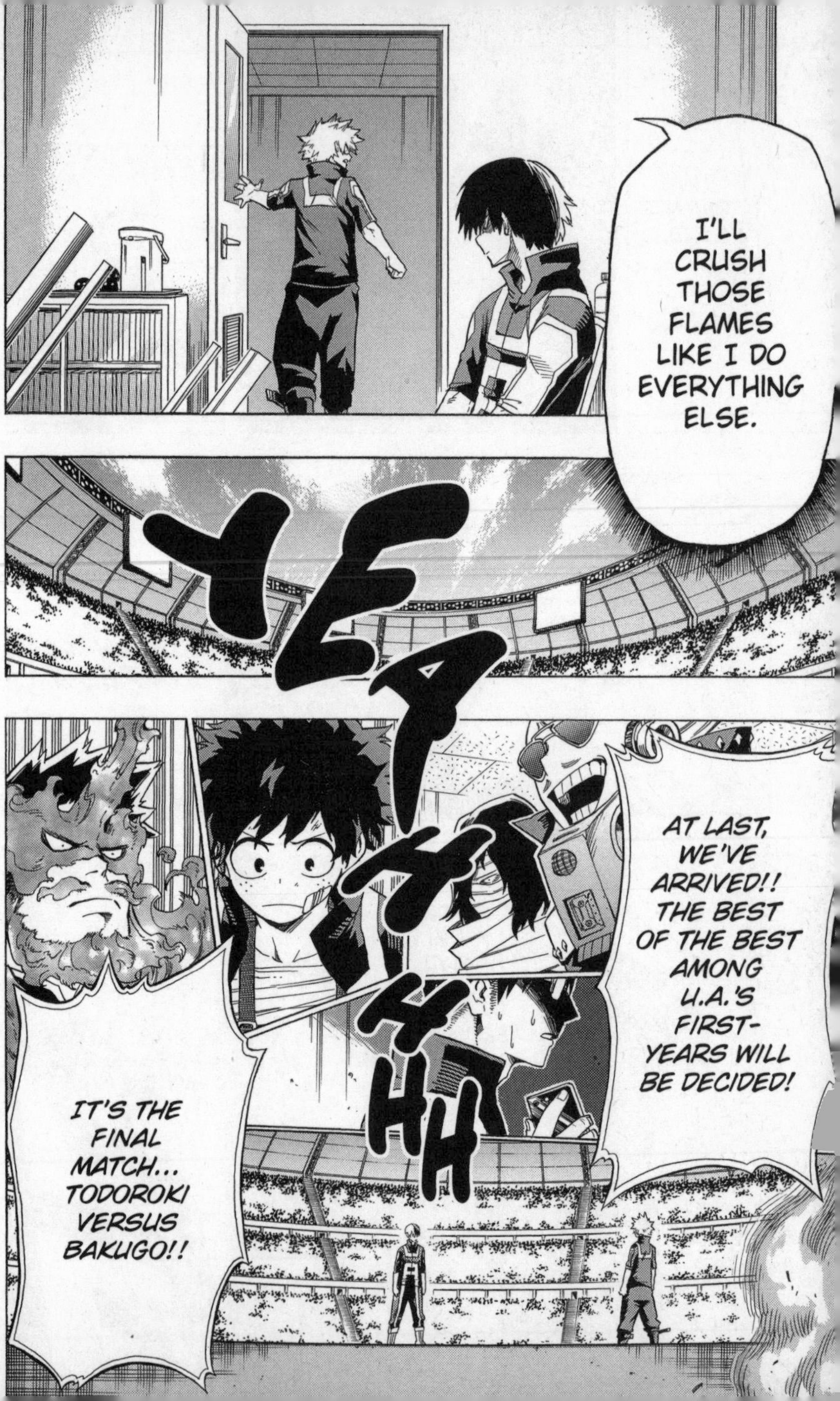
I'LL CRUSH THOSE FLAMES LIKE I DO EVERYTHING ELSE.
AT LAST, WE'VE ARRIVED!! THE BEST OF THE BEST AMONG U.A.'S FIRST-YEARS WILL BE DECIDED!
IT'S THE FINAL MATCH... TODOROKI VERSUS BAKUGO!!

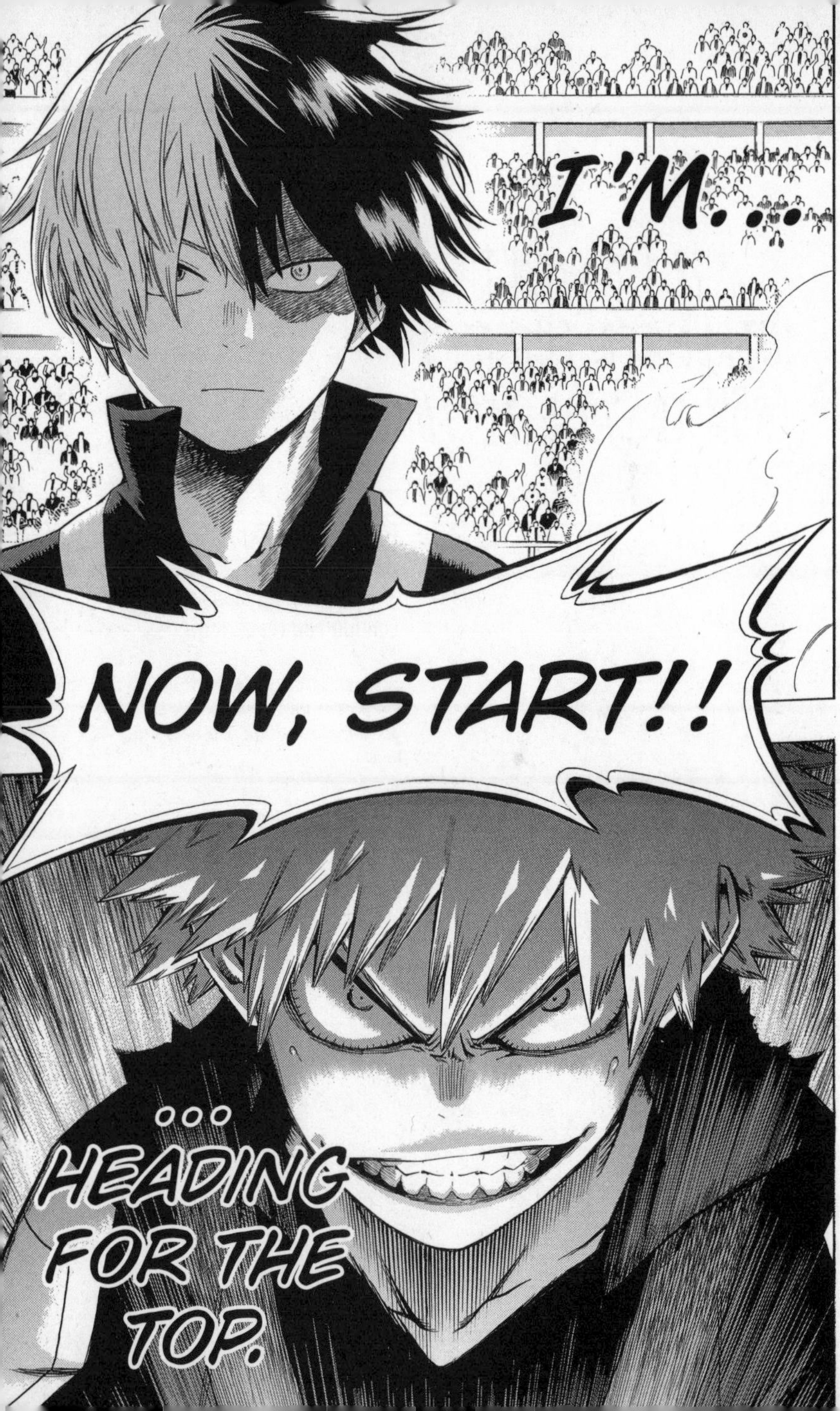
I'M...
NOW, START!!
...HEADING FOR THE TOP.

JUZO HONENUKI (15)

AH! I HAVEN'T INTRODUCED THE KIDS FROM CLASS B YET!!

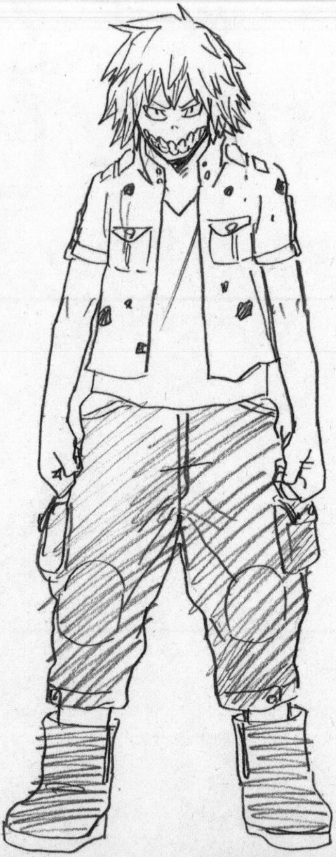

Birthday: 6/20
Height: 174 cm
Favorite Thing: Massages (giving and receiving)

BEHIND THE SCENES

Rank filler for Class B. A cool, good-looking dude. He hates to lose.

NO. 43 - TODOROKI VS. BAKUGO

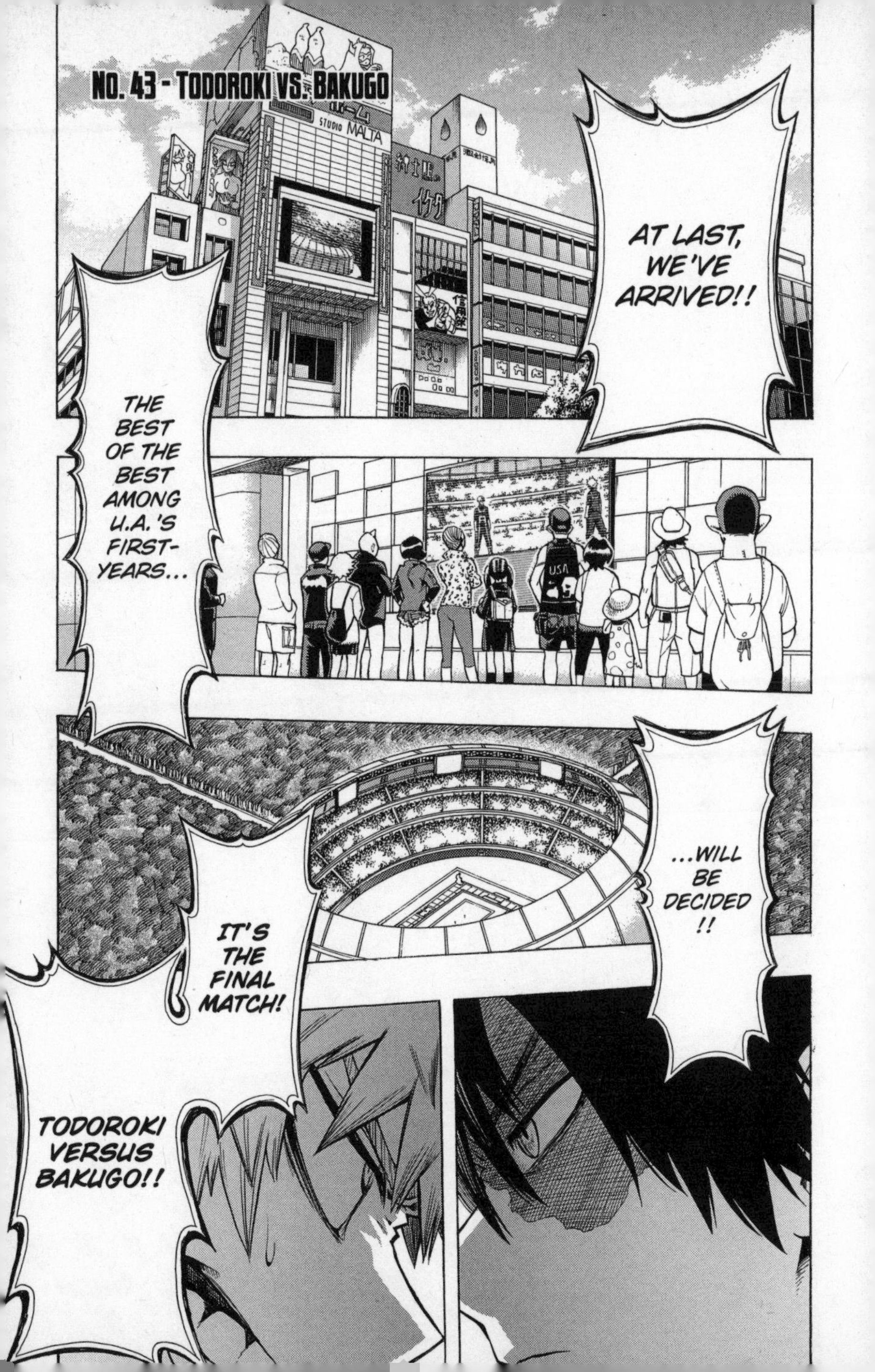
STUDIO MALTA
AT LAST, WE'VE ARRIVED!!
THE BEST OF THE BEST AMONG U.A.'S FIRST-YEARS...
USA
...WILL BE DECIDED!!
IT'S THE FINAL MATCH!
TODOROKI VERSUS BAKUGO!!

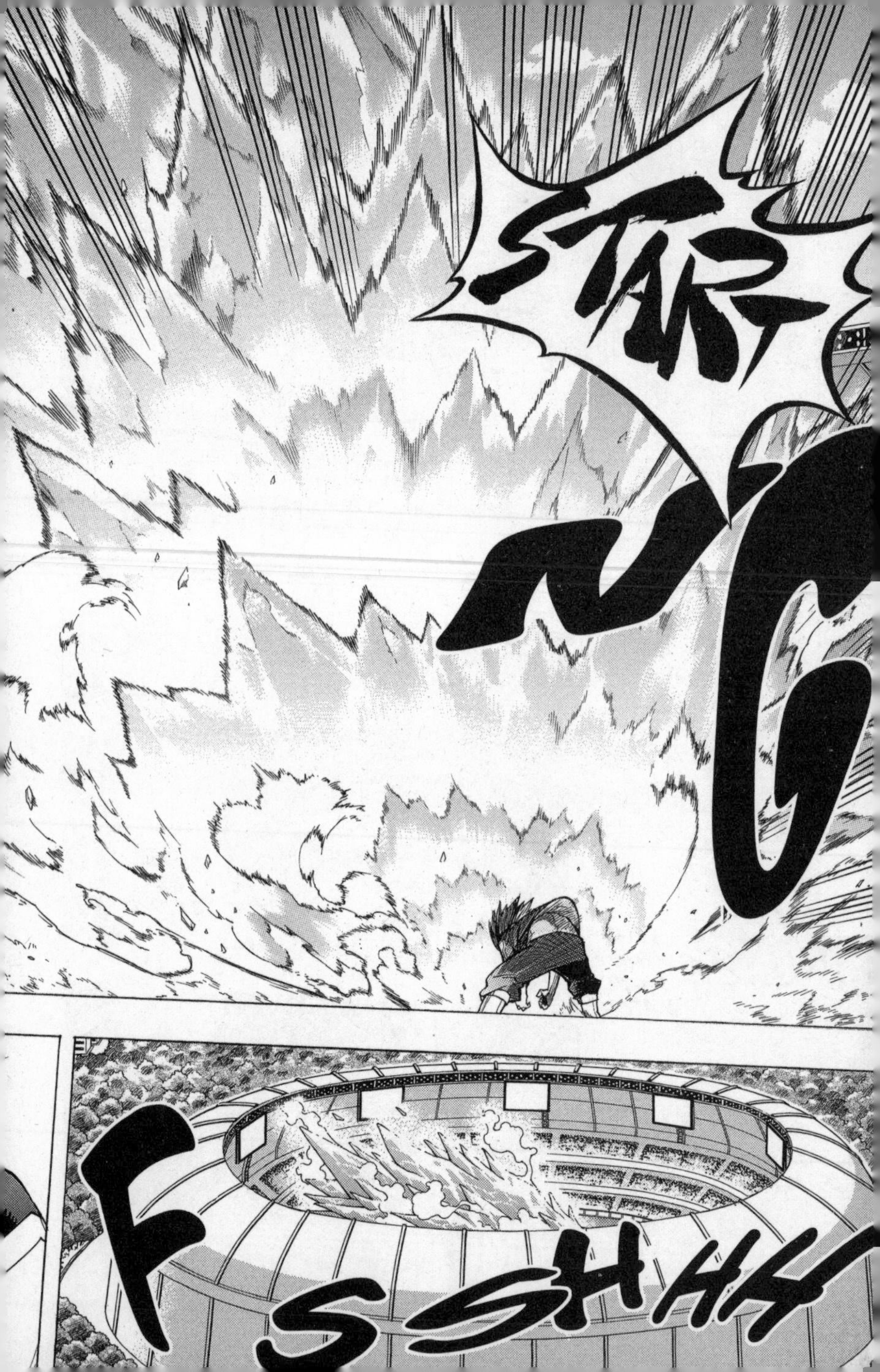
START
NG
F
SSHH

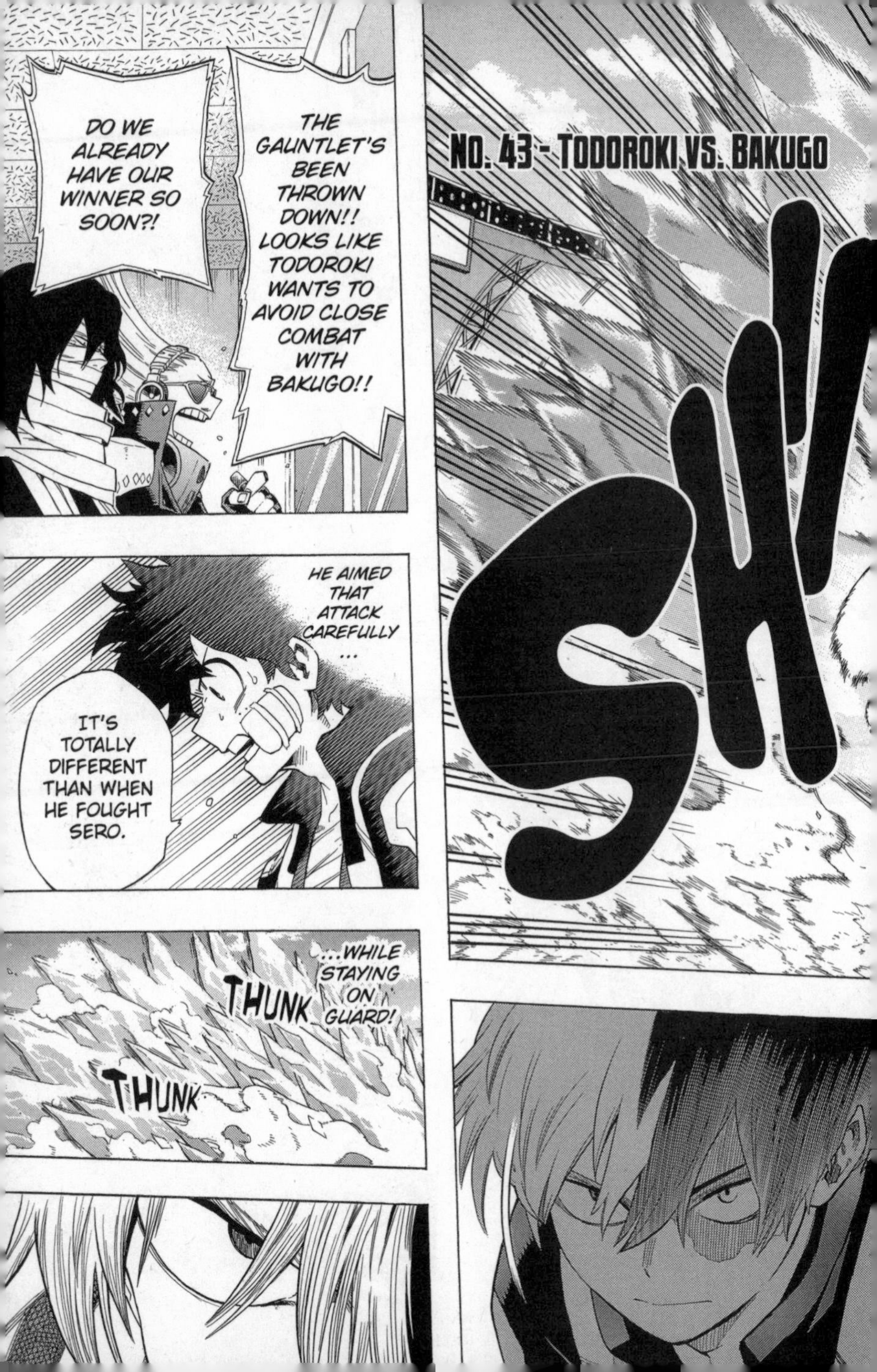
NO. 43 - TODOROKI VS. BAKUGO
SH
THE GAUNTLET'S BEEN THROWN DOWN!! LOOKS LIKE TODOROKI WANTS TO AVOID CLOSE COMBAT WITH BAKUGO!!
DO WE ALREADY HAVE OUR WINNER SO SOON?!
HE AIMED THAT ATTACK CAREFULLY...
IT'S TOTALLY DIFFERENT THAN WHEN HE FOUGHT SERO.
...WHILE STAYING ON GUARD!
THUNK
THUNK

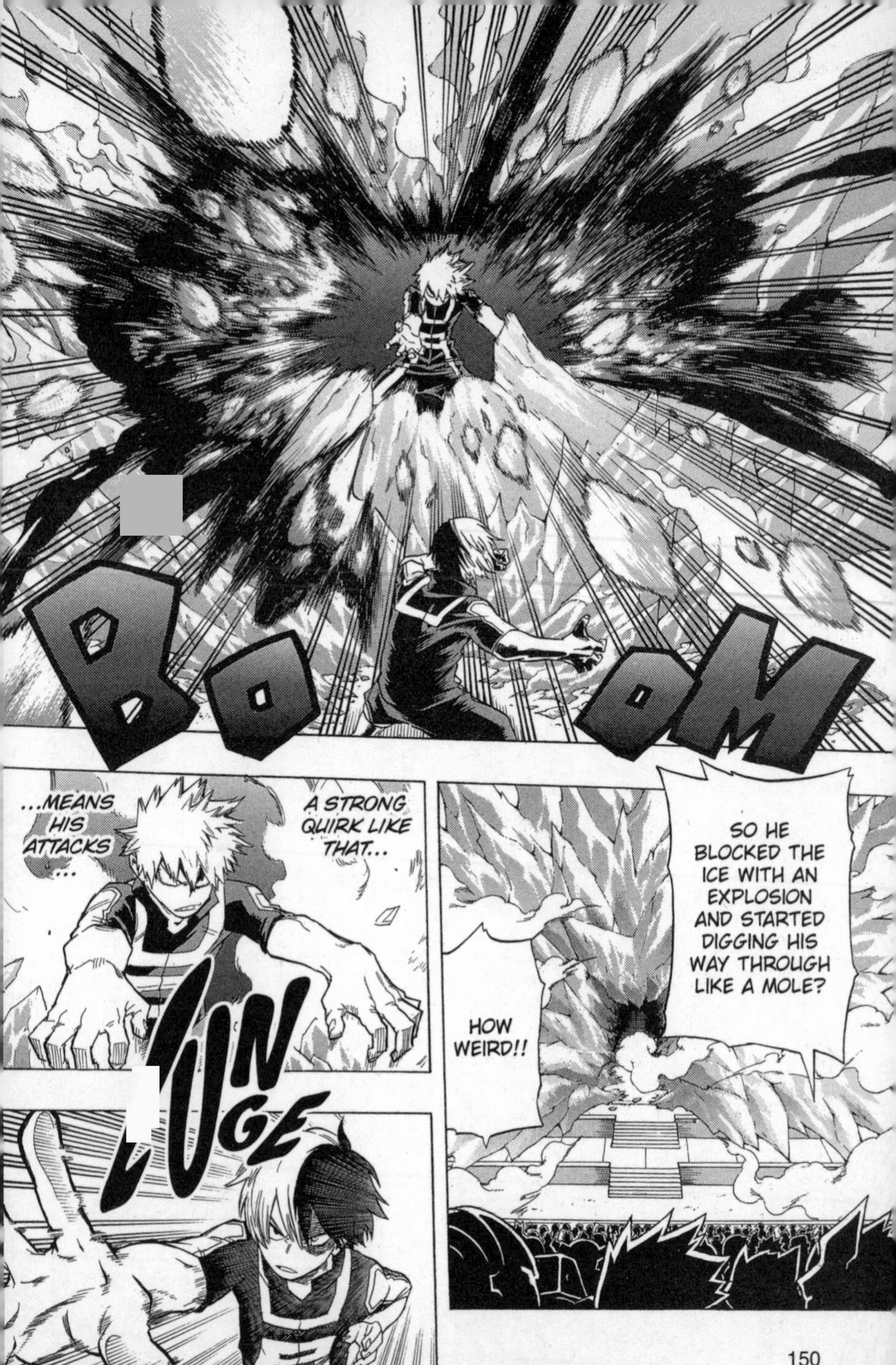
BOOM
SO HE BLOCKED THE ICE WITH AN EXPLOSION AND STARTED DIGGING HIS WAY THROUGH LIKE A MOLE?
HOW WEIRD!!
A STRONG QUIRK LIKE THAT...
...MEANS HIS ATTACKS ...

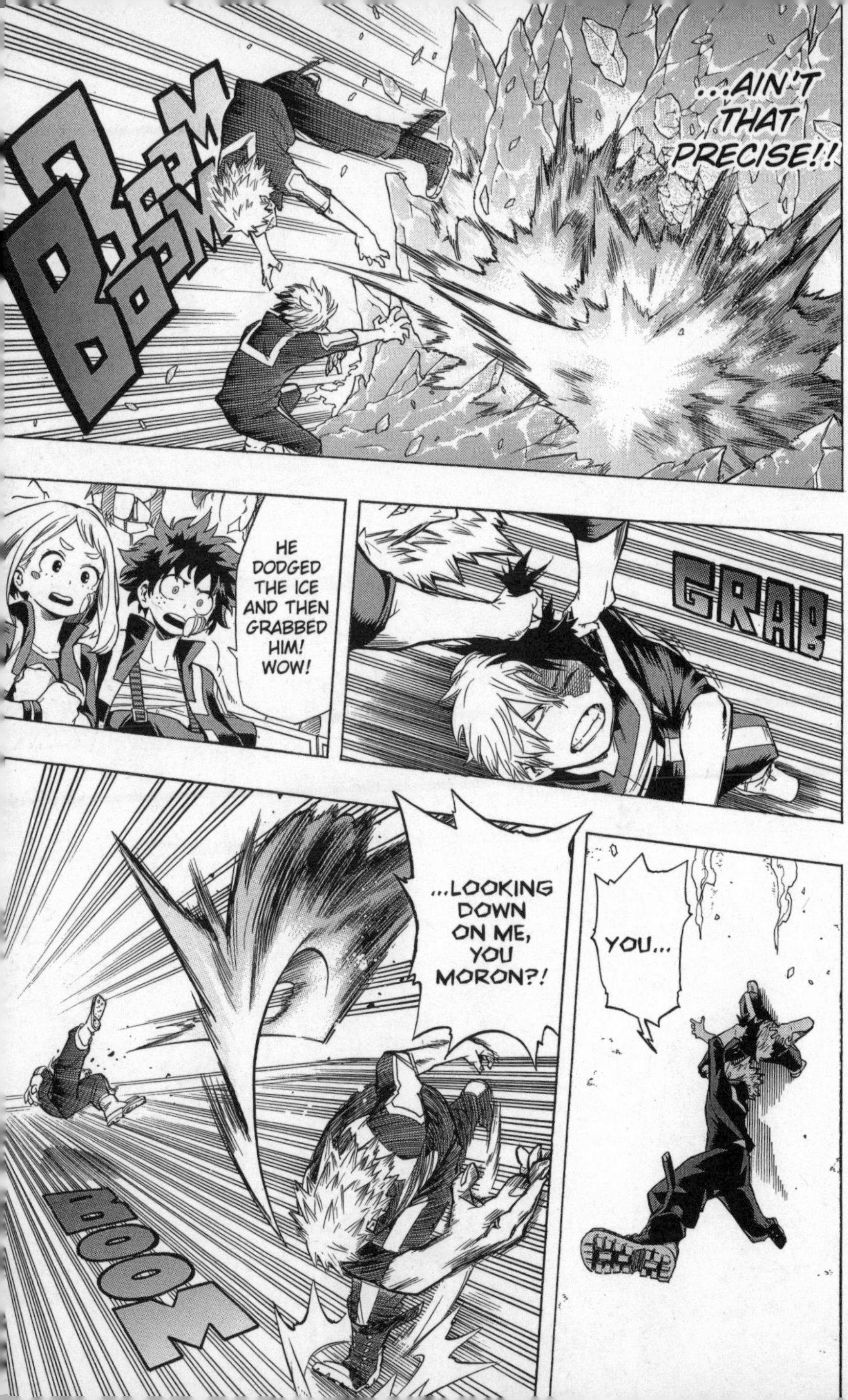
...AIN'T THAT PRECISE!!
BOOM
BOOM
GRAB
HE DODGED THE ICE AND THEN GRABBED HIM! WOW!
YOU...
...LOOKING DOWN ON ME, YOU MORON?!
BOOM

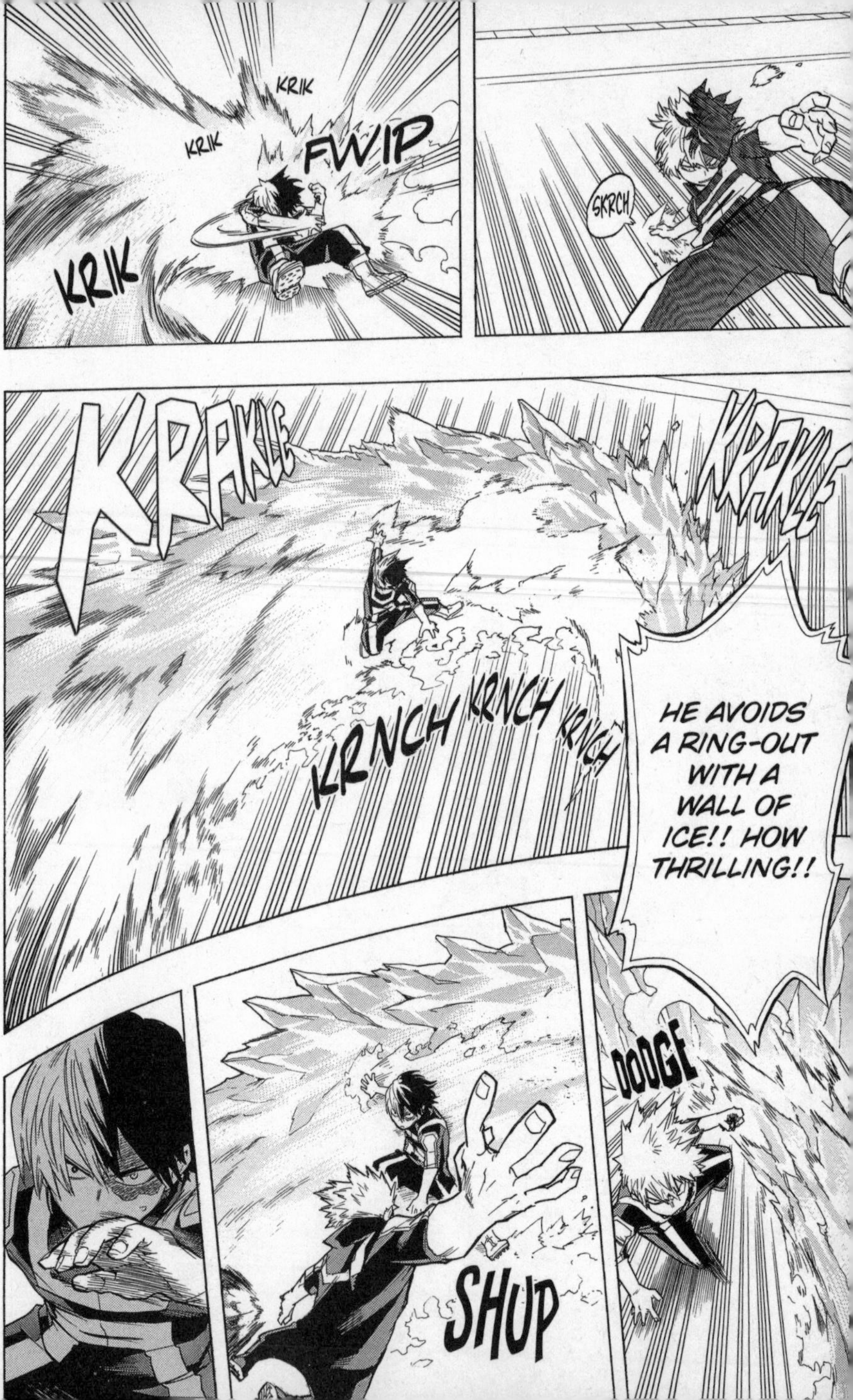
SKRCH
KRIK
FWIP
KRIK
KRIK
KRAKLE
KRAKLE
HE AVOIDS A RING-OUT WITH A WALL OF ICE!! HOW THRILLING!!
KRNCH KRNCH KRNCH
DODGE
SHUP

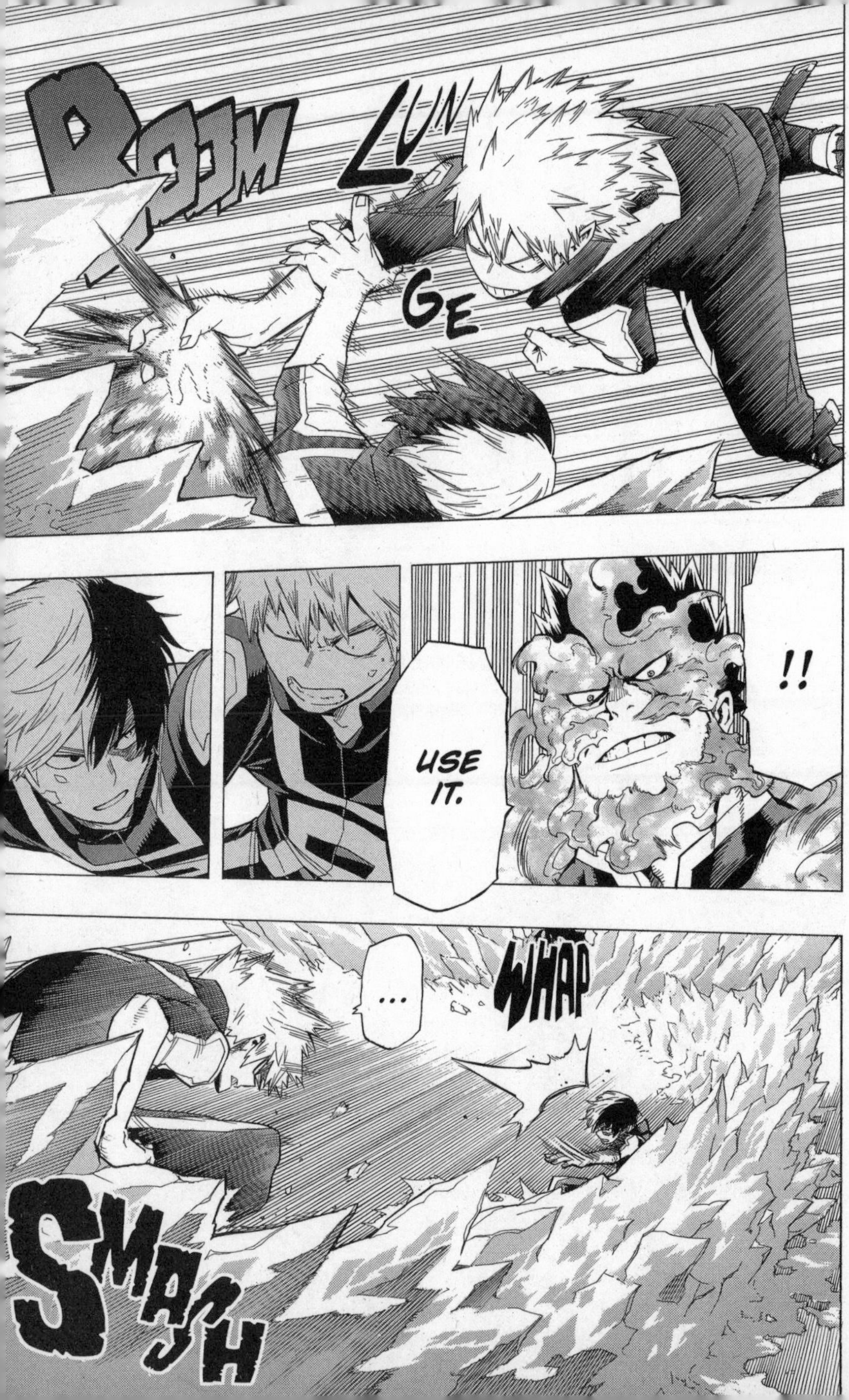
LUNGE
BOOM
!!
USE IT.
WHAP
...
SMASH

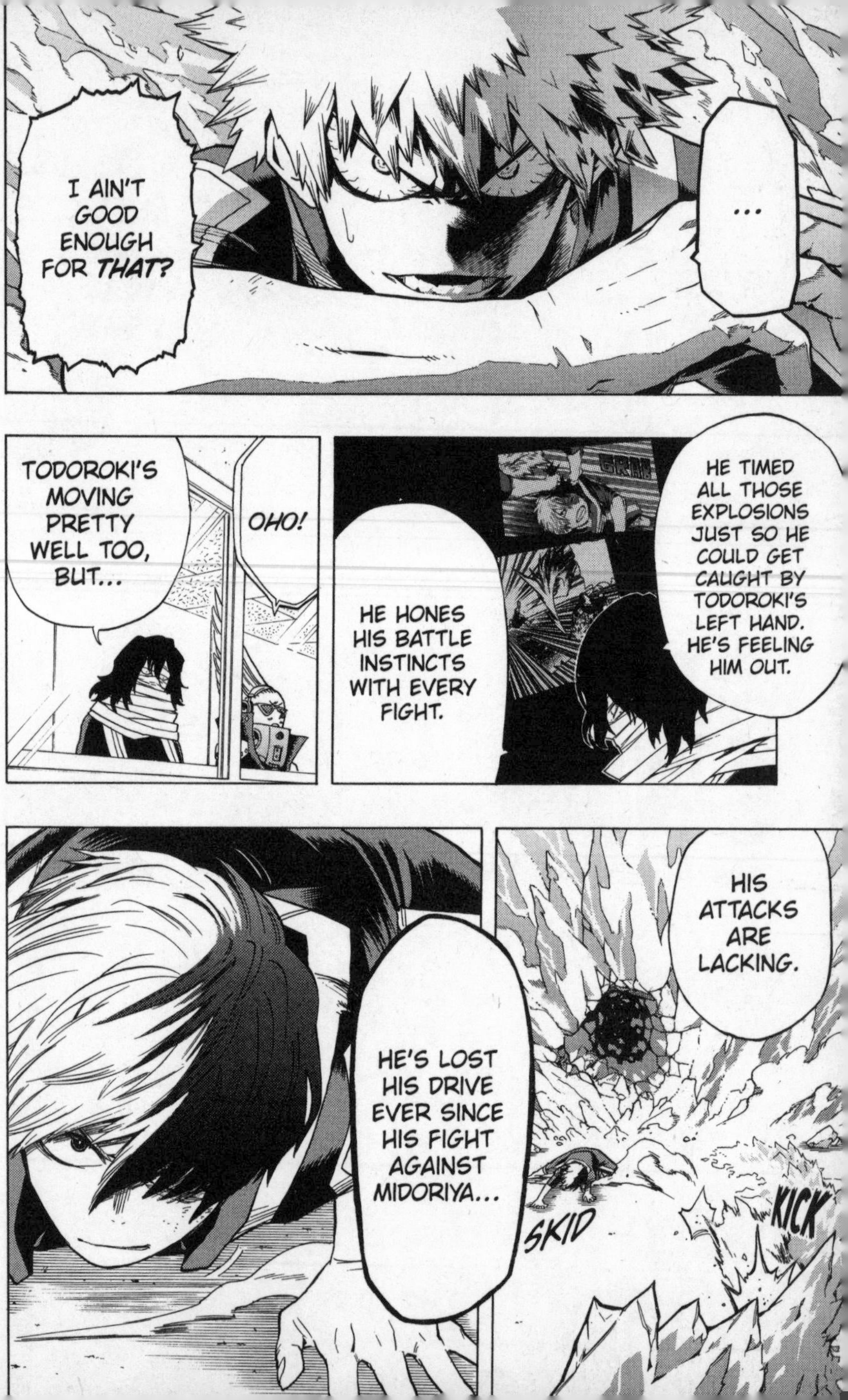
...
I AIN'T GOOD ENOUGH FOR *THAT?*
HE TIMED ALL THOSE EXPLOSIONS JUST SO HE COULD GET CAUGHT BY TODOROKI'S LEFT HAND. HE'S FEELING HIM OUT.
HE HONES HIS BATTLE INSTINCTS WITH EVERY FIGHT.
OHO!
TODOROKI'S MOVING PRETTY WELL TOO, BUT...
HIS ATTACKS ARE LACKING.
KICK
SKID
HE'S LOST HIS DRIVE EVER SINCE HIS FIGHT AGAINST MIDORIYA...

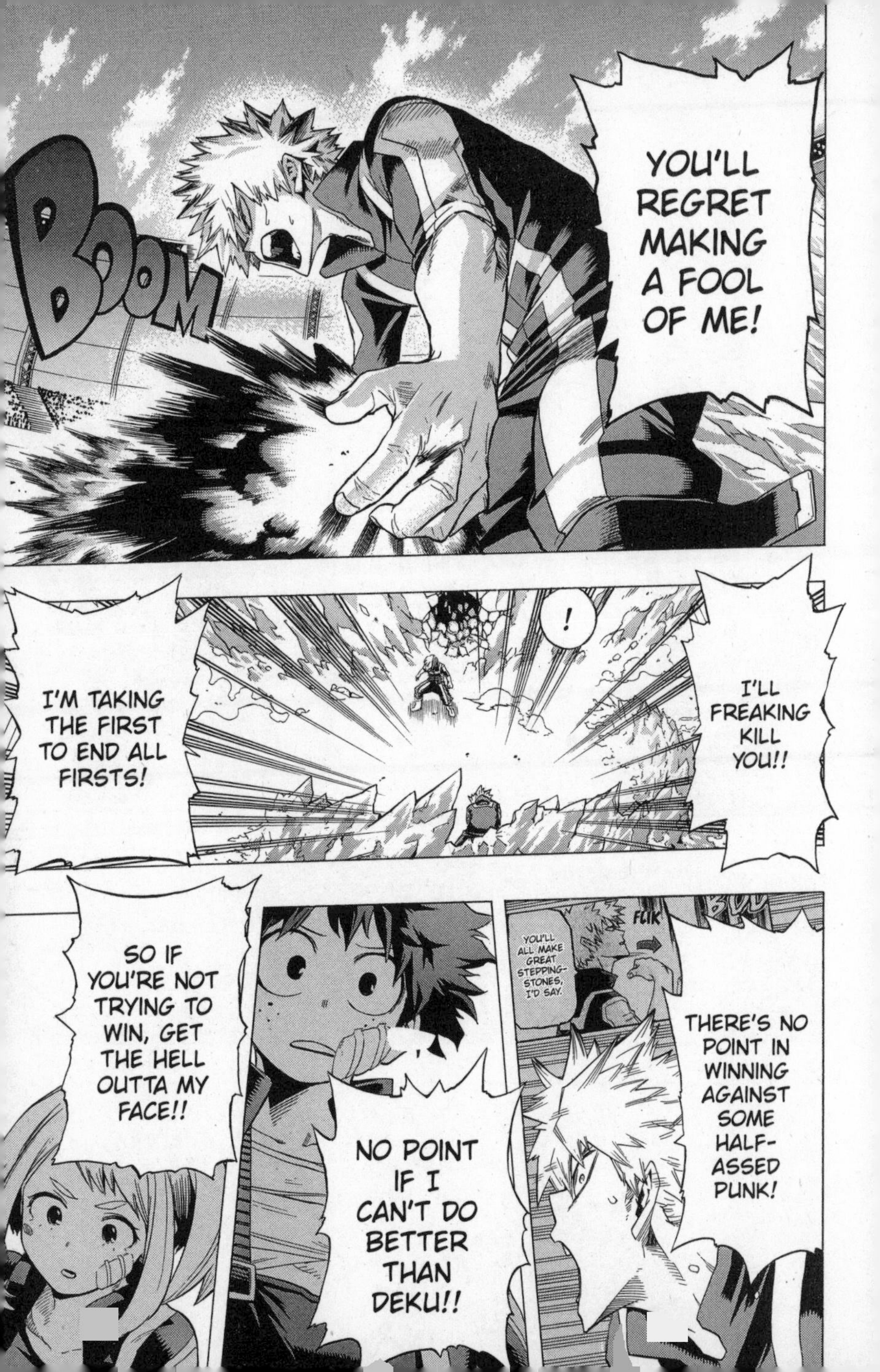
BOOM
YOU'LL REGRET MAKING A FOOL OF ME!
I'LL FREAKING KILL YOU!!
!
I'M TAKING THE FIRST TO END ALL FIRSTS!
FLIK
YOU'LL ALL MAKE GREAT STEPPING-STONES, I'D SAY.
THERE'S NO POINT IN WINNING AGAINST SOME HALF-ASSED PUNK!
NO POINT IF I CAN'T DO BETTER THAN DEKU!!
SO IF YOU'RE NOT TRYING TO WIN, GET THE HELL OUTTA MY FACE!!

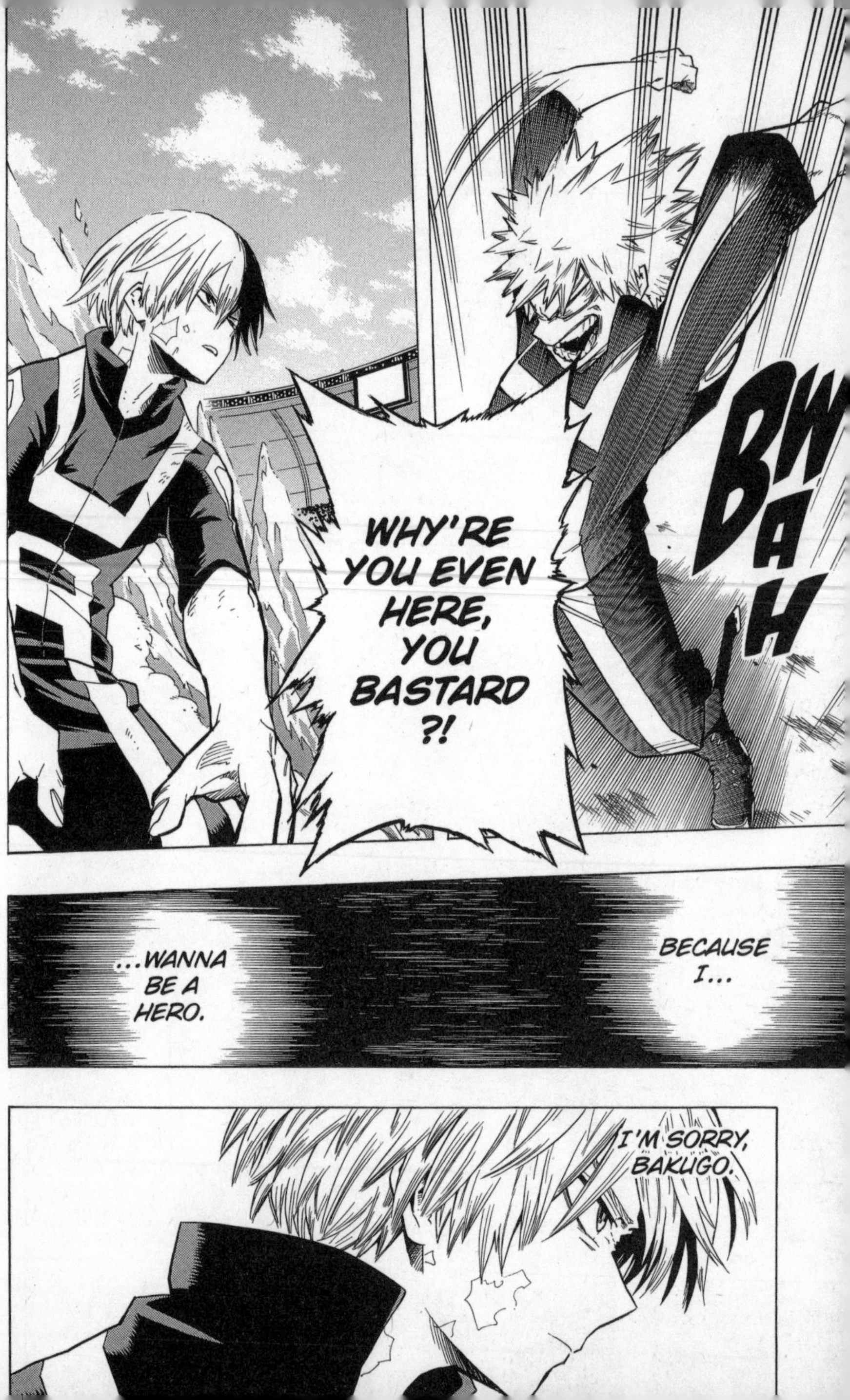
BWAH
WHY'RE YOU EVEN HERE, YOU BASTARD ?!
BECAUSE I...
...WANNA BE A HERO.
I'M SORRY, BAKUGO.

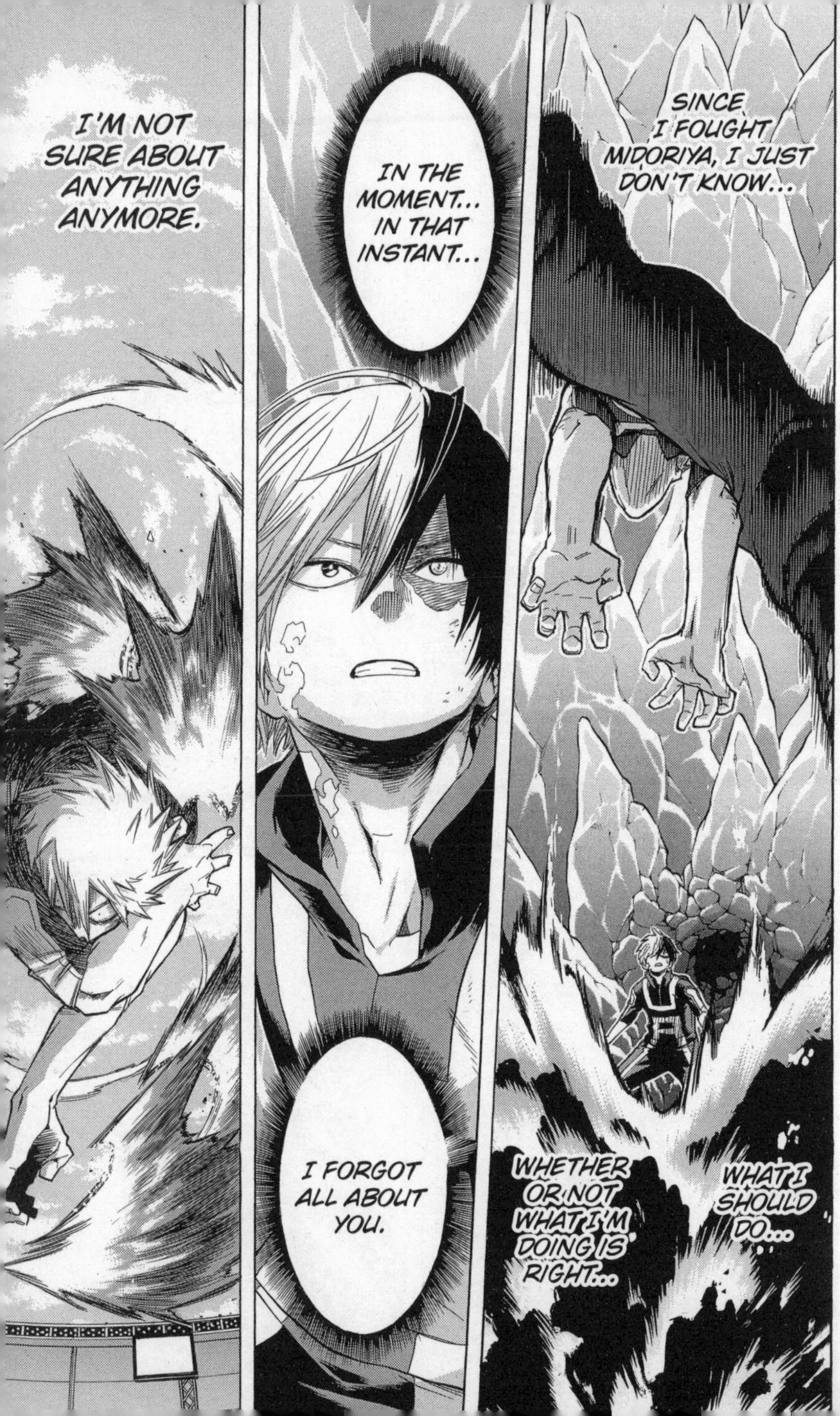
SINCE I FOUGHT MIDORIYA, I JUST DON'T KNOW...
WHAT I SHOULD DO...
WHETHER OR NOT WHAT I'M DOING IS RIGHT...
IN THE MOMENT... IN THAT INSTANT...
I FORGOT ALL ABOUT YOU.
I'M NOT SURE ABOUT ANYTHING ANYMORE.

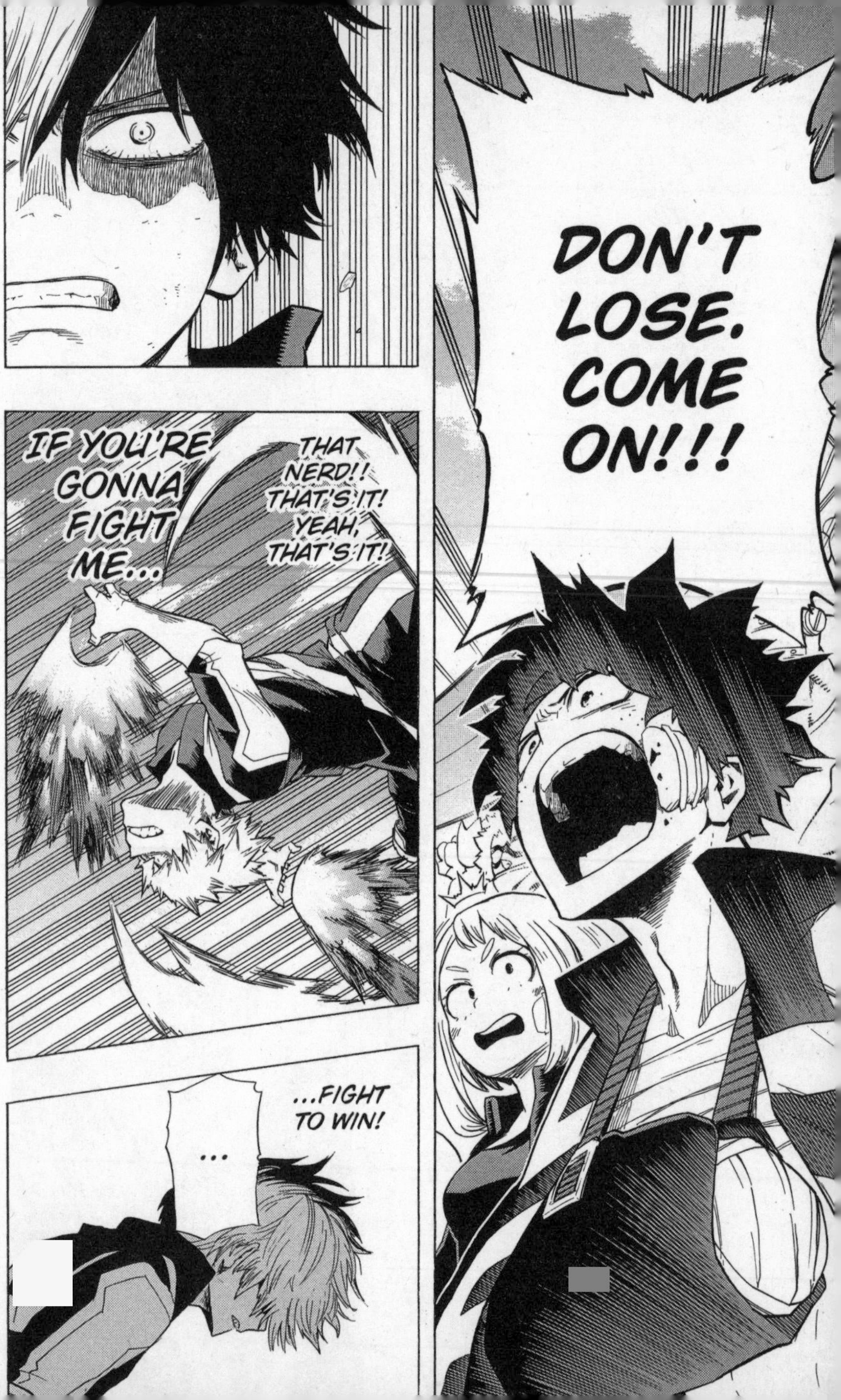
DON'T LOSE. COME ON!!!
THAT NERD!! THAT'S IT! YEAH, THAT'S IT!
IF YOU'RE GONNA FIGHT ME...
...FIGHT TO WIN!
...

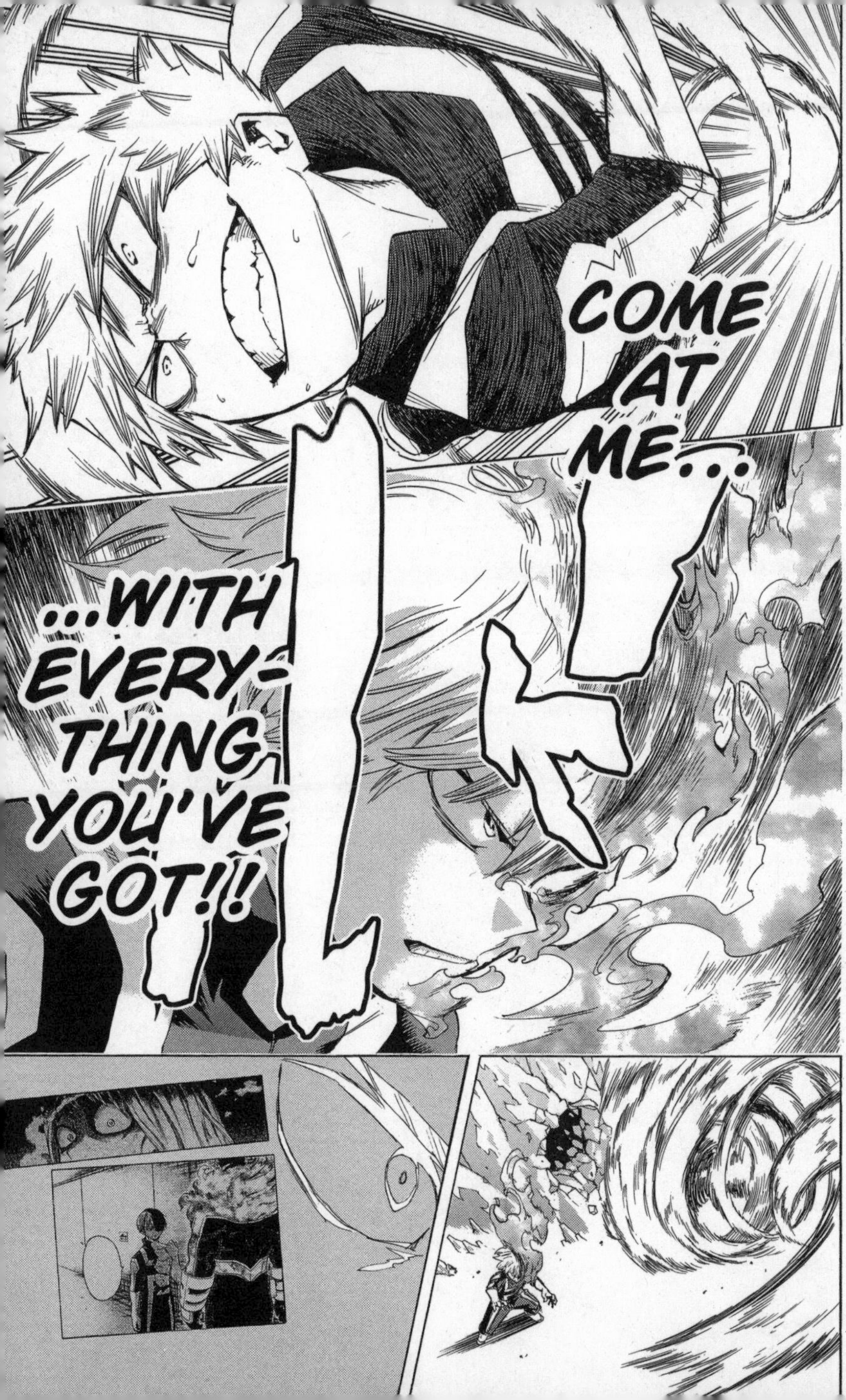
COME AT ME...
...WITH EVERY-THING YOU'VE GOT!!

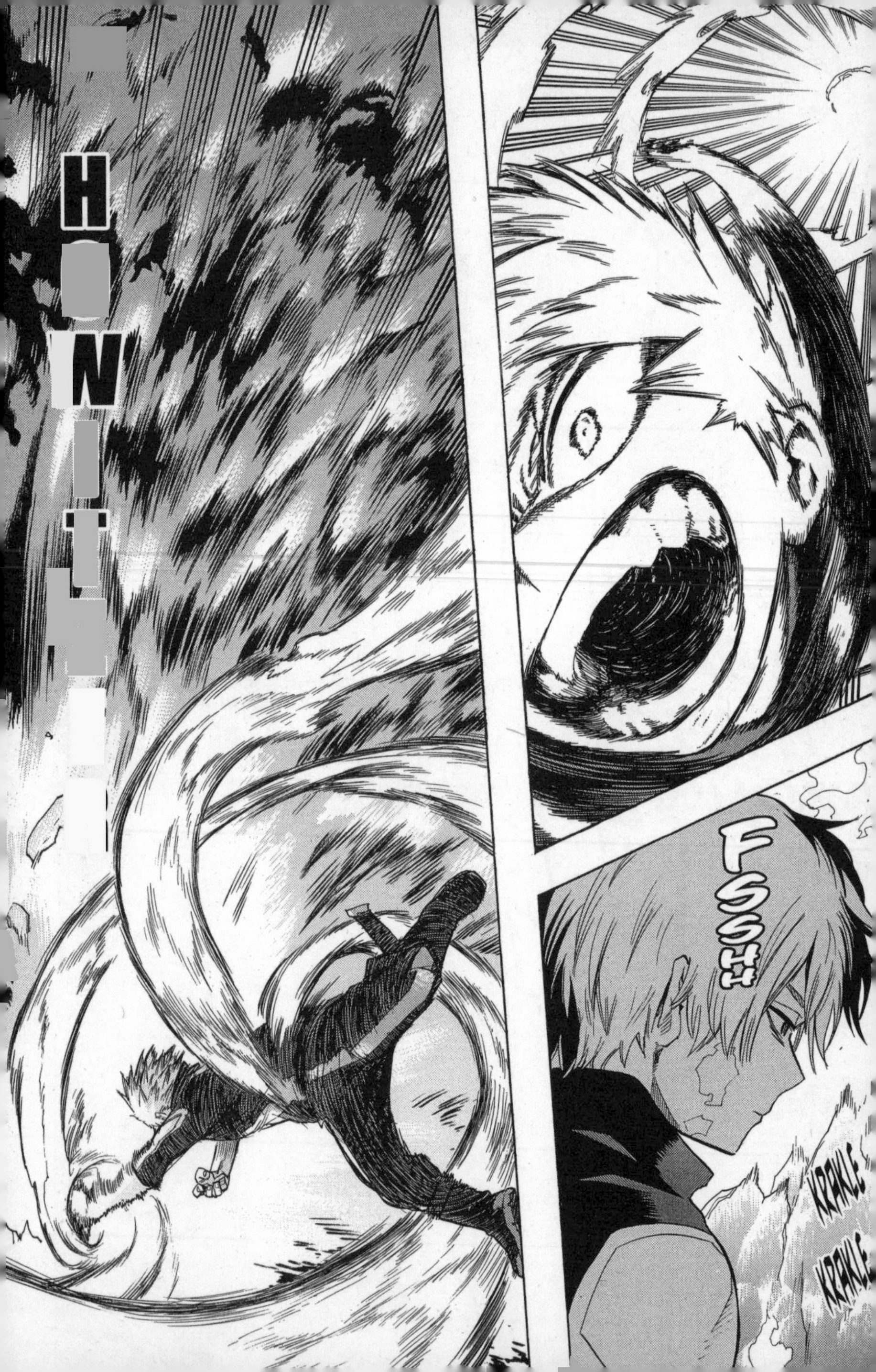
FSSHH
KRAKLE
KRAKLE

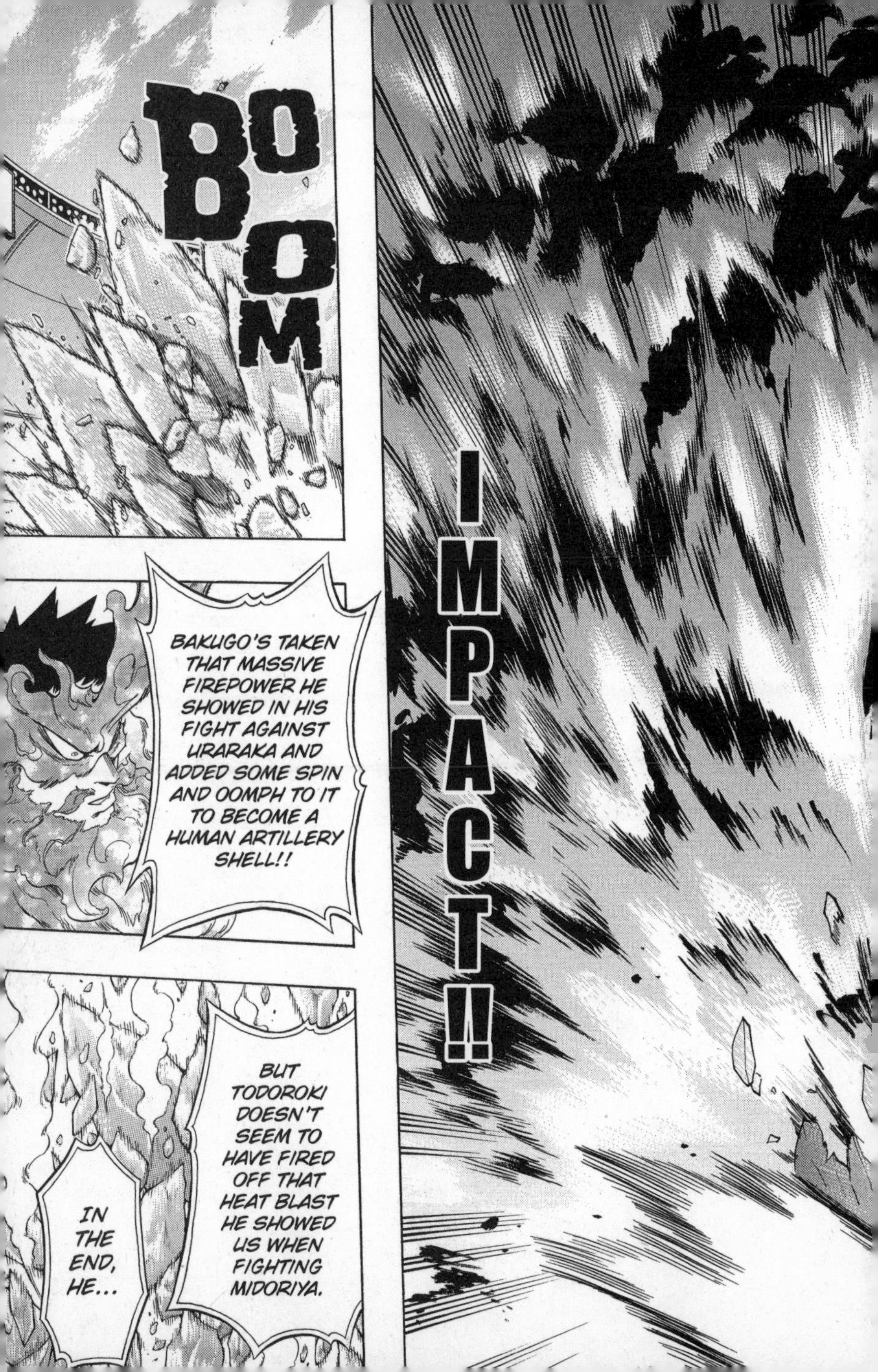
IMPACT!!
BOOM
BAKUGO'S TAKEN THAT MASSIVE FIREPOWER HE SHOWED IN HIS FIGHT AGAINST URARAKA AND ADDED SOME SPIN AND OOMPH TO IT TO BECOME A HUMAN ARTILLERY SHELL!!
BUT TODOROKI DOESN'T SEEM TO HAVE FIRED OFF THAT HEAT BLAST HE SHOWED US WHEN FIGHTING MIDORIYA.
IN THE END, HE...

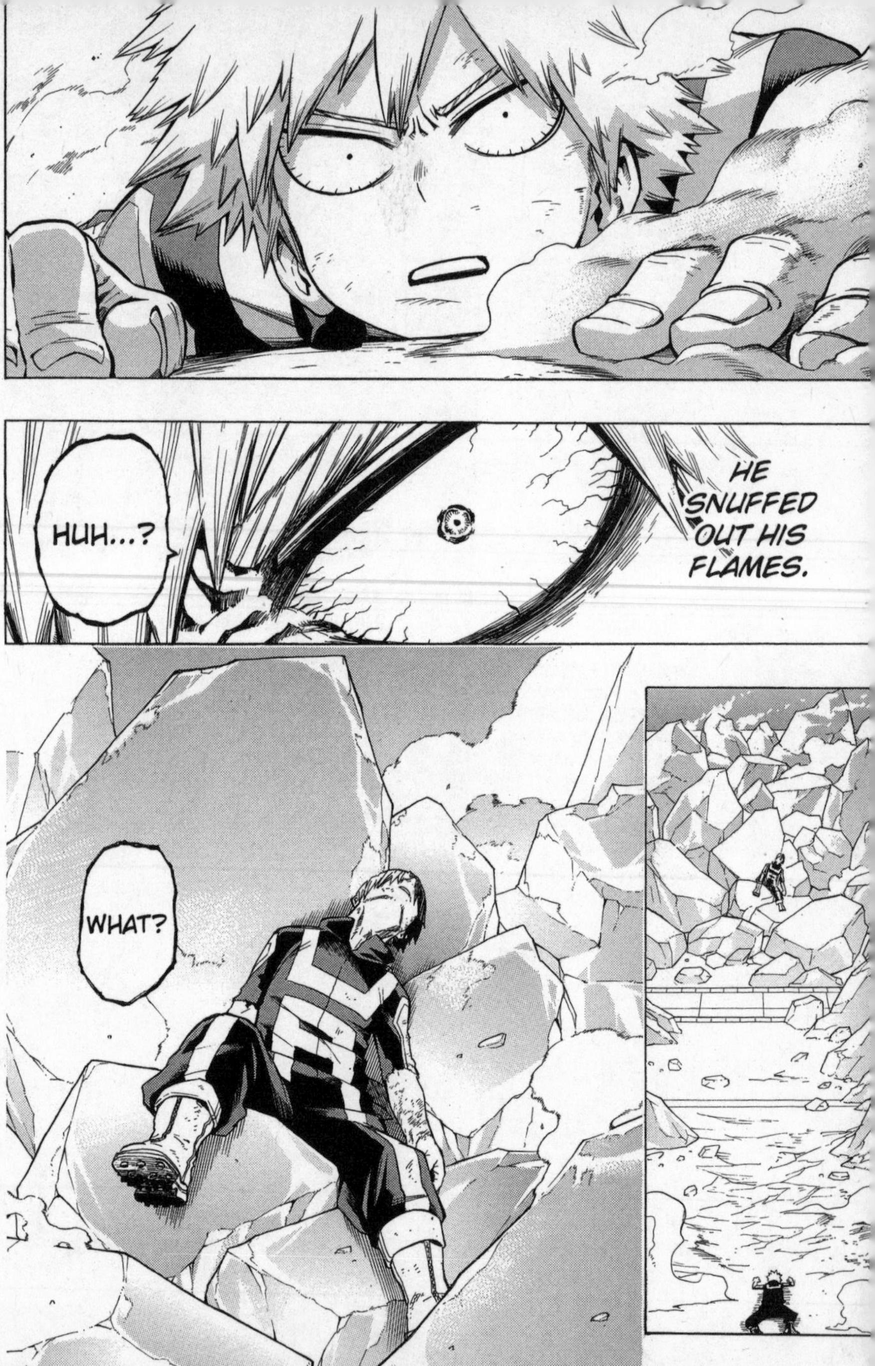
HE SNUFFED OUT HIS FLAMES.
HUH...?
WHAT?

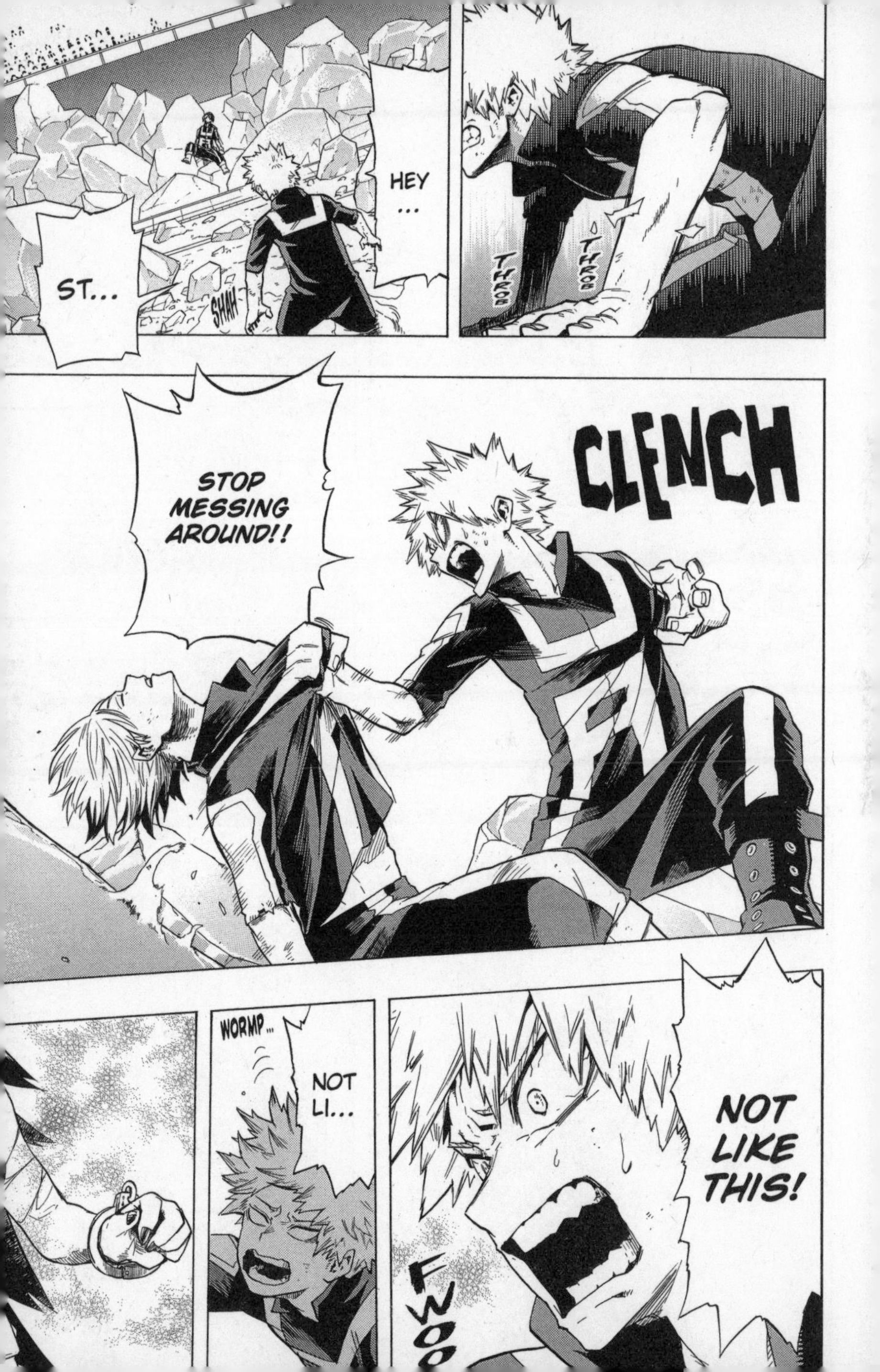
THROB
THROB
HEY ...
ST...
SHAH
CLENCH
STOP MESSING AROUND!!
NOT LIKE THIS!
FWOO
WORMP...
NOT LI...

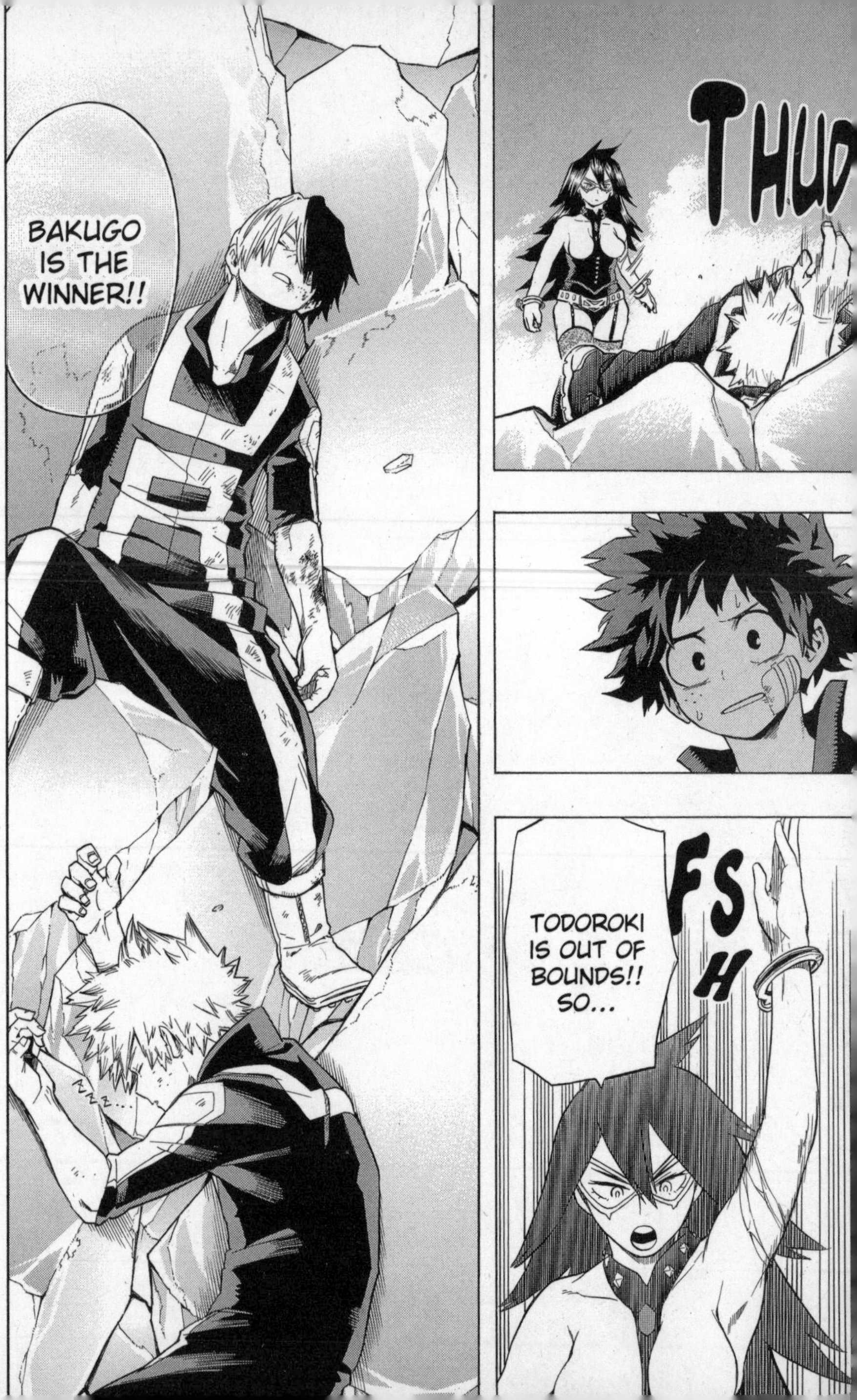
THUD
FSH
TODOROKI IS OUT OF BOUNDS!! SO...
BAKUGO IS THE WINNER!!
ZZZ...

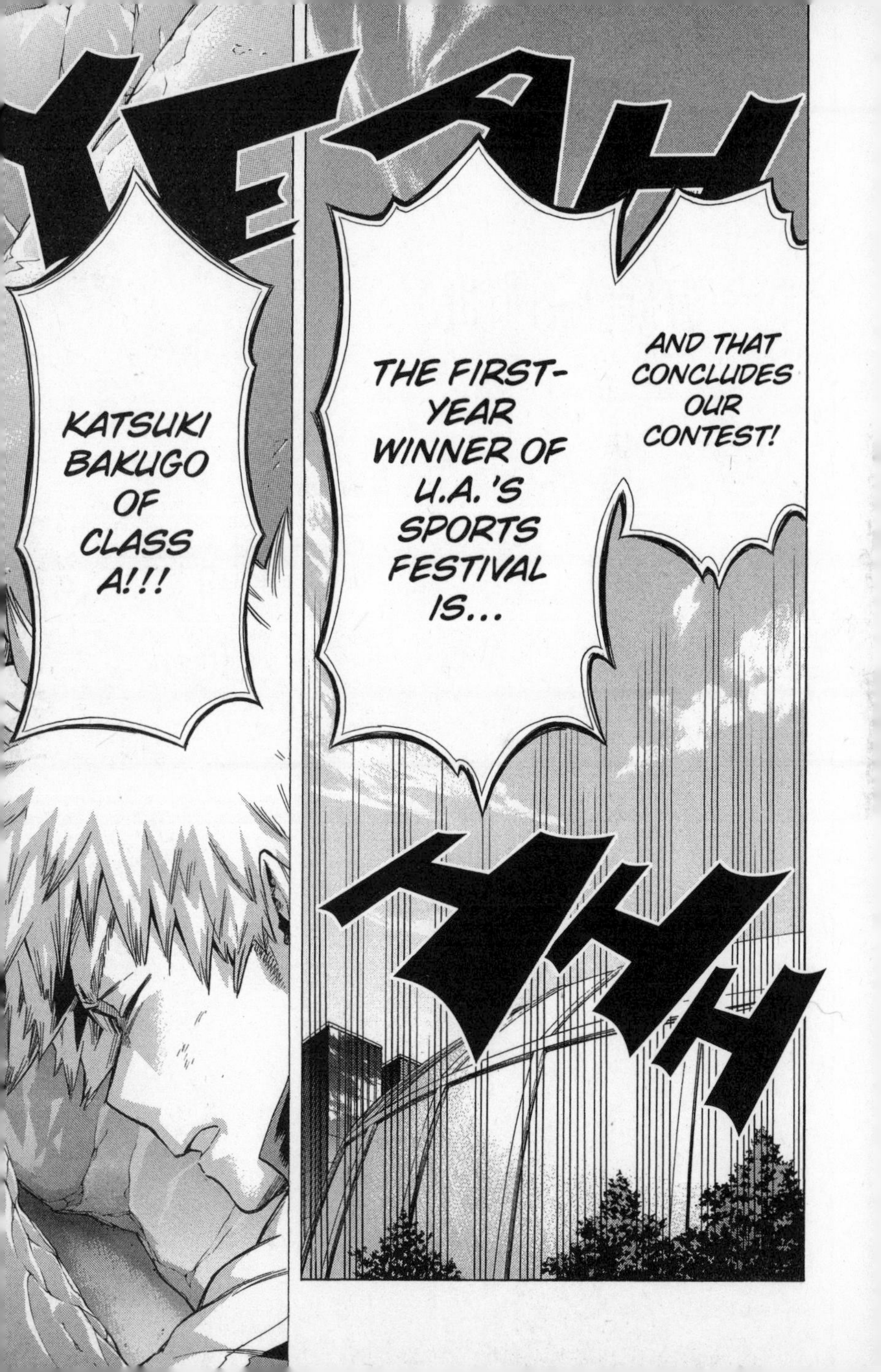
AND THAT CONCLUDES OUR CONTEST!
THE FIRST-YEAR WINNER OF U.A.'S SPORTS FESTIVAL IS...
KATSUKI BAKUGO OF CLASS A!!!
YEAH

NIRENGEKI SHODA [15]

STREET CLOTHES

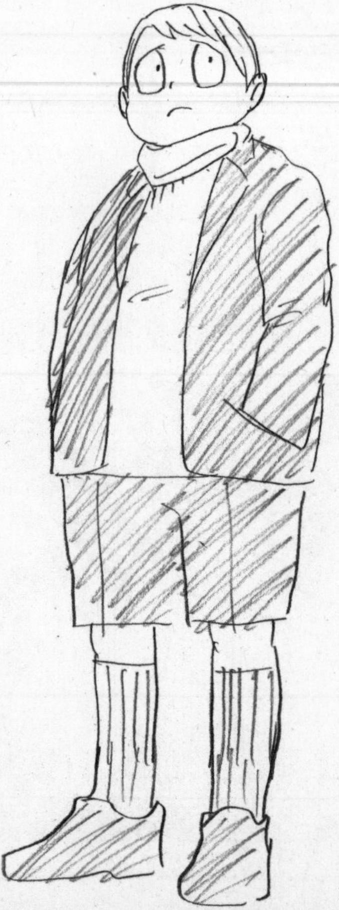

Birthday: 2/2
Height: 165 cm
Favorite Thing: Watching boxing matches

BEHIND THE SCENES
This is my greatest naming achievement to date. I feel like he's another one who was originally a member of Class A.

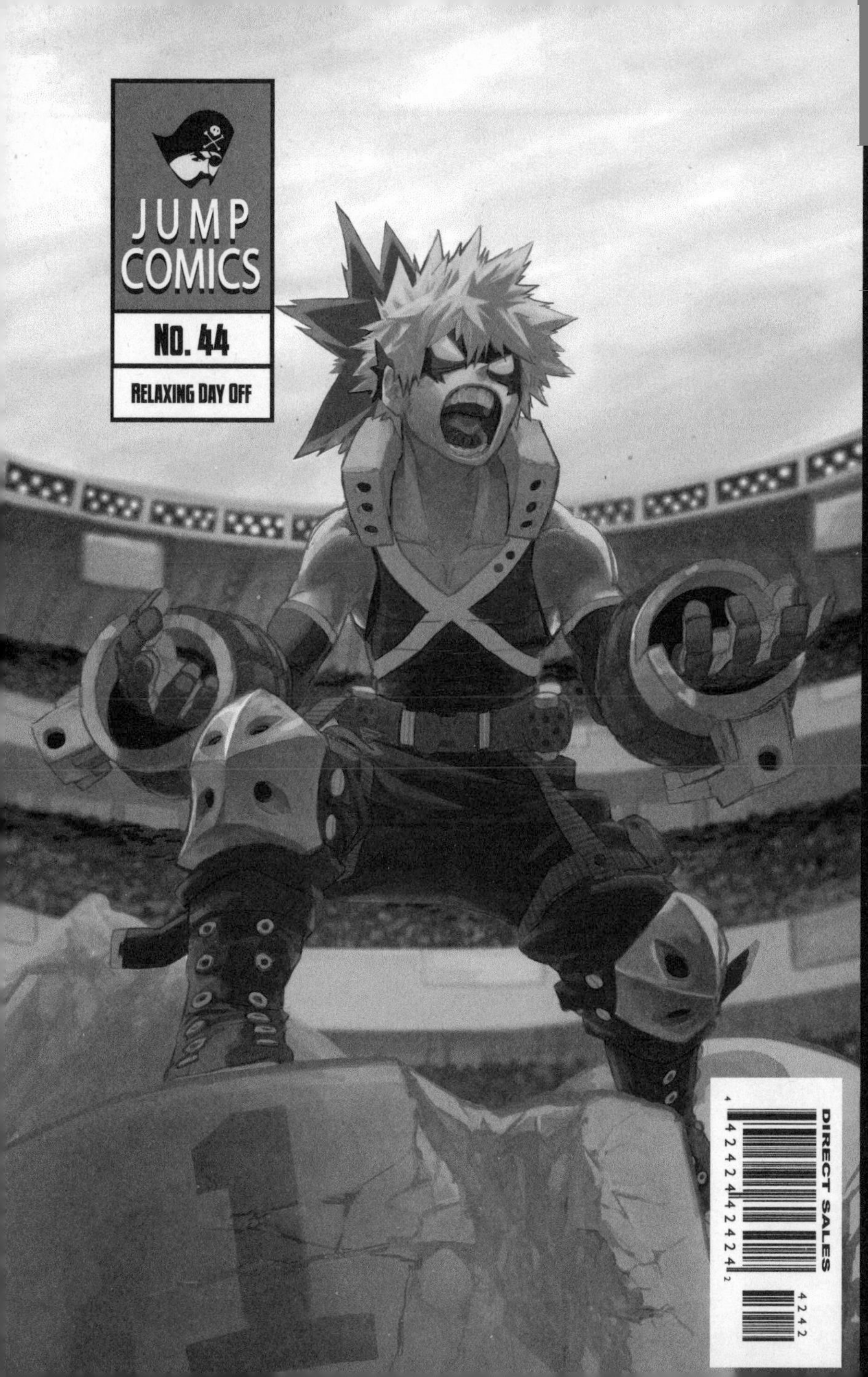
JUMP COMICS
NO. 44
RELAXING DAY OFF
DIRECT SALES

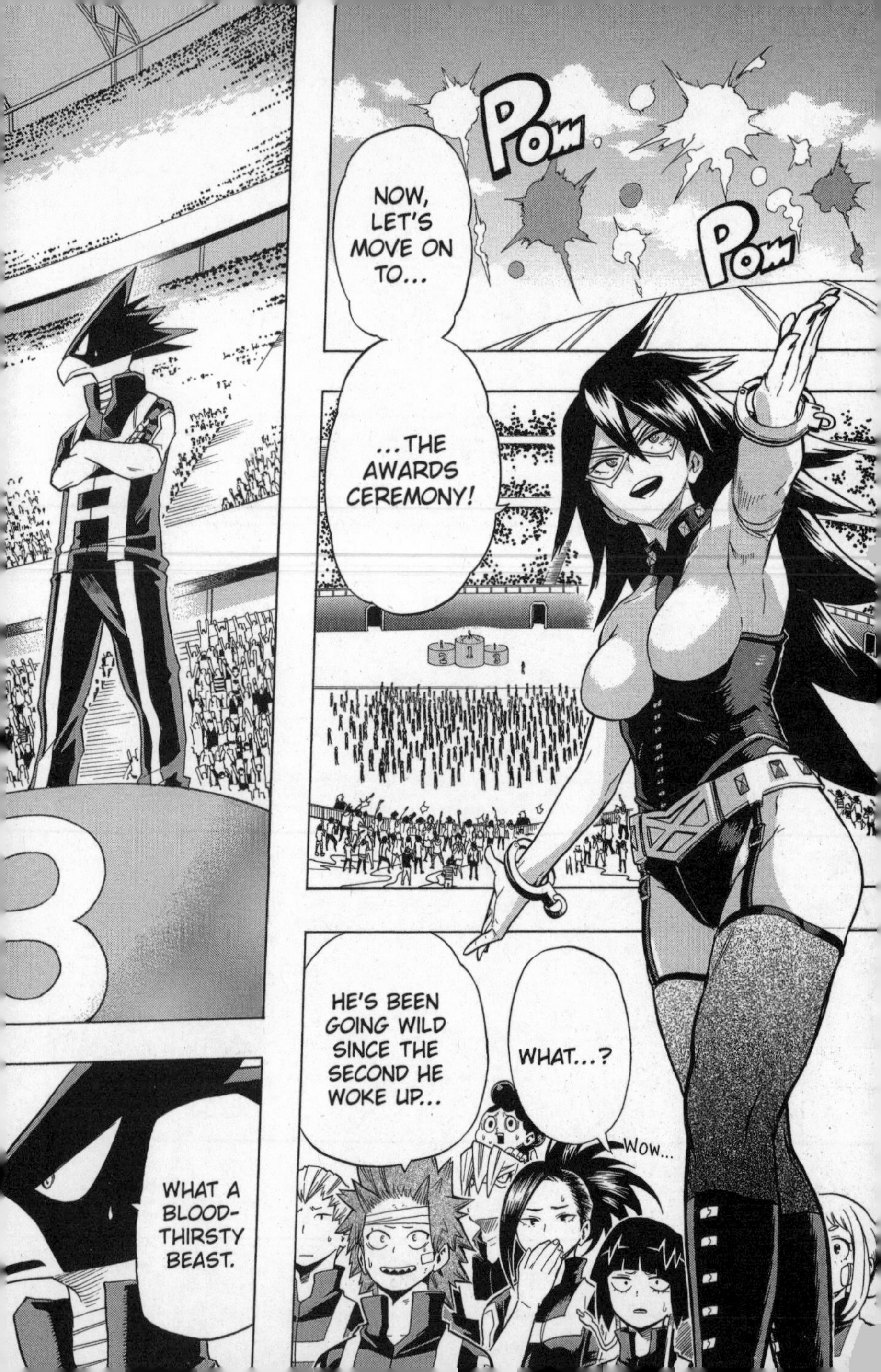
POW
POW
NOW, LET'S MOVE ON TO...
...THE AWARDS CEREMONY!
WHAT...?
HE'S BEEN GOING WILD SINCE THE SECOND HE WOKE UP...
WOW...
WHAT A BLOOD-THIRSTY BEAST.

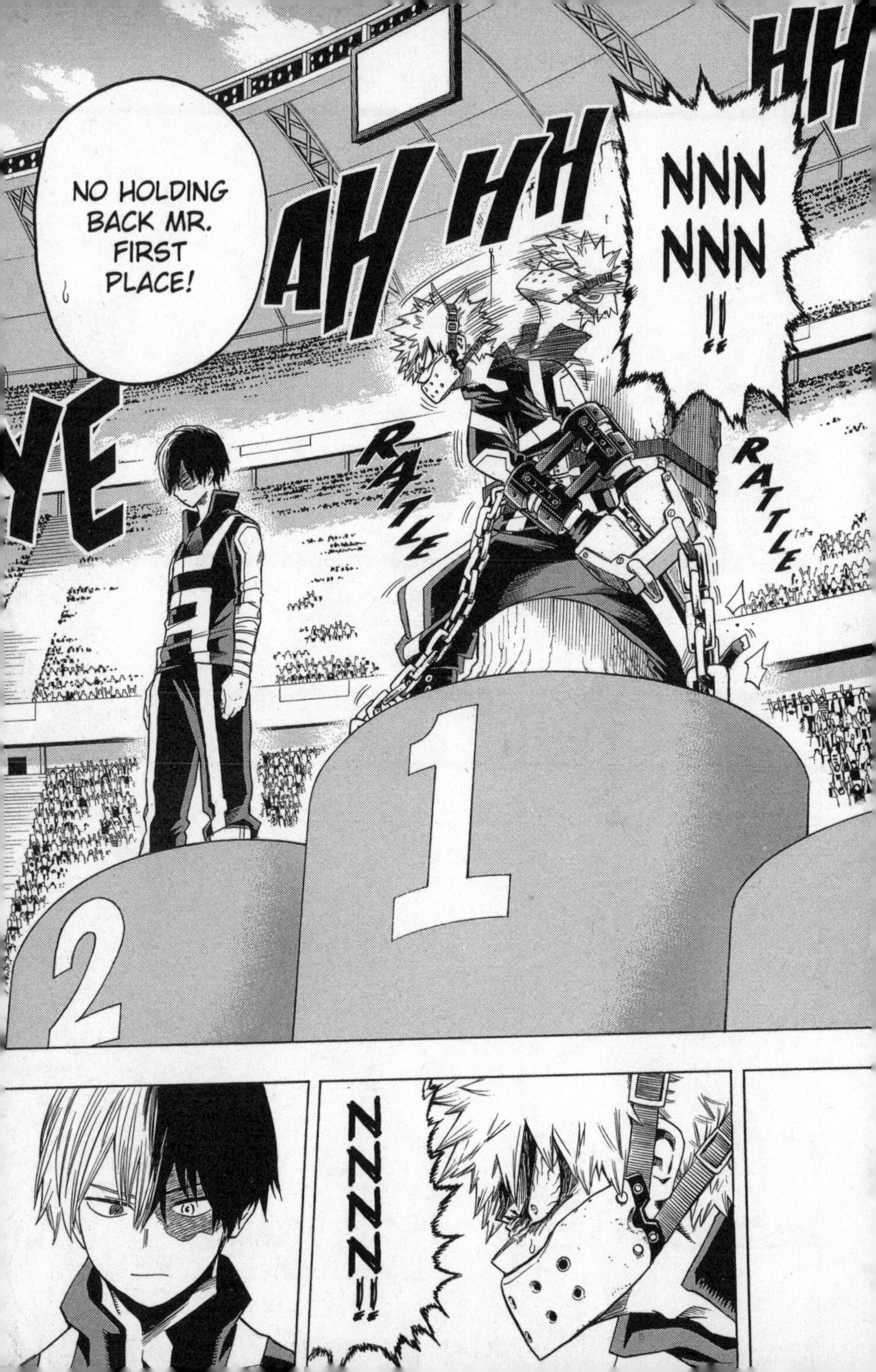
HH
NNN
NNN
!!
AH HH
NO HOLDING BACK MR. FIRST PLACE!
RATTLE
RATTLE
YE
NNNN!!

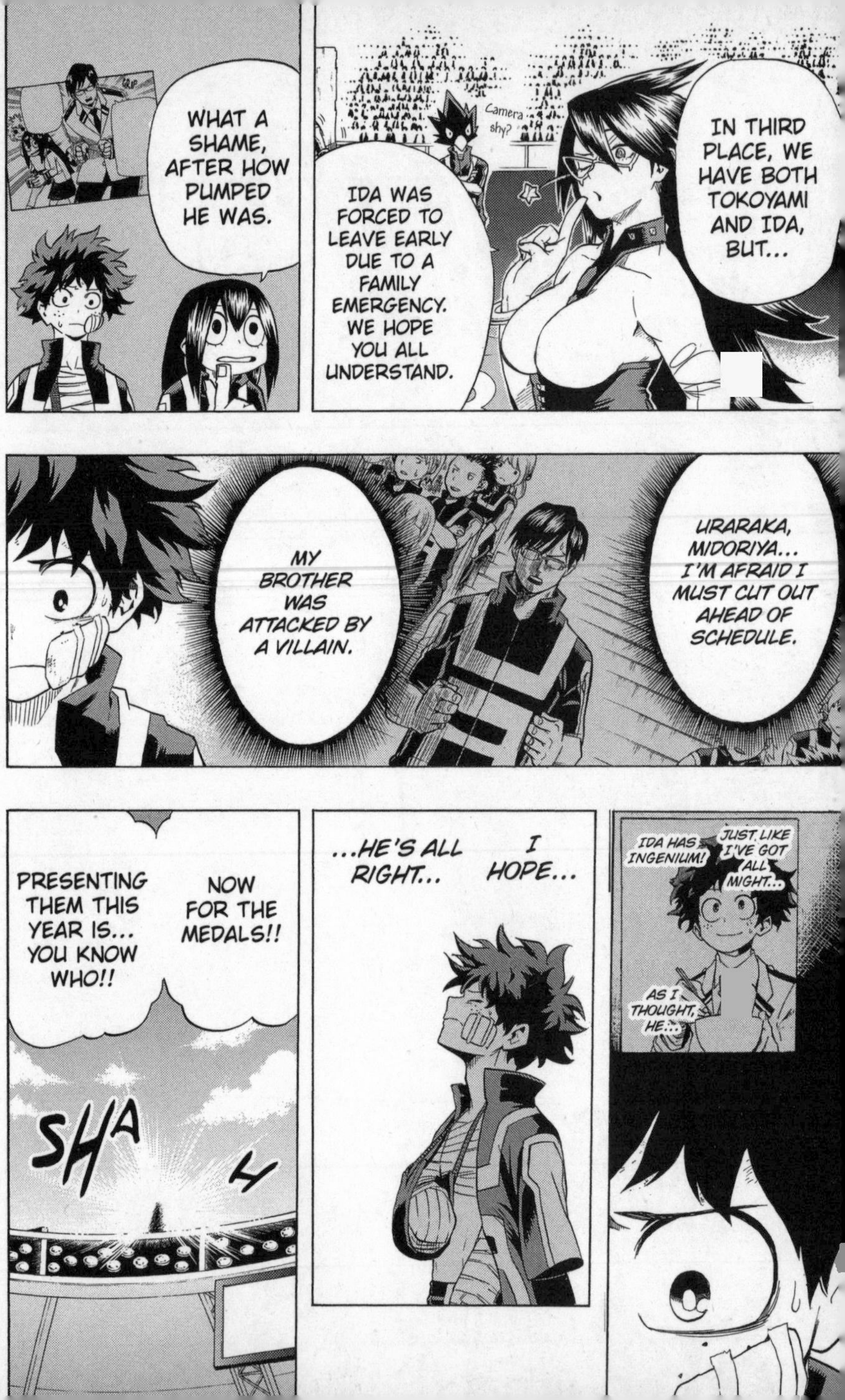
IN THIRD PLACE, WE HAVE BOTH TOKOYAMI AND IDA, BUT...
IDA WAS FORCED TO LEAVE EARLY DUE TO A FAMILY EMERGENCY. WE HOPE YOU ALL UNDERSTAND.
Camera shy?
WHAT A SHAME, AFTER HOW PUMPED HE WAS.
URARAKA, MIDORIYA... I'M AFRAID I MUST CUT OUT AHEAD OF SCHEDULE.
MY BROTHER WAS ATTACKED BY A VILLAIN.
JUST, LIKE I'VE GOT ALL MIGHT...
IDA HAS INGENIUM!
AS I THOUGHT, HE...
I HOPE...
...HE'S ALL RIGHT...
NOW FOR THE MEDALS!!
PRESENTING THEM THIS YEAR IS... YOU KNOW WHO!!
SHAAH

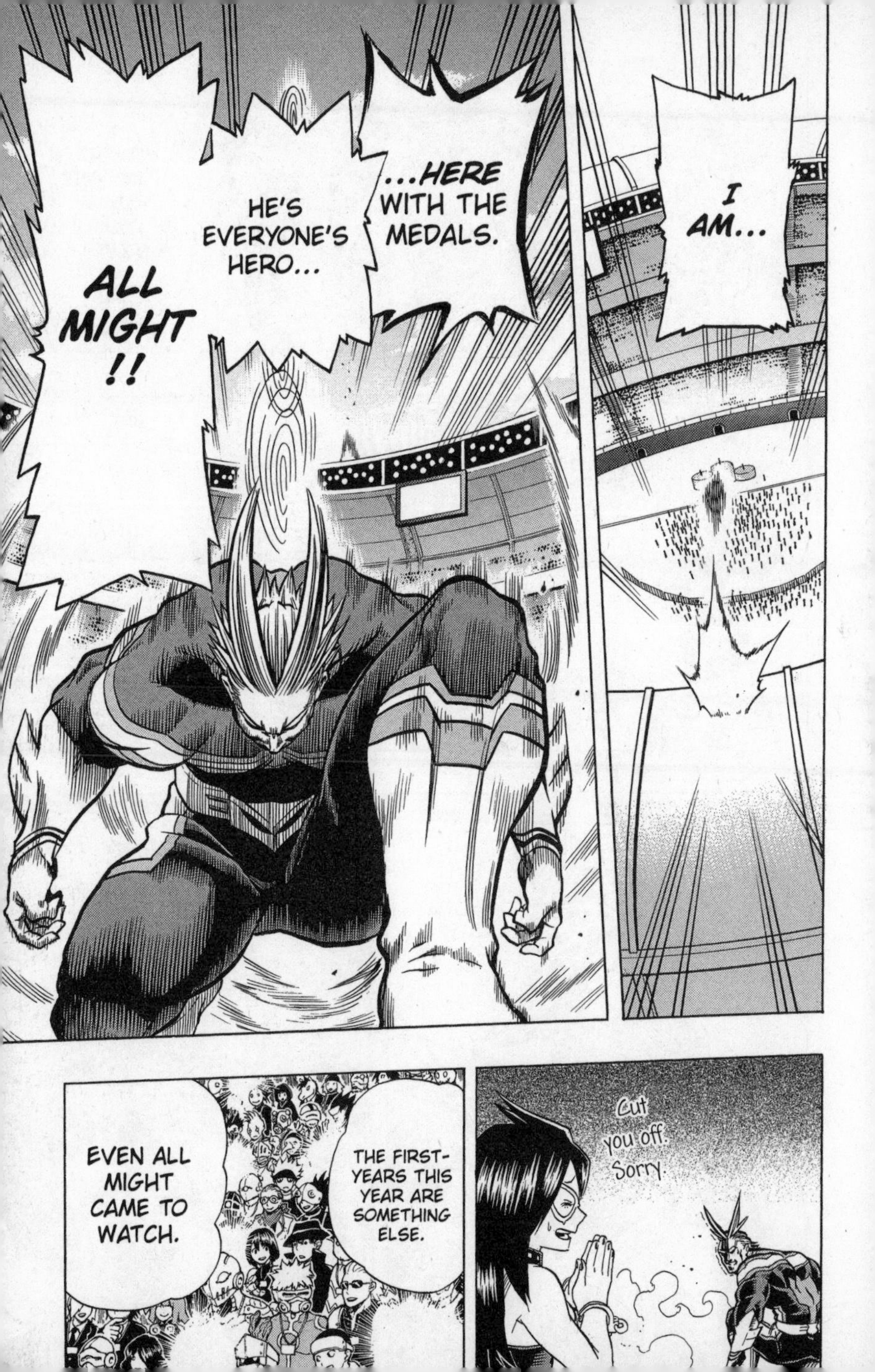
I AM...
...HERE WITH THE MEDALS.
HE'S EVERYONE'S HERO...
ALL MIGHT !!
Cut you off. Sorry
THE FIRST-YEARS THIS YEAR ARE SOMETHING ELSE.
EVEN ALL MIGHT CAME TO WATCH.

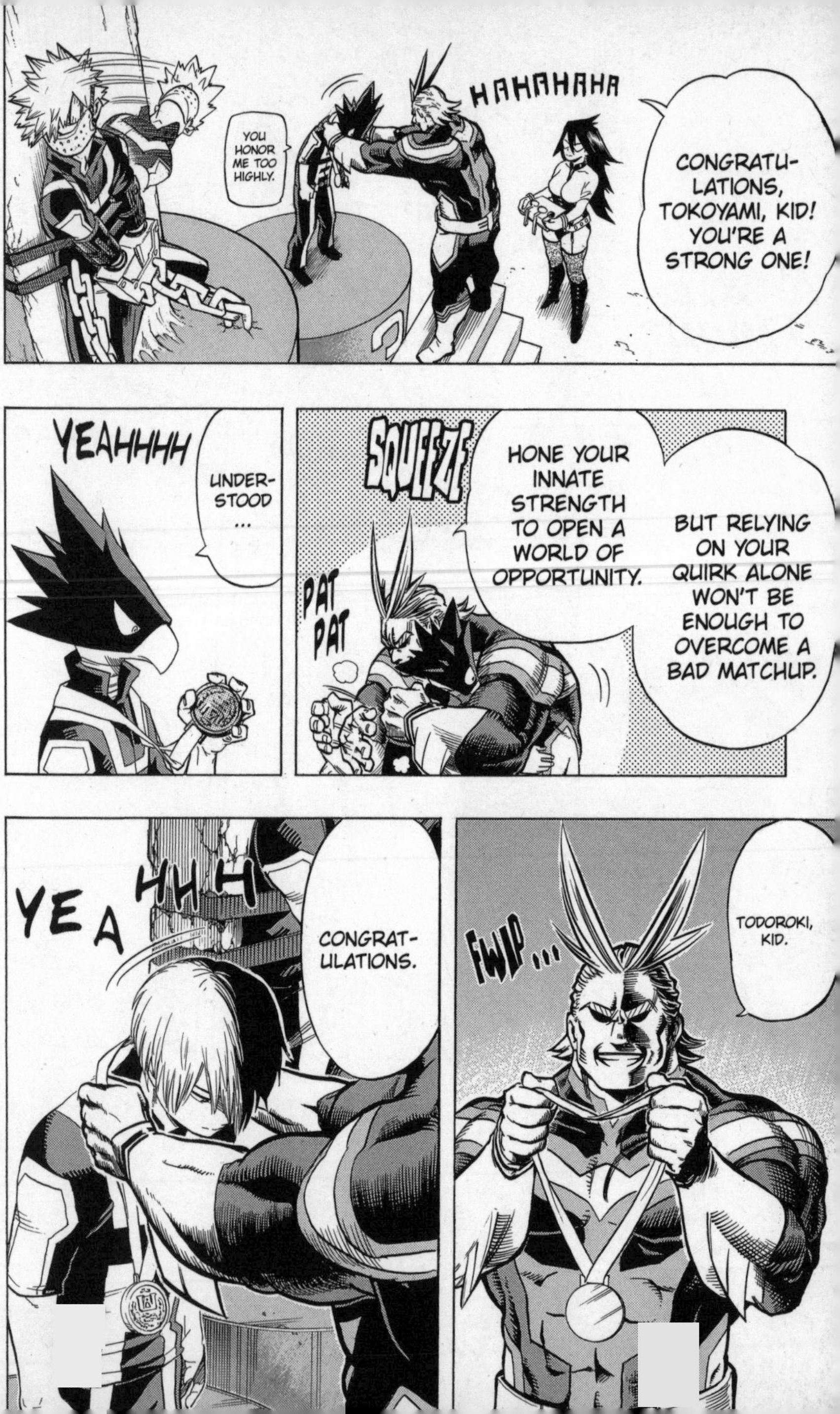
CONGRATULATIONS, TOKOYAMI, KID! YOU'RE A STRONG ONE!
HAHAHAHA
YOU HONOR ME TOO HIGHLY.
BUT RELYING ON YOUR QUIRK ALONE WON'T BE ENOUGH TO OVERCOME A BAD MATCHUP.
HONE YOUR INNATE STRENGTH TO OPEN A WORLD OF OPPORTUNITY.
SQUEEZE
PAT PAT
UNDERSTOOD ...
YEAHHHH
TODOROKI, KID.
FWIP ...
CONGRATULATIONS.
YEAHHH

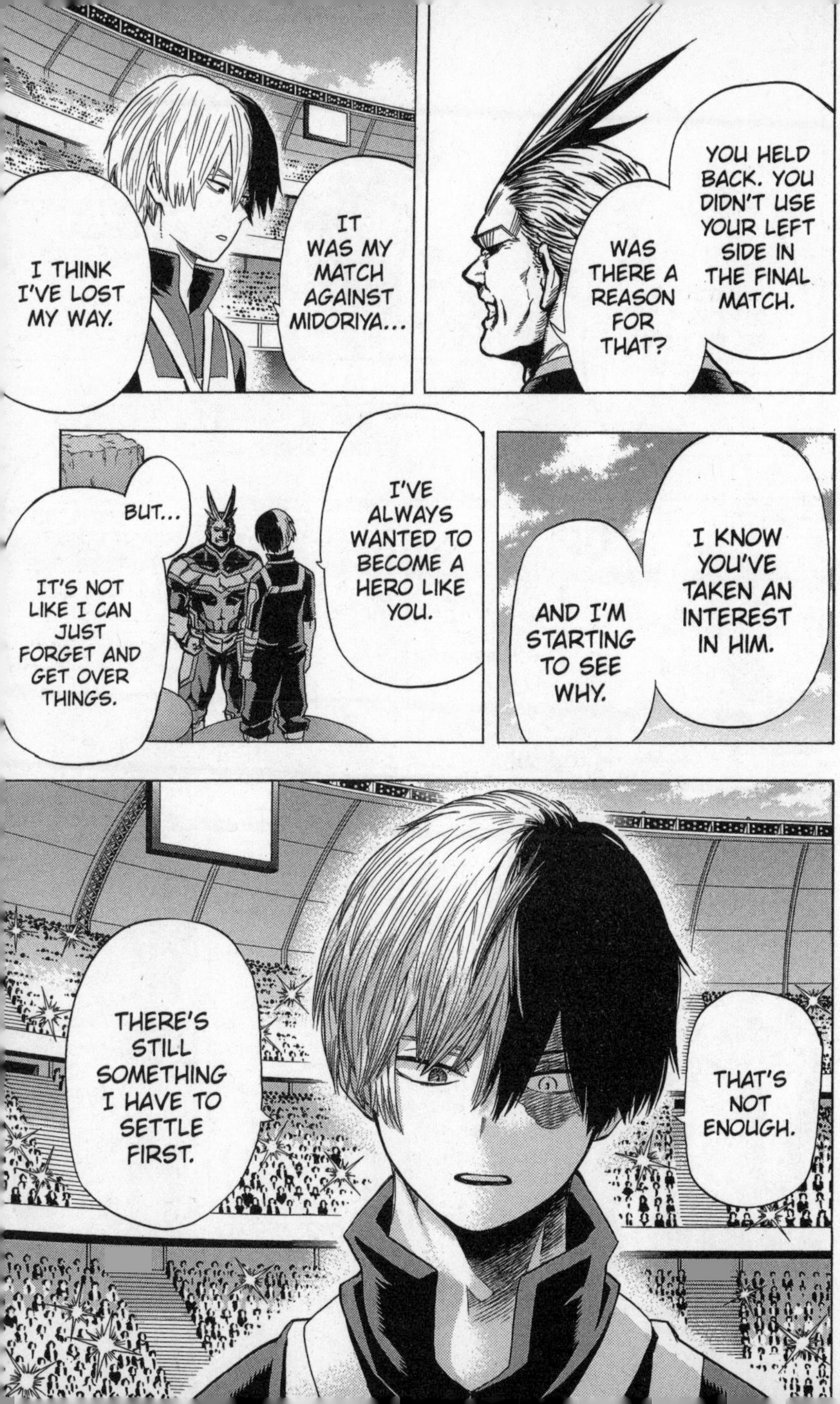
YOU HELD BACK. YOU DIDN'T USE YOUR LEFT SIDE IN THE FINAL MATCH.
WAS THERE A REASON FOR THAT?
IT WAS MY MATCH AGAINST MIDORIYA...
I THINK I'VE LOST MY WAY.
I KNOW YOU'VE TAKEN AN INTEREST IN HIM.
AND I'M STARTING TO SEE WHY.
I'VE ALWAYS WANTED TO BECOME A HERO LIKE YOU.
BUT...
IT'S NOT LIKE I CAN JUST FORGET AND GET OVER THINGS.
THAT'S NOT ENOUGH.
THERE'S STILL SOMETHING I HAVE TO SETTLE FIRST.

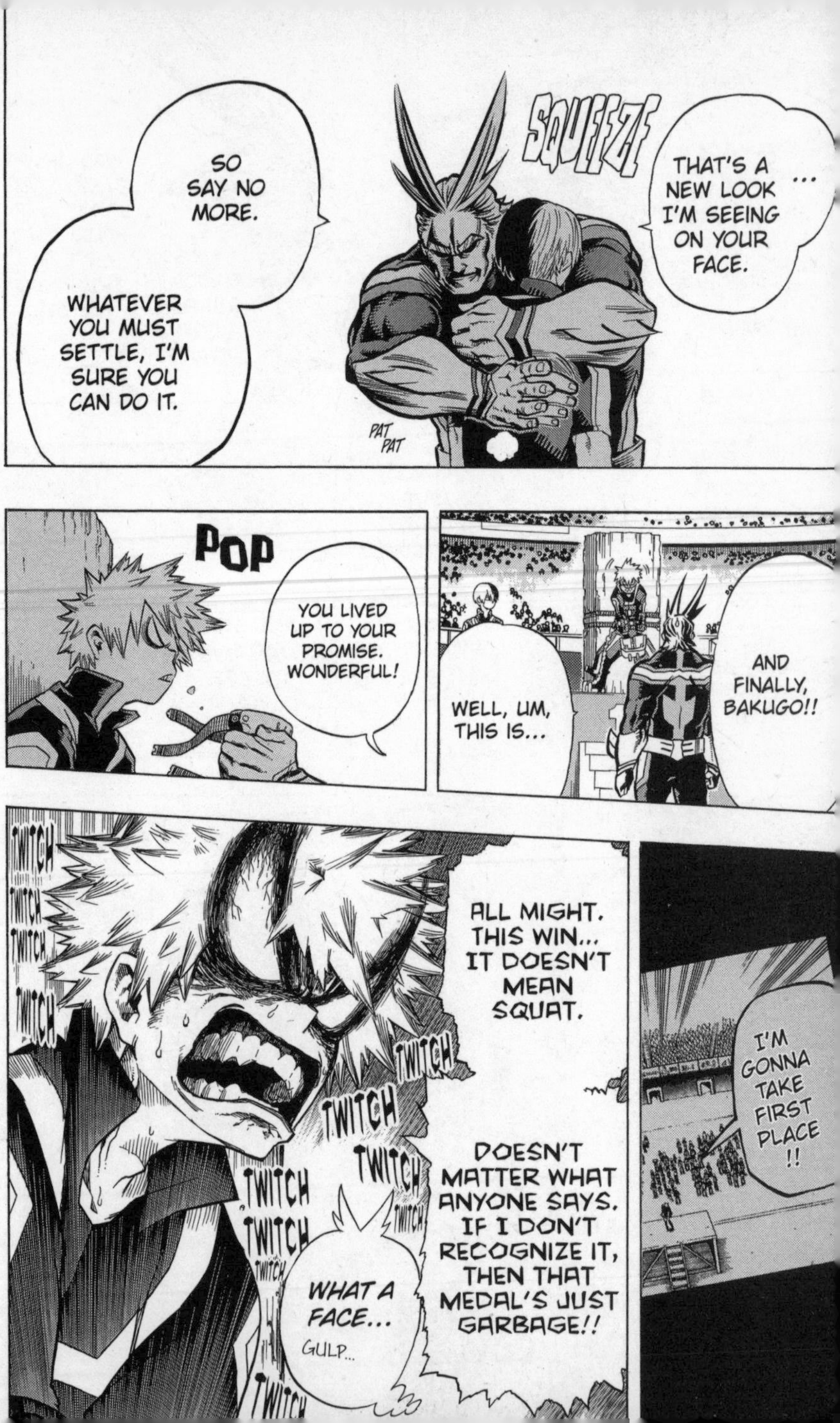
SQUEEZE
THAT'S A NEW LOOK I'M SEEING ON YOUR FACE. ...
SO SAY NO MORE.
WHATEVER YOU MUST SETTLE, I'M SURE YOU CAN DO IT.
PAT PAT
AND FINALLY, BAKUGO!!
WELL, UM, THIS IS...
POP
YOU LIVED UP TO YOUR PROMISE. WONDERFUL!
I'M GONNA TAKE FIRST PLACE!!
ALL MIGHT. THIS WIN... IT DOESN'T MEAN SQUAT.
DOESN'T MATTER WHAT ANYONE SAYS. IF I DON'T RECOGNIZE IT, THEN THAT MEDAL'S JUST GARBAGE!!
TWITCH TWITCH TWITCH TWITCH
TWITCH TWITCH TWITCH TWITCH TWITCH TWITCH TWITCH TWITCH
WHAT A FACE...
GULP...

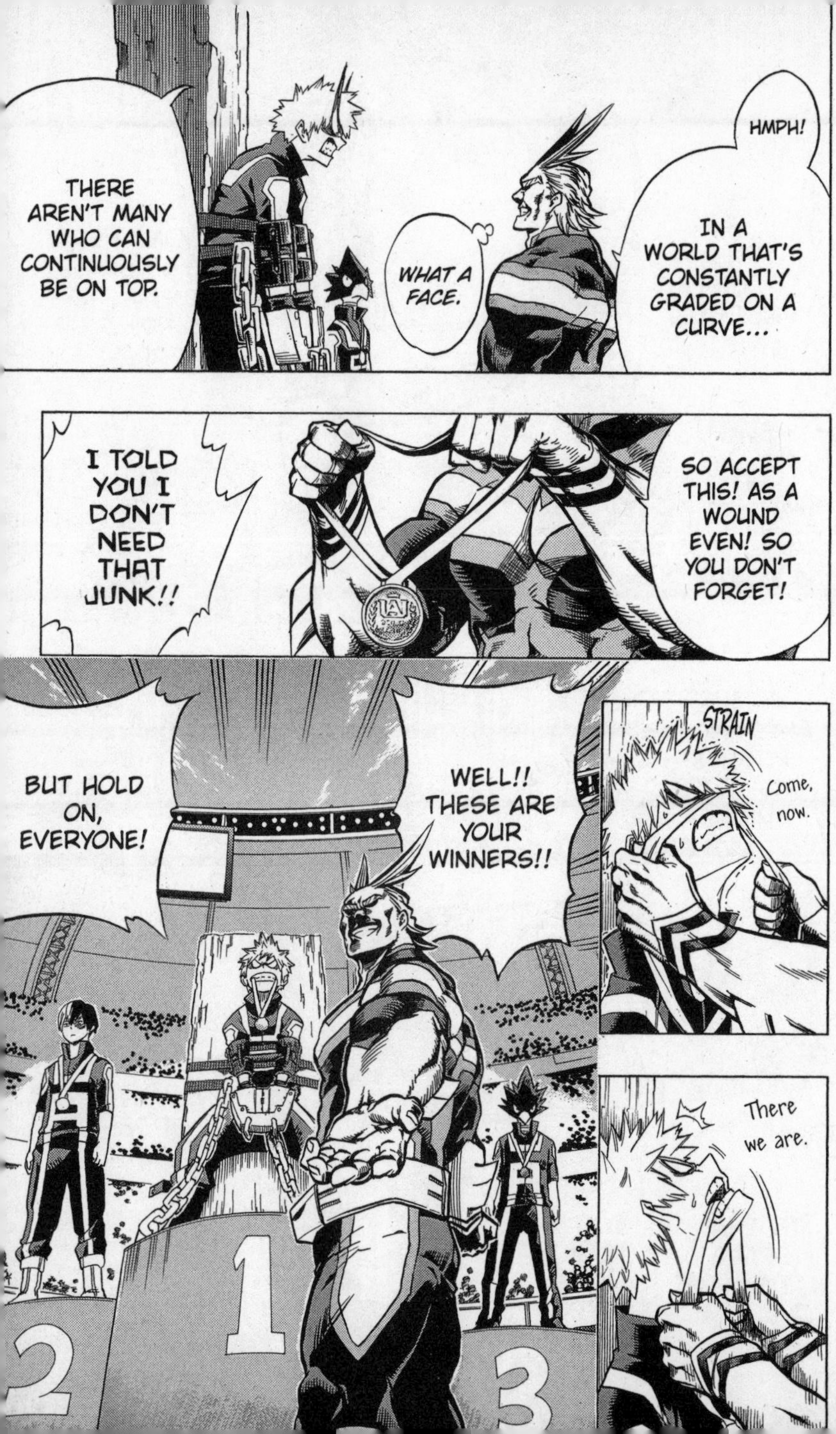
HMPH!
IN A WORLD THAT'S CONSTANTLY GRADED ON A CURVE...
WHAT A FACE.
THERE AREN'T MANY WHO CAN CONTINUOUSLY BE ON TOP.
SO ACCEPT THIS! AS A WOUND EVEN! SO YOU DON'T FORGET!
I TOLD YOU I DON'T NEED THAT JUNK!!
STRAIN
Come, now.
There we are.
WELL!! THESE ARE YOUR WINNERS!!
BUT HOLD ON, EVERYONE!

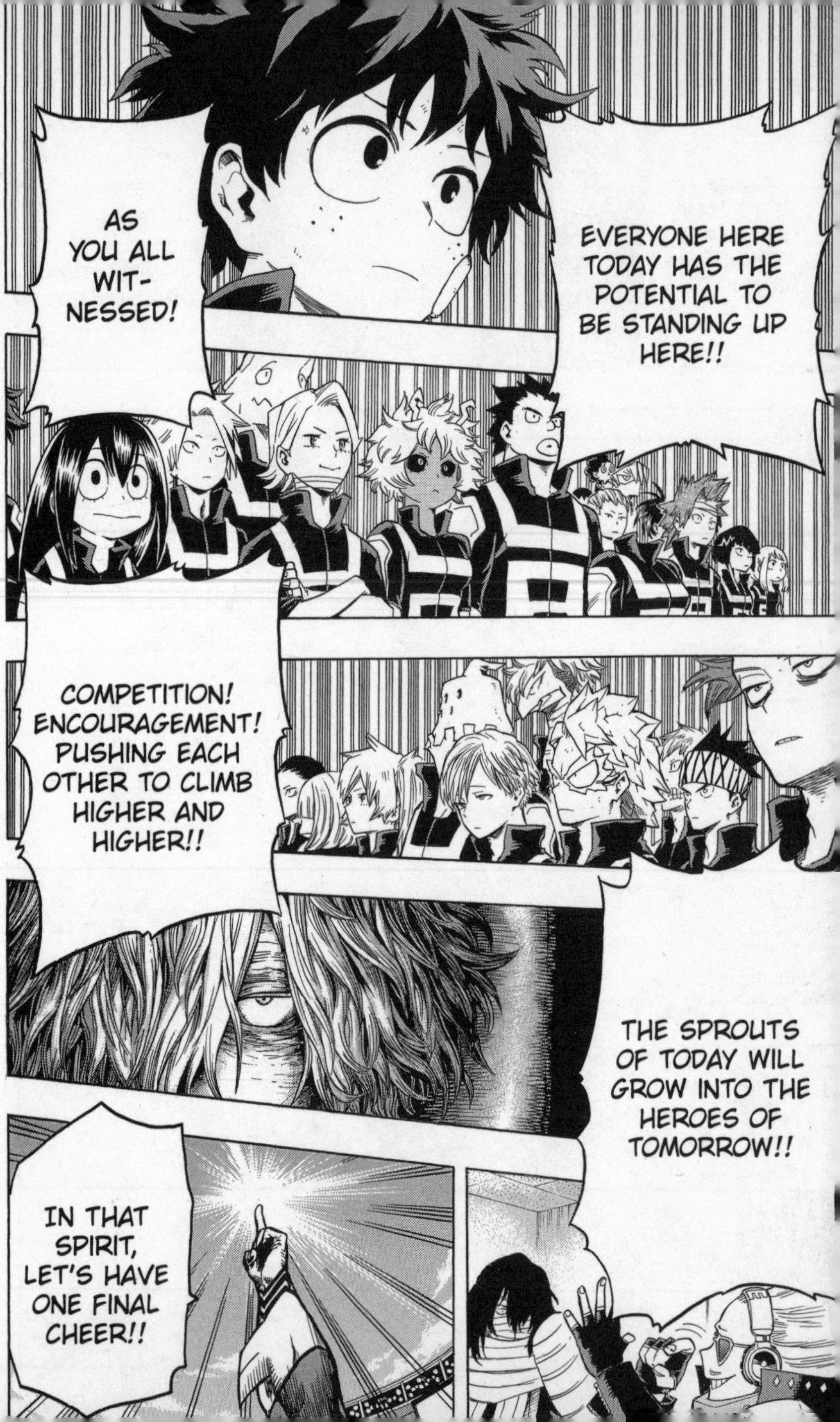
EVERYONE HERE TODAY HAS THE POTENTIAL TO BE STANDING UP HERE!!
AS YOU ALL WIT-NESSED!
COMPETITION! ENCOURAGEMENT! PUSHING EACH OTHER TO CLIMB HIGHER AND HIGHER!!
THE SPROUTS OF TODAY WILL GROW INTO THE HEROES OF TOMORROW!!
IN THAT SPIRIT, LET'S HAVE ONE FINAL CHEER!!

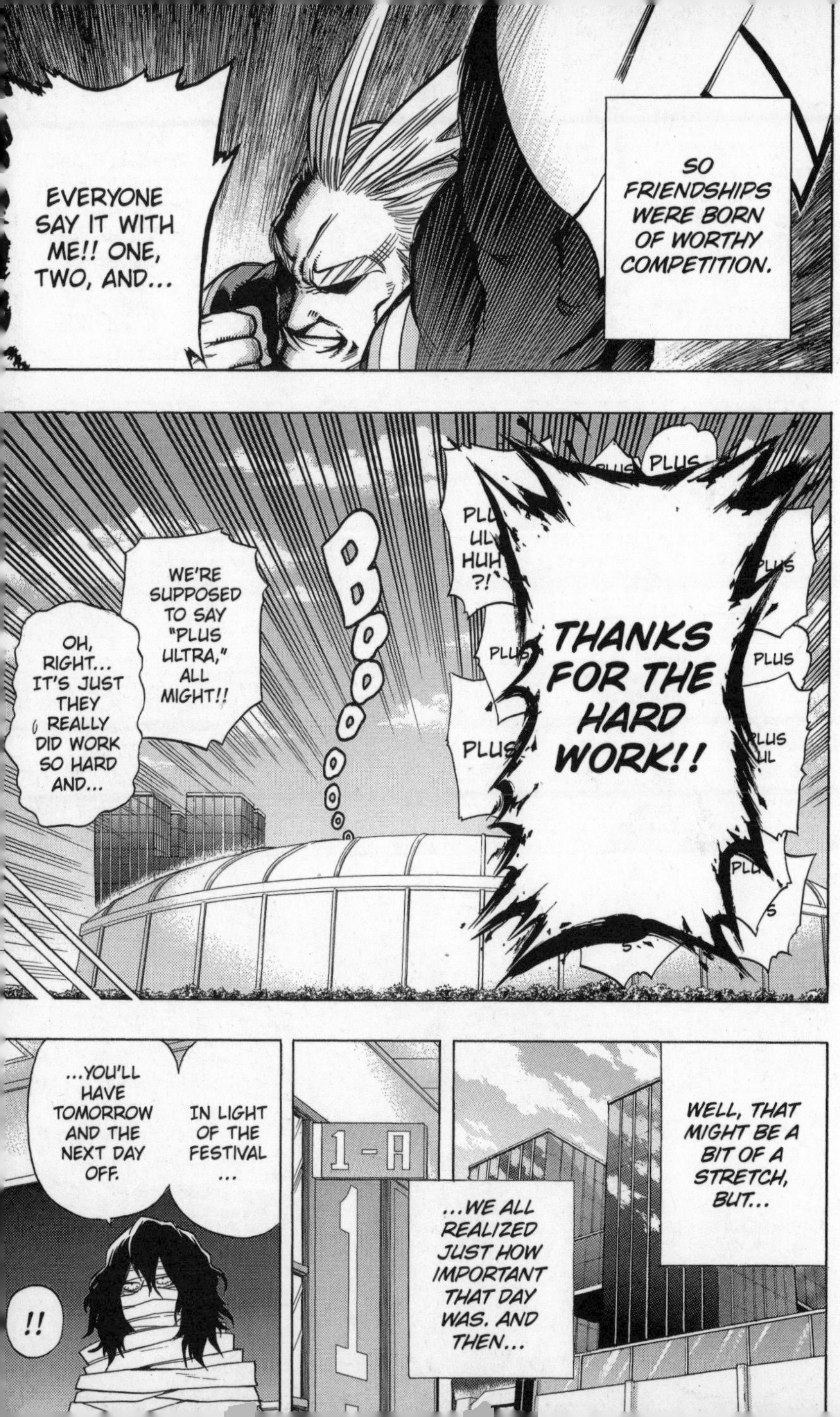
SO FRIENDSHIPS WERE BORN OF WORTHY COMPETITION.
EVERYONE SAY IT WITH ME!! ONE, TWO, AND...
THANKS FOR THE HARD WORK!!
PLUS
PLUS
PLUS
PLU UL HUH ?!
PLUS
PLUS
WE'RE SUPPOSED TO SAY "PLUS ULTRA," ALL MIGHT!!
OH, RIGHT... IT'S JUST THEY REALLY DID WORK SO HARD AND...
BOOOOOOOO
WELL, THAT MIGHT BE A BIT OF A STRETCH, BUT...
...WE ALL REALIZED JUST HOW IMPORTANT THAT DAY WAS. AND THEN...
1-A
IN LIGHT OF THE FESTIVAL ...
...YOU'LL HAVE TOMORROW AND THE NEXT DAY OFF.
!!

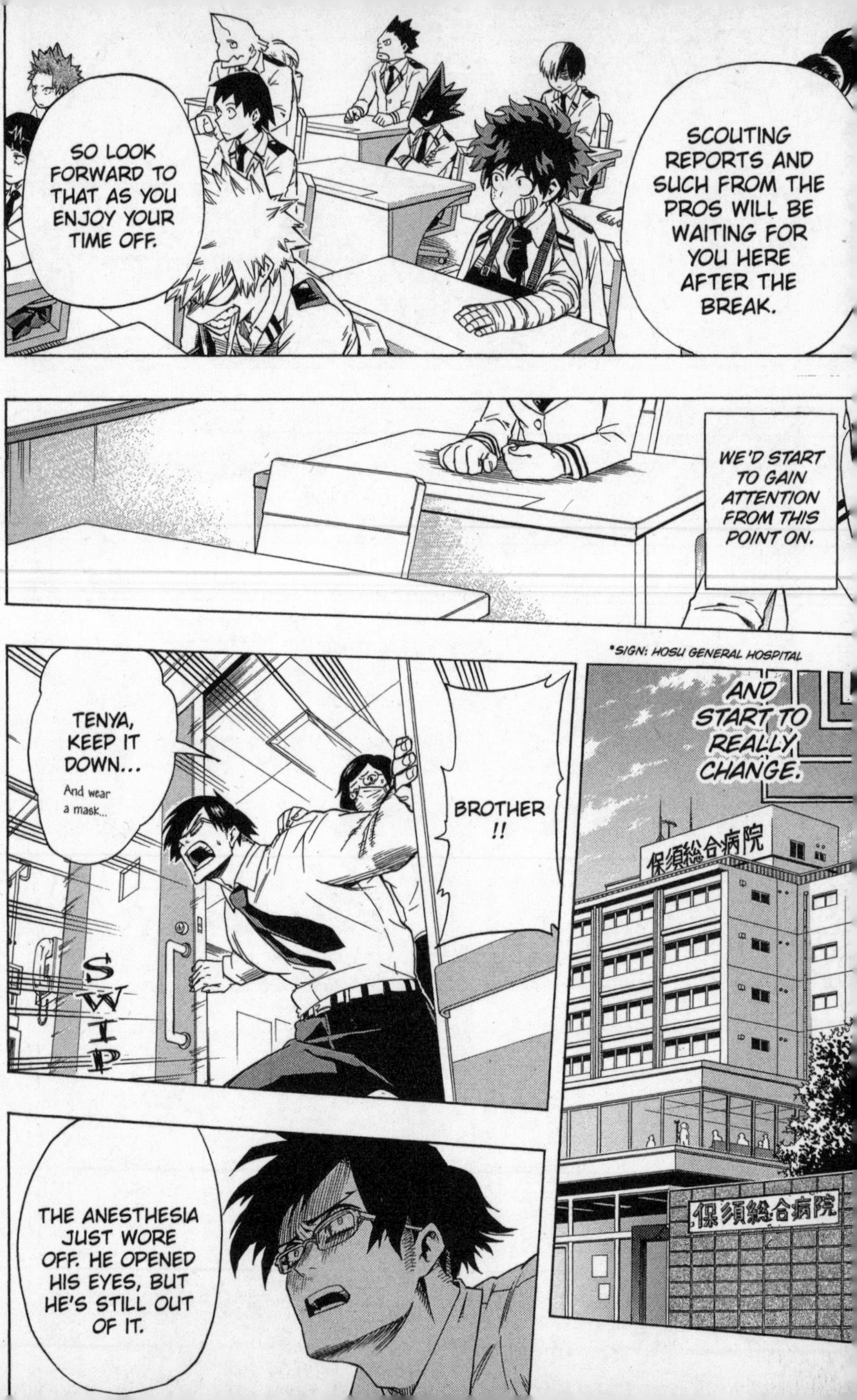
SCOUTING REPORTS AND SUCH FROM THE PROS WILL BE WAITING FOR YOU HERE AFTER THE BREAK.
SO LOOK FORWARD TO THAT AS YOU ENJOY YOUR TIME OFF.
WE'D START TO GAIN ATTENTION FROM THIS POINT ON.
*SIGN: HOSU GENERAL HOSPITAL
AND START TO REALLY CHANGE.
保須総合病院
保須総合病院
BROTHER !!
TENYA, KEEP IT DOWN...
And wear a mask...
SWIP
THE ANESTHESIA JUST WORE OFF. HE OPENED HIS EYES, BUT HE'S STILL OUT OF IT.

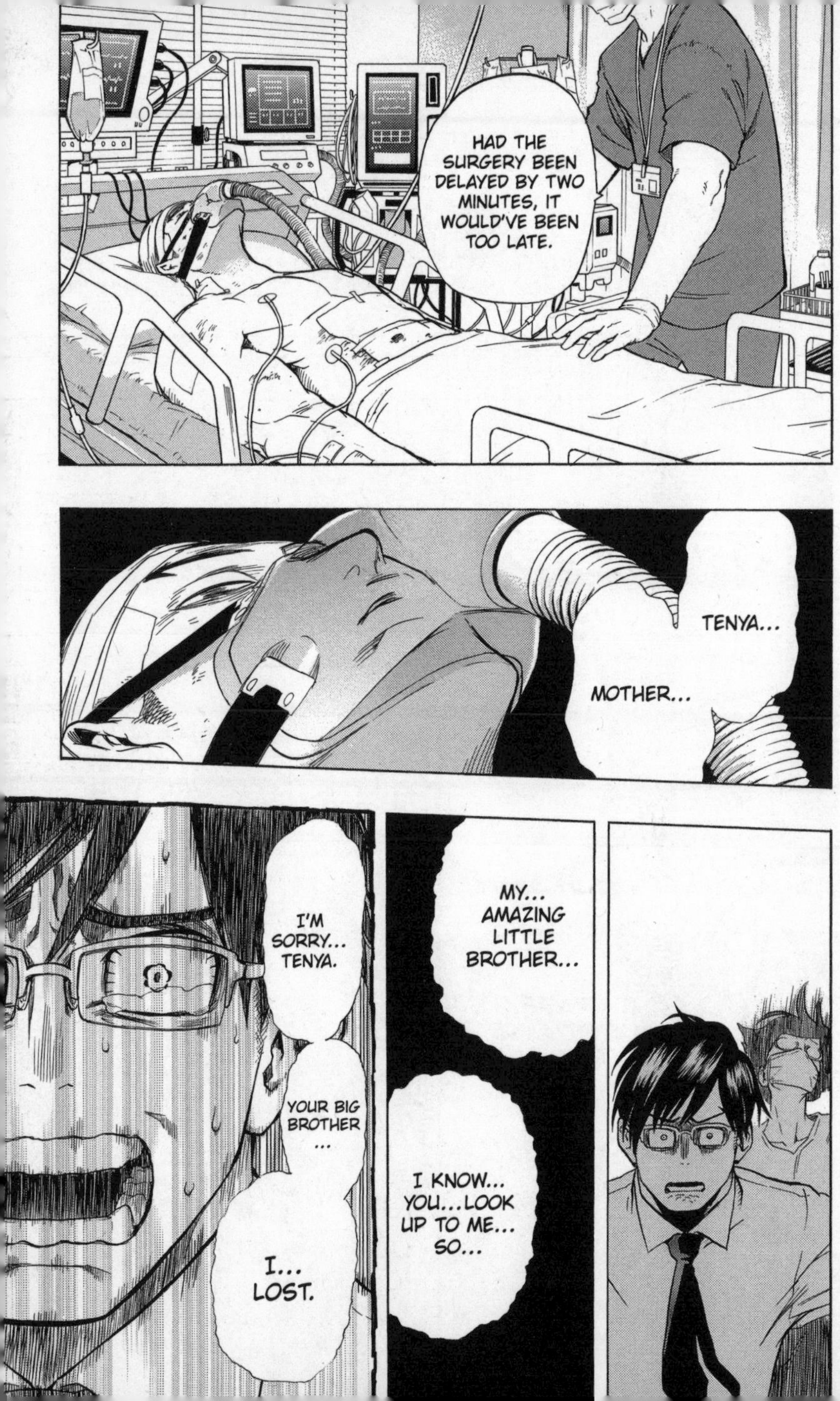
HAD THE SURGERY BEEN DELAYED BY TWO MINUTES, IT WOULD'VE BEEN TOO LATE.
TENYA...
MOTHER...
MY... AMAZING LITTLE BROTHER...
I KNOW... YOU...LOOK UP TO ME... SO...
I'M SORRY... TENYA.
YOUR BIG BROTHER ...
I... LOST.

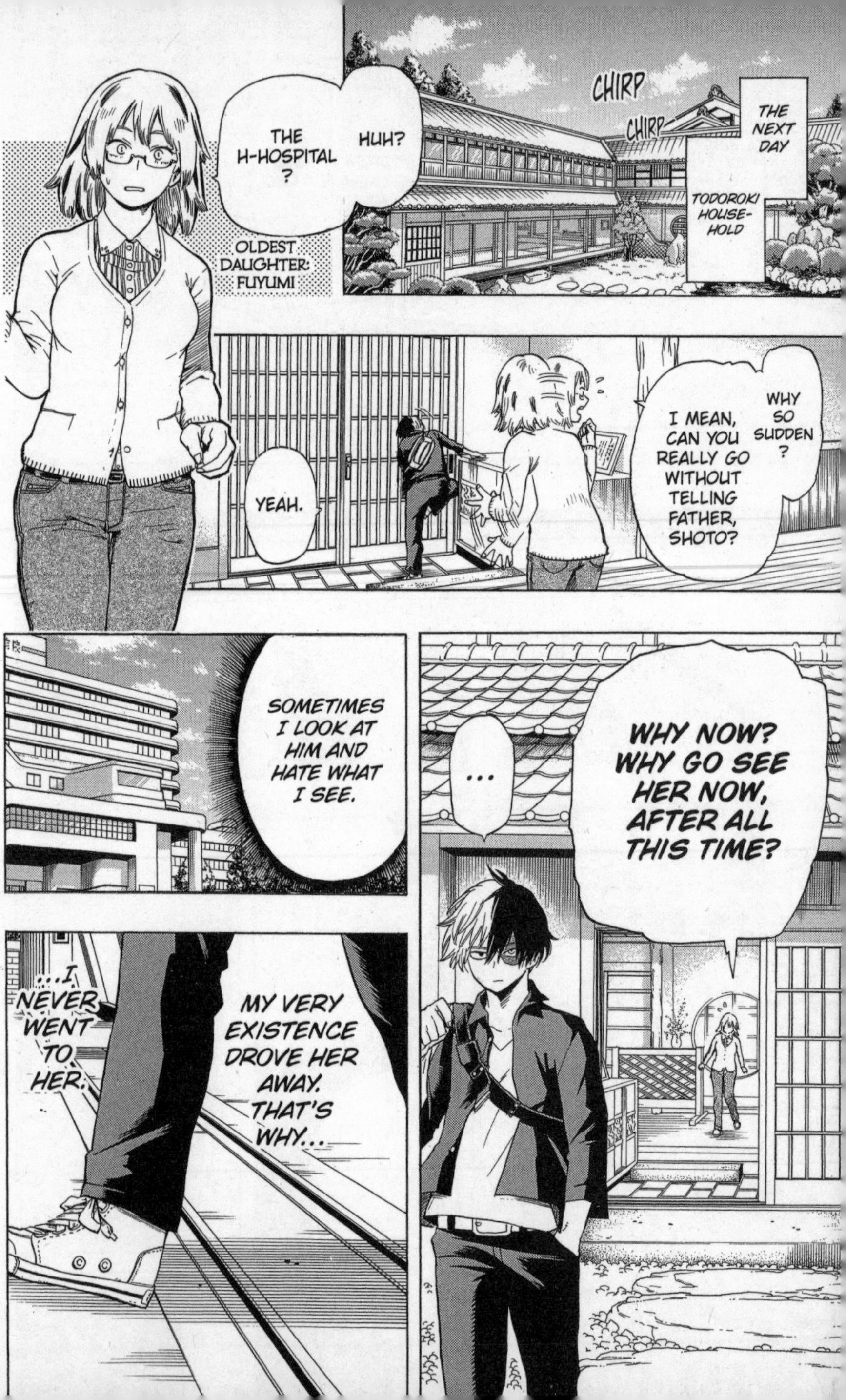
THE NEXT DAY
TODOROKI HOUSEHOLD
CHIRP
CHIRP
WHY SO SUDDEN?
I MEAN, CAN YOU REALLY GO WITHOUT TELLING FATHER, SHOTO?
YEAH.
HUH?
THE H-HOSPITAL?
OLDEST DAUGHTER: FUYUMI
WHY NOW? WHY GO SEE HER NOW, AFTER ALL THIS TIME?
...
SOMETIMES I LOOK AT HIM AND HATE WHAT I SEE.
MY VERY EXISTENCE DROVE HER AWAY. THAT'S WHY...
...I NEVER WENT TO HER.

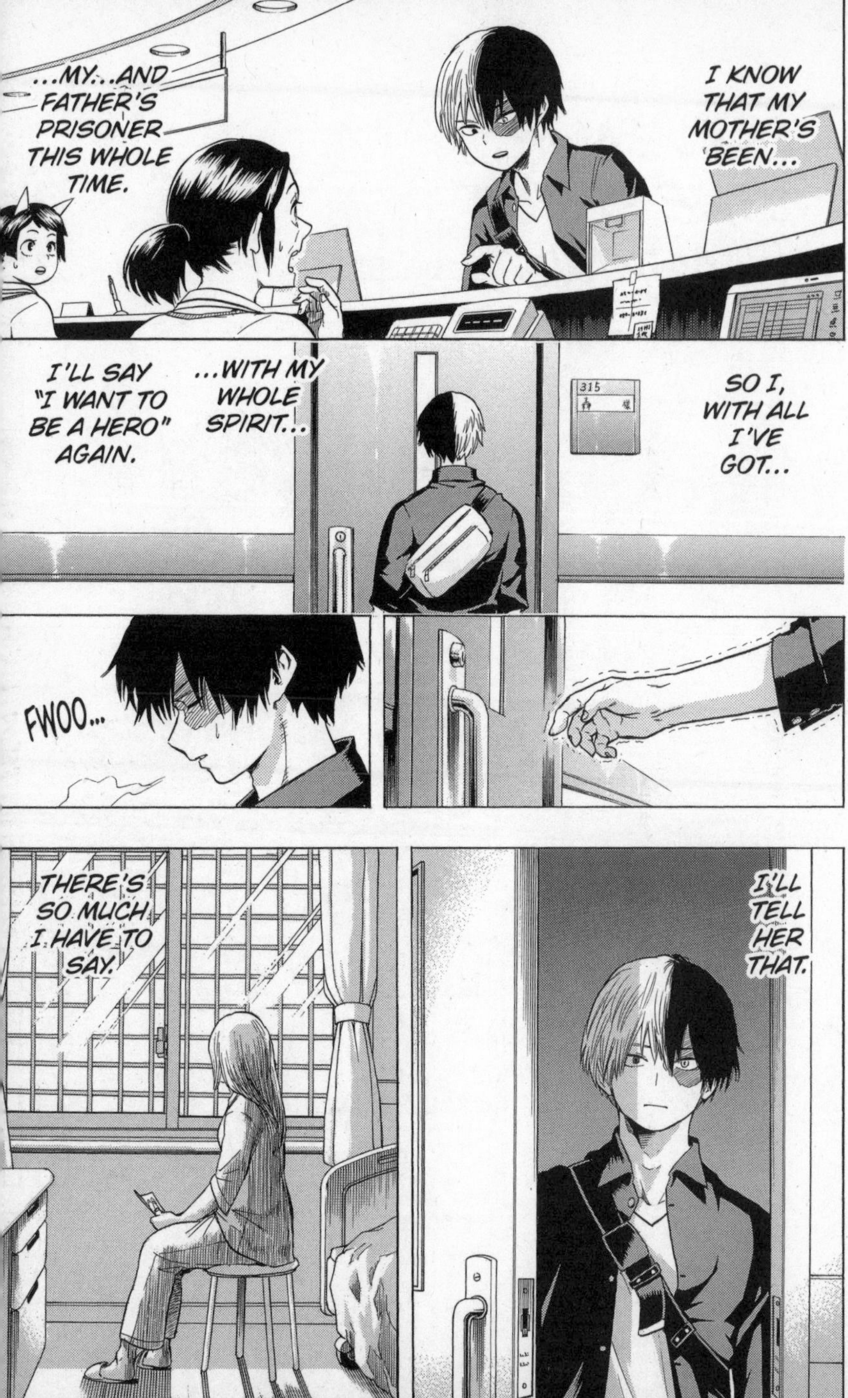
I KNOW THAT MY MOTHER'S BEEN...
...MY...AND FATHER'S PRISONER THIS WHOLE TIME.
SO I, WITH ALL I'VE GOT...
315
...WITH MY WHOLE SPIRIT...
I'LL SAY "I WANT TO BE A HERO" AGAIN.
FWOO...
I'LL TELL HER THAT.
THERE'S SO MUCH I HAVE TO SAY.

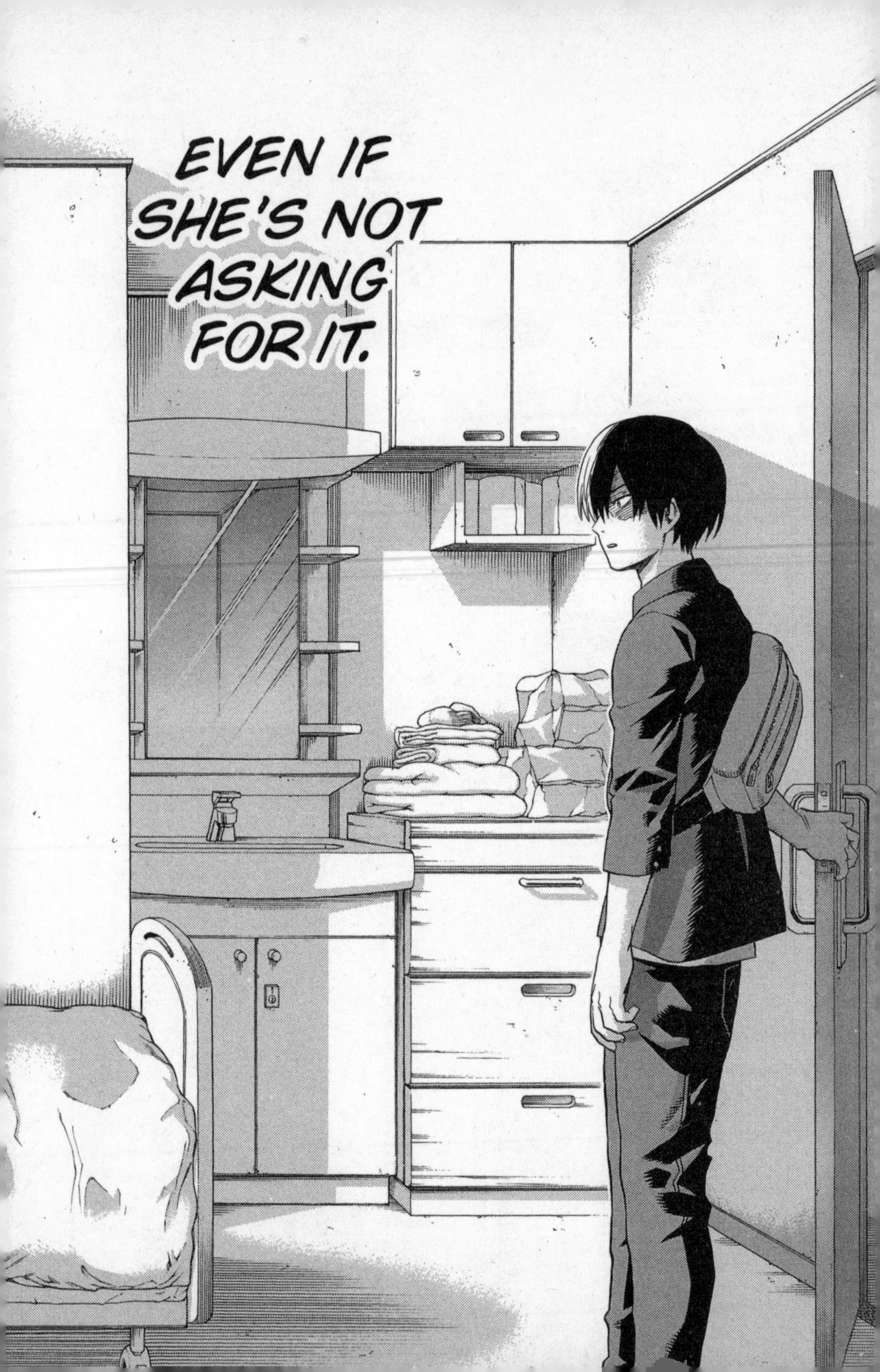
EVEN IF SHE'S NOT ASKING FOR IT.

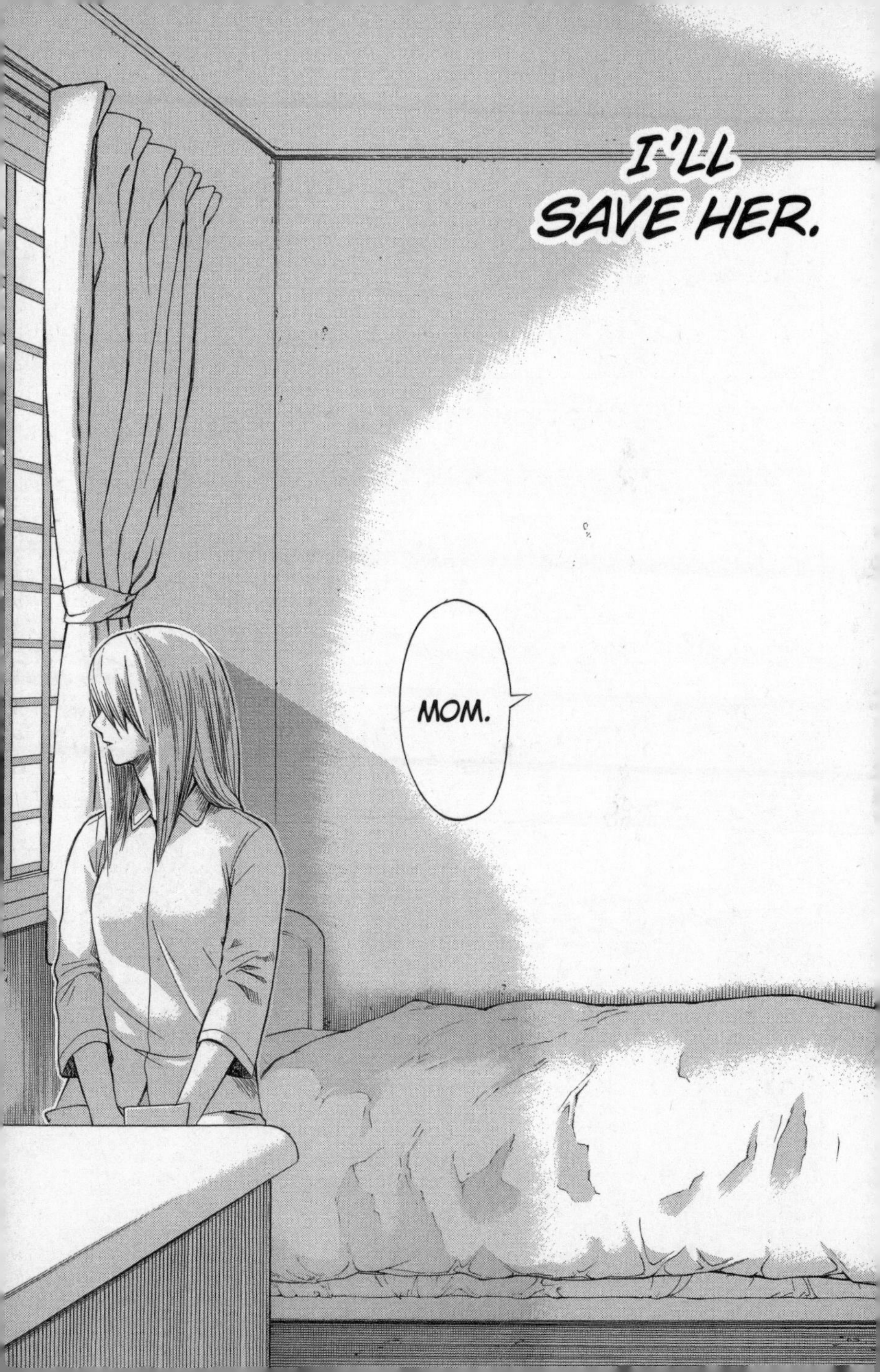
I'LL SAVE HER.
MOM.

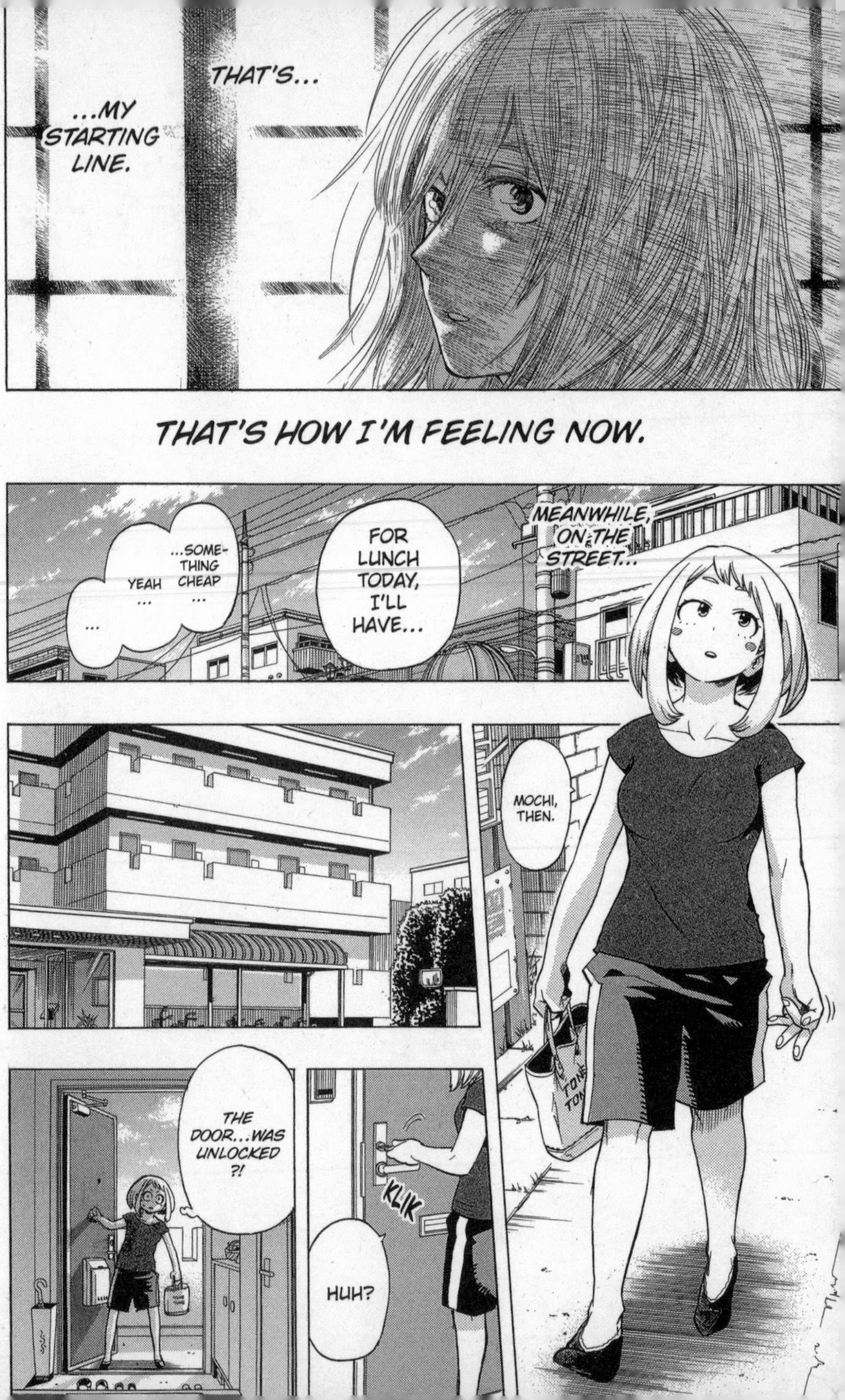
THAT'S...
...MY STARTING LINE.
THAT'S HOW I'M FEELING NOW.
MEANWHILE, ON THE STREET...
FOR LUNCH TODAY, I'LL HAVE...
...SOMETHING CHEAP...
YEAH ...
...
MOCHI, THEN.
KLIK
HUH?
THE DOOR...WAS UNLOCKED?!

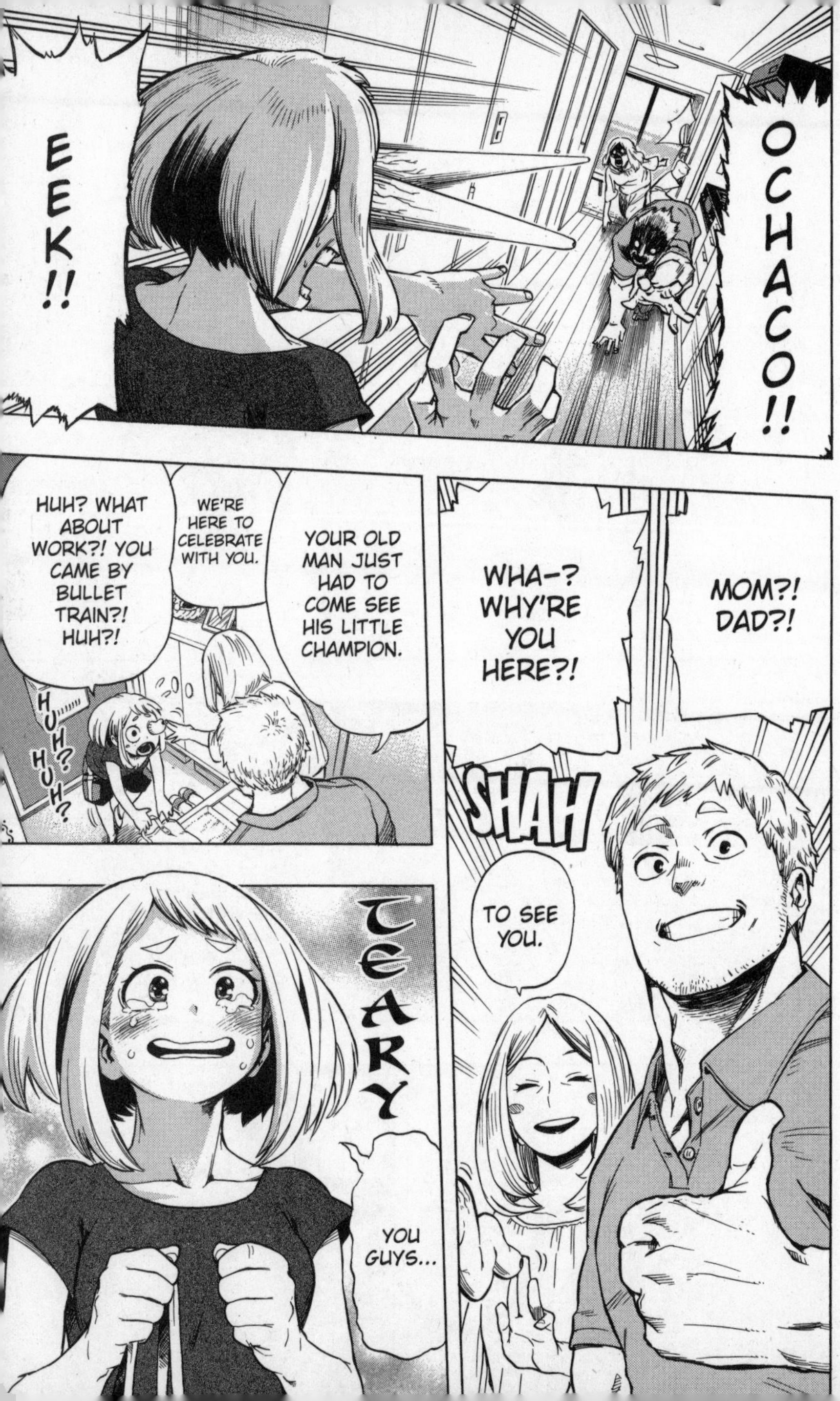
OCHACO!!
EEK!!
MOM?! DAD?!
WHA-? WHY'RE YOU HERE?!
YOUR OLD MAN JUST HAD TO COME SEE HIS LITTLE CHAMPION.
WE'RE HERE TO CELEBRATE WITH YOU.
HUH? WHAT ABOUT WORK?! YOU CAME BY BULLET TRAIN?! HUH?!
HUH? HUH?
SHAH
TO SEE YOU.
TEARY
YOU GUYS...

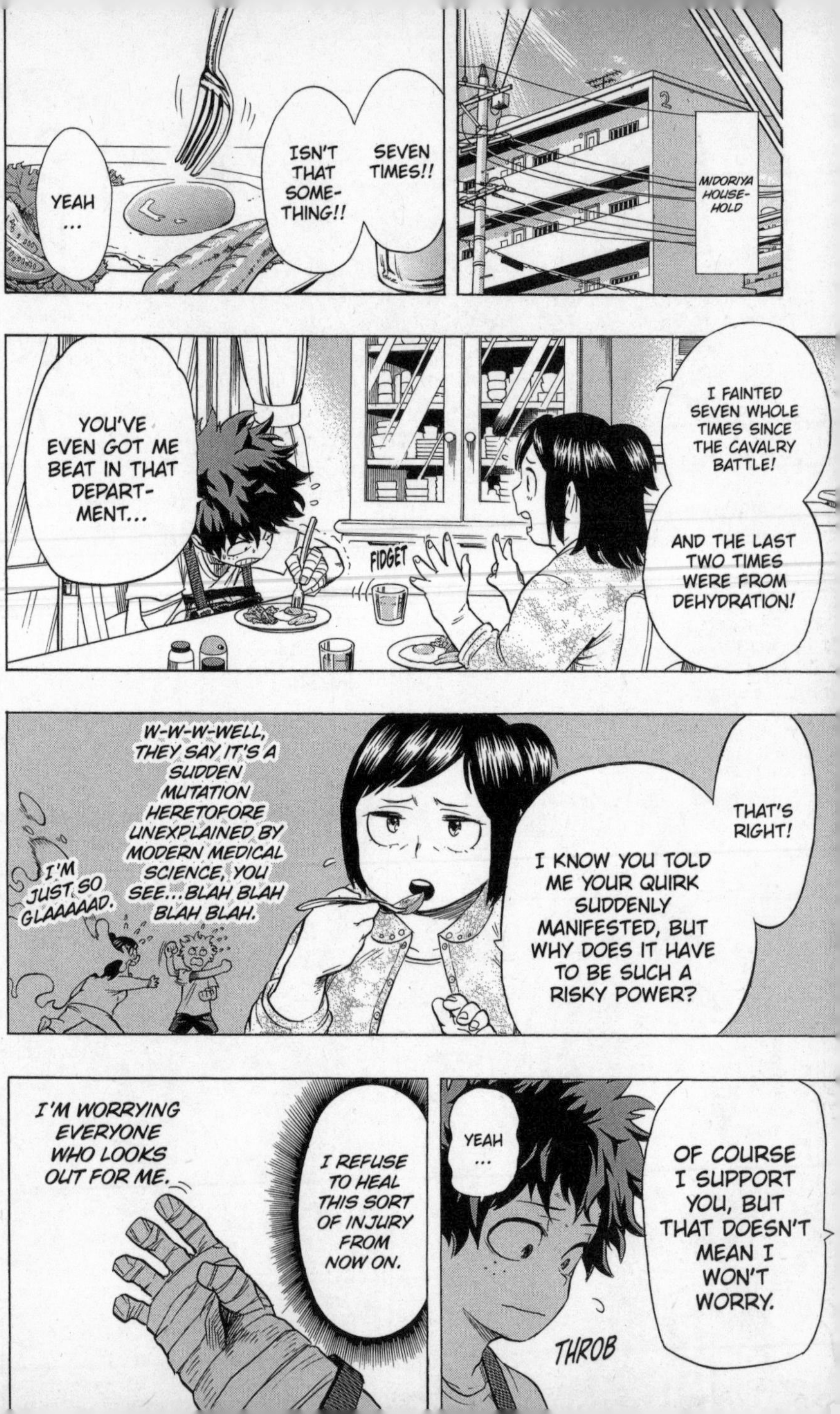
MIDORIYA HOUSEHOLD
SEVEN TIMES!!
ISN'T THAT SOMETHING!!
YEAH ...
I FAINTED SEVEN WHOLE TIMES SINCE THE CAVALRY BATTLE!
AND THE LAST TWO TIMES WERE FROM DEHYDRATION!
FIDGET
YOU'VE EVEN GOT ME BEAT IN THAT DEPARTMENT...
THAT'S RIGHT!
I KNOW YOU TOLD ME YOUR QUIRK SUDDENLY MANIFESTED, BUT WHY DOES IT HAVE TO BE SUCH A RISKY POWER?
W-W-W-WELL, THEY SAY IT'S A SUDDEN MUTATION HERETOFORE UNEXPLAINED BY MODERN MEDICAL SCIENCE, YOU SEE...BLAH BLAH BLAH BLAH.
I'M JUST SO GLAAAAAD.
OF COURSE I SUPPORT YOU, BUT THAT DOESN'T MEAN I WON'T WORRY.
YEAH ...
THROB
I REFUSE TO HEAL THIS SORT OF INJURY FROM NOW ON.
I'M WORRYING EVERYONE WHO LOOKS OUT FOR ME.

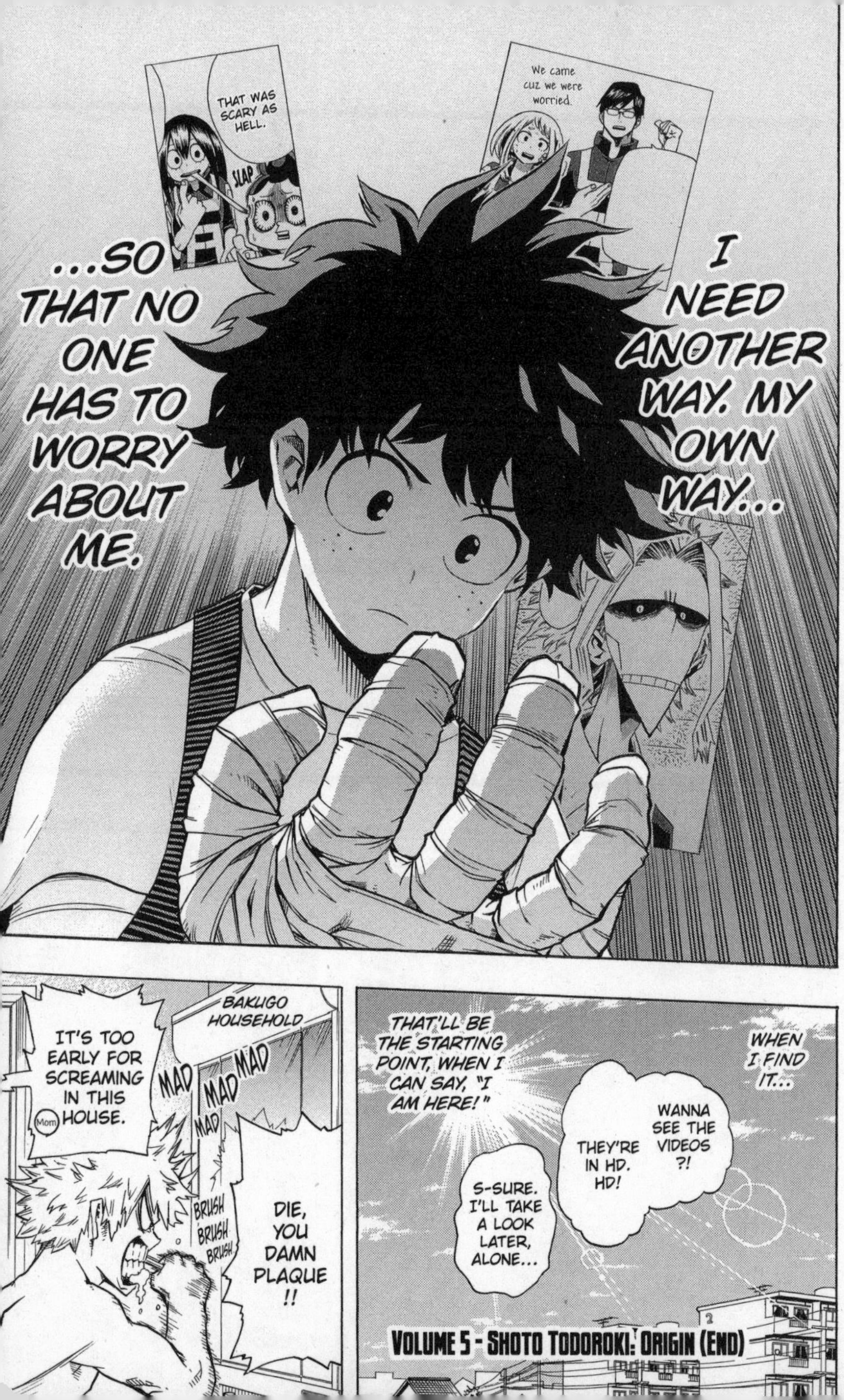
We came cuz we were worried.
THAT WAS SCARY AS HELL.
SLAP
I NEED ANOTHER WAY. MY OWN WAY...
...SO THAT NO ONE HAS TO WORRY ABOUT ME.
WHEN I FIND IT...
THAT'LL BE THE STARTING POINT, WHEN I CAN SAY, "I AM HERE!"
WANNA SEE THE VIDEOS ?!
THEY'RE IN HD. HD!
S-SURE. I'LL TAKE A LOOK LATER, ALONE...
VOLUME 5 - SHOTO TODOROKI: ORIGIN (END)
BAKUGO HOUSEHOLD
Mom
IT'S TOO EARLY FOR SCREAMING IN THIS HOUSE.
MAD MAD MAD MAD MAD
BRUSH BRUSH BRUSH
DIE, YOU DAMN PLAQUE !!

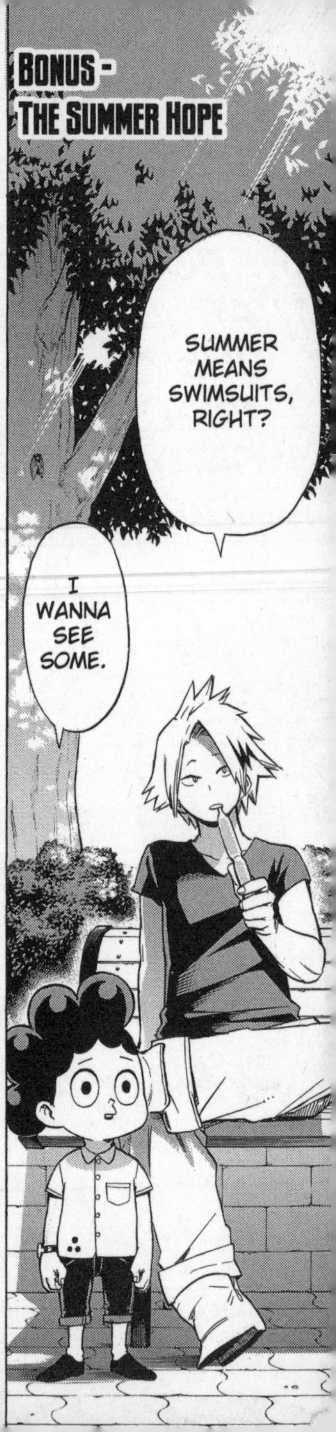
BONUS -
THE SUMMER HOPE
SUMMER MEANS SWIMSUITS, RIGHT?
I WANNA SEE SOME.
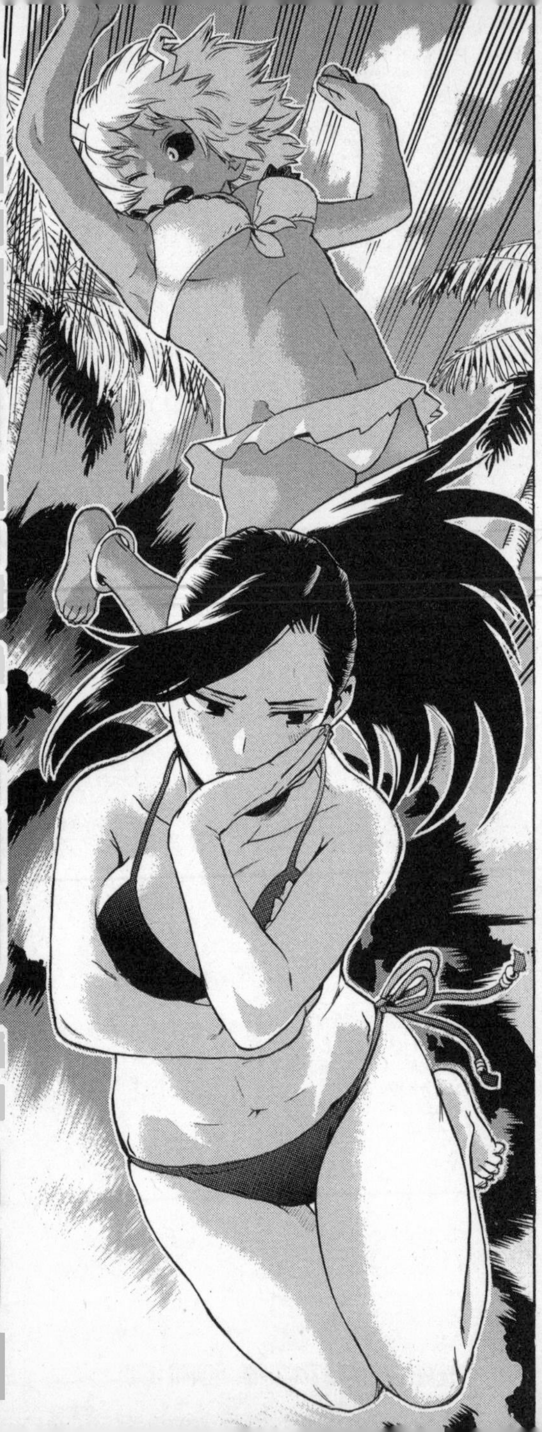

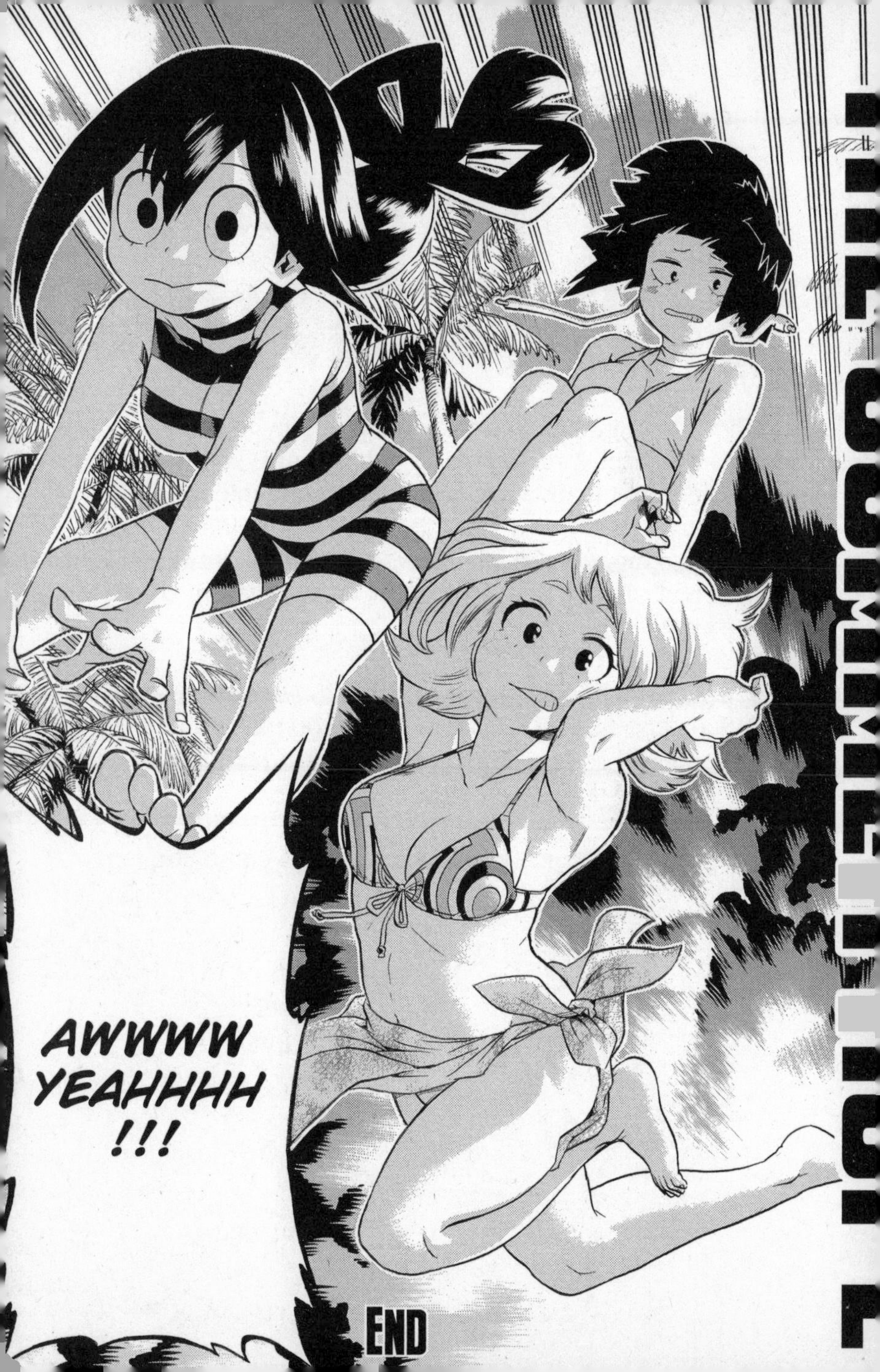
AWWWW YEAHHHH !!!
END

SPORTS FESTIVAL

When I was putting this arc together in my mind, it was going to be a vehicle for Todoroki's development. There'd be two chapters for the obstacle race, one for the interlude, two for the cavalry battle and about five for the tournament itself. That was the grand plan, but when I started drawing, I realized I needed to showcase all these different characters, so it couldn't be as succinct as I'd imagined.

Since then, I had a chance to talk with *Naruto*'s Kishimoto Sensei, and he told me, "Whenever you make an estimate for the length of an arc, count on it ballooning out to twice that length." How right he is. Wow.

I'm going full throttle with the volumes to come, too, so thanks for your support.

ALL'S WELL THAT ENDS WELL.

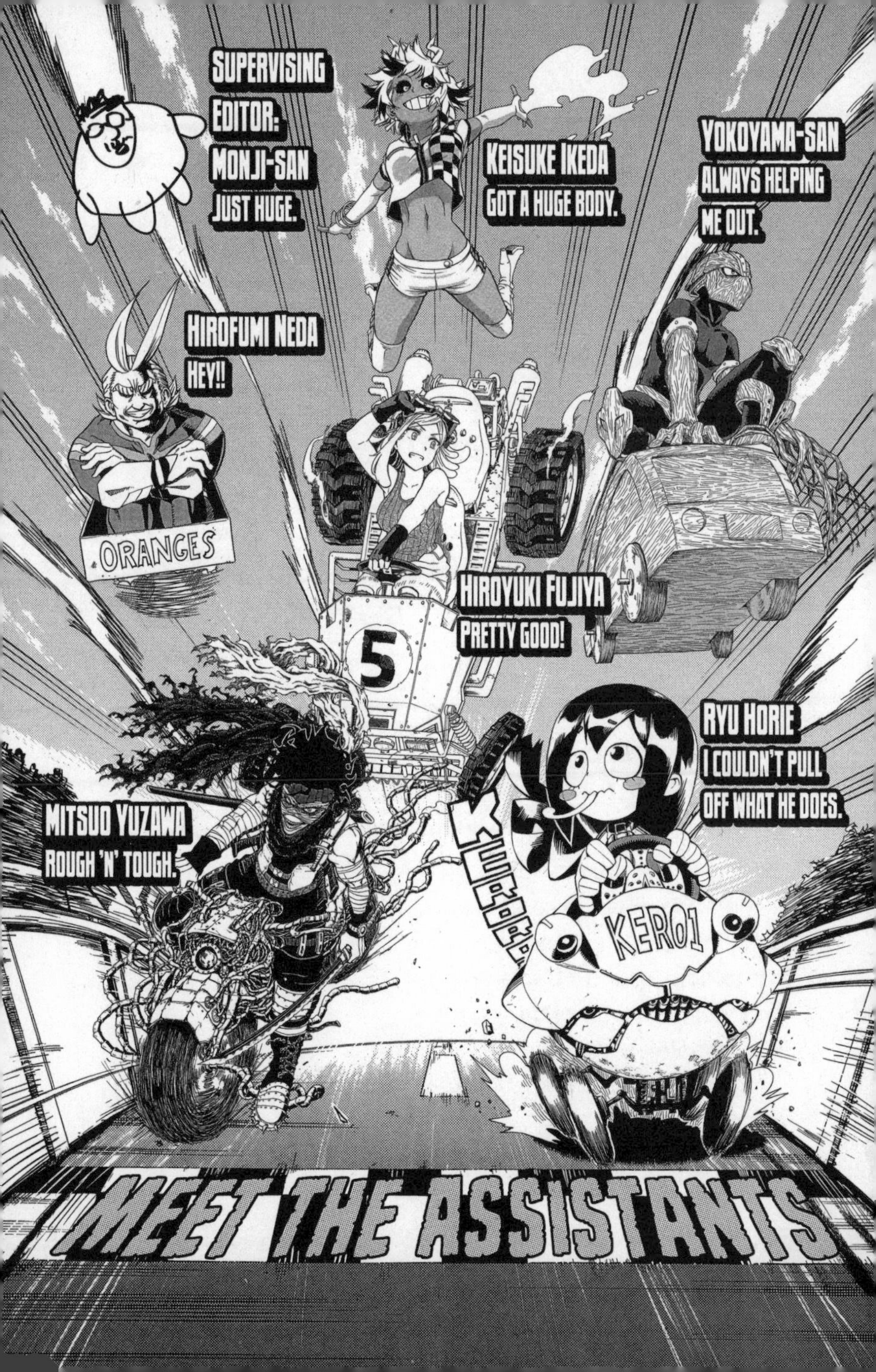
YOKOYAMA-SAN
ALWAYS HELPING ME OUT.
KEISUKE IKEDA
GOT A HUGE BODY.
SUPERVISING EDITOR: MONJI-SAN
JUST HUGE.
HIROFUMI NEDA
HEY!!
ORANGES
HIROYUKI FUJIYA
PRETTY GOOD!
5
RYU HORIE
I COULDN'T PULL OFF WHAT HE DOES.
KERO1
MITSUO YUZAWA
ROUGH 'N' TOUGH.
MEET THE ASSISTANTS

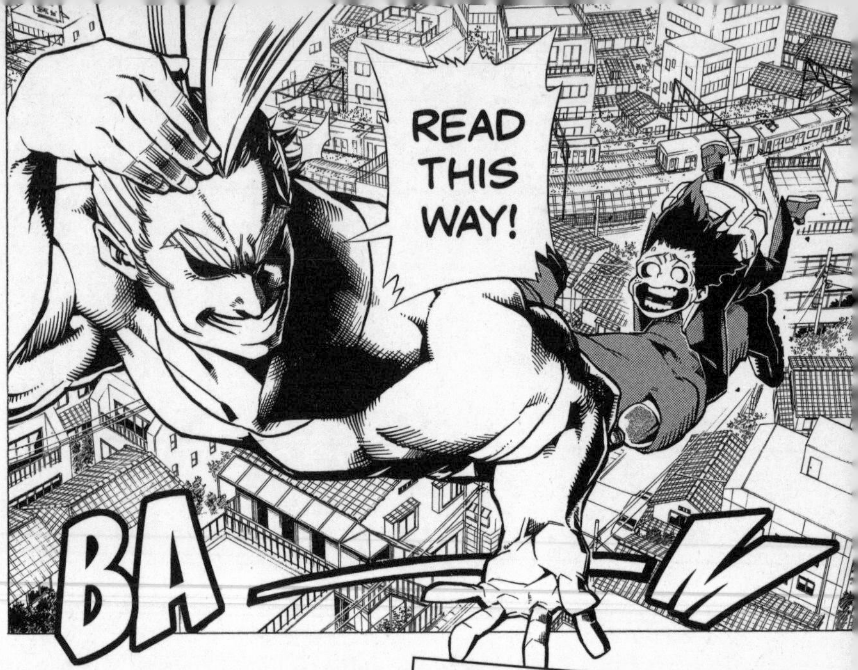
READ THIS WAY!
BA—M

MY HERO ACADEMIA

reads from right to left, starting in the upper-right corner. Japanese is read from right to left, meaning that action, sound effects and word-balloon order are completely reversed from English order.

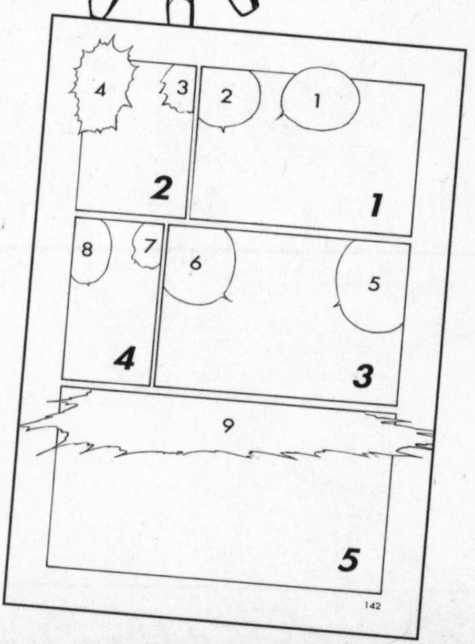
1
2
3
4
1
2
5
6
7
8
3
4
9
5
142